HISTORIC TITLES IN INTERNATIONAL LAW

HISTORIC TITLES IN INTERNATIONAL LAW

by

YEHUDA Z. BLUM

M. JUR. (JERUS.), PH. D. (LOND.)

Lecturer in International Law, Hebrew University of Jerusalem
Assistant Legal Adviser, Israel Ministry for Foreign Affairs
Member of the Israel Bar

FOREWORD BY

D. H. N. JOHNSON

Professor of International and Air Law
University of London

SPRINGER-SCIENCE+BUSINESS MEDIA, B.V. / 1965

ISBN 978-94-015-0201-6 ISBN 978-94-015-0699-1 (eBook)
DOI 10.1007/978-94-015-0699-1

Originally published by Martinus Nijhoff, The Hague, Netherlands in 1965
Softcover reprint of the hardcover 1st edition 1965

To the memory
of my grandfather

JOSEPH DUX

who perished in June 1944
in the German extermination camp of Auschwitz
at the age of 84

FOREWORD

The question of Historic Titles in International Law has been much discussed in recent years. In particular, it was an issue of some importance in several international arbitrations, such as the *Gulf of Fonseca* case, decided by the Central American Court of Justice; the *Island of Palmas* case, decided by Judge Huber as sole arbitrator, under the auspices of the Permanent Court of Arbitration; the case concerning the *Legal Status of Eastern Greenland* before the Permanent Court of International Justice; and, more recently still, the cases concerning *Fisheries* (United Kingdom v. Norway); *Minquiers and Ecrehos Islets* (United Kingdom v. France); *Certain Frontier Land* (Belgium v. Netherlands); and *Temple of Preah Vihear* (Cambodia v. Thailand), before the International Court of Justice. Historic Titles are probably also a relevant factor in a number of territorial disputes that have not yet been submitted to arbitration or judicial settlement.

The recent controversies over the proper breadth for the territorial sea and the exclusive fishing limits of coastal States have brought to the fore new aspects of the problem. There is, for instance, the question whether States, whose nationals have for a certain period of time been accustomed to fish in areas of sea relatively close to the coasts of other States, have acquired for those nationals a right, in the nature of an historic right, to continue to fish in those areas, notwithstanding an extension of their territorial sea and their exclusive fishing limits by the coastal States concerned. There is also the question whether the right of innocent passage, normally regarded as a right confined to the territorial sea, may not also exist through the internal waters of certain States where the States concerned have recently extended either their internal or their territorial waters. Whether such an exception will be permitted or not will almost certainly depend on historic factors. These questions were much discussed at the United Nations Conferences on the Law of the Sea, held at Geneva in 1958 and 1960.

The question of historic titles is not new. But, in the past, there has been a tendency not to see the problem as a whole. Writers have been apt to treat the problem as one appertaining exclusively to maritime territory e.g. the question of the so-called "historic bays" or "historic waters." Alternatively, the problem has been regarded as merely incidental to the rather sterile controversy as to whether prescription is or is not a recognised means of acquiring title to territory under international law.

The decisions of international tribunals mentioned above, and discussed at great length by Dr. Blum, show that, while the maritime factors are important, the question of historic titles deserves to be considered as a whole and not exclusively in the maritime context. It needs, for instance, to be considered in conjunction with such associated doctrines as acquiescence and estoppel. It needs to be considered too in relation to the whole process whereby international customary law is formed. Thus considered, the doctrine of historic titles can be shown to play an intelligible and constructive role in international law.

It is my belief that Dr. Blum's book contributes greatly to the clarification of these, and many other, questions. I am therefore grateful to have the opportunity in this Foreword to welcome it as a timely and valuable contribution to the literature of international law.

D. H. N. JOHNSON

London, February 1965

PREFACE

This book, which has grown out of a Ph. D. thesis submitted to the University of London in 1961, is a study of the Historic Title, one of the titles to territory recognized by international law. During my two years of study at the London School of Economics and Political Science I had the privilege of working under the supervision of Professor D. H. N. Johnson, Professor of International and Air Law in the University of London. His personal interest in the progress of my work as well as his constant guidance and encouragement carried me through the difficulties well known to those who have engaged in research of this kind.

Dr. D. W. Bowett, Fellow of Queen's College, Cambridge, external examiner of the thesis, and Dr. Shabtai Rosenne, Legal Adviser to the Israel Ministry for Foreign Affairs, Member of the International Law Commission and Associate of the Institut de Droit International, have read the manuscript and were kind enough to make valuable observations on it. Needless to say, I alone bear responsibility for the views expressed in the book.

I wish to thank the staff of the libraries of the London School of Economics and of the Institute of Advanced Legal Studies, University of London, for their patience and consideration.

I wish further to express my thanks to Mr. Henry Shaw, Director of the B'nai B'rith Hillel Foundation in London, foı his interest and the assistance he rendered to me during my stay in London.

Thanks are also due to the publishers for their courtesy and forbearance at all stages of the production of this book.

It is a time-honoured Jewish custom for an author, on completing his work, to give thanks to the Almighty. This I do now in all humility, especially as a survivor of the Bergen-Belsen concentration camp and as one belonging to a generation of Jewish youth in Europe, few of whom lived to see the end of the Second World War. This book is dedicated to the memory of my grandfather who, together with some sixty members of his family, was among the victims of what Sir Winston Churchill called "a monstrous tyranny, never surpassed in the dark, lamentable catalogue of human crime" (House of Commons, May 13th, 1940).

It is my sincere wish that this book may make a modest contribution to international law, which it is imperative to strengthen if we are to save succeeding generations from catastrophes like that which so recently threatened the very existence of humanity.

Hebrew University of Jerusalem,
Adar I, 5725 / February, 1965 Y. Z. B.

TABLE OF CONTENTS

TABLE OF CASES

A. PERMANENT COURT OF INTERNATIONAL JUSTICE

B. INTERNATIONAL COURT OF JUSTICE

C. OTHER INTERNATIONAL TRIBUNALS AND ARBITRATIONS

D. DECISIONS OF MUNICIPAL COURTS

LIST OF ABBREVIATIONS

A.C.	– Law Reports, Appeal Cases.
A.D.	– (a) Annual Digest of Public International Law Cases, London-New York, 1919–1932. (b) Annual Digest and Reports of Public International Law Cases, London, 1933–1950.
AJIL	– American Journal of International Law, Washington, 1907–
ASJG	– Nordisk Tidsskrift for International Ret (Acta Scandinavica Juris Gentium), Copenhagen, 1930–
BFSP	– British and Foreign State Papers, London, 1841–
BYIL	– British Year Book of International Law, London, 1920–
Cmd.	– Command Papers published up to 1956.
Cmnd.	– Command Papers published from 1956 onwards.
Co. Litt.	– Coke's Commentary on Littleton's *Institutes of the Laws of England.*
F. and F.	– Foster and Finlason, 1856–1867.
Fisheries case	– *Anglo-Norwegian Fisheries* case, 1951.
Hague Recueil	– Académie de Droit International, Recueil des Cours, The Hague, 1923–
Hansard (Commons)	– Parliamentary Debates (Hansard), House of Commons, Official Reports.
Hansard (Lords)	– Parliamentary Debates (Hansard), House of Lords, Official Reports.
Hertslet's Treaties	– Hertslet, L., *A Complete Collection of the Treaties*

		and Conventions... between Great Britain and Foreign Powers, London, 1840–1925, 31 volumes.
How.	–	Vol. 42–45 of the U.S. (1843–1846), edited by Benjamin C. Howard.
ICJ	–	International Court of Justice.
ICJ Reports	–	International Court of Justice, Reports of Judgments, Advisory Opinions and Orders.
ICLQ	–	International and Comparative Law Quarterly, London, 1952–
ILC	–	International Law Commission.
ILC Yearbook	–	Yearbook of the International Law Commission, 1949–
K.B.	–	Law Reports, King's Bench Division.
Moore, *International Arbitrations*	–	Moore, J. B., *History and Digest of International Arbitrations to which the United States has been a Party*, Washington, 1898, 6 volumes.
NTIR	–	Nederlands Tijdschrift voor Internationaal Recht, Leyden, 1953–
PCIJ, Series A	–	Permanent Court of International Justice, Collection of Judgments.
PCIJ, Series A/B	–	Permanent Court of International Justice, Judgments, Orders and Advisory Opinions.
PCIJ, Series C	–	Permanent Court of International Justice, Acts and Documents relating to Judgments and Advisory Opinions given by the Court.
RDI	–	Revue de Droit International, Paris, 1927–1939.
RDILC	–	Revue de Droit International et de Législation Comparée, Brussels, 1869–1940.
RGDIP	–	Revue Générale de Droit International Public, Paris, 1894–
Ser.L.o.N.P.	–	Series of League of Nations Publications.
UNRIAA	–	United Nations Reports of International Arbitral Awards, 1948–
U.S.	–	Cases Argued and Adjudged in the Supreme Court of the United States.
YBWA	–	The Year Book of World Affairs, London, 1947–

ZRV – Zeitschrift für ausländisches öffentliches Recht und Völkerrecht, Berlin-Leipzig-Stuttgart, 1929–

Unless otherwise stated:

(a) English and French texts are quoted in their original;

(b) Quotations from modern languages – other than English and French – have been translated into English by the present writer.

Tempus enim ex suapte natura vim nullam effectricem habet: nihil enim fit a tempore, quamquam nihil non fit in tempore.
(Grotius, *De Jure Belli ac Pacis*, liber II, caput IV, § I)

CHAPTER I

INTRODUCTION

1. *The acquisition of territory: the evolution of the modern concept*

The rules of international law governing the acquisition of territory have been for long among the hotly contested problems of international law. The controversial nature of the topic is augmented by the fact that the conception of State territory in general has undergone great changes ever since modern international law replaced the medieval concepts of *jus gentium*. According to Oppenheim, "when Grotius laid the foundations of modern International Law, State territory was still, as in the Middle Ages, more or less identified with the private property of the monarch of the State."[1] In accordance with this concept of State territory being the *patrimonium* of the head of the State, it was not uncommon to sell the territory of one State to another, to transfer it as a marriage gift,[2] or to dispose of it in the will of the reigning monarch. It is therefore little surprising that doctrine and practice alike displayed a natural tendency to express issues relating to the acquisition of territory in terms of analogies from private law and, in particular, Roman law. Thus, the rules of Roman law regarding the acquisition of private property were also applied to the acquisition of State territory.[3]

According to Schwarzenberger, in this primordial stage of international law "the borderline between the public and private law features of such claims [was] as blurred as might be expected during the transition from feudalism to territorial sovereignty."[4] In spite of the fact that the basic Roman law distinction between *imperium* (roughly corresponding to the modern concept of sovereignty), on the one hand, and *dominium* (i.e. the Roman law antecedent of the private law ownership), on the other hand, was well known,[5] its implications were not

[1] Oppenheim, *International Law*, 8th edition (edited by Lauterpacht), 1955, vol. I, p. 545.
[2] Thus, the policy of territorial aggrandizement followed by the Austrian Empire has been epitomized in the phrase: *Bella gerant alii – tu felix Austria nube.*
[3] Cf. Jennings, *The Acquisition of Territory in International Law*, 1963, p. 3.
[4] Schwarzenberger, *International Law*, 3rd edition, 1957, p. 291.
[5] Thus, Seneca stated that "*omnia rex imperio possidet, singuli dominio.*"

properly understood.[1] It was left to modern international law to undertake a transformation in this field. At the present stage of international law a situation has been created in which no distinction between the acquisition of *territory* and the acquisition of *sovereignty* can any longer be sustained.

Yet, the traces of Roman law in this sphere of international law can hardly be obliterated and they are clearly evidenced in the terms employed to denote various modes of acquiring territory (such as *accretio*, *avulsio*, *occupatio*). In spite of a common terminology, however, the notions underlying contemporary modes of acquisition of international titles sharply differ from private and Roman law concepts.

2. *The acquisition of territory: the differing approach of academic and practising lawyers*

The decisions rendered in recent decades by international tribunals called upon to pronounce on territorial disputes – while representing a considerable contribution towards the clarification of the process whereby a valid international title is established – have none the less failed to remove doubts and uncertainties in this field. This state of things is perhaps not so astonishing, bearing in mind the different motives underlying the approach to this matter of the international *academic* lawyer and the international *practising* lawyer, respectively. The academic lawyer's main preoccupation lies in the attempt to make neat doctrinal classifications, and he sees his chief ambition fulfilled if he succeeds in setting up a carefully planned edifice in which seemingly contradictory legal phenomena can be reconciled with each other.

The international practising lawyer, however, approaches the problems with which he is confronted from a different angle altogether. In the typical territorial controversy he will face a concrete dispute involving the conflicting claims of usually two opponents. Thus, he will not ask himself what title is *good* under international law (a question which is a matter of grave concern for the academic lawyer), but rather which title is the *better* one. Accordingly, to quote Schwarzenberger, he is "not concerned with the elaboration of the general rules governing title to territory,... but with the relative superiority of the evidence produced by the parties."[2] Understandably, the parties to such a dispute are not unduly perturbed by problems of legal classification worked

[1] See to this effect *The Collected Papers of John Westlake on International Law*, edited by Oppenheim, 1914, pp. 129–133.

[2] Schwarzenberger, *op. cit.*, p. 290.

out by writers and theoreticians – classifications, which, according to Johnson, are not in general followed by international tribunals.[1] The same writer has also drawn attention to the fact that "whereas international tribunals might be expected to indicate under which of [the] various heads they are awarding territory to State A rather than to State B, in fact they rarely do so. So much so that is is not unknown for a discussion to take place as to the appropriate head under which certain awards should be classified."[2]

3. *The various modes of acquiring territory – Classification*

Notwithstanding this hesitancy of practice to follow the classifications laid down by doctrine, it seems both pertinent and useful to mention the fact that modern international law generally distinguishes five modes of acquiring territory which are classified under the following heads: occupation, accretion, cession, conquest and prescription.[3] Oppenheim, while basically adopting this classification, substitutes the term "subjugation" for "conquest."[4]

It is also usual to divide the modes of acquiring territory into original and derivative titles "according as the title they give is derived from the title of a prior owner-State or not."[5] Thus, it is generally accepted that occupation and accretion are original modes of acquisition, whereas cession is a derivative one. The position with regard to conquest (or subjugation) and prescription is uncertain and these two modes of acquisition are occasionally classified as belonging to the former or latter group.[6] While agreeing with Johnson that "this particular classification serves no useful purpose" and that "in so far as it leads to controversy and confusion it is probably even harmful,"[7] it is felt that it might be claimed with equal justice that this lack of unanimity even in the sphere of classification is a true indication of, and reflection on, the confused state of things at present pervading this field of international law.

[1] Johnson, "Consolidation as a Root of Title in International Law," *Cambridge Law Journal* (1955), p. 215, at p. 217.

[2] *Ibid.*

[3] For references as to writers who follow this classification, see *ibid.*, p. 216, notes 5–11.

[4] See Oppenheim, *op. cit.*, pp. 566–567, where it is stated that "conquest alone does not *ipso facto* make the conquering State the sovereign of the conquered territory.... Conquest is only a mode of acquisition if the conqueror, after having firmly established the conquest, formally annexes the territory.... Such annexation makes the enemy State cease to exist and thereby brings the war to an end.... Such ending of war is named subjugation." (Italics in original).

[5] *Ibid.*, p. 546.

[6] Johnson, *loc. cit.*, p. 217, n. 14.

[7] *Ibid.*, p. 217.

4. Plan of the work

The present study does not deal with international titles in general, and its scope is confined solely to the discussion of what has come to pass under the name of an "historic title." As will be pointed out in more detail in chapter II, prescription has frequently been resorted to as the possible legal root of such an historic title. For the reasons which are set out in that chapter, however, it is believed that the employment of this term, giving rise as it does to certain well-defined associations springing into the jurist's mind on the basis of analogy with private law prescription, should be avoided when dealing with the validity in international law of an originally unlawful title.

The similarity of purpose existing between the municipal law title of prescription and the historic title in international law ought not to obscure the difference of the legal foundations on which each of these titles rests. Both of them stem from a wish not to upset unduly an existing order of things. *Quieta non movere.* Both represent a concession made by the law to a situation of fact and the occasional subordination of the generally valid maxim of *ex injuria non oritur jus* to the principle of much more limited scope which is expressed in the rule *ex facto oritur jus.* On the State and inter-State level alike the existing legal orders are, in exceptional circumstances, willing to lend their sanction – for the sake of preserving peace and stability – to certain situations of fact, even if the origins of such situations are not free from doubt.

There, however, ends the similarity between the private law title of prescription and the historic title in international law. In domestic law it is the existence of the legislative machinery – and not the operation of time as such – that sets the seal of legal validity on an originally invalid claim. Since international law has at present no such legislative machinery at its disposal, the legal basis for the existence of an historic title has to be sought elsewhere and one has to revert to a more ancient and less elaborate mechanism of law-making, namely, the formation of custom. Thus, the juridical basis of an historic title is to be found – as in the case of any customary norm of international law – in the conviction of a State that a practice followed by it is a binding rule of law (the *opinio juris*). Consequently, an historic title must be regarded – as is submitted at greater length in chapter III below – as a customary norm of international law, differing from the ordinary customary rule only in that its scope of validity and application is more limited. Both, however, share a common process of formation and maintenance.

Chapters IV and V of this study are devoted to an investigation of the various elements through which the historic claim of a State manifests itself and to an analysis of questions of procedure and evidence relating to the building up and maintenance of such a claim.

Finally, chapter VI deals with those aspects of the historic claims which are specifically related to maritime areas.

CHAPTER II

PRESCRIPTION IN INTERNATIONAL LAW

5. *The distinction between acquisitive prescription and extinctive prescription*

"In law prescription is of two kinds: it is either an instrument for the *acquisition* of property or an instrument of an *exemption* solely from the servitude of judicial process."[1]

The latter form of prescription is known in English law as "limitation" and is sometimes also called "extinctive prescription."[2]

"Limitation" means the extinction of stale claims and obsolete titles. This kind of prescription does not establish in favour of the possessor a new title of ownership which had not been existing before; "it simply extinguishes a former owner's rights to recover possession of the land"[3] and therefore "operates negatively by eliminating the claim of a person having a superior title."[4]

On the other hand, that kind of prescription which "is an instrument for the acquisition of property" has a different meaning: "it operates positively, like a conveyance,"[5] and is one of the modes of acquiring a new title to property. It is accordingly called "acquisitive prescription."

This distinction between the two forms of prescription has also been recognized in international law. But, since it is the purpose of this study only to examine the process by which historic titles are being established in accordance with international law, extinctive prescription will not be dealt with any further, and any subsequent reference to prescription should be understood in the sense of meaning solely acquisitive prescription.

6. *Prescription as a private law concept*

"Since the existence of the law of nations there has always been oppo-

[1] See *Corpus Juris Secundum*, vol. 71, 1951, p. 490. (Italics added).
[2] The corresponding expression in French is "prescription libératoire."
[3] Megarry and Wade, *The Law of Real Property*, 2nd edition, 1959, p. 954.
[4] *Ibid.*
[5] *Ibid.*

sition to prescription as a mode of acquiring territory."[1] The centuries-old controversy as to the applicability of prescription in international law has not yet been settled.

As will be shown later, international lawyers originating in English-speaking countries have, on the whole, endorsed the doctrine of international prescription, while continental European lawyers have been, as a rule, rather sceptical as to the admissibility of this doctrine in the sphere of international law.

There seem to be two main reasons for this divergence of opinion, which follows, broadly speaking, the linguistic frontier between the English-speaking countries and the rest of the world; one of them is of general character, while the other is specifically related to the field of prescription. They will be discussed, in turn, in sections 7–11 below.

7. *Private law concepts in international law*

Seen in the broad perspective, the controversy that has arisen in international law over the applicability of the doctrine of prescription cannot be isolated from the more fundamental controversy as to the place of private law concepts within international law. As has been shown by Lauterpacht,[2] this discussion – started centuries ago – is basically a clash between the "positivist school" in international law and those adhering to the concepts of "natural law." "The chief postulate of the positivist school can be expressed in one word: self sufficiency. It rejects the taking over of rules and precepts from sources other than international custom or treaties."[3] Thus, it views with the utmost suspicion any recourse being had to private law analogies. The opponents of this positivist approach to international law, on the other hand, adopt "Roman law as a living source from which its numerous gaps may be filled."[4]

The case for the positivist school has been most clearly stated in the writings of the German school of jurisprudence,[5] but "positivism" was by no means confined to the German writers: "recent Italian positivists... follow the German lead."[6]

On the other hand, British and American international lawyers

[1] Oppenheim, *op. cit.*, p. 575.
[2] Lauterpacht, *Private Law Sources and Analogies of International Law*, 1927, chap. I, pp. 3–42.
[3] *Ibid.*, p. 7.
[4] *Ibid.*, p. 24.
[5] *Ibid.*, pp. 17–19.
[6] *Ibid.*, p. 30.

have "never discarded the idea that Roman law is the source most likely to contain 'the reason of the thing' on many a question of international law.... The acknowledgment of its importance as a subsidiary source of international law [has] become one of the characteristic features of British international jurisprudence."[1] The American writers share, on the whole, the view of the British publicists.[2]

Lauterpacht, though, claims that "the influence of the English conception is not confined to English-speaking countries"[3] and cites to this effect the example set by the Swiss-Belgian writer Rivier.[4] Yet he admits that "the reign of the [positivist school] at the end of the nineteenth century is undisputed.... It is still predominant today."[5]

It may fairly be assumed that the general views held by the "positivists" and the adherents of "natural law," respectively, as to the applicability of private law concepts and analogies in the field of international law, have been shaping to a large extent their views as to the existence of international prescription.

8. Divergence of the definition of prescription between the continental and English legal systems

We now turn to the second and more specific reason which is believed to account for the divergence of opinion as to the applicability of prescription in the sphere of international law. It should be noted that the private law notions prevailing among continental and English-speaking writers, respectively, as to the exact meaning of prescription, seem to be at variance with each other (as the subsequent juxtaposition of these different concepts of prescription is intended to demonstrate). Thus, it would not seem to be too bold to say that, since the views of international lawyers are inevitably coloured by the notions prevailing in their own national legal systems, this variance of concepts as to the meaning of the doctrine of prescription in municipal law should be reckoned with as one of the main reasons for the controversy relating

[1] *Ibid.*, p. 24. It is rather extraordinary that Anglo-American international lawyers, coming from countries whose municipal legal systems have been somewhat reluctant in adopting Roman law, are, on the whole, more inclined to adopt Roman law notions for international law than jurists originating from Europe where the influence of Roman law is still strongly felt on the national legal level. A detailed analysis of this startling phenomenon would clearly go beyond the scope of this work. It is not intended here to do more than to draw attention to this intriguing problem which, no doubt, deserves a monograph of its own.

[2] *Ibid.*, p. 29.

[3] *Ibid.*, p. 30.

[4] *Ibid.*, p. 31.

[5] *Ibid.*, p. 7 (written in 1927).

to international prescription. It is for this reason that it is thought useful to contrast Roman and English law in this particular field for it is believed that by doing so some of the roots of the dispute overhanging this problem in international law may be brought more clearly into light.

9. *Prescription in municipal law – Roman law*

Roman private law distinguishes between two forms of prescription:
(a) *usucapio;*
(b) *possessio longi temporis.*

Usucapio means "the acquisition of ownership by continued possession for a certain time"[1] and was available as a mode of acquiring title to property in cases "where a person is in possession of property as owner but without legal title."[2] According to this doctrine, the possessor *justo titulo* and *bona fide*[3] during two years of land and during one year of movables acquired a property in the land or movables which had not previously belonged to him.[4]

The institution of *usucapio* was originally confined to *praedia Italica* and was available solely for Roman citizens. It was extended later to the provinces where it became known under the name of *possessio longi temporis.* Justinian blended together these two institutions and conferred the right of property on a person who had possessed movables for three years and immovables for ten years *inter praesentes* and twenty years *inter absentes*, provided that the other requirements essential for the operation of *usucapio* or *possessio longi temporis* were complied with.[5]

Thus, both *usucapio* and *possessio longi temporis* confer upon a person the right of property which he did not have previously, curing thereby an originally defective title. Both are measured by a definite period of time, the length of which is fixed by law.

In addition to these two forms of prescription there was in existence another kind of prescription, indefinite in time, which was available when the origin of possession was not capable of proof, i.e. when nobody could recollect that it had belonged to another person. This kind of prescription, known as *vetustas* or *antiquitas*,[6] does not in itself confer a right of property on the possessor, but raises a presumption of pos-

[1] Jolowicz, *Historical Introduction to the Study of Roman Law*, 2nd edition, 1952, p. 152.
[2] Lee, *Elements of Roman Law*, 3rd edition, 1952, p. 116.
[3] The requirement of good faith was dispensed with in certain exceptional cases, such as *usucapio pro herede*; see Girard, *Manuel élémentaire de droit romain*, 8th edition, 1927, p. 327.
[4] Lee, *op. cit.*, p. 119.
[5] *Ibid.*, p. 121.
[6] Other terms used are *immemoriale tempus, possessio vel praescriptic immemorialis.*

session in his favour, thus relying on a principle resembling the well-known legal maxim *omnia praesumuntur rite esse acta*. This presumption is not irrebuttable and "facts which indicate an unlawful origin, rebut the presumption of immemoriality."[1]

It should be mentioned, however, that, while *usucapio* and *possessio longi temporis* were resorted to solely as private law institutions, *vetustas*, on the other hand, found its application mainly in cases in which rights of public character were affected (e.g. rights relating to public ways or watercourses).[2] Moreover, the doctrine of *vetustas* – owing to its limited scope of application in daily life – has in fact occupied a rather subordinate place in Roman jurisprudence.

10. Prescription in municipal law – English law

English law distinguishes between common law prescription and prescription under the *Prescription Act, 1832*. At common law "the basis of prescription is that if long enjoyment of a right is shown, the Court will strive to uphold the right by presuming that it had a lawful origin."[3]

As to the length of time required for the establishment of a prescriptive title, "the conclusion reached by the courts was that [a person] must have enjoyed the right for time immemorial,"[4] or, as it has been said: "during the time whereof the memory of man runneth not to the contrary."[5] "Legal memory" was related back as far as 1189 (i.e. the first year of the reign of Richard I) and, because of the impossibility of literally fulfilling such a requirement, the courts have shown themselves willing to presume that enjoyment has lasted from 1189 if proof has been forthcoming of an actual enjoyment from as far as living witnesses could speak.[6] A period of twenty years would usually be sufficient to raise such a presumption.[7]

This presumption of "regularity," on which common law prescription is based, has also found its application in the form of the legal fiction of the "lost grant," which presumed the existence of grants in certain cases of long enjoyment of right.[8]

[1] Dernburg, *System des römischen Rechts*, 8th edition, 1911, vol. I, p. 380, where the author says: "Tatsachen welche eine unrechtmässige Entstehung dartun, entkräften die Unvordenklichkeit."

[2] *Ibid*., p. 379.

[3] Megarry and Wade, *op. cit*., p. 802.

[4] Cheshire, *The Modern Law of Real Property*, 8th edition, 1958, p. 471.

[5] *Co. Litt.* 114b.

[6] Cheshire, *op. cit*., p. 472.

[7] *Darling* v. *Clue* (1864), F. and F., p. 329, at p. 334.

[8] *Dalton* v. *Angus & Co.* (1881), 6 *A.C.*, p. 740, at p. 804, per Lord Penzance.

Following the pattern set by Roman law, English law requires for the operation of prescription the user to be as of right (*nec vi, nec clam, nec precario*).

Owing to the deficiencies inherent in the prescription at common law – in particular the difficulty of persuading juries to presume grants to have been lost when they knew this was not true – the *Prescription Act, 1832,* was enacted.[1] Section 2 of the Act provides, *inter alia,* that an easement which had been enjoyed without interruption for a period of 40 years shall be deemed absolute and indefeasible unless it was enjoyed by some consent or written agreement.[2]

However, it should be borne in mind that "the Act is only supplementary to the common law – it provides an additional method of claiming easements.... If, for instance, the claimant is unable to show enjoyment for a statutory period ... he may either prescribe at common law or invoke the doctrine of the lost grant."[3]

English law, therefore, still conceives two kinds of prescription, in each of which the time factor fulfils a different role. In prescription at common law the lapse of time is of probative value in that it contributes towards the strengthening of the presumption of regularity; in statutory prescription, on the other hand, the lapse of a certain period of time fixed by the Act is indispensable, since time is a constituent element of statutory prescription.

11. Prescription in municipal law – Conclusions

From the foregoing comparison of prescription in Roman and English law the following conclusions may be drawn:

In Roman law the time factor is a constituent element and thus of overriding importance both in *usucapio* and in *possessio longi temporis,* while *vetustas,* being an instrument of the law of evidence, is only of minor significance. The reverse is true of English law: here the common law notion of prescription still prevails. Prescription is regarded as being basically a tool of the law of evidence, and statutory prescription, which is most akin to *usucapio* and *possessio longi temporis,* is only supplementary to the common law.

Consequently, international lawyers trained in countries whose legal systems are rigidly modelled on Roman law patterns find some difficulty in reconciling the existence of prescription with the lack of a

[1] Megarry and Wade, *op. cit.,* p. 811.
[2] Cheshire, *op. cit.,* p. 477.
[3] *Ibid.,* p. 483.

definite period of time fixed by law, since the time factor is for them an essential element for the operation of prescription. Jurists originating from common law countries, on the other hand, apparently having in mind the doctrine of prescription at common law, are less impressed by this difficulty. Thus, it is not unlikely that, when reference is made to the doctrine of prescription, the minds of all lawyers are dominated by certain private law concepts drawn from their respective municipal legal systems. The result is that misunderstandings arise which tend to confuse the issues involved in this rather controversial field of international law.

It is therefore not altogether surprising that a writer and international lawyer of high distinction has gone as far as to suggest the complete abandonment of the term "prescription" and its substitution by the term "consolidation," explaining this change in terminology by saying that "to avoid useless discussion, the term 'consolidation' is preferred to 'acquisitive prescription.'"[1]

12. Doctrinal reasons for the existence of prescription in international law

A variety of reasons has been advanced in the writings of publicists to justify – from the doctrinal point of view – the existence of prescription in international law. First and foremost among them is the need to preserve international order and stability, since the repudiation of the doctrine of prescription would entail, in Grotius' words, "a very serious inconvenience in that contests about kingdoms and the boundaries of kingdoms never come to an end with lapse of time."[2]

Vattel voices the same opinion by saying that "la tranquilité des Peuples, le Salut des Etats, le bonheur du Genre-humain ne souffrent point que les Possessions, l'Empire et les autres droits des Nations demeurent incertains, sujets à contestation et toujours en état d'exciter des guerres sanglantes."[3]

This reason is given also by Wheaton,[4] Phillimore,[5] Audinet,[6] West-

[1] De Visscher, *Theory and Reality in Public International Law* (translated from the French by P. E. Corbett), 1957, p. 199.

[2] Grotius, *De Jure Belli ac Pacis*, the Classics of International Law, edited by J. B. Scott, translated by Francis W. Kelsey, 1925, book II, chapter IV, section I.

[3] Vattel, *Droit des Gens*, the Classics of International Law, edited by J. B. Scott, 1916, book II, chapter XI, para. 149.

[4] Wheaton, *Elements of International Law*, Dana's edition, 1866, sec. 164.

[5] Phillimore, *Commentaries upon International Law*, 3rd ed., 1879, vol. I, pp. 361–362.

[6] Audinet, "De la prescription acquisitive en droit international public," 3 *RGDIP* (1896), p. 313 *et seq.*

lake,[1] Hershey,[2] Nys,[3] Lawrence,[4] Hall,[5] Fauchille,[6] Lindley,[7] Verykios[8] and Oppenheim.[9]

For Ortolan[10] prescription is based on the theory that a State which has maintained order in a territory and developed it, is entitled to sovereignty over it against the former possessor who had neglected that territory.[11]

Grotius mentions as an additional reason the presumed voluntary abandonment of the former possessor's rights, since "silence for... [a] length of time will always seem sufficient to imply abandonment of ownership."[12]

Among other reasons that are occasionally advanced one might mention the argument according to which prescription is "the punishment for negligence," for "time runs against the indolent and those who are careless of their rights."[13]

Others again maintain that the real reason for the existence of prescription is that the lapse of time makes it increasingly difficult for a claimant to supply any positive evidence as to the origins of his title.[14]

All these arguments, while undoubtedly containing elements of practical wisdom and expediency, seem to ignore the fact that, although considerations of this kind might well underlie the doctrine of prescription in any given legal system, it is not the principles referred to that in fact introduce this doctrine into the law. This reasoning has therefore met with the objection – rightly, it is believed – that those founding international prescription on such doctrinal grounds "font une confusion entre l'opportunité de la prescription, les raisons abstraites qui sont à sa faveur et sa reconnaissance positive par la volonté

[1] Westlake, *International Law*, 2nd ed., 1910, part I, p. 94.

[2] Hershey, *The Essentials of International Public Law*, 1912, p. 180.

[3] Nys, *Le droit international* (revised edition), 1912, vol. II, p. 40.

[4] Lawrence, *The Principles of International Law*, 7th ed., 1923, section 78.

[5] Hall, *Treatise on International Law*, 8th ed., 1924, p. 143.

[6] Fauchille, *Traité de droit international public*, 8th ed., 1925, vol. I, part II, p. 757.

[7] Lindley, *The Acquisition and Government of Backward Territory in International Law*, 1926, p. 178.

[8] Verykios, *La prescription en droit international public*, 1934, p. 25.

[9] Oppenheim, *op. cit.*, p. 576.

[10] Ortolan, *Des moyens d'acquérir le domaine international*, 1851, p. 125.

[11] See to the same effect Verykios, *op. cit.*, p. 31 and Sørensen, "La prescription en droit international public," 3 *ASJG* (1932), p. 149. A similar argument was advanced by the United States Secretary of State Olney in a letter to Sir Julian Pauncefote, dated June 12th, 1896, as reported in 88 *BFSP*, p. 1288.

[12] Grotius, *op. cit.*, sec. VII; see also Vattel, *op. cit.*, para. 140; see also Verykios, *op. cit.*, pp. 26–28 and Audinet, *loc. cit.*, p. 315.

[13] Bracton, *De Legibus et Consuetidinibus Angliae*, ed. by Twiss, 1879, vol. II, p. 123; see also Verykios, *op. cit.*, pp. 29–30.

[14] Verykios, *op. cit.*, p. 36.

collective des Etats."[1] More recently Pinto has expressed a similar view by maintaining that "ces fondements philosophiques, éthiques ou politiques – seraient ils communs aux prescriptions du droit interne et aux institutions du droit international que l'on qualifie ainsi – n'autorisent pas à assimiler les unes aux autres. On les retrouve en effet à la base de très nombreuses institutions juridiques bien distinctes – principe de non retroactivité des lois – principe *Pacta sunt servanda* – principe de la responsabilité internationale."[2]

The same author goes on to say that "l'institution [de prescription] suppose... un état social déjà avancé. Elle suppose un système juridique évolué qui comprend des procédures établies de création des règles, des actes et des titres juridiques susceptibles de transférer des droits."[3] Thus, it is not the abstract ideas underlying the doctrine of prescription, but "le système juridique évolué" that enables any given law to adopt this principle. It is therefore not surprising that ancient legal systems did not recognize the institution of prescription. As has been shown by Pinto, the ancient legal systems of China, India and Rome ignored this institution.[4] It might be questioned whether international law, in its present rudimentary condition, has really achieved the status of a "système juridique évolué qui comprend des procédures établies de création des règles, des actes et des titres juridiques susceptibles de transférer des droits."

As for the theory of "the presumption of abandonment," it would appear that it rests on a legal inconsistency. It overlooks the fact that, if the abandonment of a disputed territory is to be presumed, that territory consequently becomes *res nullius* and is thus open to acquisition *by occupation*. Prescription, however, is based on the reverse assumption, namely, that the previous owner has *not* given up his rights. This is why "par la prescription va être acquis un titre à l'encontre de l'ancien souverain, c'est-à-dire indépendamment de l'assentiment de celui-ci."[5] In other words: prescriptive rights are acquired solely by adverse holding.[6]

The contention, according to which international prescription, like municipal prescription, amounts to "the punishment of negligence"

[1] Cavaglieri, 26 *Hague Recueil* (1929), vol. I, p. 405.

[2] Pinto, "La prescription en droit international," 87 *Hague Recueil* (1955), vol. I, p. 387 *et seq.*, at p. 400. (Italics in original).

[3] *Ibid.*, p. 392.

[4] *Ibid.*,

[5] Beckett, 50 *Hague Recueil* (1934), vol. IV, p. 248.

[6] The theory of the presumption of abandonment has also been severely criticized by Verykios, *op. cit.*, p. 27; by Cavaglieri, *loc. cit.*, p. 406; and by Fauchille, *op. cit.*, p. 757.

has been commented upon by Pierre Dupuy as long ago as 1670, when he said that prescription was "une espèce de peine que la loi inflige aux négligens. Mais les princes souverains n'ont point de lois entre eux qui les lient et obligent."[1] This notion of "punishing the negligent" is closely related to the doctrine of estoppel, and, as will be suggested elsewhere, the principle of estoppel should not be invoked either as the doctrinal basis for the formation of an historic title.[2]

It is submitted that the question whether or not prescription exists in international law should be decided in the light of purely legal – as distinct from meta-legal – considerations, as they have found expression in the works of writers, in the decisions of both national and international tribunals and in the practice of States.

13. The existence of prescription in international law – Opinions of writers

"International prescription has been for centuries the favourite subject of all learned dissertations, the main playground of pure theory and scholarly wisdom."[3] The controversial nature of the subject is well illustrated by the writings of Grotius, already containing the seeds of the arguments which were later put forward by the supporters of international prescription and their opponents alike. Grotius' views on this subject are far from being unequivocal.[4] In his *Mare liberum* (first published in 1609) he rejected the existence of international prescription. "Prescription," he argued, "is a matter of municipal law; hence it cannot be applied as between kings or as between free and independent nations;... For it is impossible to acquire by usucaption or prescription things which cannot become property, that is, which are not susceptible of possession or of quasi-possession and which cannot be alienated."[5]

In his later years Grotius' views on this subject seem to have under-

[1] As quoted by Pinto, *loc. cit.*, p. 396.

[2] See below chapter III, section 31.

[3] Heimburger, *Der Erwerb der Gebietshoheit*, 1888, part I, p. 143, where the author says: "Die völkerrechtliche Verjährung bildete Jahrhunderte hindurch das Lieblingsthema aller gelehrten Dissertationen, den hauptsächlichen Tummelplatz der reinen Theorie und Schulweisheit."

[4] As has already been pointed out by Lauterpacht, in a different context, "this contradictory attitude... is amazing only when we forget that some of the difficulties in the writings of Grotius which puzzle the student and commentator are due to the fact that exactitude of terminology cannot be regarded as one of the achievements of the great lawyer." (Lauterpacht, *op. cit.*, p. 13).

[5] Grotius, *Mare Liberum*, the Classics of International Law, edited by J. B. Scott, translated by Magoffin, 1916, chap. VII, p. 47.

gone some modification and in his *De Jure Belli ac Pacis* (first published in 1625) he qualified his former rejection of international prescription by saying that "a serious difficulty arises at this point in regard to the right of usucaption. For since this right was introduced by municipal law (time, in fact, in its own nature has no effective force; nothing is done by time, though everything is done in time), it has no place... in the relations between two independent states or kings."[1] Thus, he rejected the idea of international *usucapio*, but adopted from Roman law the concept of immemorial possession. In his view, "because a length of time exceeding the memory of man is in its essential character practically infinite, a silence for that length of time will always seem sufficient to imply abandonment of ownership, unless there are very strong reasons to the contrary."[2] He went on to argue that "possession beyond the limits of memory not interrupted nor called in question by appeal to the courts, should absolutely transfer ownership."[3] In Grotius' opinion "time exceeding the memory of man" was about a century, "because a hundred years ordinarily constitute the limit of human life,"[4] and he assumed that "the nations agreed in this, since it was of the greatest importance for the preservation of the common peace."[5]

Thus, Grotius drew a sharp distinction between *usucapio* and immemorial possession and, while rejecting the former, adopted the latter for international law. It is a matter for regret that this distinction has not always been followed since, and the widespread tendency to confound these two different aspects of prescription has undoubtedly contributed towards increasing the confusion that has ever since prevailed in this field of international law. Accordingly, these two aspects of the problem will be dealt with separately.

It may safely be maintained that the existence of immemorial possession in international law has gained general acceptance among writers. Even such fierce opponents of international *usucapio* as Heffter,[6] de Louter[7] and Rivier[8] have espoused doctrines virtually amounting to the recognition of the existence of immemorial possession in international law. They admit that a long and undisturbed possession of a

[1] Grotius, *De Jure Belli ac Pacis*, the Classics of International Law, edited by J. B. Scott, translated by Francis W. Kelsey, 1925, book II, chap. IV, sec. I.
[2] *Ibid.*, sec. VII.
[3] *Ibid.*, sec. IX.
[4] *Ibid.*, sec. VII.
[5] *Ibid.*, sec. IX.
[6] Heffter, *Das europäische Völkerrecht der Gegenwart*, 8th ed. (by Geffcken), 1888, p. 38.
[7] De Louter, *Le droit international public positif*, 1920, vol. I, p. 341.
[8] Rivier, *Principes du droit des gens*, 1896, vol. I, pp. 182–183.

territory strongly militates in favour of the presumption that the State in possession has an originally valid title over this territory. "The postulate of this form of prescription is that a state of things exists the origin of which is uncertain. It is impossible to prove whether the origin of this state of affairs is legal or illegal. It is therefore presumed to be legal."[1] Consequently, it has been argued that immemorial possession does not create new rights, but confines itself to lending its sanction to a certain state of things the origins of which it is impossible to trace and which is therefore assumed to have come into existence in conformity with the legal requirements. In other words: it does not *confer* a new title; it only *consecrates* a title which had already been in existence.[2]

However, immemorial possession in itself would be too narrow a concept – even by the widest stretch of imagination – to cope with the necessities of international order, since "there are few, very few, titles of which it can be said that they have lasted for so long, 'qu'il est impossible de fournir la preuve d'une situation différente et qu'aucune personne ne se souvient d'en avoir entendu parler.'"[3]

Owing to the longevity of the subjects of international law, the theory of immemorial possession, if literally taken, is virtually impracticable and the time-limit of 100 years, as suggested by Grotius, would certainly be too short a period to justify the assumption that the memory of States fails them whenever they have to recollect events which lie further back. This rather arbitrary suggestion put forward by Grotius in fact transforms immemorial possession into *usucapio*, the existence of which in the sphere of international law Grotius so strenuously denied.

Thus, the correct view seems to have been stated by Johnson when he said that, from the point of view of international law, immemorial possession is of comparatively minor importance and that the real field of controversy is "whether that form of 'acquisitive prescription' which presupposes an originally defective title but which relies on possession for a reasonable period of time to cure the defect, or in other words that form of prescription which is akin to *usucapio* (*prescription proprement dite*, as some authors call it), is a recognized doctrine of international law."[4]

[1] Johnson, "Acquisitive Prescription in International Law," 27 *BYIL* (1950), p. 332 *et seq.*, p. 334.

[2] The correctness of this view has been doubted by some writers. See e.g. Verykios, *op. cit.*, p. 44, n. 1.

[3] Johnson, *loc. cit.*, p. 339, where he quotes this definition of immemorial possession which was given by the tribunal in the *Meerauge* arbitration between Austria and Hungary concerning certain lakes in Galicia. The arbitral award can be found in 8 *RDILC* (*Deuxième série*) (1906), p. 196. The passage quoted may be found at p. 207 there.

[4] Johnson, *loc. cit.*, p. 336. (Italics in original).

Grotius' negative view as to the applicability of *usucapio* in international law has already been indicated. Vattel, on the other hand, maintained that *usucapio* was part of the Natural Law, and therefore of the Law of Nations. He accepted international *usucapio* which he defined as "l'acquisition du domaine fondée sur une longue possession non interrompue et non contestée."[1] He bluntly admitted that international law did not provide for the operation of *usucapio*, but he asserted that this problem could be settled by custom or by treaty.[2]

The later doctrinal developments concerning the question of the existence of international *usucapio* may be described as a constant struggle between the "Grotians" and the "Vattelians." It would appear that one is not wide off the mark if one says that, on the whole, writers coming from common law countries have turned out to be "Vattelians,"[3] whereas jurists who had been brought up by the Roman school of legal thinking have displayed a strong tendency to accept "Grotianism."[4]

Thus, one is tempted to believe that a jurist coming from a common law country has – for reasons which have been elaborated above[5] – less difficulty in conceiving a form of prescription which is devoid of requirements relating to a specified period of time than is the case with lawyers trained elsewhere, who have been taught to believe that the time element, as expressly fixed by law, is the very essence and the prerequisite for the operation of prescription.

From the legal viewpoint the adoption of *usucapio* for international law encounters yet another obstacle: the requirement of good faith. This aspect of the problem will now be touched upon briefly before reverting to the examination of the role of the time element in international *usucapio*.

Usucapio, both in Roman and in English law, assumes good faith on the part of the person claiming for himself the benefits of prescription,[6] since "le domaine de prescription est limité aux situations... *subjectives*. Elle ne trouve aucune application lorsqu'il s'agit de situations *objectives*."[7] In theory Vattel too required good faith as a condition for the

[1] Vattel, *op. cit.*, para. 140.

[2] *Ibid.*

[3] Hall, *op. cit.*, p. 143; Hershey, *op. cit.*, pp. 226–227; Lawrence, *op. cit.*, p. 160; Phillimore, *op. cit.*, pp. 353–358; Lindley, *op. cit.*, pp. 178–180; Wheaton, *op. cit.*, p. 200.

[4] As to a detailed list of writers who have declared themselves against the existence of *usucapio* in international law, see Verykios, *op. cit.*, pp. 201–203.

[5] See above, section 11.

[6] As will be recalled, in Roman law there were certain exceptional cases in which this requirement was dispensed with, as it was generally considered as belonging to an earlier and more primitive stage of Roman law. (See p. 9, n. 3 above).

[7] Pinto, *loc. cit.*, p. 394. (Italics added).

operation of international *usucapio*, although he was prepared to assume good faith in the absence of contrary evidence.[1] In this respect Vattel seems to be rather isolated even within the camp of the "Vattelians" who have come to realize that in the international sphere the requirement of good faith, if insisted upon, would virtually amount to putting the whole machinery of prescription out of operation. Thus, Fauchille – himself a "Vattelian" – admits that, at least in so far as the inhabited parts of the globe are concerned, "la prescription aura presque toujours à sa base un acte de violence."[2] Similarly, Hall states that "internationally [prescription] is allowed for the sake of interests which have hitherto been looked upon as supreme to lend itself as a sanction for wrong, when wrong has shown itself strong enough not only to triumph for a moment but to establish itself permanently and solidly."[3] And Verykios went even further by asking: "A quoi bon exiger une telle condition en droit international, alors qu'elle ne sera jamais remplie? Car nous prétendons que, spécialement pour les territoires habités, l'Etat possesseur sera toujours de mauvaise foi."[4]

If then, even in the view of the "Vattelians" themselves, international *usucapio* has been deprived of an attribute which is regarded as an essential element of *usucapio* in domestic law, namely, the requirement of good faith, the additional deficiency expressing itself in the lack of a fixed period of time is felt even more strongly. "If thus there becomes evident bad faith – a thing held to be permanent in a nation as well as in an individual – then prescription fails because of a double defect."[5] In fact, the main difficulty in recognizing the existence of international *usucapio* stems from the fact that "dans les systèmes juridiques modernes la prescription a reçu du législateur une 'armature technique' complexe.... Dans son mécanisme le temps est généralement considéré comme élément essentiel. Ce temps n'est pas la durée du philosophe."[6]

Audinet has attempted to meet this objection by distinguishing between "le droit de prescription" and "la loi de la prescription,"[7] which has been explained as a distinction between a principle and its technical applications.[8] Similarly, Fauchille maintains that, although the appli-

[1] Vattel, *op. cit.*, para. 150.
[2] Fauchille, *op. cit.*, p. 758.
[3] Hall, *op. cit.*, pp. 143–144.
[4] Verykios, *op. cit.*, pp. 74–75.
[5] Grotius, *Mare Liberum*, the Classics of International Law, edited by J. B. Scott, translated by Magoffin, 1916, pp. 50–51.
[6] Pinto, *loc. cit.*, p. 395.
[7] Audinet, *loc. cit.*, p. 315.
[8] Johnson, *loc. cit.*, p. 334.

cation of prescription in international law "ne peut être déterminée d'une manière uniforme, le principe en est inhérent à la nature des choses et essentiel à l'existence des nations."[1] And Sørensen follows suit by saying that "l'acquisition par prescription doit être possible... car on admet généralement que le droit international s'appuie... sur la nature de la chose."[2]

With due respect to the eminence of these distinguished writers it is felt that "la nature des choses" should not be invoked as evidence for the existence of any positive rule of law. The advancement of such an argument is, of course, perfectly legitimate as long as one is concerned with the desirability of introducing a certain rule into a given legal system, but would be utterly inappropriate as a means of proving its existence as a rule of positive law. The course advocated by Audinet, Fauchille and Sørensen is in fact tantamount to deducing the existence of *lex lata* from its being *lex ferenda.*

It now remains to be seen whether the judicial decisions and the manifestations of State practice usually relied upon as evidence for the recognition of prescription in the sphere of international law indeed endorse this doctrine.

14. The existence of prescription in international law – Judicial decisions rendered by international tribunals

It is a fact of considerable significance that "des décisions importantes qui pour une partie de la doctrine fondent ou consacrent le droit de prescription dans le droit international n'usent pas de mot,"[3] although, in some of these cases, the parties or one of them in their pleadings expressly argued on this ground. It is felt therefore that the persistent silence observed by the tribunals on this point should not be considered as devoid of any legal meaning.

(a) The Grisbadarna Arbitration, 1909

The *Grisbadarna* Arbitration Award of October 23rd, 1909,[4] has been frequently referred to as one of the instances in which the doctrine of prescription was accorded recognition. In fact, both Sweden and Nor-

[1] Fauchille, *op. cit.*, p. 755.
[2] Sørensen, *loc. cit.*, p. 149.
[3] Pinto, *loc. cit.*, p. 397.
[4] *UNRIAA*, vol. XI, p. 155 (in the original French). The English translation of the award has been published in 4 *AJIL* (1910), p. 226, in Wilson's *Hague Arbitration Cases*, 1915, p. 102, and in Scott's *Hague Court Reports*, 1st Series, 1916, p. 121.

way – the parties to that arbitration – expressly invoked the doctrine in their pleadings. The arbitral award, however, does not mention the term "prescription" at all. Notwithstanding this fact, Lauterpacht is of the opinion that "in the Grisbadarna case ...judgment was given on grounds amounting virtually to a recognition of prescription in international law, although the term itself was not mentioned by the tribunal."[1] It is thought, nevertheless, that this award should not be construed as a recognition of the principle of international *usucapio*, since it appears that it is based on the concept of immemorial possession. This clearly emerges from that passage of the award where the tribunal concludes that "from [the] various circumstances it appears so probable as to be almost certain that the Swedes utilized the banks in question much earlier and much more effectively than the Norwegians."[2] In the opinion of the tribunal, Sweden succeeded in establishing her rights over the Grisbadarna by utilizing that region *prior* to the Norwegians, whereas the concept of acquisition by *usucapio* would have required Norwegian utilization to precede that of the Swedes. It is in this context that one should analyze the tribunal's statement, according to which

> it is a settled principle of the law of nations that a state of things which actually exists and has existed for a long time should be changed as little as possible[3].

(b) The Chamizal Arbitration, 1911

The *Chamizal* Arbitration between the United States of America and Mexico[4] is cited as another instance in which the doctrine of international prescription is purported to have been upheld. However, it would appear that the award does not lend itself to such a sweeping interpretation. In the tribunal's own words:

> In the countercase of the United States, the contention is advanced that the United States has acquired a good title by prescription to the tract in dispute.... *Without thinking it necessary to discuss the very controversial question as to whether the right of prescription invoked by the United States is an accepted principle of the law of nations, in the absence of any convention establishing a term of prescription*, the commissioners are unanimous in coming to the conclusion that the possession of the United States in the present case was not of such a character as to found a prescriptive title.[5]

Quite obviously the tribunal entertained serious doubts as to the applicability of prescription in the sphere of international law and pre-

[1] Lauterpacht, *op. cit.*, p. 264; see also to the same effect Sørensen, *loc. cit.*, pp. 152–153.
[2] Scott, *op. cit.*, p. 131; *UNRIAA*, vol. XI, p. 161.
[3] Scott, *op. cit.*, p. 130; *UNRIAA*, vol. XI, p. 161.
[4] Award of June 15th, 1911, *UNRIAA*, vol. XI, p. 316; 5 *AJIL* (1911), p. 782 *et seq.*
[5] *UNRIAA*, vol. XI, p. 328. (Italics added).

ferred to deal with the American contention "under protest." In other words: the tribunal was prepared to accept the plea of prescription solely for the sake of argument and proceeded at once to refute it by showing that the United States' possession of the tract in dispute had not complied with the requirements which are enumerated by the protagonists of prescription themselves as the necessary prerequisites for the formation of a prescriptive title. Thus, the award constitutes a dissociation from the notion of prescription rather than its endorsement.[1]

(c) The Walfish Bay Arbitration, 1911

Nor can it be conceded that the award given in 1911 in the *Walfish Bay* Arbitration between Great Britain and Germany[2] amounts to a recognition of the doctrine of international prescription.[3] All the tribunal was prepared to say in that case was that, since "exception has not been taken to the continued possession on the part of Great Britain of the territory extending to the point on the coast where the southern frontier [of the bay]... commences, it is necessary to accept the fact of possession" as being "the evidence of a wish to acquire, and of an effective occupation, by which in any case British sovereignty could have been established over the zone in dispute, *before the adjacent territory was placed under the protection of Germany*."[4]

Thus, in this case also, the tribunal's award was based on a principle which is the very opposite of *adverse* holding and it is therefore not surprising that the term "prescription" was not mentioned at all in the award.

(d) The Anglo-Brazilian Boundary Dispute, 1904

Similarly, the use of that term was avoided in the arbitral award rendered in 1904 in the *Anglo-Brazilian Boundary* dispute concerning the boundaries of British Guiana.[5] King Victor Emanuel III of Italy, in his capacity as sole arbitrator, confined himself to saying:

That it does not appear... that there are historical and legal claims on which to

[1] See however, the opposing view held by Lauterpacht, *op. cit.*, pp. 276–277; see also to the same effect Johnson, *loc. cit.*, p. 340, and Verdross, *Völkerrecht*, 4th ed., 1959, p. 224.

[2] *UNRIAA*, vol. XI, p. 267; the award has also been reported in *Hertslet's Treaties*, vol. 26, p. 187, and in 104 *BFSP*, p. 50.

[3] This view has been expressed e.g. by Lauterpacht, *op. cit.*, p. 277.

[4] *UNRIAA*, vol. XI, pp. 307–308. (Italics added). See also 104 *BFSP*, pp. 101–102, and *Hertslet's Treaties*, vol. 26, p. 249. For some reason the italicized portion of the passage has been deleted by Lauterpacht, *op. cit.*, p. 277.

[5] *UNRIAA*, vol. XI, p. 21. The award has also been printed in 11 *RGDIP* (1904), Documents, p. 18, and in 99 *BFSP*, p. 930.

found thoroughly determined and well-defined rights of sovereignty in favour of either of the contending Powers over the whole of the territory in dispute,...[1].

He went on to say

That it cannot... be decided with certainty whether the right of Brazil or Great Britain is the stronger."[2]

Consequently, the arbitrator decided to divide the territory in dispute "in accordance with the lines traced by nature,"[3] as such course "better lends itself to a fair decision of the disputed territory."[4]

(e) The Meerauge Arbitration, 1902

As to the *Meerauge* Arbitration between Austria and Hungary,[5] it will be recalled that the tribunal in that case was confronted solely with the problem of immemorial possession which was defined in its award as being a possession "qui dure depuis si longtemps qu'il est impossible de fournir la preuve d'une situation différente et qu'aucune personne ne se souvient d'en avoir entendu parler."[6]

(f) The Fur Seal Arbitration, 1893

In the award rendered on August 15th, 1893, in the *Fur Seal* Arbitration between Great Britain and the United States of America[7] "neither the term nor the doctrine [of prescription] is mentioned in the written and oral arguments of the parties, or in the pronouncements of the arbitrators – with the exception of a casual remark by Lord Hannen [one of the British members of the tribunal]... denying the existence of prescription in international law."[8]

While "it appears clearly, both from the opinions of the American arbitrators and from the oral argument, that it was on the basis of prescription that the United States originally founded one of their main contentions... it is admitted by the agent of the United States in his final report that early in the preparation of the case the conclusion

1 *UNRIAA*, vol. XI, p. 22.
2 *Ibid.*
3 *Ibid.*
4 *Ibid.*
5 8 *RDILC* (*Deuxième série*) (1906), p. 196. (This case has been mentioned by Fauchille among those allegedly upholding the doctrine of international prescription; see Fauchille, *op. cit.*, p. 756).
6 8 *RDILC (Deuxième série)* (1906), p. 207.
7 95 *BFSP*, p. 1185. The case is also known as the *Behring Sea* Arbitration case. For a detailed report of this case, see Moore's *International Arbitrations*, vol. I, pp. 755–961; see also Smith's *Great Britain and the Law of Nations*, vol. II, 1935, pp. 369–422.
8 Lauterpacht, *op. cit.*, p. 224.

was reached that it would be difficult to sustain the plea of prescription."[1]

(g) The Alaskan Boundary Dispute, 1903

The experience that had been accumulated in the course of the deliberations in the *Fur Seal* Arbitration caused the United States in the *Alaskan Boundary* Dispute between herself and the United Kingdom[2] to forsake the plea of prescription and she "expressly disclaimed the intention of availing [herself] of the plea of prescription."[3] Nevertheless, "the Canadian arbitrator and the British counsel tried to construe the United States' argument as a plea of prescription, which they promptly proceeded to reject... as a rule of international law. In the course of this stage of the argument, the President, Lord Alverstone, associated himself with the view expressed by Lord Hannen in the course of the Behring Sea Arbitration, that... prescription so called was not recognized in international law."[4]

It is therefore somewhat startling that this case as well has been cited by some writers as yet another instance for the recognition of the principle of prescription in international law.[5]

(h) The Legal Status of Eastern Greenland Case, 1933

The case concerning the *Legal Status of Eastern Greenland*[6] has also been occasionally relied upon as evidence for the recognition of international prescription. This dispute between Norway and Denmark arose as a result of certain Norwegian decrees purporting to annex parts of Greenland and thereby affecting Danish rights over the same territories. However, as has already been pointed out by Beckett, the real issue involved in this case was not whether one of the parties had acquired any rights through adverse holding – which is what acquisition by prescription means – but whether the territory in question was *res nullius* or under Danish sovereignty.[7] Beckett went on to say that "c'est pourquoi j'ai... déclaré que dans l'affaire du Groenland [le débat portait] sur l'occupation."[8] The same view is also held by other writers.[9]

[1] *Ibid.*, pp. 224–225.
[2] The award has been printed in 98 *BFSP*, p. 152; see also *Hertslet's Treaties*, vol. 25, p. 1183, and Pitt Cobbett's *Cases on International Law*, 4th ed., 1922, vol. I, pp. 99–107.
[3] Lauterpacht, *op. cit.*, p. 235.
[4] *Ibid.*, pp. 235–236.
[5] E.g. Sørensen, *loc. cit.*, p. 152.
[6] *PCIJ*, Series A/B, No. 53.
[7] Beckett, 50 *Hague Recueil* (1934), vol. IV, p. 233.
[8] *Ibid.*, pp. 248–249.
[9] E.g. Hackworth, *Digest of International Law*, vol. I, 1940, p. 405, where this case is classified under the heading of occupation; see also Johnson, *loc. cit.*, p. 343.

(i) The Fisheries Case, 1951

As to the *Fisheries* case,[1] according to Pinto, the International Court of Justice did not resort there to the doctrine of prescription. Its traces can be found, in the opinion of this writer, only in the Separate and Dissenting Opinions.[2] The Court's reluctance to pronounce on this problem cannot be overlooked in view of the fact that in the pleadings of the parties, both oral and written, international prescription was resorted to and dealt with at great length. In the United Kingdom's Reply of November 28th, 1950, express reference was made to this notion and it was argued that the acquisition of rights over maritime territories in derogation of the generally applicable rules can be made by means of prescription only.[3] In the Rejoinder submitted by Norway on April 30th, 1951, the very existence of international prescription was challenged. It was argued by Norway, *inter alia,* that "la notion de la prescription est constamment invoquée par le Gouvernement britannique dans le présent litige.... Mais cette notion est loin d'être unaniment admise. De nombreux auteurs pensent que la prescription acquisitive n'est pas une institution du droit international et se refusent à en faire la base des titres historiques."[4]

Thus, the silence observed by the Court in its judgment on this problem can only be interpreted as meaning that the Court itself entertained some doubts as to the applicability of this doctrine in the sphere of international law. The Court contented itself with the rather obscure statement – from the doctrinal point of view – that "the general toleration of foreign States with regard to the Norwegian practice is an unchallenged fact. For a period of more than sixty years the United Kingdom Government itself in no way contested it."[5] This cautious wording can hardly be taken as an endorsement of the doctrine of prescription, which, in fact, was explicitly mentioned only in the Individual Opinion of Judge Alvarez.[6] For this Chilean jurist the doctrines of prescription and historic rights were identical.[7] Yet he deemed it appropriate to point out that "the concept of prescription in international law is quite different from that which it has in domestic law.... There is no prescription with regard to [the] territorial status [of States]."[8] In the

[1] *ICJ Reports,* 1951, p. 116 *et seq.*
[2] Pinto, *loc. cit.,* pp. 397–398.
[3] *ICJ, Fisheries case, Pleadings, Oral Arguments, Documents,* vol. II, pp. 649–651.
[4] *Ibid.,* vol. III, p. 440.
[5] *ICJ Reports,* 1951, p. 138.
[6] *Ibid.,* pp. 151–152.
[7] *Ibid.,* p. 151.
[8] *Ibid.*

Dissenting Opinions of Judge Sir Arnold (now Lord) McNair[1] and Judge Read[2] the problem of historic waters is dealt with without any recourse being had to the principle of prescription.

(j) The Minquiers and Ecrehos Case, 1953

In the *Minquiers and Ecrehos* case[3] both sides refrained from expressly invoking the doctrine of prescription. Both the United Kingdom and France, the parties to this dispute, pleaded a very long possession of the disputed islets and claimed to have acquired an original title to them. "The much criticized, but somewhat uncertain, doctrine of prescription was not invoked by either side,"[4] and it was only alternatively claimed that title had been established by long-continued "effective possession." This reluctance of the parties of availing themselves expressly of the plea of prescription has been attributed to "the tendency to regard prescription purely as a means of acquiring title through adverse possession."[5]

The Court in its judgment found for the United Kingdom on the first ground, namely, that the United Kingdom had established an original title to the contested islets, which it had never abandoned. The Court, therefore, did not find it necessary to pronounce on the alternative argument advanced by the parties.

(k) The Sovereignty over Certain Frontier Land Case, 1959

In the case concerning *Sovereignty over Certain Frontier Land*[6] the International Court of Justice had to pronounce in a dispute which had arisen between Belgium and the Netherlands relating to certain portions of territory which were claimed by Belgium as part of her domain, but over which the Netherlands seem to have exercised for a century or so diverse governmental functions. The Netherlands contended, *inter alia*, that, even if it were to be assumed that sovereignty over the disputed areas had originally been vested in Belgium by virtue of the Boundary Convention of 1843 concluded between the two countries, the acts of sovereignty performed ever since by the Netherlands in these areas firmly established the sovereignty of the Netherlands. The Court was

[1] *Ibid.*, pp. 158–185.
[2] *Ibid.*, pp. 186–206.
[3] *ICJ Reports*, 1953, p. 47 *et seq.*
[4] Johnson, "The Minquiers and Ecrehos Case," 3 *ICLQ* (1954), p. 189, at p. 208. Johnson was one of the United Kingdom Counsel before the *ICJ* in that case.
[5] Johnson, "Consolidation as a Root of Title in International Law," *Cambridge Law Journal* (1955), p. 215, at p. 220.
[6] *ICJ Reports*, 1959, p. 209.

therefore faced with the question "whether Belgium has lost its sovereignty, by non-assertion of its rights and by acquiescence in acts of sovereignty alleged to have been exercised by the Netherlands."[1] Thus, the Court approached the problem from the point of view of Belgium's alleged acquiescence without resorting to the doctrine of prescription and, having reached the conclusion that Belgium's attitude should not be construed as such acquiescence, the Court found for Belgium.

In a declaration read after the pronouncement of the Court's decision, Judge Sir Hersch Lauterpacht gave his reasons for having voted with the minority in favour of awarding the disputed territories to the Netherlands. Sir Hersch maintained that "at least during the fifty years following the adoption of the Convention there had been no challenge to the exercise, by the Government of the Netherlands and its officials, of normal administrative authority with regard to the plots in question. ...There is no room here for applying the exacting rules of prescription in relation to a title acquired by a clear and unequivocal treaty; there is no such treaty."[2]

Judge Armand-Ugon in his Dissenting Opinion pointed out that "the Netherlands Government has exercised preponderant governmental functions in respect of the disputed plots, without these having given rise on the part of the Belgian Government to any protest or any opposition. This prolonged tolerance of the Belgian Government in this respect has created an indisputable right of sovereignty in favour of the Netherlands Government."[3]

Both the majority and minority judges refrained from invoking the doctrine of prescription, and the criterion applied by majority and minority alike was whether or not Belgium was presumed to have acquiesced in the Netherlands sovereignty over the disputed plots.

(l) The Palmas Island Arbitration, 1928

One of the well-known judicial decisions relating to the acquisition of title to territory in international law is the *Palmas Island* Arbitration Case[4] in which Judge Huber acted as sole arbitrator. The award rendered in this case is frequently relied upon by the supporters of international prescription as yet another instance for the recognition of this doctrine by an international tribunal. The dispute in this case arose between the United States of America and the Netherlands concerning the sover-

[1] *Ibid.*, p. 227.
[2] *Ibid.*, p. 231.
[3] *Ibid.*, p. 250.
[4] The award has been printed in *UNRIAA*, vol. II, p. 829; see also 22 *AJIL* (1928), p. 867.

eignty over the island of Palmas (or Miangas), not far off the Philippines. The United States claimed that the original title to the island – based on discovery – rested with Spain and that, following the cession to the United States of the Spanish dependencies in the region, under the Treaty of Paris, 1898, the sovereignty over the island of Palmas as well was to be vested thereafter in the United States. The Netherlands, on the other hand, maintained that they had been exercising effective control over the island for several centuries without having encountered opposition of any kind and that consequently the legal title rested with them and not with the United States. In his award, rendered on April 4th, 1928, Judge Huber accepted the Netherlands' view and found in favour of the Netherlands because "practice, as well as doctrine, recognizes – though under different legal formulae and with certain differences as to the conditions required – that the continuous and peaceful display of territorial sovereignty (peaceful in relation to other States) is as good as a title."[1] Thus, the arbitrator evaded any reference to the notion of prescription, although the applicability of this principle was expressly put in issue by the parties. The Netherlands in their Memorandum[2] had come out strongly in favour of the existence of international prescription, while the United States in their Counter-Memorandum had vigorously opposed the invocation of this principle.[3]

The only mention of prescription in this award is by means of an oblique reference to the doctrine of "so-called prescription,"[4] which can hardly be taken as an endorsement of the principle. This, however, has not prevented a distinguished author from maintaining that "dans l'affaire... de l'île de Palmas la prescription a également été admise."[5] Jessup seems to have stated the correct view when he said that "unfortunately, Judge Huber did not deal fully with [the] question [of prescription], contenting himself with the statement that the Supreme Court of the United States had applied the doctrine as between states [of the Union] and had relied on Vattel and Wheaton."[6]

In fact, Judge Huber's reference to some decisions given by the United States Supreme Court[7] has evoked criticism in some quarters who

[1] *UNRIAA*, vol. II, p. 839; see also 22 *AJIL* (1928), p. 867.

[2] See Hyde, *International Law Chiefly as Interpreted and Applied by the United States*, 2nd revised ed., 1945, vol. I, p. 388.

[3] *Ibid.*

[4] *UNRIAA*, vol. II, p. 868; see also 22 *AJIL* (1928) p. 909.

[5] Sørensen, *loc. cit.*, p. 153.

[6] Jessup, "The Palmas Island Arbitration," 22 *AJIL* (1928), p. 735, at p. 748; see also to the same effect Pinto, *loc. cit.*, pp. 436–437.

[7] The relevant passages of the award can be found in *UNRIAA*, vol. II, p. 840 and also in 22 *AJIL* (1928), p. 877.

deplored such a practice from the point of view of international law.[1] It is not intended to proceed here with a more detailed analysis of this problem. It should be added, however, that, although decisions of national tribunals cannot be considered as binding pronouncements on problems of international law, they undoubtedly indicate the manner in which the judicial authorities of various States approach questions having a bearing on international law,[2] and this is why it is thought that these decisions too deserve to be mentioned in the present survey.

15. The existence of prescription in international law – Judicial decisions rendered by municipal courts

(a) The United States of America

Foremost among the municipal tribunals which have been called upon to deal with territorial disputes involving questions relating to the acquisition of title in international law is the Supreme Court of the United States, and in the opinion of some writers, the doctrine of international prescription was upheld in its decisions.[3]

The practice of this Court might perhaps be best summed up by saying that, on the whole, some of the early judgments did indeed recognize international prescription,[4] while later judgments have displayed a tendency to substitute for this doctrine other principles of international law. Thus, in *Indiana* v. *Kentucky*[5] the Court, after quoting Vattel and Wheaton on international prescription, summed up the legal position in the following words:

> [The] long acquiescence [of Indiana] in the exercise by Kentucky of dominion and jurisdiction over the island is more potential than the recollections of all witnesses.... Such acquiescence in the assertion of authority by the State of Kentucky, such omission to take any steps to assert her present claim by the State of Indiana, can only be regarded as a recognition of the right of Kentucky too plain to be overcome, except by the clearest and most unquestioned proof. It is a principle of public law universally

[1] E.g. Bleiber, *Die Entdeckung im Völkerrecht*, 1933, p. 41, n. 108.

[2] On the evidentiary value of decisions of national tribunals see Lauterpacht, "Decisions of Municipal Courts as a Source of International Law," 11 *BYIL* (1929), pp. 65–95; see also Hudson, *Working Paper on Article 24 of the Statute of the International Law Commission* (U.N. Document A/CN. 4/16 of March 3rd, 1950); see also Schwarzenberger, *op. cit.*, pp. 32–34.

[3] Fauchille, *op. cit.*, p. 756; see also Johnson, 27 *BYIL* (1950), p. 342.

[4] *Rhode Island* v. *Massachusetts*, 4 How. (1846), p. 591, at p. 638. It should be noticed that the Court's reasoning in that case was based on the assumption that "this dispute is between two sovereign and independent States" (*ibid.*), a conception which might appear at least questionable when applied to the states of the American Union. In fact, in its later judgments the Court itself spoke of the "quasi-sovereign states of the Union." (See e.g. *Michigan* v. *Wisconsin*, 270 U.S. (1926), p. 296, at p. 308).

[5] 136 U.S. (1890), p. 479.

recognized, that long acquiescence in the possession of territory and in the exercise of dominion and sovereignty over it, is conclusive of the nation's title and rightful authority.[1]

As may readily be seen, the Court's decision in this case was founded on the doctrine of acquiescence, rather than on the principle of prescription. The same course was followed in a series of judgments delivered at later dates. In *Louisiana* v. *Mississippi*[2] the Court declared that "*as between the states of the Union*, long acquiescence in the assertion of a particular boundary and the exercise of dominion and sovereignty over the territory within it should be accepted as conclusive, *whatever the international rule might be in respect of the acquisition by prescription* of large tracts of country claimed by both."[3]

Here again the Court plainly invoked the doctrine of acquiescence and did not rely upon the doctrine of international prescription, as to the very applicability of which in the sphere of international law the Court had serious doubts. The Court went even further and expressly confined the application of the principle of acquiescence "as between the states of the Union," thus stressing the constitutional aspects of the matter, as distinct from the international law aspect, with which the Court did not, and did not have to, deal.

The principle of acquiescence was relied upon also in *Arkansas* v. *Mississippi*,[4] where it was held by the Court that it was "unable to depart from [the *thalweg*] principle because of long acquiescence in enactments and decisions and the practices of the inhabitants of the disputed territory in recognition of a boundary, which have been given weight in a number of our cases where the true boundary line was difficult to ascertain."[5]

Similarly, in *Michigan* v. *Wisconsin*[6] the Court held that "the rule, long settled and never doubted by this court, is that long acquiescence by one state [of the Union] in the possession of territory by another and in the exercise of sovereignty and dominion over it is conclusive of the latter's title and rightful authority."[7]

More recently the issue has again been somewhat obscured by a

[1] *Ibid.*, p. 510.
[2] 202 U.S. (1906), p. 1.
[3] *Ibid.*, pp. 53 –54. (Italics added).
[4] 250 U.S. (1919), p. 39.
[5] *Ibid.*, p. 45.
[6] 270 U.S. (1936), p. 296.
[7] *Ibid.*, p. 308; see also to the same effect *Maryland* v. *West Virginia*, 217 U.S., p. 1, at pp. 41–44; *Virginia* v. *Tennessee*, 148 U.S., p. 503, at p. 522; *New Mexico* v. *Colorado*, 267 U.S., p. 30, at pp. 40–41; *Vermont* v. *New Hampshire*, 289 U.S., p. 593, at p. 613.

decision given in *Arkansas* v. *Tennessee*[1] where the Court seems to have taken the view that the terms "prescription" and "acquiescence" were interchangeable. The Court pronounced in that case, *inter alia*, that

> this principle of prescription and acquiescence... [is] essential to the 'stability of order' *as between the States of the Union.*[2]

The Court, while again confining the scope of its decision "as between the States of the Union," spoke in its decision of the "principle of prescription and acquiescence," but from the authorities relied upon in the judgment it clearly emerges that this case as well was in fact decided on grounds virtually amounting to the recognition of the principle of acquiescence, as conceived in earlier decisions rendered by the same Court.[3]

Thus, the general trend of the United States Supreme Court's decisions – as displayed in various judgments covering a period exceeding one century – has been one of steadily drifting away from the principle of prescription and of shifting the emphasis towards the doctrine of acquiescence. It can hardly be doubted that this trend has been influenced by international practice and doctrine which have become increasingly sceptical as to the very existence of international prescription.

(b) Great Britain

In comparison with the impressive number of American cases, British judicial practice is scarce indeed. The only case usually referred to as having direct bearing on the questions relating to international prescription is the *Direct United States Cable Co. Ltd.* v. *The Anglo-American Telegraph Co. Ltd.*[4] There the Judicial Committee of the Privy Council was called upon, *inter alia*, to pronounce on the status of Conception Bay from the point of view of international law. The Court held

> that in point of fact, the British Government has for a long period exercised dominion over this bay and that their claim *has been acquiesced in by other nations.*[5]

The Court went on to enumerate the acts of legislation which, in its opinion, indicated the United Kingdom's assertion of sovereignty over

[1] 310 U.S. (1940), p. 563; The case has also been reported in 35 *AJIL* (1941), p. 154, and in *A.D.*, 1938–1940, No. 43.
[2] 310 U.S. (1940), p. 570. (Italics added).
[3] *Ibid.*, pp. 569–570.
[4] 2 (1877) *A.C.*, p. 394 *et seq.*
[5] *Ibid.*, p. 420. (Italics added).

the bay and concluded by saying that, since "this assertion of dominion has not been questioned by any nation from 1891 down to 1872... this would be very strong in the tribunals of any nation to shew that this bay is by prescription part of the exclusive territory of Great Britain."[1]

Apparently the term "prescription" seems to have been interpreted here as well as being synonymous with "acquiescence." The judgment's reasoning, however, indicates that Great Britain's rights over Conception Bay – from the point of view of international law – were founded on the acquiescence of the international community in these rights, such acquiescence being inferred from the lack of any opposition whatsoever to various acts by which Great Britain asserted her sovereignty over the bay. The only fault that can be found with this judgment is that it tends to confound the issues by availing itself of the rather controversial term of prescription.

(c) Germany

The same principle of acquiescence seems to have been the basis of the decision given by the German *Staatsgerichtshof* on October 10th, 1925, in a dispute which arose between the states of Lübeck and Mecklenburg-Schwerin concerning the exercise by Lübeck of certain rights of jurisdiction in regard to fisheries over part of the territorial waters of Mecklenburg-Schwerin in the bay of Travemünde.[2] The Court found that Lübeck had exercised since the end of the 16th century the rights which formed the subject-matter of the dispute and that she had enacted in 1896 a law in which the existence of these rights had been unmistakably asserted. Commenting on this law the Court held that

> in view of the neighbourly relations between the states, it may safely be assumed that Mecklenburg-Schwerin was indeed aware of the promulgation and contents of this law. She has certainly not taken exception to it and has thereby *tacitly recognized* the sovereignty of Lübeck.[3]

The dispute which arose in the 19th century between the Duchies of Lippe-Detmold and Schaumburg-Lippe – both members of the Confederation of the Rhine – and which was submitted in 1839 to the Supreme Court of Appeal of Baden,[4] in accordance with two resolutions passed

[1] *Ibid.*, p. 421.

[2] For the full text of the Court's order see Wenzel, *Die Hoheitsrechte in der Lübecker Bucht*, 1926, pp. 9–21; the case has also been reported in *A.D.*, 1925–1926, No. 85.

[3] Wenzel, *op. cit.*, pp. 14–15: "Dass Mecklenburg-Schwerin vom Erlass und Inhalt dieses Gesetzes alsbald Kenntnis erhalten hat, entspricht dem nachbarlichen Verhältnis und ist ohne weiteres anzunehmen. Widerspruch hat es unstreitig nicht erhoben und damit die Hoheit Lübecks *stillschweigend anerkannt.*" (Italics added).

[4] The judgments delivered in this case have been printed in Martens' *Nouveau recueil de*

by the German Federal Diet on May 27th, 1829, and on August 5th, 1830, has been mentioned by Fauchille as yet another example for the recognition of international prescription.[1] The bones of contention in this case were certain plots of land which had formerly been part of the possession of Count Simon of Lippe, the founder of the House of Lippe, from which the rival houses of Lippe-Detmold and Schaumburg-Lippe took their origin. The differences between the parties touched upon the problem as to which of them was the legal heir to the disputed plots of land. The original claim was put forward by the House of Schaumburg-Lippe and a counter-claim was lodged by the House of Lippe-Detmold. The Court, accordingly, delivered two separate judgments in each of which it dwelt at some length upon the problem of prescription, as this argument had been raised by the parties in the course of their pleadings. From a perusal of the Court's judgments, however, it emerges that it was not concerned at all with international prescription and that it examined this problem solely from the municipal law aspect. Thus, the plea of prescription raised by Lippe-Detmold in opposition to Schaumburg-Lippe's claim was rejected on the ground that the conditions required by municipal private law for the operation of prescription had not been fulfilled.[2]

In the judgment delivered on Detmold-Lippe's counter-claim the Court made it plain that it was led solely by considerations based on the municipal constitutional law. Referring to the plea of prescription, the Court said:

> As far as... prescription is concerned, in cases where rights of sovereignty as against subjects are involved, the only recognized form of prescription is that of immemorial prescription, which has no application in the present case.... As far as prescription is being pleaded not as between the State and one of its subjects, but as between two parties to a dispute, one may speak only of acquisitive prescription and not extinctive prescription, and a claimant may successfully rely on the non-exercise of rights by his adversary only if he himself has exercised his rights during the period of prescription.[3]

traités, vol. XVI, p. 432. For a history of the case and a shortened French version of the judgment see Lapradelle and Politis, *Recueil des arbitrages internationaux*, vol. I, 1905, p. 401.

[1] Fauchille, *op. cit.*, p. 756.

[2] Martens, *op. cit.*, p. 464. See also Lapradelle-Politis, *op. cit.*, pp. 413–414. In the Court's words, the dispute was "nicht zugleich um die Landeshoheit, jetzt Souverainetät, sondern nur um das Dominial – oder Privat-Eigenthum des Amtes Lipperode." (*Ibid.*).

[3] Martens, *op. cit.*, p. 497. In the original German: "Was die Verjährung betrifft, so findet bei Hoheitsrechten gegenüber den Unterthanen nur die hier überall nicht vorhandene, unfürdenkliche statt.... Insofern nur aber auch da, wo das Hoheitsrecht nicht gegenüber den Unterthanen, sondern zwei Berechtigten eintritt, so kann dies denn doch nur eine erwerbende und keine blos erlöschende seyn, und ein Berechtigter kann sich auf die Nichtausübung des Andern mit Erfolg nur in sofern berufen, als er selbst während der Verjährungszeit das

Moreover, the whole dispute must be viewed against the background of the Confederation of the Rhine and its unique structure which enabled the member-States to retain some of the characteristically feudal features of public institutions, thus causing a good deal of confusion between the aspects of property and sovereignty.[1]

16. The existence of prescription in international law – Practice of States

From the judicial decisions delivered by both national and international tribunals, it is intended to turn now to a brief survey of the practice of States relating to the problem of the existence of international prescription, such practice being manifested in both oral and written statements emanating from the duly authorized agents and representatives of the States.[2] This practice, which seems to be rather meagre,[3] hardly warrants the conclusion that the community of nations or even any given nation have irrevocably committed themselves in favour of one attitude or another. The practice of the different States in this field is indeed not marked by an uncompromising consistency and is obviously dependent – as elsewhere – on the real or imaginary political interests of the States in question. Attention to this fact has been drawn by Hyde, who has rightly pointed out that "in the Chamizal Arbitration with Mexico... the United States invoked without success the principle of prescription. In the Island of Palmas Arbitration, it vigorously opposed the applicability and invocation of that principle by The Netherlands."[4]

Similarly, the United Kingdom seems to have recognized the ex-

Recht ausgeübt hat." The above-quoted passage has not been reproduced in its entirety by Lapradelle-Politis and the misleading impression created by this omission may well account for Fauchille's attitude towards this judgment.

[1] See the doctrinal note of Laband in Lapradelle-Politis, *op. cit.*, pp. 423–438.

[2] One of the main reasons for the relative scarcity of State practice in this field seems to be the fact that any reliance by a State on the doctrine of prescription implies its admission that its rights over the territory in question are adverse rights and that the original title to that territory rests with another State, which, in most cases, would be the rival party to the dispute. For reasons which are not difficult to understand, States are not prone to make such admissions and to concede that the opposing party has acquired any rights prior to the emergence of their own rights. Thus, they prefer not to rely – as far as possible – on a prescriptive title.

Similarly, States are hesitant to rely on the doctrine of immemorial possession, because the invocation of this doctrine may be construed as an admission on their part that the origins of their titles to the territories in question are uncertain. In order to avoid any possible misapprehension, States refrain, therefore, from invoking, as far as possible, international prescription and immemorial possession alike.

[3] Various instances of the application of the doctrine of prescription in State practice have already been cited while dealing with judicial decisions rendered by municipal courts and international tribunals and will not be gone into again in this section.

[4] Hyde, *op. cit.*, vol. I, p. 388.

istence of international prescription in the Arbitration Treaty concluded in 1897 between herself and Venezuela concerning the settlement of the *Boundary Dispute between British Guiana and Venezuela*[1] and in the course of her pleadings in the *Fisheries* case,[2] while she rejected the applicability of the same doctrine in the *Alaskan Boundary* Dispute.[3]

It has been alleged that article III of the treaty concluded between the United States and Great Britain on October 20th, 1818, and article I of the treaty concluded between the same countries on August 6th, 1827, relating to Oregon, impliedly recognized the doctrine of international prescription, "one of their objects... being to negative the inference of title from long continued possession by either party of a particular portion of such territory."[4] It is thought, however, that these and similar treaty stipulations should be construed rather as aiming at the removal of any doubts as to one party having acquiesced in the possession of a given territory by the other.[5]

Nor would it appear justified to maintain that the British Agent's argument before the Commission constituted under article IV of the Treaty of Ghent of 1794, relating to the *Title to the Islands in Passamaquoddy Bay*, amounts to having put forward the plea of prescription. In his Memorial of June 11th, 1817, Mr. Chipman, the British Agent, confined himself to saying that "the United States... '*remained silent spectators*' of the settlements and improvements... upon these islands... during a period of... more than thirty years,"[6] and that this uncontroverted fact "will justly furnish an argument, that the United States have *no claim* at this day to any of those islands."[7]

This passage, it is submitted, does not intend to say more than that the United States' silence raises against her the presumption of her acquiescence in a certain state of things.

The notion of international prescription was, however, expressly mentioned by Mr. Olney, the United States Secretary of State, in a letter written on June 22nd, 1896, to Sir Julian Pauncefote, the British Ambassador,[8] although he admitted that there was no fixed period for

[1] 89 *BFSP*, p. 57.

[2] *ICJ*, *Fisheries case, Pleadings, Oral Arguments, Documents*, vol. I, pp. 649–650.

[3] Lauterpacht, *op. cit.*, p. 235.

[4] Moore, *Digest of International Law*, vol. I, 1906, p. 296.

[5] This aspect of the problem will be dealt with more extensively when the requirements for the formation of an historic title will be elaborated upon, and in particular the requirement for the possession being *à titre de souverain*. (See below section 37).

[6] Moore, *International Adjudications (Modern Series)*, vol. VI, 1933, p. 213. (Italics in original).

[7] *Ibid.* (Italics in original).

[8] 88 *BFSP*, p. 1288. This letter was part of the correspondence which preceded the *Venezuelan Boundary* Arbitration to which reference will be presently made.

the operation of international prescription. On the other hand, it is difficult to construe the letter sent on January 5th, 1818, by Don Luis de Onis, the Spanish Minister, to Mr. Adams, the United States Secretary of State, concerning the disputed boundary of Florida,[1] as an endorsement of international prescription. The Spanish Minister justified the Spanish claim on the ground that "the French themselves never disputed the rights of the Spaniards to possession and property, nor laid claim to these parts of the Territories of the Spanish Monarchy."[2]

One of the best-known instances in which the doctrine of international prescription is alleged to have been recognized is the Arbitration Treaty signed on February 2nd, 1897, between Great Britain and the United States of Venezuela respecting the *Settlement of the Boundary between British Guiana and Venezuela.*[3] The first of the rules laid down in article IV of the Treaty stipulates that "adverse holding or prescription during a period of fifty years shall make a good title."[4]

While this provision appears at first sight to be an express acknowledgment of the notion of international prescription, it may also be contended that it impliedly indicates the lack of recognition of this principle rather than its existence and that it constitutes a sort of "contracting out" from the general rules of international law. This argument seems to find some support in the second rule enumerated in article IV which authorizes the arbitrators "to give effect to rights and claims resting on any... ground whatever valid according to international law."[5] Had the doctrine of prescription really been part and parcel of international law, there would not have arisen the need for inserting a specific rule to this effect into the treaty, and the express stipulation contained in the first rule would appear to be superfluous in view of the more general provisions of the second rule.[6]

Whatever the correct interpretation of this treaty may be, the fact cannot be ignored that, in the arbitral award rendered by the tribunal on May 22nd, 1899,[7] the doctrine of prescription was not resorted to (in fact, the tribunal refrained from giving the reasons for its decision)

[1] 5 *BFSP*, p. 425.
[2] *Ibid.*, p. 436.
[3] 89 *BFSP*, pp. 57–65. For the diplomatic correspondence preceding the conclusion of this treaty see 87 *BFSP*, pp. 1061–1107, and 88 *BFSP*, pp. 1242–1327.
[4] 89 *BFSP*, p. 60.
[5] *Ibid.*
[6] It could, however, be argued, that the first rule was concerned not with the principle of prescription as such, but solely with the fixing of the period of 50 years for the operation of prescription. Such an argument would have had more to commend it had the first rule been inserted *after* the second rule and not before it.
[7] 92 *BFSP*, p. 160.

and "unfortunately the actual Award... added little to the law of prescription."[1]

In the case concerning the *Legal Status of Eastern Greenland*, which has already been mentioned in a different context, de Visscher, Counsel for Denmark in that case, expressly refuted the allegation made earlier by the Agent for Norway that Denmark was founding her rights over the disputed territories upon the principle of prescription. Moreover, he questioned the very existence of this institution in international law, by expressing the view that "la détermination d'un délai préfixe est, dans l'institution de la prescription, une condition de caractère technique que le droit international positif n'a pas encore consacrée jusqu'à présent."[2]

[1] Johnson, 27 *BYIL* (1950), p. 340.
[2] *PCIJ*, Series C, No. 66, p. 2873.

CHAPTER III

ACQUIESCENCE AS THE JURIDICAL BASIS OF AN HISTORIC TITLE

17. General

Although "it cannot be denied that the traditional development of custom is ill suited to the present pace of international relations,"[1] it is true to say that customary rules of international law still occupy a prominent place among the binding rules of international law. In fact, custom is still one of the chief formal sources of international law, standing alongside treaties at the apex of the hierarchy of the law-determining agencies of international law.[2]

In view of the fact that historic claims put forward by different States cannot be founded on international treaties – if this were feasible, there would not arise the need to invoke the theory of historic titles – the attempt has to be made to find the legal basis of such claims in the field of customary international law. Accordingly, a brief analysis of the process of formation of customary rules of international law has to be undertaken. A thorough and comprehensive investigation of this problem is not intended, since such an analysis of the mechanism by which customary rules of international law are shaped and developed would clearly be beyond the compass of this work. The present excursion into one of the most fundamental – and also one of the most controversial – fields of international law, which has been the subject of a voluminous literature, is meant only to facilitate a comparison of the processes by which general rules of customary international law and historic rights, respectively, are formed. Particular emphasis will be placed on the doctrine of acquiescence, which, it is submitted, underlies not only the process of formation of general customary rights under international law, but is also the very pillar of the mechanism with the aid of which special or historic rights take shape.

[1] De Visscher, "Reflections on the Present Prospects of International Adjudication," 50 *AJIL* (1956), p. 467, at p. 472.

[2] See Article 38 of the Statute of the International Court of Justice.

18. The creation of a customary rule of international law – The generality of practice and the time element

The nature of customary law is a general problem of law. The reasons for the pre-eminence of this problem in the sphere of international law are not far to seek. They are derived from the fact that, on the one hand, in the municipal legal order the impact of custom has been steadily on the decline, as a result of the rigid structure of the modern State, while in the international legal order, on the other hand, owing to the deficiencies and shortcomings inherent in the present structure of international society, custom is still a vital and fundamental factor in the growth and development of the law.

Article 38(1)(b) of the Statute of the International Court of Justice defines international custom as "evidence of a general practice accepted as law." This wording is far from being free of ambiguity and has frequently given rise to difficulties.[1] Oppenheim, in an apparent attempt to evade the controversial issues pertaining to the definition of international custom, describes it as "a clear and continuous habit of doing certain actions... under the aegis of the conviction that these actions are, according to International Law, obligatory or right."[2] This definition, in spite of its presumably intentional vagueness, clearly bears out the twofold nature of the process which brings an international custom into being, namely,

(a) the habit must be continuous; and

(b) it must spring from the conviction that the course of action taken is obligatory or right (the so-called *opinio juris sive necessitatis*).

Thus, first of all, there is an element of repetition. "Historically", says Tunkin, "a 'customary' norm of international law arises out of repeated actions of States."[3] This element of repetition, continuity or the element of time usually plays, according to Tunkin, an important role in the process of creation of a customary rule. It is, however, essential to

[1] It would appear that this drafting was meant to evade the controversy as to whether the consensual element in the creation of custom – which will be elaborated upon in the next section – is *creative* of the customary rule or merely *cognitive* of it, i.e. a recognition of a rule as being already established. In the opinion of Kunz, the reason for what he calls "the extremely bad drafting of Article 38 (1) of the Statute of the International Court of Justice" is "the idea of seeing in custom not a procedure for creating norms of international law, but merely the 'proof,' 'evidence,' '*la constatation*' of a pre-existing rule of law. This is the typical approach of the natural law doctrine." (See Kunz, "The Nature of Customary International Law," 47 *AJIL* (1953), p. 662, at p. 664). (Italics in original). As to references for the said concept, among whose exponents Kunz mentions Duguit, Scelle, François and Lauterpacht, see *ibid.*, n. 13-16.

[2] Oppenheim, *op. cit.*, p. 26.

[3] Tunkin, "Co-existence and International Law," 95 *Hague Recueil* (1958), vol. III, p. 5, at p. 9.

remember, he goes on to say, that "though time plays historically, as a matter of fact, a considerable role in the process of formation of a customary rule of conduct, it is juridically irrelevant."[1]

Commenting on the juridical irrelevance of the time factor in the establishment of a new customary norm of international law, MacGibbon observes that "the judgments and Advisory Opinions of the Permanent Court of International Justice provide no exact criterion with regard to the length of time which must pass before a usage becomes a custom."[2] On this point MacGibbon echoes the views put forward earlier by Sørensen, who has drawn attention to the fact that, in the jurisprudence of the Permanent Court of International Justice, the element of time or repetition seems to be fused with the problem of the generality of practice. According to Sørensen, a practice followed by a great majority of States will be deemed sufficient for the creation of a new custom, in spite of its recent origin; an ancient norm of conduct, on the other hand, will require fewer adherents for its being regarded as a binding rule of law.[3]

Thus, in Sørensen's view, the time factor in the creation of a new customary norm of international law is closely and inextricably linked up with the question of the generality of practice. It is not intended here to give a definite answer to the question under what circumstances a practice may be considered as being a "general" practice. All that can be said in this connection is that international law does not require the practice to be unanimous. As has been pointed out by Kunz, "the practice must be 'general,' not universal; but a mere majority of states is not enough. The practice must have been applied by the overwhelming majority of states which hitherto had an opportunity of applying it."[4]

[1] *Ibid.*, p. 10; see also to the same effect Lauterpacht, 27 *BYIL* (1950), p. 393, and Fitzmaurice, 30 *BYIL* (1953), p. 31.

[2] MacGibbon, "Customary International Law and Acquiescence," 33 *BYIL* (1957), p. 115, at p. 120.

[3] Sørensen, *Les sources du droit international*, 1946, p. 102, where the author writes: "C'est un trait caractéristique de la jurisprudence de la Cour [Permanente de Justice Internationale] que l'élément de temps ou de durée n'est pas considéré indépendamment de la généralité de la pratique en question. L'envergure et l'ancienneté de la pratique semblent se fondre en une unité, de sorte que la pratique suivie par une grande majorité d'Etats suffit pour la création d'une coutume, même d'origine assez récente; d'un autre côté, une pratique de grande ancienneté n'a peut-être pas besoin d'autant d'adhérents."

[4] Kunz, *loc. cit.*, p. 666. Similarly, it has been maintained in the Norwegian Counter-Memorial in the *Fisheries* case that "la notion de généralité est relative. On n'exige pas que l'existence de la règle soit attestée par la pratique de tous les Etats. Il faut cependant qu'un grand nombre d'Etats aient manifesté par leur attitude l'acceptation de cette règle." (*ICJ, Fisheries case, Pleadings, Oral Arguments, Documents*, vol. I, p. 380).

In the United Kingdom Reply it was pointed out, likewise, that "it is common ground that ...a customary practice invoked as law must be general but that generality is relative and does not connote universality." (*Ibid.*, vol. II, p. 427).

Lauterpacht explains the readiness of international law to dispense with the requirement of universality of practice as a condition for the application of customary rules by pointing out that any insistence on the requirement of universality would render doubtful the existence of numerous rules of law. "To say," he argues, "...that with regard to any particular matter no rule of international law exists unless practice is unanimous or approaching unanimity may result in giving judicial imprimatur to the existence of wide gaps in international law."[1]

19. The creation of a customary rule of international law – Opinio juris *and acquiescence*

The element of time, repetition and continuity of practice usually raises questions of fact which can be ascertained with relative ease by examining the practice of States and international case law. This element is therefore sometimes called the "objective factor" in the formation of a customary norm of international law, as distinct from the second element, the so-called "subjective factor," or "psychological factor," which makes it necessary to investigate whether or not the States concerned acted in the belief that their actions were "obligatory or right."

The necessity of introducing this second element into the process of formation of a customary norm of international law springs from the fact that a rule of conduct does not become law by its mere repetition. According to Tunkin, "only a recognition on the part of the States of such a rule as legally binding, i.e. recognition of such a rule as a rule of international law, has a decisive influence and consummates the process of creating a customary norm of international law."[2]

The essence of this recognition or acceptance by a State of a certain international practice as a rule of law is for Tunkin "an expression of a will of a State, it is a consent to consider this customary rule as a rule of international law and therefore as a juridically obligatory rule. ...It is a tacit offer, there are no conferences or negotiations; this offer is implied in actions of State constituting its recognition of a certain rule as a legal norm."[3]

Thus, for Tunkin, whose approach reflects a rather widespread concept, the psychological element in the formation of a customary norm of international law might be looked upon as yet another mani-

[1] Lauterpacht, *The Development of International Law by the International Court,* 1958, p. 370.
[2] Tunkin, *loc. cit.,* p. 12.
[3] *Ibid.,* p. 13.

festation of the general device of recognition. For him, and for those who share his view, international custom gains its ultimate legal validity from the recognition granted to it by the community of nations.

For the sake of completeness it should be noted, however, that the above-mentioned interpretation of the term *opinio juris*, though presumably governing the field, is by no means the only one in existence. According to another theory, "it suffices if [the practice] is regarded as something which it is morally incumbent (as opposed merely to convenient, expedient or correct)."[1]

Both these theories share the belief that, for the States acting as they do, there arises an obligation to behave as others would behave under similar circumstances, and that this obligation is not merely a rule of courtesy. It is this subjective element that distinguishes a binding customary rule from a usage followed from mere convenience or comity.

There exists, however, a third theory which maintains that the subjective element in the formation of international custom may be dispensed with altogether. In the view of Guggenheim, who is one of the leading exponents of this trend, "la doctrine du 18e siècle examinée plus haut, ignore l'élément de l'*opinio juris*. La formule, en effet, ne remonte pas plus haut qu'au début du 19e siècle.... C'est... en Allemagne, ...qu'est née l'idée que la répétition des mêmes faits n'était pas le seul élément constitutif de la coutume et qu'il fallait également considérer comme tel l'*opinio juris*."[2] Yet, while himself denying the necessity of this element in the formation of international custom, he admits that "selon l'opinion dominante, cette *opinio iuris sive necessitatis* serait l'élément spécifique de la coutume, l'élément qui permet de distinguer la coutume obligatoire de l'usage simplement facultatif."[3]

In fact, both the Permanent Court of International Justice and the International Court of Justice seem to have upheld the traditional and commonly accepted doctrine which lays stress on the existence of the subjective element in the formation of an international customary norm. In the well-known *Lotus* case[4] the Permanent Court of International Justice held that "even if the rarity of the judicial decisions to

[1] Fitzmaurice, "The General Principles of International Law Considered from the Standpoint of the Rule of Law," 92 *Hague Recueil* (1957), vol. II, pp. 101–102.

[2] Guggenheim, "Contribution à l'histoire des sources du droit des gens," 94 *Hague Recueil* (1958), vol. II, p. 53 (italics in original); see also to the same effect Kopelmanas in 18 *BYIL* (1937), pp. 127–151, and Kelsen, "Théorie du droit international coutumier," *Revue Internationale pour la Théorie du Droit* (1953), p. 253 *et seq.*

[3] Guggenheim, *loc. cit.*, p. 53 (italics in original). For a rejection of this theory denying the necessity of *opinio juris*, see Fitzmaurice, *loc. cit.*, pp. 103–105; see also Lauterpacht, *op cit.*, pp. 379–381.

[4] *PCIJ*, Series A, No. 10.

be found among the reported cases were sufficient to prove in point of fact the circumstance alleged by the Agent for the French Government, it would merely show that States had often, in practice, abstained from instituting criminal proceedings, and not that they recognized themselves as being obliged to do so; for only if such abstention were based on their being conscious of having a duty to abstain would it be possible to speak of an international custom."[1]

In the *Asylum* case[2] the International Court of Justice re-affirmed this principle by stating that "the Party which relies on a custom... must prove that this custom is established in such a manner that it has become binding on the other Party... [and] that the rule invoked is in accordance with a constant and uniform usage practised by the States in question, and that this usage is the expression of a right appertaining to the State... and a duty incumbent on the [other]... State."[3]

This idea was further reiterated in the *Morocco* case[4] where the International Court of Justice, after quoting the relevant passage from the judgment delivered in the *Asylum* case, found that "there has not been sufficient evidence to enable the Court to reach a conclusion that a right to exercise consular jurisdiction founded upon custom or usage has been established in such a manner that it has become binding on Morocco."[5]

More recently the International Court of Justice had to concern itself again with the same problem in the case concerning *Right of Passage over Indian Territory*.[6] Judge *ad hoc* Chagla, in his Dissenting Opinion, pointed out that for the establishment of a custom under international law "it is not enough to have its external manifestation proved; it is equally important that *its mental or psychological element must be established*. It is this all-important element that distinguishes mere practice or usage from custom. In doing something or in forbearing from doing something the parties must feel that they are doing or forbearing out of a sense of obligation. They must look upon it as something which has the same force as law.... There must be an overriding feeling of compulsion – not physical but legal. That is what the jurisprudence on the subject calls the conviction of necessity."[7]

[1] *Ibid.*, p. 28.
[2] *ICJ Reports*, 1950, p. 266.
[3] *Ibid.*, p. 276.
[4] *ICJ Reports*, 1952, p. 176.
[5] *Ibid.*, p. 200.
[6] *ICJ Reports*, 1960, p. 6.
[7] *Ibid.*, p. 120. (Italics added). See also the definition of *opinio juris* given by Judge Armand-Ugon in his Dissenting Opinion, at p. 82.

The distinction made by the Court in the *Asylum* case between "a right appertaining to the State and... a duty incumbent on the [other]... State"[1] is significant in that it focuses attention on the basically two-fold aspect of the customary norm: it emphasizes the fact that, with the emergence and development of a customary right, a correlative customary duty also develops. This same idea was expressed again by the Court in its judgment in the case concerning *Right of Passage over Indian Territory*, where it found "that that practice [allowing free passage between the various Portuguese possessions] was accepted as law by the parties and has given rise to a right and a correlative obligation."[2] Similarly, Judge Sir Percy Spender in his Dissenting Opinion pointed out that "a right of passage having been established, there was a correlative obligation on India not to prevent the exercise of that passage."[3]

This distinction seems to have prompted one author to make it the starting-point of a theory aiming at reconciling the seemingly irreconcilable concepts concerning the role of *opinio juris* in the formation and growth of international custom. In an article published in 1957,[4] MacGibbon suggested that a distinction be drawn between the processes of formation of customary rights and customary obligations. In his view "generalizations concerning the process by which rules of customary international law are formed do not always acknowledge that a rule may be expressed in terms either of a right or of an obligation and that it may involve both the protection of the right in question and the acknowledgement of the correlative duty. Considerations which apply to a rule expressed as a right or as a liberty may well be inappropriate to a rule expressed as a duty or as a prohibition."[5] This contention is warranted by the fact which has been observed by McDougal that, in the sphere of international relations, the same nation-state officials are alternatively, in a process of reciprocal interaction, both claimants and external decision-makers, passing upon the claims of others.[6] According to the same writer, this duality of function "merely reflects the present lack of specialization and centralization of policy functions in international law generally."[7] MacGibbon offers the following explana-

[1] *ICJ Reports*, 1950, p. 276.
[2] *ICJ Reports*, 1960, p. 40.
[3] *Ibid.*, p. 110.
[4] MacGibbon, "Customary International Law and Acquiescence," 33 *BYIL* (1957), p. 115.
[5] *Ibid.*, p. 116.
[6] McDougal, "The Hydrogen Bomb Test and the International Law of the Sea," 49 *AJIL* (1955), p. 356, at pp. 357–358.
[7] *Ibid.*

tion concerning the growth of a new customary obligation of international law:

In the early stages of the development of a customary right other States are faced with the choice of objecting or remaining passive. From their inaction the inference of consent in and acceptance of the validity of the claim may be drawn and... strengthened by the passage of time, the growth in the number of States participating in the claim and the extent to which the claim is enforced. So far, the conduct of States other than participants in the claim and practice may amount but not exceed voluntary acquiescence, and this may remain the position while the possibility of simple passivity is open to them. However, at the same time as the right is developing its correlative duty is developing....The right claimed may be such that its fulfilment may continue to require no more than passive submission on the part of other States. If that is so, the validity of the claim... may be gauged solely by reference to the continued acquiescence of other States.... On the other hand, once the correlative duty involves for its implementation a course of positive action, as opposed to simple tolerance, then the *opinio juris* may become an essential element in the absence of which that course of action cannot become endowed with the binding force of a customary obligation. If the practice continues with uniformity and is asserted as of right and if the States assuming the obligation share the conviction that the action taken to give effect to the objection is enjoined by law, the latter course of action has at that stage ripened into a definitive customary obligation.[1]

As a result of the foregoing considerations MacGibbon is led to the conclusion that *opinio juris* is to some degree distinct from acquiescence, although it is nothing more than its logical outcome, and acquiescence "would have permitted the right correlative to the obligation to be perfected in any event."[2] He suggests, however, that "in the case of a customary obligation expressed in terms of prohibition... it is not unreasonable that emphasis should be placed on the *opinio juris* rather than on acquiescence."[3] On the other hand, "the part which that concept plays in the acquisition of customary rights is ... indirect ... and its place is taken in this context by the doctrine of acquiescence."[4]

The explanation offered by MacGibbon would appear to remove the theoretical difficulty which puzzles the scholar who devotes more than cursory attention to this problem. On the one hand, it is said that usage coupled with *opinio juris* leads to the creation of a customary norm of international law, while on the other hand it is claimed that, in order to enable the creation of such a norm, the States involved must initiate such practice because of the *opinio juris*. In other words: the coming into being of a new norm would presuppose that the States acted

[1] MacGibbon, *loc. cit.*, p. 130. (Italics in original).
[2] *Ibid.*
[3] *Ibid.*, p. 131. (Italics in original).
[4] *Ibid.*, p. 126.

in legal error. As suggested, the emphasis placed by MacGibbon on the distinction between customary rights and customary obligations might provide the answer to this theoretical challenge.

In fact, some writers appear to have formulated the requirements for the establishment of an international custom so as to embrace both the notion of *opinio juris* and the doctrine of acquiescence within a single definition. Hudson requires for the international custom "the concordant and recurring action of numerous States in the domain of international relations, the conception in each case that such action was enjoined by law, and the failure of other States to challenge that conception at the time."[1] Similarly, Kunz expresses the view that "not only must the states which applied the practice have had the conviction, but this conviction must not have been challenged by other states."[2] However, the inadequacy of these and similar formulations of the requirements necessary for the formation of international custom stems from the fact that "failure to protest against the *conviction that the practice is enjoined by law*... is not equivalent to acquiescence in the practice itself."[3]

20. The consensual basis of customary international law

The assertion, according to which acquiescence is the prerequisite for the coming into existence of the *opinio juris*, and consequently for the establishment of a customary norm of international law, would appear to be tantamount to upholding the consensual basis of customary international law. In fact, Scelle expressly equated *opinio juris* with consent when he wrote that "le second élément essentiel de la coutume est d'ordre psychologique: c'est le consensus ou l'opinio necessitatis, c'est à dire le faisceau des consentements individuels prêts à reconnaître et à subir la règle de Droit ainsi découverte et extériorisée."[4]

Similarly, it has been pointed out by Morelli that international custom is, according to the traditional doctrine, nothing more than an agreement, differing from international treaties in only one respect, namely, that it is a *tacit* agreement.[5] From this assumption it follows,

[1] Hudson, *The Permanent Court of International Justice, 1920–1942*, 1943, p. 609.

[2] Kunz, *loc. cit.*, p. 667.

[3] MacGibbon, 31 *BYIL* (1954), p. 151. (Italics in original).

[4] Scelle, *Droit international public*, 1944, p. 398; the same idea has been voiced less explicitly by Sørensen, *op. cit.*, p. 104.

[5] Morelli, "Cours général de droit international public," 89 *Hague Recueil* (1956), vol. I, p. 441 *et seq.*, at pp. 453–454, where he says: "La coutume internationale, d'après la doctrine traditionnelle, n'est qu'un accord. La caractéristique pour laquelle la coutume, configurée

in the view of Morelli, that customary international rules can legally bind only those States which participated in the creation of such norms and persistently followed them as binding rules of conduct. Their validity in respect of other States can, however, be based solely on their voluntary acts, i.e. on their *recognition* of the customary norms.[1] (Morelli though, does not approve of this concept and proceeds to refute the consensual theory of the binding force of customary international law).[2]

The concept of the consensual and essentially voluntarist basis of customary international law has found support in the judgment delivered by the Permanent Court of International Justice in the *Lotus* case[3] where the majority of the Court took the view that "the rules binding upon States ... emanate from their own free will as expressed in conventions or by usages generally accepted as expressing principles of law."[4]

This concept is not unchallenged[5] and, although it is not intended here to enlarge on this subject, one of the objections raised against the consensual basis of the binding force of customary international law appears to deserve mention, since it seems to be directly relevant to the subject-matter of this work. Kelsen has objected to this theory by pointing out the apparent fact that "general international law is binding upon many states which never, expressly or tacitly, consented to it"[6] and which had been in existence long before those States were established. He therefore insists that the assumption, according to which international law draws its binding force from the recognition of all States, is fictitious and cites to this effect the case of a newly-established community in respect of which "international law becomes applicable ... when the latter is recognized as a state by the other states."[7] This contention, however, has been met by Lauterpacht who argues that the consent of States is essential and indispensable merely in the process of the

comme un accord, se distingue des autres accords internationaux (c'est-à-dire des traités) consiste seulement dans le fait qu'il s'agit d'un *accord tacite*." (Italics in original).

[1] *Ibid.*, p. 455, where Morelli states: "La coutume internationale, en tant qu'accord, ne peut produire des règles de droit que pour les Etats qui ont pris part à l'accord, à savoir pour les Etats qui ont effectivement suivi une certaine ligne de conduite. La valeur de la règle coutumière pour les autres Etats... que personne ne saurait nier, ne pourrait être expliquée qu'au moyen d'un acte de volonté de ces Etats, c'est-à-dire de ce que l'on appelle la *reconnaissance* de la coutume." (Italics in original).

[2] *Ibid.*, pp. 455–458.

[3] *PCIJ*, Series A, No. 10.

[4] *Ibid.*, p. 18.

[5] For a detailed discussion and rejection of the objections raised against this concept, see MacGibbon, 33 *BYIL* (1957), pp. 131–138; see also Fitzmaurice, 92 *Hague Recueil* (1957), vol. II, pp. 101–105.

[6] Kelsen, *Principles of International Law*, 1952, p. 316.

[7] *Ibid.*, p. 154.

formation of new rules of international law, but has no reference to the question of whether or not a new State is bound by the already existing rules of customary international law.[1] The only conclusion that follows from the adoption of the consensual basis of customary international law is, according to Lauterpacht, that "new obligations cannot be imposed upon an unwilling State by any international legislature,"[2] but the contention that existing rules of international law are binding upon newly recognized States independently of their consent does not exclude the propriety of insisting on a consensual basis for the formation of *new* customary rules.[3]

A State is therefore entitled to dissociate itself from a *new* customary rule during its process of formation. Such dissociation will as a rule manifest itself by the recalcitrant State declaring itself not to be bound by the new rule. A State cannot, however, dissociate itself from an already existing rule of international law, i.e. it cannot "contract out" from the applicability of that rule once such a norm has become a general norm of customary international law. This point was vividly illustrated by the arguments of the parties in the *Fisheries* case and will be dealt with in detail in due course. In her pleadings in that case Norway contended that certain alleged rules of international law were not general rules at all, and that, even if they were, they could not be applied as against Norway, because she had consistently and unequivocally manifested her refusal to accept them from the time these rules were taking shape. In Norway's opinion, if a State "a manifesté, soit expressément, soit par une attitude constante et non équivoque, la volonté de ne pas soumettre à la règle, alors que celle-ci n'avait pas encore pris à son égard le caractère d'une règle obligatoire, il reste en dehors de son champ d'application."[4] In the United Kingdom's Reply the Norwegian contention was not basically questioned, although it was deemed appropriate to point out that "the right of a State to dissent from a customary rule cannot be regarded as absolute.... Where a fundamental principle is concerned, the international community does not recognize the right of any State to isolate itself from the impact of the principle."[5] It was conceded, however, that a State might "acquire an exceptional position with regard to some general rule of customary law by some process which is analogous to that of acquiring an historic

[1] Lauterpacht, *The Function of Law in the International Community*, 1933, p. 419.
[2] *Ibid.*, p. 420.
[3] MacGibbon, 33 *BYIL* (1957), p. 137.
[4] *ICJ*, *Fisheries case, Pleadings, Oral Arguments, Documents*, vol. I, pp. 382–383.
[5] *Ibid.*, vol. II, pp. 428–429.

title."[1] Sir Gerald Fitzmaurice takes the view that "the position jointly taken up by Norway and the United Kingdom on this point (for their disagreement regarding it related to the facts rather than to the principle) must be regarded as correct."[2]

21. Recognition and acquiescence

The adoption of the consensual basis as the source of the binding force of international law practically amounts to introducing into this field the well-known and much-contested doctrine of recognition, which is one of the main means of expressing consent in international relations. It has by now become common ground that the scope of the concept of recognition is by no means confined to the topics of recognition of States and Governments; this device of international law is, in fact, of a general character and has, according to Schwarzenberger, a "wide actual, and a still greater potential, scope."[3] As has been pointed out by the same writer, it is only through recognition that the principle of sovereignty – the very pillar of international society – acquires any meaning, and it would be non-existent in practice "unless at least two sovereign States had established legal relations with each other and recognised each other as independent communities."[4] The same author further points out that "the manifoldness of the functions of recognition [in the sphere of international law] must not obscure the fact that, in each case, this device serves one and the same legal purpose. It is a means by which States express their willingness to acknowledge *vis-à-vis* themselves the existence, and legal effect, of a situation or transaction which, in the absence of such recognition, would not be *opposable* to them."[5] He goes on to say that "a sovereign State which has recognised a situation, act or transaction of international relevance can no longer maintain that, *vis-à-vis* itself, it is not *opposable*. From this angle, recognition appears as an effective agency of peaceful change in international law."[6]

Although Schwarzenberger does not define the precise meaning of the term "opposability," he seems to apply it in the meaning given to it in the judgment of the International Court of Justice in the *Fisheries*

[1] *Ibid.*, p. 429.

[2] Fitzmaurice, 92 *Hague Recueil* (1957), vol. II, p. 100.

[3] Schwarzenberger, "The Fundamental Principles of International Law," 87 *Hague Recueil* (1955), vol. II, p. 195, at p. 228.

[4] *Ibid.*

[5] *Ibid.*, pp. 228–229. (Italics in original).

[6] *Ibid.*, p. 249. (Italics in original).

case. There, in a well-known and frequently-quoted passage of the judgment, the Court declared that "the application [by Norway] of a well-defined and uniform system... would reap the benefit of general toleration,"[1] which, in the words of the French text, is "fondement d'une consolidation historique qui le rendrait *opposable* à tous les Etats."[2] From the context in which this term was applied by the Court it seems to emerge that "opposability" is the consequence of the conduct of a particular State in the face of certain circumstances, this consequence being that the conduct of such State might be held out against it as a practice binding it. It is a kind of estoppel which is created by the conduct of the State and which precludes it from acting contrary to what has become binding upon it by its behaviour. Thus, it has been maintained by the Government of India in the course of the *Sino-Indian Boundary Dispute* that, in the absence of any Chinese protest against various Indian manifestations of sovereignty over the territories in question, "China must be held to have accepted and *acquiesced* in the Indian alignment and to be *estopped* from raising claims to Indian territory."[3] In this respect the function of "opposability" seems to be closely related to the notion of "estoppel" and, in fact, "the legal effect of... recognition is to create an estoppel."[4] This inevitable and logical consequence of every act of recognition was clearly borne out in the judgment delivered by the Permanent Court of International Justice in the *Legal Status of Eastern Greenland* case,[5] where the Court said:

> Norway reaffirmed that she recognized the whole of Greenland as Danish; and thereby she has debarred herself from contesting Danish sovereignty over the whole of Greenland.[6]

While the foregoing interpretation of the term "opposability," as given by Schwarzenberger, seems to be the correct one, as emerging from the pronouncements of international tribunals, it might be added, for the sake of completeness, that it is not the only one in existence. Contrary to Schwarzenberger, who seems to conceive "opposability"

[1] *ICJ Reports*, 1951, p. 138.

[2] *Ibid.* (Italics added). The corresponding expression in English for the italicized word is "enforceable."

[3] See the *Summary of the Report of the Officials of the Governments of India and the People's Republic of China on the Boundary Question*, published by the Ministry of External Affairs of the Government of India (undated), *MEA*. 32, p. 10. (Italics added).

[4] Schwarzenberger, *loc. cit.*, p. 253. For a more detailed discussion of the doctrine of estoppel in relation to acquiescence, see below, section 31.

[5] *PCIJ*, Series A/B, No. 53.

[6] *Ibid.*, pp. 68–69; see the Advisory Opinion of the International Court of Justice concerning the *International Status of South-West Africa, ICJ Reports*, 1950, p. 128 *et seq.*, at pp. 135–136, and at p. 142.

as the result and outcome of recognition, resembling in its function and scope the doctrine of estoppel, Charpentier avails himself of this term in a somewhat different meaning. He distinguishes between two different aspects of recognition, the first being "la *manifestation de volonté* par laquelle l'Etat tiers adhère à une modification qui s'était réalisée sans sa participation,"[1] while the second is defined as "*l'extension* à l'Etat tiers des effets de la modification."[2] He goes on to explain that "le premier sens est *volontaire ou formel*. Le deuxième sens est *matériel ou fonctionnel*,"[3] indicating "non l'attitude de l'Etat tiers, mais la modification elle-même, non pas un acte, mais un fait juridique."[4] It is this second kind of recognition which is called by Charpentier "opposabilité."

The line of cleavage between the two approaches seems to become clearer owing to Charpentier's assertion that "rien ne prouve que l'extension à un Etat tiers des effets de la modification nécessite sa reconnaissance.... Rien ne prouve non plus que la reconnaissance ait pour effet d'étendre à l'Etat qui l'accorde les effets de la modification."[5]

Conversely, as will be recalled, recognition, in one form or another, is for Schwarzenberger the prerequisite for a situation to become opposable. Such recognition does not necessarily express itself in a formal act. In some cases it takes the form of passive toleration in circumstances where a different conduct would have been expected from a party which meant to object to that situation. A recognition of this kind, such a passive toleration, is what Schwarzenberger calls "acquiescence." According to this writer, acquiescence "differs from recognition merely in its mode of expression: passive toleration; for even implied recognition presupposes some acts which are capable of being interpreted as such. When... it is accompanied by a positive act by which acquiescence is expressed, it amounts to recognition."[6] Thus, while differing from recognition in its mode of expression, acquiescence produces likewise "an estoppel in circumstances when good faith would require that the State concerned should take active steps of some kind in order to preserve its rights of freedom of action."[7] Similarly, another author described acquiescence as "the inaction of a State which is faced with

[1] Charpentier, *La reconnaissance en droit international et l'évolution du droit des gens*, 1956, p. 5. (Italics in original).
[2] *Ibid.* (Italics in original).
[3] *Ibid.* (Italics in original).
[4] *Ibid.*
[5] *Ibid.*
[6] Schwarzenberger, *loc. cit.*, p. 257. Cf. also Jennings, *op. cit.*, p. 36.
[7] Schwarzenberger, *loc. cit.*, p. 256.

a situation constituting a threat or infringement of its rights.... [It] takes the form of silence or absence of protest in circumstances which generally call for a positive reaction signifying an objection."[1]

If acquiescence is looked upon from this angle, it matters little whether it is regarded as a branch of the doctrine of recognition or of the principle of consent properly so called. For the only essential difference between consent and recognition is that recognition becomes effective with unilateral communication, while consent requires a meeting of wills and acceptance of a proposal made by one party to another.[2]

22. The role of the time element in the creation of special customary or "historic" rights

The foregoing considerations as to the nature of customary international law, its process of growth, its constituent elements and its binding force were of a general character. It is now intended to focus attention upon one of the more specific categories of customary rights – limited both in quantity and in its scope of application. The subsequent analysis will be devoted to a discussion of the so-called "special customary rights" among which, it is submitted, historic rights too might be classified.

Special customary rights have been defined by Fitzmaurice as rights "such as would not exist under ordinary law."[3] While leaving aside at this stage the distinguishing characteristics of general customary rights and special customary rights, respectively, it cannot be overemphasized that special customary rights share with general customary rights "a common process of development which involves, on the one hand, the constant assertion of the right in question and, on the other hand, consent or acquiescence in that assertion on the part of the affected States.... The two elements are complementary and... interdependent."[4] Similarly, it has been said that both general and special customary rights depend on the establishment of a practice or usage – one general and the other particular – and each derives its eventual legal sanction from some form of consent on the part of States, either general acceptance in the one case, and, in the other, specific recognition or tacit acquiescence. However, the method (practice and assent)

[1] MacGibbon, 31 *BYIL* (1954), p. 143.
[2] Schwarzenberger, *loc. cit.*, p. 260.
[3] Fitzmaurice, 30 *BYIL* (1953), p. 69.
[4] MacGibbon, 33 *BYIL* (1957), p. 119.

is the same.[1] It has also been pointed out by Fitzmaurice that "the acquisition of a historic right... is merely a special case of the creation of right by custom or usage, similar in principle to the creation of a general rule of law by those means."[2]

It should be noted, however, that special customary rights differ in at least two respects from the general rules of customary international law: "In the first place," says MacGibbon, "they are, or were in origin, apparently or in actual fact, essentially adverse rights. In the second place, they are, *ex hypothesi*, deprived of the benefit accruing to rights which the generality of States exercise: in place of general participation which raises strongly the presumption of consent with regard to general customary rights, special and exceptional customary rights are validated entirely by the consent or acquiescence of the States affected manifested in relation to a passage of a comparatively prolonged period of time."[3]

Thus, the time factor assumes with regard to the formation of special customary rights a role which it does not fulfil in respect of the general customary rights. As has already been pointed out, the efflux of time as such is not regarded as an essential element in the establishment of general customary norms of international law. In the words of Lauterpacht, "a 'consistent and uniform usage practiced by the States in question' – to use the language of the International Court of Justice in the *Asylum* case – can be packed within a short space of years. The 'evidence of a general practice accepted as law' – in the words of Article 38 of the Statute – need not be spread over decades."[4] Similarly, Sir Gerald Fitzmaurice noted that a new rule of customary law, based on the practice of States, can in fact emerge very quickly and even almost suddenly if new circumstances have arisen that imperatively call for legal regulation.[5] From the juridical point of view, however, "the length of time within which the customary rule of international law comes to fruition is irrelevant."[6]

Thus, in the growth of general rules of customary international law the time factor is not of decisive importance, although in the nature of things some time elapses between the initiation of a usage, its development into a general practice and its final acceptance as law. However,

[1] Fitzmaurice, 30 *BYIL* (1953), p. 31, note 3.
[2] *Ibid.*, p. 39.
[3] MacGibbon, 33 *BYIL* (1957), p. 123. (Italics in original).
[4] Lauterpacht, 27 *BYIL* (1950), p. 393. (Italics in original).
[5] Fitzmaurice, 30 *BYIL* (1953), p. 31.
[6] Lauterpacht, *loc. cit.*

all that can be said as to the length of time required for the crystallization of a new custom is that "it must be proportionate to the degree and the intensity of the change that it purports, or is asserted, to affect."[1] It necessarily follows that such crystallization of a usage and its transformation into a binding custom of international law will be hastened by the general participation of the States affected by its growth and development.

Conversely, a practice which runs counter to the prevailing international order and is in derogation of it will require a longer period of time for its ripening into a special customary right. The acquisition of such exceptional rights by individual States "contrary to the existing (and otherwise still subsisting) international order, involves... considerations and criteria that make the passage of time, and of an appreciable period of time at that, essential at any rate in all those cases... where the positive consent or express recognition of States cannot be shown."[2]

Indeed, it is the lack of such positive consent or express recognition that characterizes historic claims put forward by the different States. For obvious reasons there is no need to invoke the theory of historic rights – i.e. the theory of special customary rights – which relies heavily on the time factor for the establishment of such rights, in cases where a departure by a State from the generally accepted rules of international law has met with the explicit approval of the States which are likely to be affected by such a departure. Nor does the need for the invocation of this doctrine arise in cases where, without explicitly consenting, the affected State has acted in such a manner that its consent can be inferred in a positive sense from its actions. "Where, however," says Fitzmaurice, "other States have neither consented expressly, nor, by their conduct, actively implied their consent, but have simply been *inactive*, only the historic element in a claim can supply the necessary presumption of (tacit) acquiescence arising out of the fact that the practice in question has continued for a long time without encountering active opposition."[3] Consequently, "*the theory of historic rights comes into play... where an absence of express consent by States might otherwise lead to an inference of opposition.*"[4] This idea found its expression in the United Kingdom's Reply in the *Fisheries* case in the following words:

[1] *Ibid.*
[2] Fitzmaurice, 30 *BYIL* (1953), p. 31.
[3] *Ibid.*, p. 29. (Italics in original).
[4] *Ibid.* (Italics in original).

The relevance of an historic title is to raise an inference of the acquiescence of States in a claim which is exceptional and which, apart from such acquiescence, would be illegal and invalid.[1]

In all the cases where an historic title is asserted, the time factor fulfils the function that is usually assigned to express recognition or positive consent; the need for the efflux of a considerable period of time for the growth of historic rights is explained by the fact that "the presumption of general or particular acceptance which may be raised by absence of protest... [will be] strengthened in proportion to the length of time silence persists."[2] The primary function of the theory of historic rights is therefore to make up for the lack of express evidence of the acquiescence of a particular State against whom such a claim is meant to be invoked. This attitude was taken up in the Reply of the United Kingdom in the *Fisheries* case, commenting on the function of the theory of historic waters. With due allowance to the existence of some characteristic features appertaining to maritime historic rights which distinguish them from historic rights in general, one is tempted to subscribe to the statement that "there would have been no need for a theory of historic waters if only waters covered by express acquiescence were to be included. Frequently, however, evidence of express acquiescence by the particular State is lacking and then the claimant State is entitled, if it can, to raise an inference of... acquiescence... *by proving the historic character of its claim by long usage*. The historic element is thus relevant precisely in regard to the acquiescence of other States in an appropriation of maritime territory which, apart from the acquiescence implied from long usage, they would be entitled to regard as an invasion of their rights."[3] This statement applies, *mutatis mutandis*, also to historic rights in general, i.e. historic rights concerning other than maritime areas.[4]

23. Some historic rights viewed as remainders of more extensive ancient rights

The logical consequence of the adoption of the consensual basis as the source of the binding force of customary international law appears

[1] *ICJ, Fisheries case, Pleadings, Oral Arguments, Documents*, vol. II, p. 651.
[2] MacGibbon, 33 *BYIL* (1957), p. 120.
[3] *ICJ, Fisheries case, Pleadings, Oral Arguments, Documents*, vol. II, pp. 609–610. (Italics added).
[4] As to the juridical aspects specifically related to maritime historic titles, see below, chapter VI.

to be that, if it can be proved that a particular State opposed a new customary rule from the time of its inception and gestation – i.e. during the period when such a rule was in the process of taking shape – such a rule will not be held binding on the recalcitrant State. Thus, we are faced with a second way of establishing historic rights, which, in fact, is nothing but a further extension of the doctrine of the consensual basis of customary international law. If a State consistently declines to accept, and unequivocally opposes, a nascent customary rule from the beginning of its taking shape, this rule does not become binding on the opposing State, and such State acquires an historic right to the effect that such a rule cannot be applied against it. Sir Cecil Hurst seems to have had in mind this possibility while dealing with some of the problems pertaining to the ownership of the bed of the sea. In his view "the ownership of the bed of the sea within the three-mile limit is the survival of more extensive claims to the ownership of and sovereignty over the bed of the sea. The claims have become restricted by the silent abandonment of the more extended claims. Consequently, where effective occupation has been long maintained of portions of the bed of the sea outside the three-mile limit, those claims are valid and subsisting claims, entitled to recognition by other States."[1]

Similarly, Baldoni, commenting on the status of historic bays, poses the question whether "les zones comprises dans ces baies ont jamais été assujetties au principe de la mer libre."[2] He comes to the conclusion that

> la recherche historique nous permet de donner une réponse négative à cette question. En effet, à l'époque où la règle de la liberté des mers s'affirmait, les baies de Cancale, de Chaleurs, de Chesapeake, de Conception, de Delaware, de Fonseca et de Miramichi étaient déjà assujetties à la souveraineté effective et permanente des Etats riverains. Le principe de la liberté des mers n'a partant jamais été en vigueur pour elles. Il n'est donc pas nécessaire pour expliquer leur appartenance à l'Etat riverain, de recourir aux prétendus principes de la prescription, ou, comme d'autres l'estiment, à de prétendues règles spéciales créées en derogation au principe de la liberté de la haute mer.[3]

This concept was readily taken up by the Norwegian Government in its Rejoinder in the *Fisheries* case, where it was quoted with approval, and it was further alleged that "les eaux pour lesquelles un titre historique... peut être invoqué, ne sont pas des eaux qui auraient fait partie de la haute mer et que l'Etat riverain se serait appropriées. Ce sont

[1] Hurst, "Whose is the Bed of the Sea?," 4 *BYIL* (1923–1924), p. 34, at p. 43.

[2] Baldoni, "Les navires de guerre dans les eaux territoriales étrangères," 65 *Hague Recueil* (1938), vol. III, p. 185, at p. 221.

[3] *Ibid.*, pp. 221–222.

des eaux qui ont toujours été comprises dans son territoire et que la haute mer n'a jamais entamées."[1]

Thus, the Norwegian concept of historic waters was presented as being in contrast with the British concept, which relied upon the acquiescence of other nations as the basis for the establishment of an historic title. In the words of the United Kingdom's Reply in the *Fisheries* case, "where the claim goes beyond what is accepted under general customary international law, it is the acquiescence of other States, express or implied from long usage, that sets the seal of legal validity upon the exceptional claim."[2]

It is submitted, however, that the apparent incompatibility of the two conflicting views might be removed by bearing in mind that historic rights are no more than specific customary rights, and that customary norms of international law derive their legal validity from the acceptance and consent of the member-States of the international community. Seen against this background, the apparently contradictory concepts as to the origins of the theory of historic waters would not appear to be irreconcilable. The United Kingdom seems to have argued on the assumption that Norway had not dissociated herself from the general rules of maritime international law, at the time these rules were taking shape, and that she could therefore have acquired historic rights over maritime areas only after the coming into force of these rules, and with the consent of the international community. Norway, however, took the view that these rules had never become binding on her, since she had from the outset declined to accept them. Thus, the dispute between the parties seems to have touched upon the facts rather than upon the principles. It can only be regretted that this point seems to have been overlooked by the parties to the dispute who argued at great length the legal issues, thereby somewhat obscuring the questions of fact.

24. Non-exclusive historic rights

In the foregoing sections a distinction has been made between:

(a) customary rights and obligations; and

(b) general customary rights and special customary rights.

The present section deals with a further distinction within the sphere of the special customary rights themselves.

[1] *ICJ, Fisheries case, Pleadings, Oral Arguments, Documents*, vol. III, p. 445.

[2] *Ibid.*, vol. II, p. 621.

Sir Gerald Fitzmaurice has drawn attention to the fact that special customary rights fall in two different categories:

(1) "Special [customary] right[s] different from, and in principle contrary to, the ordinary rule of law applicable... built up by a particular State or States... leading to the emergence of a usage or customary or historic right in favour of such State or States."[1] In the formation of such rights which are acquired as against the world in general and which are valid *erga omnes* "the element of consent, that is to say, acquiescence... on the part of other States is not only present, but necessary."[2] Special customary rights of this kind might well be termed "historic rights properly so called."

(2) "Rights... as would not exist under ordinary law, [which] may, however, be acquired by one State, not as against the world in general... but against another particular State, e.g. in its territory or waters or with reference to its vessels or nationals.... While the element of consent may be more difficult to detect here, and may have been lacking at the origin of the matter, it is believed that if the right has developed into a legal right, this is because consent, in the form of acquiescence, was given or can be presumed."[3]

The distinction made by Sir Gerald amounts, in fact, to a distinction between historic rights proper (namely, historic rights involving the acquisition of full territorial sovereignty) and non-exclusive historic rights, occasionally referred to as "international servitudes," which imply the acquisition by one State over the territory of another State of rights falling short of sovereignty, such as the right of transit or the right of fishing. Since claims belonging to this category of non-exclusive historic rights are raised in our days mainly in respect of maritime areas, it is felt that a more thorough discussion of their nature and scope should be deferred to the chapter dealing with the specific legal aspects attendant upon maritime historic claims.[4]

Incidentally, the existence of non-exclusive historic rights over land territories has met of late with the approval of the International Court of Justice in the case concerning *Right of Passage over Indian Territory*.[5] In the judgment delivered in this case, the Court explicitly recognized the existence in international law of a doctrine sanctioning the acquisition by a State against another State of special customary rights

[1] Fitzmaurice, 30 *BYIL* (1953), p. 68.
[2] *Ibid.*
[3] *Ibid.*, p. 69.
[4] See below, chapter VI, section 73.
[5] *ICJ Reports*, 1960, p. 6.

falling short of sovereignty. The Court confirmed the validity of certain Portuguese rights of transit over Indian territory, and, by a majority of 11 against 4, held that

with regard to private persons, civil officials and goods in general there existed during the British and post-British periods a constant and uniform practice allowing free passage.... This practice having continued over a period extending beyond a century and a quarter, unaffected by the change of regime in respect of the intervening territory which occurred when India became independent, the Court is, in view of all the circumstances of the case, satisfied that that practice was accepted as law by the Parties and has given rise to a right and a correlative obligation.[1]

In another passage of the judgment the Court stressed that the number of States required for the establishment of such historic rights does not necessarily have to be larger than two. The Court stated that

it is difficult to see why the number of States between which a local custom may be established on the basis of long practice must necessarily be larger than two. The Court sees no reason why continued practice between two States accepted by them as regulating their relations should not form the basis of mutual rights and obligations between the two States.[2]

25. Acquiescence versus prescription as the legal basis of historic rights

Special customary rights, like general customary rights, have no fixed period of gestation for such rights to mature. "[It is] the great cardinal characteristic of acquiescence... that it does not require any particular length of time to perfect it; it depends in each particular case upon all the circumstances of the case."[3] And it is this cardinal characteristic of acquiescence that removes the besetting difficulty which confronts the exponents of international prescription, namely, that it can dispense with the exacting requirements for the efflux of a fixed period of time. The doctrine of acquiescence "reduces the significance of the necessity for a fixed prescriptive period by constituting a conclusive test by which the validity of a prescriptive claim may be evaluated, namely, the test of the existence or otherwise of a general conviction that the situation which has been created is in conformity with the requirements of international stability and order."[4]

Moreover, the doctrine of acquiescence is indifferent to the question whether or not the State purporting to have acquired a certain right

[1] *Ibid.*, p. 40.
[2] *Ibid.*, p. 39.
[3] *Proceedings of the Alaskan Boundary Tribunal*, vol. VII, p. 619.
[4] MacGibbon, 30 *BYIL* (1953), p. 306.

on the basis of acquiescence acted in good faith. (*Bona fides*, as will be recalled, is usually required for the operation of prescription, but can hardly be assumed where the establishment of adverse territorial rights is concerned). Acquiescence takes account of the consensual basis of international law and it is its great virtue that "it looks for its determining force to the root of the processes which give rise to new rules of international law, finding its justification in the final resort in the consent of the States."[1] Instead of resorting to the institution of prescription, which represents a development of custom, its ascendancy to a higher stage and its refinement, international law which, in its present rudimentary form, has not yet achieved such a high degree of development, "remonte au principe, à la coutume. Source reconnue par le droit international, la coutume crée, transforme, éteint les règles et les obligations, conformément à son régime juridique propre."[2]

Acquiescence, which is instrumental in the establishment of any customary right of international law, is indispensable indeed in the formation of historic rights. The doctrine of acquiescence "mitigates the rigours of the positivist view and imparts a welcome measure of controlled flexibility to the process of formation of rules of customary international law."[3]

26. Acquiescence as the juridical basis of historic rights – Opinions of writers

In the works of publicists who have examined the legal foundations of historic rights, acquiescence – taking the form of absence of protest under circumstances which would have warranted such a protest as evidence of opposition – has been assigned a prominent role. As has been observed by MacGibbon, to these publicists "belongs in great measure the credit for exposing the fundamental antinomy which tribunals may be called upon to resolve in questions of disputed title, namely, the rival claims to consideration of the maxim *quieta non movere*, on the one hand, and the concept of good faith, on the other."[4]

According to Hyde, "it has been deemed more desirable to the family of nations that an adverse occupant long in possession should be suffered to remain in unmolested control, than that the existing sovereign, although unjustly deprived of possession, should retain its rights of such, at least

[1] MacGibbon, 31 *BYIL* (1954), p. 166.
[2] Pinto, *loc. cit.*, p. 449.
[3] MacGibbon, 33 *BYIL* (1957), p. 145.
[4] MacGibbon, 31 *BYIL* (1954), p. 152. (Italics in original).

when it has failed to make constant and appropriate efforts to keep them alive, as by ceaseless protests against the acts of the wrongdoer."[1]

In view of the fact that disputes involving the claim of historic rights have arisen in recent times chiefly in respect of maritime territories, it is easy to understand why the process of formation of historic rights has been subjected to examination mainly by writers who have devoted particular attention to problems relating to the establishment of maritime historic rights. Commenting on the territorial character of historic bays, Westlake maintains that the general rule as to the territoriality of bays with entrances not exceeding twice the width of the maritime belt "often meets with an exception in the case of bays which penetrate deep into the land.... Many of these are *recognized by immemorial usage* as territorial sea of the States into which they penetrate, notwithstanding that their entrance is wider than the general rule for bays would give as a limit for such appropriation."[2]

In the opinion of Heimburger, "the legality of the actually consolidated possession of a State does not rest on the concept of prescription – analogous to the municipal law prescription – neither definite, nor indefinite; it is founded solely and exclusively on the title of international recognition which is a specifically international law title. Such recognition may be granted expressly; in the majority of cases, however, it will be granted by the States tacitly and will be inferred from such State acts, the commission of which presupposes recognition on their part. Recognition will be extended to every possession which is accepted by general conviction as a possession manifesting actual consolidation and constant necessity. For the establishment of such a general conviction, however, the efflux of a period of time is required, during which a possession, the origins of which are uncertain, will be gradually consolidated and will become capable of asserting its intrinsic necessity."[3]

Perels maintains that "the laying of claims of sovereignty to maritime areas which strictly speaking are parts of the high seas, has oc-

[1] Hyde, *op. cit.*, vol. I, p. 387.

[2] Westlake, *op. cit.*, part I, pp. 191–192. (Italics added).

[3] Heimburger, *op. cit.*, p. 151, where the author says: "Die Rechtmässigkeit des thatsächlich befestigten Staatenbesitzes beruht überhaupt nicht auf einer der privatrechtlichen analogen Verjährung, weder auf einer bestimmten, noch auf einer unbestimmten; sie gründet sich vielmehr einzig und allein auf den spezifisch völkerrechtlichen Rechtsgrund der internationalen Anerkennung. Diese kann ausdrücklich geschehen; sie wird aber meist stillschweigend durch staatliche Willensäusserungen erfolgen welche dieselbe voraussetzen. Sie wird jedem Besitz zu Teil der sich dem allgemeinen Bewusstsein als ein thatsächlich befestigter und dauernd notwendiger offenbart. Zur Begründung einer derartigen allgemeinen Überzeugung ist jedoch der Ablauf einer gewissen Zeit erforderlich während der sich ein seinem Ursprung nach unsicherer Besitz allmählich befestigen und seine innere Notwendigkeit bewähren kann."

casionally found express or tacit recognition."[1] Referring to various British claims of sovereignty over maritime territories, the same author states that "the exceptional claims of the British Crown have gained... recognition of other States, either tacitly or as manifested through the conclusive acts of those States."[2]

Raestad, dealing with problems relating to the acquisition by States of rights over maritime territories in derogation of the normally applicable rules of international law, takes the view that "l'important, c'est de savoir *quand et comment a eu lieu le consentement exprès ou tacite des nations* qui donne à l'occupation ou à l'usurpation la qualité d'un titre de droit."[3] He further states that "la prescription telle qu'elle a été introduite dans les législations nationales n'existant pas... dans le droit international, un état de choses qui existe depuis longtemps n'est sanctionné par le droit des gens que si *l'existence prolongée de cet état de choses prouve le consentement tacite des nations*."[4]

Fauchille, referring to the problem of historic bays, explains that "ce sont les grands golfes et les grandes baies dont le caractère de territorialité a été *reconnu par un usage longuement accepté et une coutume non-controversée*."[5] The same author goes on to say that "c'est... *l'acquiescement des Etats* qui, d'après des décisions judiciaires *explique le caractère de territorialité des baies historiques*."[6]

Jessup contends that "holding in abeyance the general rule which is to govern all bays it must be admitted that there are certain bodies of water to which individual states *by general acquiescence or long usage* have acquired the absolute right or title."[7] He further claims that the legality of such excessive claims "is to be measured not by the size of the area affected but by the definiteness and duration of the assertion and *the acquiescence of foreign powers*."[8]

Gidel expresses the view that "il ne suffit pas que l'Etat riverain émette la prétention de considérer telles ou telles eaux comme lui étant 'propres' pour que les autres Etats aient le devoir de s'incliner devant

[1] Perels, *Das internationale öffentliche Seerecht*, 1903, p. 33, where this writer states: "Die Inanspruchnahme von Staatshoheitsrechten in Seegebieten die eigentlich zur hohen See gehören hat zuweils ausdrückliche oder stillschweigende Anerkennung gefunden."

[2] *Ibid.* In the original German: "Die Sonderansprüche der britischen Krone hatten... die stillschweigende oder durch konkludente Handlungen bezeugte Anerkennung für sich."

[3] Raestad, *La mer territoriale*, 1913, p. 167. (Italics added).

[4] *Ibid.*, p. 174. (Italics added).

[5] Fauchille, *op. cit.*, vol. I, part II, p. 380. (Italics added).

[6] *Ibid.* (Italics added).

[7] Jessup, *The Law of Territorial Waters and Maritime Jurisdiction*, 1927, pp. 362–363. (Italics added). Jessup seems to regard "long usage" as the alternative to "general acquiescence" rather than the evidence of it.

[8] *Ibid.*, p. 382. (Italics added).

cette prétention; la consécration de ces prétentions ne peut dériver... que de *l'acquiescement international; c'est l'usage prolongé* qui, généralement, en fournira la manifestation."[1]

Canada's claim to Hudson Bay as an historic bay has been justified by Johnston "on the basis of occupation [by Canada], and acquiescence by other states in that occupation."[2]

Balladore Pallieri claims that "the legal basis... of these claims to a 'historic' bay is constituted by continued usage *with the explicit or implicit consent of the members of the international community*."[3]

Colombos takes the view that "the territorial State is entitled to claim a wider belt of marginal waters [in bays], provided it can produce evidence of a long and consistent dominion over that bay and that its claim has been accepted, expressly or tacitly, by the great majority of other nations."[4]

Schwarzenberger, discussing the term "historic waters," contends that "all it means is that the title on which the incorporation of portions of the high seas into the territorial sea, or of parts of the territorial sea into national waters, rests is based upon an *uncontested usage*. As time passes, the presumption increases that the silence of other States amounts to acquiescence and creates an estoppel against such a historically consolidated title being contested."[5]

The Soviet international lawyer Kozhevnikov claims for the Soviet Union, on historical grounds, the Gulf of Peter the Great, the Kara Sea, the Laptev Sea, the East Siberian Sea and the Chukotsk Sea, as Soviet internal waters. He asserts that

> so-called historical bays, the width of whose entrance considerably exceeds ten sea miles, are considered to be the internal territory of a State.
>
> For example... the waters of the Gulf of Peter the Great up to a line joining Cape Povorotny and the mouth of the river Tumen-Ula are historically internal waters of the Soviet Union.... Soviet jurists rightly consider the Siberian seas which are akin to gulfs (Kara Sea, Laptev Sea, East Siberian Sea and Chukotsk Sea) as Soviet internal waters. *These seas*, which in effect constitute gulfs and *which are of exceptional economic and strategic importance to the Soviet Union, have over a prolonged period of history been used by Russian seafarers*. This point of view corresponds to international

[1] Gidel, *Le droit international public de la mer*, 1934, vol. III, p. 651. (Italics added).

[2] Johnston, "Canada's Title to Hudson Bay and Hudson Strait," 15 *BYIL* (1934), p. 1, at p. 20.

[3] Balladore Pallieri, *Diritto internazionale pubblico*, 7th revised ed., 1956, p. 377, as quoted in English in the United Nations *Memorandum on Historic Bays*, prepared by the Secretariat of the United Nations for the first U.N. Conference on the Law of the Sea, Document A/CONF. 13/1, p. 20. (Italics added).

[4] Colombos, *The International Law of the Sea*, 5th revised ed., 1962, pp. 154–155.

[5] Schwarzenberger, *op. cit.*, pp. 326–327. (Italics added).

practice and is in line with the Judgement of the International Court of Justice... in the... Anglo-Norwegian dispute, in which... the sea route along the Norwegian coast was held to be Norwegian internal waters, having been marked for navigation by Norway.[1]

Vishnepolskii founds Soviet historic claims to the Kara Sea on the alleged recognition of these claims by foreign Powers at different times and on the lack of opposition to various Russian enactments which purported to regulate the regime of navigation in the said sea. He maintains that

notwithstanding direct knowledge of the Kara Sea on the part of several representatives of the Western and Scandinavian countries, the latter did not deem it possible to interfere with the regulations issued by the Russian authorities concerning that sea. The right of Russia, and, by virtue of succession, that of the U.S.S.R. to establish autonomously any legal regime of navigation in the Kara Sea, a right exercised for centuries, was never subject to any protest on the part of the foreign Powers and must be considered as an 'uninterrupted and indisputable custom.'[2]

In addition to the Kara Sea, the same writer also lays claim, on behalf of the Soviet Union, to the seas of Chukostk and Laptev, as well as to the Eastern Siberian Sea, which he regards as "our national waters... whose legal regime must be determined in virtue of the recognition of the sovereignty of the U.S.S.R. over these seas."[3]

Commenting on the *North Atlantic Fisheries* Arbitration award of September 7th, 1910,[4] Drago, one of the judges in that arbitration, explained the theory of historic bays, in an article published in 1912, in the following words:

Ces baies exceptionnelles apparaissent dans plusieurs traités, et la doctrine les reconnaît expressément... et font... une catégorie spéciale et distincte, dont la propriété appartient aux pays qui les entourent. Ces pays, lorsqu'ils ont procédé à l'affirmation de leur souveraineté, en acquièrent la possession et les incorporent à leur domaine, *du consentement des autres nations.*[5]

[1] See *International Law,* a textbook for use in law schools, Academy of Sciences of the U.S.S.R., Institute of State and Law, translated from the Russian by Dennis Ogden, Foreign Languages Publishing House, chapter VI, by F. I. Kozhevnikov, pp. 205–206. (Italics added).

[2] Vishnepolskii, in *Sovietskoe Gosudarstvo i Pravo,* issue No. 7, July 1952, pp. 36–45; the passage quoted above has been translated into English by Kulski, 47 *AJIL* (1953), p. 132.

[3] *Ibid.,* p. 133. For a more detailed account of Soviet claims, on historic grounds, to various maritime areas, and in particular to the gulf of Peter the Great, see Hartingh, *Les conceptions soviétiques du droit de la mer,* 1960, pp. 33–38. At pp. 35–36 there the author, herself a member of the French delegation to the 1958 Geneva Conference on the Law of the Sea, has reproduced the text of a Soviet Note of January 7th, 1958, containing the reply to Japanese protests against the Soviet assertions that the Gulf of Peter the Great is to be regarded, on historic grounds, as internal waters of the Soviet Union.

[4] *UNRIAA,* vol. XI, pp. 173–211; Scott, *Hague Court Reports,* 1st Series, 1916, pp. 141–225.

[5] Drago, "Un triomphe de l'arbitrage," 19 *RGDIP* (1912), p. 5, at p. 37. (Italics added).

Referring to the estuary of Rio de la Plata which he regards as an historic bay, Drago points out that it constitutes

[une] baie historique par excellence, et une baie historique de toute ancienneté, présentant un caractère très net et acceptée comme telle *par le consentement de toutes les nations* depuis de longues années.[1]

27. Acquiescence as the juridical basis of historic rights – Opinions of learned bodies

Since the end of the nineteenth century numerous attempts have been made by various learned societies to codify the law of the sea. The problem of historic rights had to be faced by these societies while dealing with the formulation of the draft provisions relating to bays. Although the term "acquiescence" has not been mentioned in the various drafts, it would appear that the wording of these drafts justifies the conclusion that in the opinion of their authors the attitude taken up by the international community *vis-à-vis* such historic claims is of direct relevance in ascertaining whether or not an historic title has been established.

Thus, article 3 of the draft regulations concerning the territorial sea in time of peace, as adopted by the Institute of International Law at its Stockholm session in 1928, lays down the rule that the territorial sea is measured in the case of bays from a straight line drawn across the bay at the nearest opening to the sea, at a point where the distance between the two shores does not exceed ten miles, "*unless international usage has sanctioned a greater width.*"[2] It has therefore been claimed – rightly it is believed – that the word "international" in this context was meant "to express the principle that a *unilateral national pretension is not sufficient.* The national usage must have received *international recognition.*"[3]

Article 7 of the Draft Convention submitted in 1926 to the 34th Conference of the International Law Association, by a committee appointed by the Executive Council, provided that, with regard to bays and gulfs, the territorial waters should follow the sinuosities of the coast, "unless an established usage has sanctioned a greater limit."[4] In the course of the debate the exact meaning of the term "established"

[1] *Ibid.* (Italics added).
[2] 34 *Annuaire de l'Institut de Droit International*, Stockholm session, August 1928, pp. 755–756. (Translated from the French; italics added).
[3] *ICJ*, *Fisheries case*, *Pleadings*, *Oral Arguments*, *Documents*, vol. II, pp. 623–624. (Italics in original).
[4] International Law Association, *Report of the 34th Conference*, 1926, p. 143.

seems to have given rise to some doubts and in the draft Convention, as adopted by the Conference, this passage was deleted. In its final wording the saving clause speaks of "an established usage generally recognized by Nations"[1] as the prerequisite for the departure from general rules governing the regime of bays and gulfs. This amendment, illuminating in itself, only gains additional significance from the fact that in an earlier draft relating to the same subject the International Law Association, at its Brussels session in 1895, adopted a draft rule which in its relevant passage referred to a "continuous usage of long standing" ("usage continu et séculaire").[2]

In article 6 of Project No. 10, prepared in 1925 by a Committee set up by the American Institute of International Law for the codification of American international law, a "continued and well-established usage" is required for the sanctioning of a width of a territorial belt in derogation of the generally applicable rules relating to the regime of bays.[3] Although the precise meaning of the expression "well-established" is not quite clear, one is tempted to agree with the proposition that "when international jurists speak of well-established usage, they necessarily mean a usage wellestablished among States, or, in other words, a well-established *international* usage."[4]

Article 22 of the Harvard Research draft of 1929 on territorial waters stipulates that "the provisions of this convention relating to the extent of territorial waters do not preclude the delimitation of territorial waters in particular areas in accordance with established usage."[5] In the comment on this article – the scope of which is of a general character and is not confined to bays only – it is stated that the article "seems

[1] *Ibid.*, p. 102.

[2] International Law Association, *Report of the 17th Conference*, 1895, p. 115, article 3. This issue has been somewhat obscured owing to the fact that in the same article "occupation" has been inserted as an alternative to "established usage." In the opinion of the United Kingdom, as expressed in its Reply in the *Fisheries* case, the words "generally recognized by nations" apply also to occupation (see *ICJ, Fisheries case, Pleadings, Oral Arguments, Documents*, vol. II, p. 624), thus rejecting the Norwegian contention, according to which, in addition to "an established usage generally recognized by nations," there was another mode of acquiring exceptional rights over maritime territory, namely, by means of simple occupation. (*Ibid.* vol. I, p. 557).

[3] 20 *AJIL* (1926), Special Supplement, p. 318.

[4] *ICJ, Fisheries case, Pleadings, Oral Arguments, Documents*, vol. II, p. 624. (Italics in original). See, however, the project submitted in 1933 to the 7th International Conference of American States by the American Institute of International Law where historic bays and estuaries were defined as bays or estuaries "over which the coastal State or States, or their constituents, *have traditionally exercised and maintained their sovereign ownership*." (*Ibid.*, vol. III, p. 455; italics added). Here no reference has been made to the reaction of foreign States to the assertion of State sovereignty.

[5] Harvard Law School, *Research of International Law (Nationality, Responsibility of States, Territorial Waters)*, 1929, p. 288.

necessary because of historic claims made by certain States and *acquiesced in by other States* with reference to certain bodies or with reference to particular areas of water."[1]

28. Acquiescence as the juridical basis of historic rights – Decisions of international tribunals

The doctrine of acquiescence was frequently resorted to by both national and international tribunals when called upon to pronounce on the question of disputed territorial titles. Some of these pronouncements expressly mention the term "acquiescence," while others virtually amount to recognizing that principle without explicitly referring to it.

(a) The Alaskan Boundary Dispute, 1903

In the *Alaskan Boundary* Dispute between Great Britain and the United States the tribunal took note of the fact that for more than sixty years "Russia, and in succession to her the United States, occupied, possessed and governed the disputed territory ...*without any protest or objection.*"[2] This absence of objection on the part of Great Britain was construed by the tribunal as her acquiescence in the rights of Russia and later of the United States and was among the main considerations prompting the tribunal to decide the case in favour of the United States' contention. In fact, the American members of the tribunal had earlier laid particular emphasis on the statement made by the Prime Minister of Canada in the Canadian Parliament, admitting that no protest whatsoever had been lodged with the United States against her occupation of the disputed territory, and from this fact they drew the following conclusion:

It is manifest that the attempt to dispute that possession... is met by the practical, effective construction of the Treaty, presented by the long-continued acquiescence of Great Britain in the construction which gave the territory to Russia and the United States and to which the Prime Minister testifies. Only the clearest case of mistake could warrant a change of construction after so long a period of acquiescence in the former construction, and no such case has been made out before this Tribunal.[3]

(b) The Anglo-Brazilian Boundary Dispute, 1904

In the award rendered by the King of Italy in the border dispute between Great Britain and Brazil concerning the delineation of the

[1] *Ibid.* (Italics added).
[2] *Cmd.* 1877 (1904), p. 49 *et seq.*, at p. 79. (Italics added).
[3] *Ibid.*, p. 87.

Boundary between Brazil and British Guiana[1] the arbitrator, while admitting that "it cannot... be decided with certainty whether the right of Brazil or Great Britain is the stronger,"[2] found that "acts of authority and jurisdiction over traders and native tribes were... continued in the name of British sovereignty... [and] such effective assertion of rights of sovereign jurisdiction was generally developed *and not contradicted* and by degrees became accepted."[3] He therefore concluded that by virtue of the said facts the acquisition of authority by Great Britain had been effected over a certain part of the disputed territory.

(c) The Island of Bulama Arbitration, 1870

In the dispute that arose between Great Britain and Portugal in the latter part of the nineteenth century over the *Title to the Island of Bulama*, off the coast of Sierra Leone, General Grant (then President of the United States), in his capacity as sole arbitrator, held that Great Britain's claim over the disputed island ought to be rejected owing to the fact that Portugal had never acquiesced in the acts which were alleged to have established the British claim.[4]

(d) The Delagoa Bay Arbitration, 1875

Five years later, in another dispute between the same parties relating to the *Territorial Rights over the Delagoa Bay*, the arbitrator, President MacMahon of France, in his award of July 24th, 1875, found in favour of Portugal, explaining his decision, *inter alia*, in the following words:

> Les actes par lesquels le Portugal a appuyé ses prétentions n'ont soulevé aucune réclamation de la part du Gouvernement des Provinces Unies [to which the territory adjoining had formerly belonged]; ...en 1782 ces prétentions ont été tacitement acceptées par l'Autriche, à la suite d'explications diplomatiques échangées entre cette puissance et le Portugal;... en 1817 l'Angleterre elle-même n'a pas contesté le droit du Portugal [by signing with her a treaty, article 12 of which specifically referred to the disputed territory].[5]

It was on this basis of total lack of objection to the exercise of Portuguese authority by the States affected by such exercise of authority that the arbitrator founded his conclusions as to the legal validity of the Portuguese claims.

[1] *UNRIAA*, vol. XI, pp. 21–23; 99 *BFSP*, pp. 930–932.
[2] *UNRIAA*, vol. XI, p. 22.
[3] *Ibid.* (Italics added).
[4] Lapradelle – Politis, *op. cit.*, vol. II, 1924, p. 612.
[5] Martens, *Nouveau recueil général de traités* (*Deuxième série*), vol. III, p. 517.

(e) The Grisbadarna Arbitration, 1909

In the *Grisbadarna* Arbitration of 1909 between Sweden and Norway[1] the Permanent Court of Arbitration gave among the reasons which prompted it to allot the Grisbadarna bank to Sweden the circumstance

that Sweden has performed various acts in the Grisbadarna region, especially of late, owing to her conviction that these regions were Swedish... which involved considerable expense... whereas Norway... showed much less solicitude in this region....[2]

The Court concluded by saying that

the stationing of a light-boat, which is necessary to the navigation in the regions of Grisbadarna, was done by Sweden without meeting any protest and even at the initiative of Norway, and likewise a large number of beacons were established there without giving rise to any protests.[3]

Thus, it clearly emerges from the perusal of the tribunal's award that Norway's acquiescence in certain acts of authority performed by Sweden in the Grisbadarna was reckoned with as one of the decisive factors in upholding the validity of the Swedish claim.

(f) The Chamizal Arbitration, 1911

In the *Chamizal* Arbitration between the United States and Mexico[4] the Commissioners in their award indicated that one of their reasons for the dismissal of the American claim was the fact that

the Mexican Government had done all that could be reasonably required of it by way of protest against the alleged encroachment.[5]

The Commissioners apparently took the view that the Mexican protests, obviating any presumption of Mexican acquiescence in the alleged American rights and expressing Mexican opposition to such alleged rights, prevented the American rights from maturing.

(g) The Island of Palmas Arbitration, 1928

In the *Island of Palmas* Arbitration[6] between the United States of America and the Netherlands, Judge Huber, the arbitrator, in upholding the Netherlands claim, expressly relied on the acquiescence of

[1] Scott, *Hague Court Reports*, 1st Series, 1916, p. 121; *UNRIAA*, vol. XI, p. 155.
[2] Scott, *op. cit.*, p. 130; *UNRIAA*, vol. XI, p. 161.
[3] Scott, *op. cit.*, p. 131; *UNRIAA*, vol. XI, p. 161.
[4] *UNRIAA*, vol. XI, pp. 316–347; 5 *AJIL* (1911), p. 782 *et seq.*
[5] *UNRIAA*, vol. XI, p. 329; 5 *AJIL* (1911), p. 807.
[6] *UNRIAA*, vol. II, p. 829 *et seq.*

Spain and of other States in the exercise of authority by the Netherlands over the disputed island. He stated that

since the moment when the Spaniards, in withdrawing from the Moluccas in 1666, made express reservations as to the maintenance of their sovereign rights, up to the contestation made by the United States in 1906, no contestation or other action whatever or protest against the exercise of territorial rights by the Netherlands... has been recorded.... The peaceful character of the display of Netherlands sovereignty for the entire period to which the evidence concerning acts of display relates (1700–1906) must be admitted.[1]

In a later passage the arbitrator reverted once more to the same principle when he pointed out that

the acquiescence of Spain in the situation created after 1677 would deprive her and her successors of the possibility of still invoking conventional rights at the present time.[2]

(h) The Colombia-Venezuela Boundary Arbitration, 1922

The doctrine of acquiescence was also resorted to in some of the territorial disputes relating to the precise delineation of the boundaries of the Latin-American States, which are usually referred to as the *uti possidetis*[3] cases. In the award rendered in Berne on March 24th, 1922, in the *Colombia-Venezuela Boundary* Arbitration,[4] the Swiss Federal Council, which had been appointed by the parties to act as arbitrator in this case, found in favour of Colombia, pointing out, *inter alia,* that in a treaty of cession signed in 1907 by Colombia and Brazil, Colombia had ceded to Brazil parts of the disputed territory. The Swiss Federal Council stressed the fact that

cette cession n'a pas provoqué aucune réclamation de la part du Vénézuela et les occupations colombiennes de 1900 dans le bassin de l'Orénoque ont été subies par le Vénézuela sans protestation claire et explicite.[5]

The Swiss Federal Council regarded the absence of objection by Venezuela as amounting to acquiescence on her part in the Colombian jurisdiction over the disputed territory and accordingly awarded it to Colombia.[6]

[1] *Ibid.*, p. 868.
[2] *Ibid.*, p. 869.
[3] As to the meaning and scope of this term in international law, see Appendix below.
[4] *UNRIAA*, vol. I, pp. 223–298.
[5] *Ibid.*, p. 280.
[6] For a more detailed discussion of this case see Scott, "The Swiss Decision in the Boundary Dispute between Colombia and Venezuela," 16 *AJIL* (1922), p. 428 *et seq.*

(i) The Guatemala-Honduras Boundary Arbitration, 1933

Similar reasoning seems to underlie the award given on January 23rd, 1933, in the *Guatemala-Honduras Boundary* Arbitration,[1] in which Chief Justice Hughes of the United States acted as president of the tribunal, the other two members having been appointed by the parties to the dispute themselves. By the terms of the Arbitration Treaty of July 16th, 1930, the parties agreed that the boundary between the two countries should follow the line which had divided them in 1821, at the time of the cessation of Spanish rule. In its search for evidence of the administrative frontier at the crucial time, the tribunal deemed itself

> at liberty to resort to all manifestations of [the] will [of the Spanish Crown]... and also, in the absence of precise laws and prescripts, to conduct indicating royal acquiescence in colonial assertions of administrative authority. The Crown was at liberty at all times to change its royal commands or to interpret them by allowing what it did not forbid. In this situation the continued and unopposed assertion of administrative authority by either of the colonial entities, under claim of right, which is not shown to be an act of usurpation because of conflict with a clear and definite expression of the Royal will, is entitled to weight and is not to be overborne by reference to antecedent provisions or recitals of an equivocal character.[2]

The tribunal went on to say that, in determining this question, the actions and behaviour of the new States

> in establishing their independent Governments and in formally describing the extent of the territory to the sovereignty over which they regarded themselves as succeeding is significant.... The Constitutions of the new States and the governmental acts of each, *especially when unopposed, or when initial opposition was not continued,* are of special importance.[3]

The tribunal reverted to the same topic in a later passage where it stated that

> while no State can acquire jurisdiction over territory in another State by mere declarations on its own behalf, it is equally true that these assertions of authority by Guatemala... show clearly the understanding of Guatemala that this was her territory. These assertions invited opposition on the part of Honduras if they were believed to be unwarranted.[4]

Starting from these premises the tribunal reached the conclusion that

> if it had been considered that Honduras was being deprived of territory to which she was entitled, and especially that Guatemala was asserting authority over territory

[1] *UNRIAA*, vol. II, pp. 1307–1366.
[2] *Ibid.*, pp. 1324–1325.
[3] *Ibid.*, p. 1325. (Italics added).
[4] *Ibid.*, p. 1327.

which was, or prior to independence had been, under the administrative control of Honduras, it can hardly be doubted that these assertions by Guatemala would have aroused immediate antagonism and would have been followed by protest and opposition on the part of Honduras.[1]

(j) The Gulf of Fonseca Case, 1917

In the judgment delivered in 1917 by the Central American Court of Justice[2] in the *Gulf of Fonseca* case[3] the Court, in giving its reasons for declaring the bay as the common property of the littoral States – to the exclusion of all other Powers – stated that

> the representative authorities [of the former central American provinces and subsequently of the newly established independent States in the region] have notoriously affirmed their peaceful ownership and possession in the Gulf; that is, *without protest or contradiction by any nation whatsoever*.... A secular possession such as that of the Gulf could only have been maintained *by the acquiescence of the family of nations*.[4]

In a later passage of its judgment the Court once more resorted to the same concept by saying that the Gulf of Fonseca constituted an historic bay, since

> it combines all the characteristics and conditions... prescribed as essential to territorial waters to wit, secular or immemorial possession accompanied by *animo domini* both peaceful and continuous and by *acquiescence on the part of other nations*.[5]

(k) The Minquiers and Ecrehos Case, 1953

In the *Minquiers and Ecrehos* case[6] the International Court of Justice, in upholding the British claim, drew attention, *inter alia*, to the fact that in respect of the Ecrehos

> by a British Treasury Warrant of 1875, constituting Jersey as a Port of the Channel Islands, the 'Ecrehou Rocks' were included within the limits of that port. This legislative Act was a clear manifestation of British sovereignty over the Ecrehos at a time when a dispute as to such sovereignty had not yet arisen. The French Government protested in 1876 on the ground that this Act derogated from the Fishery Convention of 1839. But this protest could not deprive the Act of its character as a manifestation of sovereignty.[7]

In other words: the Court attached considerable importance to the fact that the French protest had been confined to the alleged breach

[1] *Ibid.*, p. 1328. For a detailed discussion of the history of this dispute leading up to the arbitration and for a comprehensive analysis of its legal aspects and of the award, see Fisher, 27 *AJIL* (1933), pp. 403–428.

[2] Now defunct.

[3] 11 *AJIL* (1917), p. 674 *et seq.*

[4] *Ibid.*, pp. 700–701. (Italics added).

[5] *Ibid.*, p. 705. (First italics in original; second added).

[6] *ICJ Reports*, 1953, p. 47 *et seq.*

[7] *Ibid.*, p. 66.

of the Fishery Convention of 1839 and had not found any fault with the United Kingdom legislating at all for the "Ecrehou Rocks." From this absence of objection on the part of the French Government the Court drew the inference of French acquiescence in this manifestation of British sovereignty.

Likewise, with regard to the Minquiers, the Court deemed it appropriate to refer to the fact that

> when the British Embassy in Paris, in a Note of November 12th, 1869, to the French Foreign Minister, had complained about alleged theft by French fishermen at the Minquiers and referred to this group as 'this dependency of the Channel Islands', the French Minister, in his reply of March 11th, 1870, refuted the accusation against French fishermen, but made no reservation in respect of the statement that the Minquiers group was a dependency of the Channel Islands.[1]

The function of the doctrine of acquiescence, taking the form of absence of objection, was perhaps even more emphatically resorted to in the Individual Opinions delivered in the *Minquiers and Ecrehos* case by Judges Basdevant and Levi Carneiro, both of whom approached the problem from a similar angle. Judge Basdevant found in favour of the United Kingdom on the ground that

> for a long time and in a consistent manner the Jersey authorities have taken an interest in what was happening on the Ecrehos and the Minquiers and that they took action in this connection to an extent and in a way appropriate to the character of these islets and the use which was made of them. They did this *without encountering any competing action*, still less any exclusive action on the part of the French authorities.[2]

This complete absence of any "competing action" on the part of the French authorities was apparently given due weight by Judge Basdevant in awarding the disputed islets to the United Kingdom.

Judge Carneiro in his turn pointed out that

> there can... no longer be any excuse for the failure of the French Government to protest against the acts by which the British Government exercised sovereignty over the disputed islets.... As regards to Ecrehos no protests were made after 1888 for sixty years."[3]

Again, the absence of any French objection to the exercise of governmental functions by the United Kingdom over the disputed islets was invoked as one of the main reasons for deciding this case in favour of the United Kingdom.

[1] *Ibid.*, p. 71.
[2] *Ibid.*, p. 83. (Italics added). As to the problems surrounding the relative worth of competing claims, see below, chapter V, section 57.
[3] *Ibid.*, p. 106.

(l) The Walfish Bay Arbitration, 1911

In the *Walfish Bay* Arbitration[1] between Great Britain and Germany the tribunal found for Great Britain and gave among its reasons the fact that

> *exception has not been taken* to the continued possession on the part of Great Britain of the territory extending to the point on the coast where the southern frontier [of the bay]... commences.[2]

It was on this ground that the tribunal reached the conclusion that British sovereignty had been established over the disputed territory.

(m) The Fisheries Case, 1951

The significance of the doctrine of acquiescence in relation to the establishment of historic rights was perhaps most emphatically borne out by the International Court of Justice in the *Fisheries* case.[3] In examining the legal validity of the Norwegian system of delimiting territorial waters the Court considered

> whether the application of the Norwegian system encountered any opposition from foreign States.[4]

The Court found that

> Norway has been in a position to argue without contradiction that neither the promulgation of her Delimitation Decrees in 1869 and in 1889, nor their application, gave rise to any opposition on the part of foreign States.... *The general toleration of foreign States* with regard to the Norwegian practice is an unchallenged fact. For a period of more than sixty years *the United Kingdom Government... in no way contested it.*[5]

[1] *UNRIAA*, vol. XI, p. 267 *et seq.*; 104 *BFSP*, p. 150 *et seq.*
[2] *UNRIAA*, vol. XI, p. 307. (Italics added).
[3] *ICJ Reports*, 1951, p. 116 *et seq.*
[4] *Ibid.*, p. 138.
[5] *Ibid.* (Italics added). The somewhat loose phrase "general toleration" used by the Court several times in its judgment has given rise to some doubts. It has been suggested by Johnson that "general toleration" was "probably intended to have a rather weaker meaning than acquiescence." (See Johnson, "The Anglo-Norwegian Fisheries Case," 1 *ICLQ* (1952), p. 145 *et seq.*, at p. 165, note 33). This contention, however, has been questioned by MacGibbon who holds the view that "the remainder of the Judgment [in the *Fisheries* case] hardly supports the view that such a distinction was intended.... The use of the phrase 'general toleration' where 'general acquiescence' might have been expected is of no apparent significance: the terms are synonymous." (See MacGibbon, 31 *BYIL* (1954), p. 160, note 5). Whatever the precise meaning of this phrase, one is tempted to subscribe to MacGibbon's submission that "confusion may well arise from the looseness of terminology employed by jurists in this particular matter." (*Ibid.*, p. 161).

In a later passage the Court once more reverted to the same idea when it noted that

in respect of a situation which could only be strengthened with the passage of time, the United Kingdom Government refrained from formulating reservations.... [The Norwegian] method had been consolidated by a constant and sufficiently long practice, in the face of which the attitude of governments bears witness to the fact that they did not consider it to be contrary to international law.[1]

Judge Hsu Mo in his Separate Opinion justified Norway's method of delimitation "because of her special geographical conditions and her consistent past practice which is acquiesced in by the international community as a whole."[2]

Judge McNair, while dissenting from the majority judgment, approached the problem in a manner not unlike that of the majority. He posed the question

whether the United Kingdom had precluded herself from objecting to [the Norwegian system of delimitation] by acquiescing in it.[3]

In assessing the evidence which was before the Court, he reached the conclusion that the conduct of the United Kingdom leading up to the dispute before the Court should not be construed as acquiescence on her part in the Norwegian method. Thus, although Judge McNair differed from the majority of the Court in his appraisal of the available evidence, and consequently reached a different conclusion, he approached the problem in practically the same manner as the majority and applied the same legal principles.

Judge Read, the other dissenting judge in this case, dealt with the question confronting him in a very similar manner. He defined historic waters as waters which, regardless of breadth, the coastal States could treat as internal waters, provided that sovereignty had been exercised in those waters by the said States "without challenge for a long time."[4] Dealing more specifically with Norway's historic claims, Judge Read expressed the view that, in order to establish such rights, it would be sufficient for Norway to prove that she had "consistently and persistently asserted the right to apply the System to the Norwegian coast generally, and that *there had been acquiescence in this claim* by the international community."[5] In examining the pattern of behaviour

[1] *Ibid.*, p. 139.
[2] *Ibid.*, p. 154.
[3] *Ibid.*, p. 171.
[4] *Ibid.*, p. 188.
[5] *Ibid.*, p. 197. (Italics added). See also *ibid.*, pp. 194–195.

followed by the United Kingdom Government in respect of the Norwegian claims, as it found expression in the correspondence exchanged in 1913 between Great Britain and Norway, Judge Read came to the conclusion that "the information [i.e. the information passed on by Norway to the British Government concerning the application of her system of delimitation] was received in such circumstances that the failure to make immediate protest could not have been regarded as acquiescence."[1]

(n) The Sovereignty over Certain Frontier Land Case, 1959

As will be recalled, in the case concerning *Sovereignty over Certain Frontier Land*[2] relating to a territorial dispute between Belgium and the Netherlands, the International Court of Justice was confronted with the question "whether Belgium has lost its sovereignty, by non-assertion of its rights and by acquiescence in acts of sovereignty alleged to have been exercised by the Netherlands."[3]

The Court examined the available evidence in the light of this question and found for Belgium on the ground that her conduct could not be construed in the given circumstances as acquiescence in the Netherlands' rights. Judge Sir Hersch Lauterpacht, while dissenting from the majority and while taking the view that the disputed plots of territory should have been awarded to the Netherlands, made it clear that his conclusion was warranted solely by the fact that "at least during the fifty years following the adoption of the [Boundary] Convention [of 1843] there had been no challenge to the exercise, by the Government of the Netherlands and its officials, of normal administrative authority with regard to the plots in question."[4]

Similarly, Judge Armand-Ugon, one of the dissenting judges, stated that the Netherlands had acquired an indisputable right of sovereignty over the contested territory owing to the fact that

> the Netherlands Government has exercised preponderant governmental functions in respect of the disputed plots, without these having given rise on the part of the Belgian Government to any protest or any opposition. This prolonged tolerance of the Belgian Government in this respect has created an indisputable right of sovereignty in favour of the Netherlands Government.[5]

[1] *Ibid.*, p. 204.
[2] *ICJ Reports*, 1959, p. 209.
[3] *Ibid.*, p. 227.
[4] *Ibid.*, p. 231.
[5] *Ibid.*, p. 250.

Judge Moreno Quintana seems to have relied upon the same principle when he stated that

Belgium, which was not separated from Holland until 1831, has since that date, and up to 1921 perhaps – almost a century – made no formal protest against the exercise of sovereignty by the other country.[1]

(o) The Right of Passage over Indian Territory Case, 1960

More recently, in the case concerning *Right of Passage over Indian Territory*,[2] the International Court of Justice held that

the exclusive authority of the Portuguese over the villages [comprised in the Maratha grant] was never brought in question. Thus Portuguese sovereignty over the villages was recognized by the British in fact and by implication and was subsequently tacitly recognized by India. As a consequence the villages... acquired the character of Portuguese enclaves within Indian territory.[3]

In Judge Wellington Koo's Separate Opinion this point was borne out even more explicitly when he stated that

although during the early years of British succession the attitude of the British authorities on the subject was obscure, their *tacit recognition* of Portuguese sovereignty over the enclaves became increasingly clear as time went on.[4]

Referring to the Indian contention that India had never recognized Portugal's territorial sovereignty over the said enclaves, Judge Wellington Koo pointed out that

under international law such recognition need not always be express or explicit. It does not always call for an open declaration; *it may be tacit.*[5]

Judge Armand-Ugon in his Dissenting Opinion founded Portuguese rights of passage over Indian territory, *inter alia*, on the fact that "during the British period, *no difficulty or obstacle was raised* concerning the existence of this obligation to allow passage."[6]

The Portuguese judge *ad hoc* Fernandes stated in his Dissenting Opinion that

it is sufficient... to record the Court's finding that Portugal has been for a long time *the undisputed sovereign* of the enclaves. That is what is important in order to determine whether Portugal possesses the right it claims.[7]

[1] *Ibid.*, p. 255.
[2] *ICJ Reports*, 1960, p. 6 *et seq.*
[3] *Ibid.*, p. 39.
[4] *Ibid.*, p. 65. (Italics added).
[5] *Ibid.*, p. 65. (Italics added).
[6] *Ibid.*, pp. 80–81. (Italics added).
[7] *Ibid.*, p. 126. (Italics added).

He further maintained that

Portuguese sovereignty was recognized by the British in fact and by implication and... was subsequently *tacitly recognized* by India.[1]

(p) The Temple of Preah Vihear Case, 1962

The function of acquiescence in the establishment of new territorial rights was again discussed by the International Court of Justice, in the *Temple of Preah Vihear* case.[2] There Cambodia asserted that Thailand's lack of reaction to the publication by the French authorities of maps showing the disputed area as falling within the domain of French Indo-China should be regarded as acquiescence on her part in the French claims. (Cambodia had been part of French Indo-China until 1953, when she became independent). The Court found for Cambodia and held:

It is clear that the circumstances were such as called for some reaction... on the part of the Siamese authorities, if they wished to disagree.... They did not do so, either then or for many years, and thereby must be held to have acquiesced.[3]

(q) The North Atlantic Fisheries Arbitration, 1910

It appears worth mentioning that in the award of September 7th, 1910, given in the *North Atlantic Fisheries* Arbitration,[4] only passing reference was made to the theory of historic bays when the Tribunal stated that "conventions and *established usage* might be considered as the basis for claiming as territorial those bays which on this ground might be called historic bays."[5]

29. Acquiescence as the juridical basis of historic rights – Decisions of municipal courts

In the previous chapter reference was made to some of the pronouncements of municipal courts relating to territorial disputes;[6] it was submitted there that those pronouncements did not amount to an endorsement of the principle of international prescription, but were founded rather on the doctrine of acquiescence. It is not intended here to revert to the same authorities; however, a number of further pro-

[1] *Ibid.*, p. 138. (Italics added).
[2] *ICJ Reports*, 1962, p. 6 *et seq.*
[3] *Ibid.*, p. 23. See also *ibid.*, pp. 27–31, and Sir Gerald Fitzmaurice's Separate Opinion, *ibid.*, p. 55.
[4] *UNRIAA*, vol. XI, pp. 173–211; Scott, *Hague Court Reports*, 1st Series, 1916, pp. 141–225.
[5] *UNRIAA*, vol. XI, p. 197; Scott, *op. cit.*, p. 185.(Italics added).
[6] See above, chapter II, section 15.

nouncements of national courts on the same topic will be mentioned presently.

In *Virginia* v. *Tennessee*[1] it was held by the Supreme Court of the United States that

> a boundary line between states or provinces, as between private persons, which has been run out, located and marked upon the earth, and afterwards recognized and acquiesced in by the parties for a long course of years, is conclusive, even if it be ascertained that it varies somewhat from the courses given in the original grant.[2]

In *Maryland* v. *West Virginia*[3] the same Court was concerned with an action instituted by Maryland alleging that the boundary line originally fixed between herself and West Virginia (the so-called "Deakins line") had been violated by West Virginia. The Court, however, declined to uphold the Maryland claim on the ground that

> a perusal of the record satisfies us that for many years occupation and conveyance of the lands on the Virginia side has been made with reference to the Deakins line as the boundary line. The people have generally accepted it and have adopted it, and the facts in this connection cannot be ignored.[4]

The Court summed up by saying that even on the assumption that the actual boundary line was in derogation of that agreed upon originally by the rival States, "a right... has arisen, has been practically undisturbed for many years [and should] not... be overthrown without doing violence to principles of established right and justice equally binding upon states and individuals."[5]

In *New Mexico* v. *Colorado*[6] the Court was called upon to pronounce in a boundary dispute between the two States and held that

> from 1868, when [the surveyor] Darling ran and marked the line of the 37th parallel, to 1919, when this suit was brought, a period of more than half a century, his line was recognized and acquiesced in, successively, as the boundary between the two territories, between the State of Colorado and the territory of New Mexico, and between the two states [after the admission of New Mexico to the Union in 1912].[7]

1 148 U.S. (1893), p. 503 *et seq.*
2 *Ibid.*, p. 522.
3 217 U.S. (1909), p. 1 *et seq.*
4 *Ibid.*, p. 41.
5 *Ibid.*, p. 44.
6 267 U.S. (1924–25), p. 30 *et seq.*
7 *Ibid.*, p. 40.

In *Vermont* v. *New Hampshire*[1] the Court found in favour of Vermont and explained its decision, *inter alia*, by the fact that

the New Hampshire representatives in Congress were familiar with the terms of [its] resolutions and could not have been unaware of the fact that in all the formal representations made to Congress on behalf of Vermont and in the various reports and resolutions of committees and the resolutions of Congress itself, the eastern boundary of Vermont was described interchangeably as the west side of the Connecticut River. ...Although these were public acts of notoriety, New Hampshire does not appear ever to have made any objection to these definitions of the boundary line. The conclusion we have reached... finds support... in the long continued failure of New Hampshire to assert any dominion over the west bank of the river and in her long acquiescence in the dominion asserted there by Vermont.[2]

In *New Jersey* v. *Delaware*[3] the Supreme Court was called upon to determine the boundary in the Delaware Bay and River. The Court quoted, with approval, a statement made by the Master, according to which

'at no time has the State of Delaware ever abandoned its claim, dominion or jurisdiction over the Delaware River within the said twelve-mile circle, nor has it at any time acquiesced in the claim of the State of New Jersey thereto....' The truth indeed is that almost from the beginning of statehood Delaware and New Jersey have been engaged in a dispute as to the boundary between them. There is no room in such circumstances for the application of the principle that long acquiescence may establish a boundary, otherwise uncertain.... Acquiescence is not compatible with a century of conflict.[4]

It was on this ground – the lack of acquiescence – that the claim put forward by New Jersey was bound to fail.

The same principle was also applied as the criterion for the Court's decision in *Massachusetts* v. *New York*[5] where it was held that

long acquiescence in the possession of territory and the exercise of dominion and sovereignty over it may have a controlling effect in the determination of a disputed boundary.[6]

On the evidence produced, the Court reached the conclusion that Massachusetts must be considered as having acquiesced in the state of things of which it was complaining and her claim of title to the disputed territory was accordingly dismissed.

[1] 289 U.S. (1932), p. 593 *et seq.*
[2] *Ibid.*, p. 613.
[3] 291 U.S. (1934), p. 361 *et seq.*
[4] *Ibid.*, p. 376–377.
[5] 271 U.S. (1926), p. 65 *et seq.*
[6] *Ibid.*, p. 95.

In *Stetson* v. *United States*[1] the United States Second Court of Commissioners set up to deal with the so-called "Alabama Claims" arising out of the American Civil War, was faced with a claim based on the sinking of the vessel *Alleganean* by Confederate forces in Chesapeake Bay. The Court dismissed the claim on the ground that the capture of the ship had taken place not on the high seas, but within the internal waters of the United States. Among the reasons which prompted the Court in arriving at this conclusion, which presupposed the territoriality of Chesapeake Bay and its incorporation within the maritime domain of the United States, the Commissioners mentioned the fact that

> from the earliest history of the country [Chesapeake Bay] has been claimed to be territorial waters, and that... claim has never been questioned.[2]

In *Annakumaru Pillai* v. *Muthupayal and others*[3] the Supreme Court of Madras was called upon to pronounce on the legal status of Palk's Bay and it found amongst other reasons that

> considering the evidence that exists as to the occupation of Palk's Bay by the British with the acquiescence of other nations, we have no hesitation in holding that it is... an integral part of His Majesty's Dominions.[4]

In an earlier passage of the same judgment the Court declared that

> considering that the various European maritime powers who from about the 16th century were contending for supremacy in the Indian Seas, raised no question as to the right of the Sovereigns... to their respective fisheries, there can be little doubt that such right was regarded by one and all of them as unassailable.[5]

30. Acquiescence as the juridical basis of historic rights – State practice

Turning now to the practice of States and to the attitude adopted by State authorities with regard to territorial disputes involving conflicting claims over the disputed territories, it is submitted that this practice too seems to support the contention that it is the behaviour of States affected by the claim of historic rights – usually taking the form of tacit recognition or acquiescence – that establishes such historic rights.

In the course of the proceedings under article IV of the Treaty of

[1] Scott, *Cases on International Law*, 1922, p. 232.
[2] *Ibid.*, p. 237.
[3] [1903] 27 *Indian Law Reports* (Madras Series), p. 551 *et seq.*
[4] *Ibid.*, p. 573.
[5] *Ibid.*, p. 566.

Ghent of 1794 concerning the *Title to the Islands in the Passamaquoddy Bay*, the British Agent maintained that

the simple uncontroverted fact, that all... islands now in question... were in the possession of His Majesty, and... continued in his possession, with the tacit consent and acquiescence not only of the Government of the United States but that of the State of Massachusetts, always vigilant and tenacious of all her rights... must to any unprejudiced mind most strongly evince the sense of both nations at that time with regard to the right to these islands....[1]

In the prolonged controversy between Great Britain and Spain in the middle of the 19th century relating to the "*Cuban Cays*" Great Britain protested against the Spanish practice of arresting alleged smugglers at distances exceeding the conventional three-mile limit. Spain justified these actions by relying on various acts of national legislation purporting to vindicate such a course of action.[2] Lord Howden, the British Ambassador in Madrid at the time, in a despatch dated February 9th, 1853, asked for instructions as to how to approach these problems in his dealings with the Spanish Government. As a result of this request a memorandum was prepared by Hertslet and submitted on March 10th, 1853. In this memorandum, Hertslet claimed, *inter alia*, that

it is not stated that Great Britain has at any time objected to this jurisdiction [to the extent of six miles].[3]

In the Colombian argument presented to the Swiss Federal Council in the course of the *Colombia-Venezuela Boundary* Arbitration[4] reference was made to Venezuela's failure to protest on two occasions on which such protest would have been expected from a party which deemed its rights to have been encroached upon. It was stated in the Colombian argument that "le Vénézuela n'a soulevé aucune réclamation."[5] And it was further asserted that

l'absence de protestation est en droit international une des formes de l'acceptation de la reconnaissance de certains faits.[6]

(As will be recalled, the Swiss Federal Council upheld the Colombian claim).

[1] Moore, *International Adjudications (Modern Series)*, vol. VI, 1933, p. 213.

[2] For a selection of the extremely voluminous correspondence on this subject, see Smith, *Great Britain and the Law of Nations*, vol. II, 1935, pp. 169–198.

[3] F.O. 72/839, as quoted by Smith, *op. cit.*, p. 171.

[4] *UNRIAA*, vol. I, pp. 223–298.

[5] *Ibid.*, p, 251.

[6] *Ibid.*

The Preparatory Committee of the Hague Codification Conference of 1930[1] circulated a questionnaire among the various Governments requesting their replies to a number of points which were due to be raised at the Conference. Some of the Governments asked about their views availed themselves of that opportunity to express their opinion on the subject of historic bays, and they resorted to the principle of acquiescence as the basis of historic rights.

The Australian Government defined as "historic bays" certain bays "whose width exceeds six or even ten miles which are regarded by general acquiescence as territorial waters."[2] In the view of the Belgian Government any claims by States to a breadth of territorial waters exceeding the limits agreed upon in an international convention "could only be accepted if justified by undisputed international usage."[3] Germany required for historic bays the proof that such bays have acquired an exceptional status "through long usage generally recognised by other States."[4] Great Britain took the view that "by general acquiescence, certain historic bays have been recognised as forming part of the national territory."[5] Japan required "time-honoured and generally accepted usage."[6] Poland expressed the view that "if a State exercises sovereignty over a bay and no objection has been raised by other States, the waters of the bay should be regarded as territorial waters."[7]

The Netherlands, while recognizing in principle the existence of historic rights, did not enlarge on the subject and did not specify what requirements they deemed necessary for the establishment of such rights.[8]

Norway and Portugal referred to the attitude of other States only indirectly by an oblique reference mentioning this element among a variety of other factors. In the Norwegian reply it was claimed that "there may be historical, economic or geographical factors, such as a traditional conception of territorial limits, the undisturbed possession of the right of fishing, exercised by the coastal population since time

[1] This Committee was appointed under a resolution adopted by the Council of the League of Nations on September 28th, 1927. At its session in Geneva in January and February 1929, the Committee examined the replies of the Governments and drew up bases of discussions for the use of the Conference. As to Basis of Discussions No. 8, which is directly relevant to the subject-matter of this chapter, see *Ser. L.o.N.P.*, 1929, V. 2, p. 45.

[2] *Ibid.*, p. 117.

[3] *Ibid.*, p. 120.

[4] *Ibid.*, p. 111.

[5] *Ibid.*, p. 163.

[6] *Ibid.*, p. 168.

[7] *Ibid.*, p. 182.

[8] *Ibid.*, p. 177.

immemorial and necessary for its subsistence, and also the natural limits of fishing-grounds."[1] Portugal, likewise, spoke of "the domestic legislation of... States, their higher interests and necessities and long-established usages and customs... the security and defence of the land territory and ports, and the well-being and even the existence of the State."[2] Reference was also made in the Portuguese reply to recognized fishing interests and to the fact that "on the shores of certain bays [the local inhabitants] enjoy the exclusive right of fishing through immemorial and unbroken usage."[3]

After having received the Governments' replies, the Preparatory Committee drew up bases of discussions for the Hague Codification Conference of 1930. Basis of Discussion No. 8 provided that

> the belt of territorial waters shall be measured from a straight line drawn across the entrance of the bay, whatever its breadth may be, if by usage the bay is subject to exclusive authority of the coastal State;...[4]

The debate on Basis of Discussions No. 8 was opened by the Japanese delegate, Viscount Mushakoji, who proposed an amendment which was aimed at taking account of other States' attitude in the formation of an historic title. He stated that in the opinion of the Japanese delegation "a mere claim on the part of the State concerned – which seems to be the sole condition according to the present text, to judge from the words 'by usage' – is not enough. For that reason, the Japanese delegation proposes that the words 'long established and universally recognised' should be inserted before the word 'usage'.... The Japanese delegation cannot agree that the sole condition should be the proof furnished by the coastal State."[5] The British delegate, Sir Maurice Gwyer, who intervened after the Japanese delegate, pointed out that the United Kingdom delegation "agrees with the Japanese delegation that something more than mere usage is required – that some definite acts, if you like, of dominion exercised over this piece of water are necessary.... The coastal State has to prove that it has exercised exclusive dominion over this piece of water."[6] (Referring to this statement made by Sir Maurice, the United Kingdom Reply in the *Fisheries* case explained that "the word 'usage' was intended to mean more than

[1] *Ibid.*, p. 174.
[2] *Ibid.*, p. 184.
[3] *Ibid.*
[4] *Ibid.*, p. 45.
[5] *Ser. L.o.N.P.*, 1930, V. 16, p. 103.
[6] *Ibid.*, p. 104.

mere national usage; it meant an exercise of exclusive dominion, and has, in other words, to be an *international* usage.")[1]

In a further statement made by Sir Maurice in the course of the debate, he maintained that

every State which claims jurisdiction over an historic bay... is claiming jurisdiction over part of the high seas, and that... is a claim which must necessarily be regulated by some recognised rules of international law. Otherwise, we return to the old state of affairs in which every State claimed the right to annex as part of its own territory some part of the high seas.[2]

At the conclusion of the debate in the Plenary Committee, the question of historic waters was referred to Sub-committee No. I, to which the United Kingdom delegation submitted three different draft texts, in all of which acquiescence was explicitly mentioned as a requirement for the establishment of a title to historic waters. In the relevant paragraph of text No. 1 reference was made to the exercise "of exclusive authority in virtue of long usage and *with the general acquiescence of other States*."[3] In the second text the requirement for other States' consent has been expressed in the following words: "if the jurisdiction of the State has been *generally acquiesced in by other States*."[4] The third text, prepared at a later stage of the deliberations of the drafting committee, read as follows:

If, in virtue of uninterrupted usage, a coastal State has exercised exclusive authority over an area of water, surrounded to a very large extent by land or lands belonging to the territory of that State, the area in question shall, if the authority of the State has been generally recognized or admitted by other States, be deemed to form part of the inland waters of the State. If a tacit or express consent, though very general, is not unanimous, the rights of the non-consenting States continue to be reserved.[5]

The minutes of the Second Committee of the Conference and of Sub-committee No. I appointed by it were canvassed at great length by the parties to the *Fisheries* case,[6] but they seemed to have been at one in their assessment of the work done by the Conference on this subject. In the Reply of the United Kingdom it is asserted that "the whole discussion of historic waters in the Plenary Committee was far from

[1] *ICJ, Fisheries case, Pleadings, Oral Arguments, Documents*, vol. II, p. 633. (Italics in original).
[2] *Ser. L.o.N.P.*, 1930, V. 16, p. 111.
[3] The text of this draft has been reproduced by Gidel, *op. cit.*, vol. III, p. 635, n. 1. (Italics added).
[4] *Ibid.* (Italics added).
[5] Quoted in *ICJ, Fisheries case, Pleadings, Oral Arguments, Documents*, vol. II, p. 635.
[6] *Ibid.*, vol. I, pp. 557–562; see also *ibid.*, vol. II, pp. 628–640.

scientific,"[1] whilst the Norwegian Rejoinder claims that "la discussion, qui s'est déroulée au sein de la 2me Commission a été confuse."[2] Moreover, as is well known, the Conference broke up without any tangible results and no excessive significance can therefore be attached to its deliberations. Unfortunately, the views expounded there by a great number of delegates are far from being masterpieces of precision – as is clearly evidenced by the conflicting interpretations given to these views by the rival parties in the *Fisheries* case – and can hardly be relied upon as an endorsement in favour of one view or another.

In the written arguments submitted to the Permanent Court of International Justice in the *Legal Status of Eastern Greenland* case, Denmark maintained that her sovereignty over Greenland

> a été exercée en fait pendant de longues périodes, d'une manière entièrement publique et avec la reconnaissance et l'adhésion de tous les autres Etats. Un tel exercice prolongé, ininterrompu, paisible, public et *incontesté* de la souveraineté constitue un titre valable... à la possession d'un territoire.[3]

In his oral pleadings on behalf of Denmark, de Visscher drew attention to the fact that "le Danemark, pendant plus de deux siècles, *n'a jamais rencontré au Groenland une prétention qui se soit élevée contre sa souveraineté.*"[4]

In view of the attitude taken up later by Norway in the course of her arguments in the *Fisheries* case and the interpretation given there by her to the role of acquiescence in the formation of an historic title, it is worth noting that in the *Legal Status of Eastern Greenland* case she rallied to the support of the Danish contention and quoted with approval the opinion expressed by Anzilotti, according to which "ce n'est pas l'écoulement du temps comme tel, mais *la volonté manifestée par la reconnaissance*, grâce a l'écoulement du temps, qui transforme ainsi les situations de fait en situations juridiques."[5]

In the dispute relating to the *Territorial Rights over the Delagoa Bay*, Portugal maintained that the validity of her claims rested, *inter alia*, on "*la non-contestation de ces droits par les autres nations.*"[6]

During the *Alaskan Boundary* Dispute between the United States and Canada the failure of Canada to protest was referred to in a speech

[1] *Ibid.*, vol. II, p. 640.
[2] *Ibid.*, vol. III, p. 454.
[3] *PCIJ*, Series C, No. 62, p. 101. (Italics added).
[4] *PCIJ*, Series C, No. 66, p. 2873. (Italics added).
[5] Anzilotti, *Cours de droit international* (French edition, translated by Gidel), 1929, vol. I, p. 347. (Italics added). Reference to this passage has been made in the Norwegian Rejoinder, *PCIJ*, Series C, No. 63, p. 1305.
[6] *Cmd.* 1361 (1875), p. 87. (Italics added).

made by the Canadian Minister of the Interior in the Canadian parliament on February 11th, 1898, when he said that Canada was estopped from challenging the United States' possession of the disputed territory "when there has been no protest made against the occupation of that territory by the United States."[1] He regarded this failure to protest as "an unfortunate thing for us."[2]

In the course of the *Alaska Dispute* that arose in the years 1821-1825 between Great Britain and Russia, foreshadowing the later controversy between Great Britain and the United States which culminated in the *Fur Seal* Arbitration of 1898, it was argued in a Russian Memorandum of November 23rd, 1822, dispatched by Count Lieven to the Duke of Wellington that "la Russe était donc pleinement autorisée en profiter d'un consentement qui, pour être tacite, n'en étoit pas moins solennel."[3]

The notion of acquiescence was again explicitly referred to at great length by the parties to the *Fisheries* case. However, the United Kingdom and Norway did not seem to have been at one as to the precise meaning of this term and as to the function which the doctrine of acquiescence was designed to fulfil in the formation of an historic title. The United Kingdom's contention was that "an historic title has its whole legal basis in the express or implied recognition of the title by other States, that is, in their express or implied acquiescence in the enforcement of the exceptional claim."[4]

Norway, on the other hand, seems to have taken the view that the function of the historic element in the establishment of an historic title – at least in so far as a maritime historic title is concerned – is merely to provide confirmation for the intrinsical validity of the coastal State's claim, which in itself is justified on other grounds. Norway "n'invoque pas l'Histoire pour justifier des droits exceptionnels, pour revendiquer des espaces maritimes que le droit commun lui refuserait; il invoque l'Histoire, avec d'autres facteurs, pour justifier la manière dont il applique le droit commun."[5] Norway also challenged the United Kingdom's concept "d'après laquelle le titre historique aurait pour seul fondement l'acquiescement des autres Etats,"[6] since in her view this would mean that "le phénomène se confondrait avec celui de la

[1] *Proceedings of the Alaskan Boundary Tribunal*, vol. VII, p. 910.
[2] *Ibid.*
[3] F.O. 92/51, printed in Smith, *op. cit.*, vol. II, p. 5.
[4] *ICJ*, *Fisheries case*, *Pleadings*, *Oral Arguments*, *Documents*, vol. IV, p. 121. (Statement by Sir Frank Soskice.)
[5] *Ibid.*, vol. IV, p. 308. (Statement by Bourquin on behalf of Norway).
[6] *Ibid.*

reconnaissance."[1] Bourquin, on behalf of Norway, contrasted the notions of historic title and recognition by saying that in the formation of an historic title "la *durée* devient une condition majeure. Au contraire, dans la théorie de la reconnaissance ce facteur n'a aucune importance... parce qu'elle est uniquement fondée sur la *volonté* de l'Etat."[2]

The Norwegian objection to the British concept of the function of acquiescence in the formation of an historic title has been met by MacGibbon, who charges Norway with misrepresenting the United Kingdom's attitude in this respect. He points out – rightly, it is believed – that "if due weight is given to the consideration that acquiescence is primarily dependent for its legal effect upon the fact that it is necessarily conjoined with the passage of time, it will be seen that the part played by the historic element was recognized to be of major importance by both parties."[3]

The Court, while finding for Norway on the merits of the case, seems to have upheld the United Kingdom's contention in this respect – as has been submitted above – thus granting her some partial satisfaction in the doctrinal sphere which, however, hardly counterbalances Norway's substantial success on the merits of the case.

In the course of the oral pleadings in the *Minquiers and Ecrehos* case, Counsel for the United Kingdom drew attention to France's failure to protest against diverse manifestations of British sovereignty over the disputed islets and concluded that "these omissions related to acts of sovereignty so definite and significant that the failure to take any notice of them amounted to virtual acquiescence."[4]

Acquiescence, taking the form of absence of opposition, was impliedly mentioned by Mr. Randolph, the United States Attorney-General, in his well-known opinion of 1793 concerning the legal status of Delaware Bay. The problem arose as a result of the capture of the English vessel *Grange* by the French frigate *L' Embuscade* inside the bay. Randolph expressed the view that this capture had taken place within the inland waters of the United States and was therefore illegal. Among the considerations that led him to pronounce in favour of the

[1] *Ibid.*

[2] *Ibid.*, p. 309. (Italics in original). See to the same effect the Norwegian Rejoinder, *ibid.*, vol. III, p. 442. The same idea was also expressed by Charpentier, *op. cit.*, p. 75, where the author criticizes some of the judgments delivered by the United States Supreme Court for their requiring the proof of "long acquiescence." Charpentier asks: "De plus, pourquoi exiger un'long acquiescement'?Un acquiescement est instantané; une fois donné il produit des effets définitifs."

[3] MacGibbon, 31 *BYIL* (1954), p. 165.

[4] *ICJ, Minquiers and Ecrehos case, Pleadings, Oral Arguments, Documents*, vol. II, p. 337.

territoriality of Delaware Bay he mentioned the facts that the bay "communicates with no foreign dominion; no foreign nation has, ever before, exacted a community of right in it, as if it were a main sea; under the former and present governments the exclusive jurisdiction has been asserted."[1] He further pointed out that "from the establishment of the British provinces on the banks of the Delaware to the American Revolution, it was deemed the peculiar navigation of the British Empire;... by the Treaty of Paris, on the third day of September, 1783, his Britannic Majesty relinquished, with the privity of France, the sovereignty of those provinces, as well as of the other provinces and colonies."[2] Commenting on Attorney-General Randolph's opinion, it was stated in the United Kingdom's Reply in the *Fisheries* case that in view of the fact that "in 1793 the modern rules for the delimitation of maritime territory were in their infancy... it is really somewhat striking that... Attorney-General Randolph in his opinion gave so much attention to the attitude of other States to the United States claim."[3]

When in 1911 the English fishing vessel *Lord Roberts* was arrested in the Varangerfjord for having fished within what Norway considered her territorial waters and was subsequently found guilty by a Norwegian Court in Vardö of having infringed Norwegian law, the British Government protested against this procedure. As a result of this protest a Royal Commission was appointed which, in its report of February 29th, 1912, justified the Norwegian practice on the ground that Norway had enjoyed over the Varangerfjord "un long usage qui n'avait jamais été contesté par les gouvernements étrangers."[4]

In her applications for the institution of proceedings in the *Antarctica* cases, the United Kingdom pointed out that the administration of State authority by the Falkland Islands Government over the territories in dispute was exercised "*without any objection* from the Republic of Argentina."[5]

Similarly, in the recent *Sino-Indian Boundary Dispute* the Government of India took the view that in the face of China's failure to lodge any protest against long-standing Indian assertions, China must be held to have accepted and acquiesced in the Indian alignment.[6]

[1] Moore, *Digest of International Law*, vol. I, 1906, p. 738.
[2] *Ibid.*, p. 735.
[3] *ICJ*, *Fisheries case, Pleadings, Oral Arguments, Documents*, vol. II, p. 611.
[4] Quoted after Mochot, *Le régime des baies et des golfes en droit international*, 1938, pp. 137.
[5] *ICJ*, *Antarctica cases, Pleadings, Oral Arguments, Documents*, p. 9 (italics added); see to the same effect, *ibid.*, p. 49, where reference is made to the lack of objection by Chile.
[6] See the *Summary of the Report of Officials of the Governments of India and the People's Republic*

31. *Acquiescence and estoppel*

Closely related to the notion of acquiescence is the principle of estoppel, as understood in the common law countries. Although the term "estoppel" is not widely used among jurists educated under a legal system other than the Anglo-American school, the meaning of the principle is well known to them and, where an Anglo-American lawyer would refer to estoppel, his continental counterpart would say that a party is "precluded."[1] The same idea is known to Scottish lawyers as a "personal bar."[2]

The rule of estoppel "operates so as to preclude a party from denying before a tribunal the truth of a statement of fact made previously by that party to another whereby that other has acted to his detriment or the party making the statement has secured some benefit."[3] In continental law the same result is achieved by relying on the principles of *venire contra factum proprium* and *allegans contrario non audiendus est.*[4]

Until recently a certain hesitancy seems to have prevailed as to the operation of the rule of estoppel in the sphere of international law,[5] stemming from the belief that this concept is a rule of evidence rather than a rule of substantive law.[6]

For obvious reasons the doctrine of estoppel could be invoked as a root of title in international law only if it were considered a rule of substantive law, since otherwise its function would be limited to the field of procedure, thus creating effects closely resembling those of extinctive prescription, as distinct from acquisitive prescription.[7]

However, recent trends in English and American law have led towards a reconsideration of the scope of the rule of estoppel, and the

of China on the Boundary Question, published by the Ministry of External Affairs of India, *MEA* 32, p. 10.

On the Sino-Indian Boundary Dispute in general, see K. K. Rau, "The Sino-Indian Boundary Question and International Law," 11 *ICLQ* (1962), p. 375.

An Indian White Paper of November 28th, 1961, contains the text of 108 Notes exchanged between India and China on the border dispute during 1961. By October 1962 in all some 400 Notes had been exchanged between the two Governments. For a summary of the developments leading up to the Chinese offensive in October 1962, see *Keesing's Contemporary Archives*, vol. XIII, 1961–1962, pp. 19121–19127, and pp. 19137–19142.

[1] Lauterpacht, *Private Law Sources and Analogies of International Law*, 1927, p. 204.

[2] MacGibbon, "Estoppel in International Law," 7 *ICLQ* (1958), p. 468, n. 1.

[3] Bowett, "Estoppel before International Tribunals and its Relation to Acquiescence," 33 *BYIL* (1957), p. 176.

[4] Strupp-Schlochauer, *Wörterbuch des Völkerrechts*, 2nd edition, vol. I, 1960, p. 441.

[5] McNair, "The Legality of the Occupation of the Ruhr," 5 *BYIL* (1924), pp. 34–37.

[6] Lauterpacht, *op. cit.*, p. 203, and Friede, "Das Estoppel-Prinzip im Völkerrecht," 5 *ZRV* (1935), p. 517.

[7] Both terms are used here with reference to their respective meanings in municipal law.

tendency seems now to be in favour of treating it as a rule of substantive law.[1]

In his Separate Opinion in the *Temple of Preah Vihear* case, Vice-President Alfaro, while stressing the pliability of the rule of estoppel in the sphere of international law, emphasized that

> the principle that condemns contradiction between previous acts and subsequent claims is not to be regarded as a mere rule of evidence.... The principle is substantive in character. It constitutes a presumption *juris et de jure* in virtue of which a State is held to have abandoned its right if it ever had it, or else that such a State never felt that it had a clear legal title on which it could base opposition to the right asserted or claimed by another State. In short, the legal effects of the principle are so fundamental that they decide by themselves alone the matter in dispute and its infraction cannot be looked upon as a mere incident of the proceedings.[2]

Judge Sir Gerald Fitzmaurice, in his Separate Opinion in the same case, concurred in Judge Alfaro's view and stated that "the principle of preclusion... is certainly applied as a rule of substance and not merely as one of evidence or procedure."[3]

The close relationship existing between the doctrines of acquiescence and estoppel finds its explanation in the fact that in certain situations one party's failure to act or his acquiescence "will prejudice his rights against another who has been misled by that party's inaction or silence."[4] It is this inaction or silence – sometimes amounting to acquiescence – which operates like an estoppel.

Recourse to the doctrine of estoppel was had in the sphere of international law on various occasions, both in judicial judicions and in pronouncements emanating from competent State authorities.

Thus, in the *Island of Palmas* case, Judge Huber invoked this notion when he asserted that "the acquiescence of Spain in the situation created after 1677 would deprive her and her successors of the possibility of still invoking conventional rights at the present time."[5]

More recently any doubt which may have persisted as to the applicability of this rule in the sphere of international law has been most explicitly removed by the International Court of Justice in its judgment rendered in the case concerning the *Arbitral Award made by the King of*

[1] See *Canada and Dominion Sugar Co. Ltd.* v. *Canadian National West Indies Steamships Ltd.* [1947] *A.C.* (P.C.), p. 46, at pp. 55–56; see also Wigmore on *Evidence*, 3rd ed., 1942, s. 2589.

[2] *ICJ Reports*, 1962, pp. 41–42. (Italics in original).

[3] *Ibid.*, p. 62.

[4] Bowett, *loc. cit.*, p. 198; see also to the same effect McNair, *Law of Treaties*, 1961, p. 488.

[5] *UNRIAA*, vol. II, p. 869. Cf. the *Costa Rican-Nicaraguan Boundary* case, as reported in Moore's *International Arbitrations*, vol. II, p. 1961; cf. also the *Chamizal* Arbitration Award, as reported in *UNRIAA*, vol. XI, p. 316, at p. 328, and in 5 *AJIL* (1911), p. 782, at p. 805.

Spain on 23 December, 1906.[1] Here the Court was confronted with a dispute between Nicaragua and Honduras with regard to an arbitral award made in 1906 by King Alfonso XIII of Spain. In that award the King of Spain fixed the frontier line between the two rival States. The arbitral award handed down by King Alfonso was, on the whole, in favour of Honduras, and this fact was recognized in a telegram dispatched by the President of Nicaragua to the President of Honduras on the day following the handing down of the award. In that telegram, the President of Nicaragua stated that "having regard to this decision, it appears that you have won the day, upon which I congratulate you. A strip of land more or less is of no importance when it is a question of good relations between two sister nations."[2]

The arbitral award was, however, never put into effect, for ever since 1912 Nicaragua challenged its validity on different legal grounds, and a protracted dispute ensued among the parties until they finally agreed in 1957 to submit this dispute to the International Court of Justice.

On behalf of Nicaragua it was argued before the Court that the arbitral award of 1906 had never come into effect for various legal reasons, which may be summarized under the following headings:

(a) King Alfonso had been appointed arbitrator in violation of the Arbitration Treaty of 1894 concluded between the rival parties;
(b) The Arbitration Treaty had expired at the time when King Alfonso was designated arbitrator and, alternatively, at the time of handing down his award;
(c) The arbitrator had exceeded his jurisdiction;
(d) The arbitral award was beset with obscurities and contradictions.

The Court dismissed the first two Nicaraguan contentions in the following words:

> Having regard to the fact that the designation of the King of Spain as arbitrator was freely agreed to by Nicaragua, that no objection was taken by Nicaragua to the jurisdiction of the King of Spain as arbitrator... on the ground that the... [Arbitration] Treaty had lapsed even before the King of Spain had signified his acceptance of the office of arbitrator, and that Nicaragua fully participated in the arbitral proceedings before the King, *it is no longer open* to Nicaragua to rely on either of these contentions as furnishing a ground for the nullity of the Award.[3]

[1] *ICJ Reports*, 1960, p. 192.

[2] *Ibid.*, p. 210. Commenting on the Court's judgment in general, Johnson observed that "although there is little reason to dispute the finding that Nicaragua acquiesced in the Award of December 23, 1906, some of the evidence relied upon (*e.g.*, the telegram of December 25, 1906, from the President of Nicaragua to the President of Honduras...) is not very convincing." (Johnson, 10 *ICLQ* (1961), pp. 336–337).

[3] *ICJ Reports*, 1960, p. 209. (Italics added).

As to the two remaining Nicaraguan contentions the Court noted the fact that

Nicaragua, by express declaration and by conduct, recognized the Award as valid and *it is no longer open to Nicaragua to go back upon that recognition* and to challenge the validity of the Award. Nicaragua's failure to raise any question with regard to the validity of the Award for several years after the full terms of the Award had become known to it further confirms the conclusion at which the Court has arrived.[1]

The Court went on to say that the recognition by Nicaragua of the award, as evidenced by various acts and by her conduct, "*debars* it from relying subsequently on complaints of nullity."[2]

It is noteworthy that the Court – having found for Honduras by a majority of 14 to 1 – carefully avoided the use of the term "estoppel," which occurs only in the legal literature of the common law countries, and contented itself with paraphrases virtually amounting to the same effect. Judge Sir Percy Spender, the only judge to append a Separate Opinion of his own to the majority judgment of the Court, followed the same line and cautiously steered his way by circumventing the term "estoppel," while at the same time relying on this principle in rejecting the Nicaraguan contentions. Thus, Judge Spender maintained that the Nicaraguan claim was bound to fail, "because that State is *precluded* by its conduct prior and during the course of the arbitration from relying upon any irregularity in the appointment of the King as a ground to invalidate the Award."[3]

As to the two arguments of substance put forward by Nicaragua, Judge Spender once again stated that this aspect of the case also rested "exclusively on the ground of *preclusion*. It is unnecessary to determine whether but for this preclusion any of these contentions of Nicaragua would have afforded a cause of nullity. To attempt to do so would be, in my view, an irrelevant excursion."[4]

It can be readily seen that Judge Spender's dismissal of the Nicaraguan argument rested solely on the ground of preclusion, yet he too carefully avoided the invocation of the term "estoppel." This ominous reluctance to have recourse to a well-known legal term of the common law school of jurisprudence can only indicate Judge Spender's intention to forestall any possible objection to his Separate Opinion on the ground that this doctrine was not recognized by international law. Hence, it is believed, his attempt to evade the controversial term. In

[1] *Ibid.*, p. 213. (Italics added).
[2] *Ibid.*, p. 214. (Italics added).
[3] *Ibid.*, p. 219. (Italics added).
[4] *Ibid.*, p. 220. (Italics added).

this respect he merely follows the pattern set by the majority judgment which, as will be recalled, makes no explicit mention of this term.[1] Yet, the very applicability of the principle underlying the doctrine of estoppel and the permissibility of its invocation as the legal basis of the Court's decision can hardly be called in question.

It is also worth mentioning that the only dissenting judge in this case, Judge *ad hoc* Urrutia Holguín of Colombia, who had been appointed by Nicaragua, did not challenge the assumption that the doctrine of estoppel was a principle recognized in international law, and his objection to the majority judgment on this point was prompted by his belief that Nicaragua's acts and conduct on this particular issue did not debar her from challenging the validity of the 1906 award.[2]

In the judgment delivered by the International Court of Justice in the *Temple of Preah Vihear* case, the Court rejected the Thai contention, according to which Siam had not accepted the validity of the 1907 maps delimiting the frontier in the disputed area. The Court based its conclusion on the principle of preclusion and held:

> Even if there were any doubt as to Siam's acceptance of the map in 1908, and hence of the frontier indicated thereon, the Court would consider, in the light of the subsequent course of events, that *Thailand is now precluded* by her conduct from asserting that she did not accept it. She has, for fifty years, enjoyed such benefits as the Treaty of 1904 conferred on her.... *It is not now open to Thailand*, while continuing to claim and enjoy the benefits of the settlement, to deny that she was ever a consenting party to it.[3]

The doctrine of estoppel, its meaning and scope, were also discussed at some length in the Separate and Dissenting Opinions appended to the Court's judgment. In fact, Vice-President Alfaro's Separate Opinion is devoted, in its entirety, to an examination of this principle and contains a useful list of the cases in which this doctrine was applied by the Permanent Court of International Justice, by the International Court of Justice and by various arbitral tribunals. Judge Alfaro starts by stating that "Spanish jurists, showing an objective criterium, call... [the doctrine of estoppel] '*doctrina de los actos propios*'"[4] and goes on to say:

[1] According to Johnson, "the use of the neutral term 'preclusion' is perhaps to be preferred in international law to the essentially Anglo-American, and somewhat technical, doctrine of 'estoppel.'" (Johnson, 10 *ICLQ* (1961), p. 335, n. 7).

[2] *Ibid.*, p. 222, where Judge Urrutia Holguín states: "The objection on the grounds of good faith which exists in almost all legal systems and which prevents a party from profiting by its own misrepresentation and which, in Anglo-Saxon law, is known as estoppel, would be applicable in the present case if it were proved that the action and behaviour of one of the States caused the other State to place reliance upon its acts of acquiescence...."

[3] *ICJ Reports*, 1962, p. 32. (Italics added).

[4] *Ibid.*, p. 39. (Italics in original).

When compared with definitions and comments contained in Anglo-American legal texts we cannot fail to recognize that... there is a very substantial difference between the... clear-cut rule adopted and applied in the international field and the complicated classifications, modalities, species, sub-species and procedural features of the municipal system. It thus results that in some international cases the decision may have nothing in common with the Anglo-Saxon estoppel, while at the same time notions may be found in the latter that are manifestly extraneous to international practice and jurisprudence.[1]

Judge Alfaro further states that "the primary foundation of this principle is good faith that must prevail in international relations, inasmuch as inconsistency of conduct or opinion on the part of a State to the prejudice of another is incompatible with good faith."[2] He also asserts that "this principle, known to the world since the days of the Romans, is one of the 'general principles of law recognized by civilized nations' applicable and in fact frequently applied by the International Court of Justice in conformity with Article 38, para. 1(c), of its Statute."[3]

The principle of "preclusion" was also invoked by Sir Gerald Fitzmaurice, in his Separate Opinion, in which he defined this principle as "the nearest equivalent in the field of international law to the common-law rule of estoppel."[4] Judges Wellington Koo and Sir Percy Spender, who dissented from the majority decision in this case, did not challenge the applicability of this rule in the sphere of international law, but took the view that, having regard to the circumstances which had come to light in the course of the proceedings in this case, the requirements necessary for the application of this principle had not been met.[5]

Some passages in the judgment delivered by the International Court of Justice in the *Fisheries* case seem to have created the impression that the Court treated the United Kingdom's acquiescence in the Norwegian system of delimitation as an estoppel and that the Court's decision did, in fact, rest on applying the doctrine of estoppel against the United Kingdom.[6] But, as has already been pointed out by Bowett – rightly,

[1] *Ibid.*, pp. 39–40.

[2] *Ibid.*, p. 42.

[3] *Ibid.*, p. 43. See, however, the contrary view expressed by Sir Percy Spender, in his Separate Opinion, where he maintains that "phrases such as 'a party may not blow hot and cold' or '*allegans contraria non est audiendus*' and others to the same effect do not... express general principles of international law. They are but a convenient and compendious way in which, in a general sense, the reasons which underlie certain legal principles and rules may be described." (*Ibid.*, p. 143; italics in original).

[4] *Ibid.*, p. 62.

[5] For the relevant passages see *ibid.*, p. 97 (Judge Wellington Koo), and pp. 142–143 (Judge Spender).

[6] *ICJ Reports*, 1951, pp. 130 and 139; Judge McNair in his Dissenting Opinion seems to have approached the whole problem from this angle, by saying: "The question would arise

it is believed – the "similarity in effect tends to confuse the notion of acquiescence with the doctrine of estoppel."[1] Another writer has expressed the same view by saying: "A measure of ambiguity is perhaps introduced by treating estoppel as the equivalent of recognition or acquiescence rather than their consequence."[2]

In his Separate Opinion in the *Temple of Preah Vihear* case, Judge Sir Gerald Fitzmaurice has defined the relationship existing between the principle of preclusion (or estoppel) and the notion of acquiescence in the following words:

> The principle of preclusion [which] is the nearest equivalent in the field of international law to the common-law rule of estoppel... is quite distinct theoretically from the notion of acquiescence. But *acquiescence can operate as a preclusion or estoppel* in certain cases, for instance where silence, on an occasion where there was a duty or need to speak or act, implies agreement, or a waiver of rights, and can be regarded as a representation to that effect....[3]

Different reasons seem to militate against such an identification of the doctrines of acquiescence and estoppel.

Firstly, one of the essential conditions for the operation of the rule of estoppel is the ignorance of the State purporting to have acquired some right or interest as to another State's conflicting rights or interests; conversely, it is this same element of ignorance which prevents the concept of acquiescence from coming into operation, since acquiescence, as is submitted elsewhere,[4] cannot be presumed without the knowledge of the acquiescing State.

Secondly, the rule of estoppel presupposes – *ex definitione* – some detriment suffered by the State which claims to have acquired some right or interest as a direct result of its reliance upon another State's silence or inaction.[5] However, in the sphere of acquisition of title to territory such a detriment would be more frequently than not on the other side[6]

whether the United Kingdom had precluded herself from objecting to [the Norwegian system of delimitation] by acquiescing in it." (*Ibid.*, p. 171).

[1] Bowett, *loc. cit.*, p. 200.

[2] MacGibbon, 7 *ICLQ* (1958), p. 475.

[3] *ICJ Reports*, 1962, p. 62. (Italics added).

[4] See below, section 40.

[5] Judge Sir Gerald Fitzmaurice has pointed out in his Separate Opinion in the *Temple of Preah Vihear* case that "the essential condition of the operation of the rule of preclusion or estoppel... is that the party invoking the rule must have 'relied upon' the statements or conduct of the other party, either to its own detriment or to the other's advantage." (*Ibid.*, p. 63). Similarly, Judge Wellington Koo, in his Dissenting Opinion, has expressly stated that "the legal basis of... [the] principle [of preclusion] is that one party has relied on the statement or conduct of the other, either to its own detriment or to the other's advantage." (*Ibid.*, p. 97.)

[6] There are of course instances where a State, in genuine ignorance of another State's rights over a portion of territory considered by the first State to be within its own boundaries, undertakes some scheme involving considerable financial expenses. Considerations of this

and "the doctrine of estoppel cannot operate to protect the State which has been placed in an improved position as a result of the silence or inaction of another."[1]

Thirdly, it should not be overlooked that the invocation of the doctrine of estoppel would be inconceivable without the assumption that the State claiming the benefit of estoppel has acted in good faith. This was made abundantly clear by the late Sir Hersch Lauterpacht when, in his capacity as Special Rapporteur to the International Law Commission on the Law of Treaties, he commented on paragraph 2 of draft article 11 of his report in the following words:

A State cannot be allowed to avail itself of the advantages of the treaty when it suits it to do so and repudiate it when its performance becomes onerous. It is of little consequence whether that rule is based on what in English law is known as the principle of estoppel or the more generally conceived requirement of good faith. The former is probably no more than one of the aspects of the latter.[2]

This dependence of the doctrine of estoppel on the element of good faith was also clearly brought out in the case concerning the *Arbitral Award made by the King of Spain on 23 December, 1906*, where Judge Sir Percy Spender stressed the close relationship existing between the principle of estoppel and the presumption of good faith on the part of the State relying on this doctrine. He declined to accept the Nicaraguan arguments as to the nullity of the arbitral award rendered by the King of Spain, giving as one of his reasons the fact that

it would be contrary to the principle of good faith governing the relations between States were it permitted now to rely upon any irregularity in the appointment to invalidate the Award. Its conduct up to the moment the Award was made operated in my opinion so as to preclude it thereafter from doing so, irrespective of any subsequent conduct on its part.[3]

As will be recalled, Judge Urrutia Holguín also, in his Dissenting Opinion, emphasized the close relationship between the doctrines of

kind seem to have motivated – amongst other reasons – the award given in the *Grisbadarna* Arbitration between Norway and Sweden and are clearly reflected in the following passages of the award: "Sweden has performed various acts in the Grisbadarna region, especially of late, owing to her conviction that these regions were Swedish, as, for instance, the placing of beacons, the measurement of the sea and the installation of a light-boat, being acts which involved considerable expense..." (see Scott, *Hague Court Reports*, 1st series, 1916, p. 121, at p. 130; *UNRIAA*, vol. XI, p. 161). And again: "Sweden had no doubt as to her rights over the Grisbadarna and ... she did not hesitate to incur the expenses incumbent on the owner and possessor of these banks..." (Scott, *op. cit.*, p. 131; *UNRIAA*, vol. XI, p. 162).

[1] Bowett, *loc. cit.*, p. 201.

[2] *Report on the Law of Treaties*, U.N. Doc. A/CN. 4/63 of March 24th, 1953, published in *ILC Yearbook*, 5th session, 1953, vol. II, p. 90 *et seq.*, at p. 144. See also to the same effect the commentary on article 47 of the draft articles on the law of treaties, adopted by the *ILC* at its 14th session. (U.N. Doc. 5509, p. 24).

[3] *ICJ Reports*, 1960, p. 220.

good faith and preclusion by virtually equating "the objection on the grounds of good faith" with what "in Anglo-Saxon law is known as estoppel."[1]

Good faith, however, may be lacking altogether in some cases in which States claim rights over territories, relying upon other States' acquiescence in the acquisition of their alleged rights. Commenting on Vattel who postulated good faith as one of the requirements for the operation of acquisitive prescription in international law, Johnson states that "if the doctrine of acquisitive prescription... was in the interests of international order and stability, it was hardly to be supposed that the requirement of good faith would be maintained."[2]

Fourthly and lastly, the plea of estoppel is made solely *inter partes* and does not therefore affect third parties. On the other hand, any claim to territory is aimed at ultimately achieving validity *erga omnes*.[3]

It is therefore submitted that the doctrine of estoppel cannot be invoked as the basis for the formation of an historic title in international law, in spite of the wide application of that doctrine[4] and its close resemblance to the concept of acquiescence. In applying the rule of estoppel in the sphere of international law one should always be mindful of Schwarzenberger's warning and avoid "the temptation of pressing the available judicial and diplomatic material into apparently ready-made molds of private law analogies... which [are] more often than not – fallacious analogies from private law."[5]

At the same time it should be recognized that the doctrine of estoppel, "apart from introducing a valuable element of stability in the rights of the parties to particular cases ... may also have a significant bearing on the crucial question of proof of customary law."[6]

[1] *ICJ Reports*, 1960, p. 222.

[2] Johnson, 27 *BYIL* (1950), p. 337, and the authorities cited there.

[3] This aspect of the problem is of particular significance when national pretensions are being put forward over maritime areas, since in such cases it is the international community as a whole whose interests are affected.

[4] The pliability of the rule of estoppel has been vividly illustrated by MacGibbon, 7 *ICLQ* (1958), p. 475.

[5] Schwarzenberger, "Title to Territory: Response to a Challenge," 51 *AJIL* (1957), pp. 308–309.

[6] Jenks, *The Prospects of International Adjudication*, 1964, p. 416. On the relationship between acquiescence and estoppel, see *ibid.*, pp. 540–542.

CHAPTER IV

THE REQUIREMENTS FOR THE FORMATION OF AN HISTORIC TITLE AND ITS CONSTITUENT ELEMENTS

32. *Introductory*

In the previous chapter it was submitted that the legal basis for the formation of historic rights was the presumption of acquiescence. The present chapter is devoted to a closer perusal of this doctrine and to an analysis of the various factors which, in their entirety, contribute towards raising the presumption that the State or States affected by the historic claim have acquiesced in it. As will be shown below, acquiescence is a basically negative concept, inferred from the silence and inaction of the affected States in circumstances where a State wishing to signify its objection would have been expected to do so in a manner actively indicating its opposition. It necessarily follows that acquiescence can be presumed only if the factual situation on which this presumption is founded really warrants such a conclusion.

As will be explained in this chapter, doctrine and practice alike require for the establishment of an historic title an exercise by the claimant State of authority which is both continuous and peaceful. If these two requirements are more thoroughly scrutinized, it emerges that the first, in fact, amounts to requiring a clear and unmistakable display of authority by the claimant State over the disputed territory – usually referred to as effective possession – while the other – the requirement of peacefulness – is the invocation of acquiescence in disguise, for it indicates the lack of opposition to such an effective possession on the part of the State or States purportedly affected by the display of authority over the disputed territory. From the legal point of view it is of course not the fact of effective possession, but rather the presumption of acquiescence, that sets the seal of legal validity on the historic claim. Such presumption, however, cannot be raised if there is no factual situation to justify it. Thus, these two prerequisites for the formation of an historic title are mutually interdependent, and the relationship between the two concomitant factors instrumental in the shaping of an historic title has therefore been correctly summed up by Johnson in the following words: "Display of authority by the one party, acquiescence in that display by the other party – those are the *sine qua non* of acquisitive prescription."[1]

The exercise of State authority cannot be regarded as effective unless it was displayed continuously and uninterruptedly. The manifestations of authority required in each case will, of course, vary according to circumstances. But, whatever these circumstances, no exercise of authority can reasonably be imputed to a State unless it was displayed *on behalf* of the State, i.e. exercised *à titre de souverain.*

The first part of this chapter will accordingly be concerned with an inquiry of the actual meaning of effectiveness and continuity in the sphere of territorial possession, with a closer investigation of the various manifestations in which State authority displays itself (with special reference to the question to what extent domestic legislation may be regarded as a manifestation of such authority) and with a treatment of the problems arising from the requirement of the possession being *à titre de souverain.*

The second part of this chapter deals with the problems attendant upon the requirement of peacefulness or acquiescence proper. Since acquiescence expresses itself mainly through the lack of protest against a given practice by the States affected by the initiation of such practice, the role of protest in the formation of an historic title will be elaborated upon at some length, and an attempt will be made to draw a distinction between cases in which a presumption of acquiescence may properly be inferred from mere silence and those cases in which a simple lack of objection does not, of itself, warrant such a conclusion. Acquiescence being regarded as amounting to passive consent, it is only understandable that it cannot be presumed in those cases where it can be shown that the allegedly acquiescing State had no knowledge of the situation in which it purportedly acquiesced. This aspect of the problem raises the question of the notoriety of territorial situations which is also dealt with in this chapter.

Then follow three sections in which the relevance of the so-called "geographical factor," the "legitimate interests" (e.g. economic, social, strategical factors), as well as the function of the time element in the formation of an historic title are more closely examined.

[1] Johnson, 27 *BYIL* (1950), p. 345. (Italics in original). Johnson regards acquisitive prescription as the root of an historic title.

33. *Effective display of State authority – General*

The rule, according to which no State is entitled to raise a claim of territorial sovereignty based merely on an abstract right, is of comparatively recent origin. Since about the eighteenth century it has become generally recognized that a State can make a successful claim to territorial sovereignty only if such a claim is supported by evidence of an effective display of State authority over the territory in question.

The precise meaning of the notion of effectiveness as regards territorial situations is susceptible of different interpretations. According to a broad concept of this doctrine, effectiveness "est constituée d'éléments composites: le fait, la durée, la tolérance des Etats tiers, éléments dont l'importance et la rôle varient d'une espèce à une autre.... Il en est ainsi même de l'aspect matériel de la possession (*corpus possessionis*)."[1]

The foregoing definition seems to conceive the notion of effectiveness as embracing – in addition to the purely material element of physical possession – also considerations of a different kind, like the time factor and the reaction of other States, thus incorporating under a single heading elements which are usually distinguished as the objective and subjective factors required for the formation of a territorial title. In this context, effectiveness denotes a degree of reality which a social phenomenon must display in order to justify its inclusion and integration into international law.[2]

While such a wide and sweeping statement may unquestionably serve a useful purpose from the doctrinal point of view, it is felt that it departs to a considerable extent from what has become generally accepted as meaning "effectiveness" in international law. According to the concept prevailing in contemporary international practice, this term has a much narrower scope and is basically confined to the material and physical aspects of diverse territorial situations. It indicates a certain degree of political, military or administrative power deemed appropriate in the given conditions and varying from case to case according to circumstances. In fact, international jurisprudence still envisages "effectiveness" as meaning "l'exercice régulier de fonctions étatiques, étroitement liées à des responsabilités internationales."[3]

The weight attached to the principle of effectiveness in international law is far greater than that given to it in the modern systems of domestic

[1] De Visscher, "Observations sur l'effectivité en droit international public," 62 *RGDIP* (1958), p. 601 *et seq.*, at p. 604. (Italics in original).
[2] *Ibid.*, p. 602.
[3] *Ibid.*, p. 604.

law. In the words of de Visscher, "international law concedes to effective territorial possession consequences that private law would by no means admit in relation to property."[1] In his submission, a State which has ceased to exercise any effective authority over a given territory will not be entitled to preserve indefinitely its territorial title by simply resorting to verbal protests and the territorial title will pass into the hands of another State which for a sufficient length of time has exercised effective authority over the disputed territory, discharging the responsibilities which are usually incumbent on the territorial sovereign. "Considerations of stability, order and peace... are here preponderant."[2]

Thus, an international tribunal confronted with the duty of pronouncing on questions relating to territorial sovereignty over disputed areas will primarily be concerned with the question which of the contesting parties has in fact succeeded in establishing its effective control over the territory in question. Effective control is, in the words of Schwarzenberger, an element "which is of central importance for purposes of both the acquisition and maintenance of title."[3] This statement – the scope of which is of a general character regarding the acquisition and maintenance of territorial titles – deserves to be somewhat qualified as regards the acquisition of an historic title. No doubt, in this case too, effective control over the territory to which an historic claim has been laid is essential for the acquisition of title and cannot be dispensed with. No historic title will be allowed to perfect and mature unless evidence of such "effective control" has been forthcoming. However, it cannot be overemphasized that it is not effective control *per se* that forms the legal basis of such a title. The mere fact of physical possession or effective control is in law – both on the domestic and on the international level – devoid of any legal significance. Its value rests completely in the field of evidence. The probative weight of the fact of effective possession is considerable indeed and its cardinal purpose is to raise the inference of other States' acquiescence in a situation which has adversely affected their original rights. The requirements for the effective display of authority by the State building up an historic claim "must be viewed in the light of the ... consideration that acquiescence is a prerequisite for the valid formation of such titles."[4] Thus, the effectiveness of State authority displayed by the State putting forward an

[1] De Visscher, *Theory and Reality in Public International Law* (translated from the French by P. E. Corbett), 1957, p. 201.
[2] *Ibid.*
[3] Schwarzenberger, *op. cit.*, p. 298.
[4] MacGibbon, 30 *BYIL* (1953), p. 306.

historic claim is relevant precisely to the extent to which it is capable of supplying evidence of other States' acquiescence in a situation which has given rise to the formation of such a title.

The authorities on this aspect of the formation of an historic title are not particularly abundant. Nor would it appear that the validity of a claim to territorial sovereignty based solely on effective possession has ever been the subject of a decision rendered by an international tribunal. The dearth of specific authority on this point may be explained by the fact that "not only is the proposition as such self-evident, but, where a State... has continued to exercise effective possession over... [a] territory, it is in the nature of things unlikely that its sovereign rights will be the subject of legal challenge."[1]

The concept, according to which effective possession is vital for the formation of a territorial title, has been explicitly recognized in the *Clipperton Island* case where King Victor Emanuel III of Italy, in his capacity as sole arbitrator, observed that

> la prise de possession matérielle... est une condition nécessaire de l'occupation. Cette prise de possession consiste dans l'acte ou la série d'actes par lesquels l'Etat occupant réduit à sa disposition le territoire en question et se met en mesure d'y faire valoir son autorité exclusive.[2]

The same principle was most lucidly stated in the *Island of Palmas* Arbitration, dealing with a dispute which had arisen between the United States and the Netherlands concerning the sovereignty over the Island of Palmas (or Miangas) in the Pacific. The main American contention was that the United States ought to be regarded as the territorial sovereign of the island by virtue of the fact that they succeeded to Spain, who in her turn had established her title to the island by means of discovery. The Netherlands, on the other hand, founded their claim on a continuous and peaceful display of authority over the disputed island.

Judge Huber, the sole arbitrator, in his award found in favour of the Netherlands, holding that a title based on effective exercise of sovereignty is superior to a claim founded on discovery. In a well-known and frequently-quoted passage of the award the distinguished arbitrator observed that

> practice, as well as doctrine, recognizes – though under different legal formulae and with certain differences as to the conditions required – that the continuous and peace-

[1] *ICJ, Minquiers and Ecrehos case, Pleadings, Oral Arguments, Documents*, vol. I, p. 103.
[2] *UNRIAA*, vol. II, p. 1110. (For the English translation of the award, see 26 *AJIL* (1932), pp. 390–4).

ful display of territorial sovereignty... is as good as a title. The growing insistence with which international law, ever since the middle of the eighteenth century, has demanded that the occupation shall be effective would be inconceivable, if effectiveness were required only for the act of acquisition and not equally for the maintenance of the right.[1]

It should not be overlooked that both these awards, namely, the *Clipperton Island* Award and the *Island of Palmas* Award, deal with the question of effective control as it poses itself from the specific angle relating to the acquisition of a territorial title by occupation (as a mode of acquiring title). But "if the effectiveness has above all been insisted on in regard to occupation, this is because the question rarely arises in connection with territories in which there is already an established order of things."[2] It is therefore submitted that the considerations underlying the need for effective possession in the case of occupation do apply to the same – if not to a larger – extent to the acquisition of an historic title, where it is only through the proof of effective control that there can be raised a presumption of acquiescence which – as has already been amply illustrated in the previous chapter – is the legal basis for such an exceptional title.

In the case concerning the *Legal Status of Eastern Greenland* the Permanent Court of International Justice, relying on the criteria laid down in the *Island of Palmas* case, reaffirmed the principle that "a claim to sovereignty based not upon some particular act or title such as a treaty of cession but merely upon continued display of authority, involves two elements each of which must be shown to exist: the intention and will to act as sovereign, and some actual exercise or display of such authority."[3]

This approach is clearly reflected in the application of the United Kingdom instituting proceedings against the Argentine Republic in the *Antarctica* cases where it was pointed out that the territories in dispute "have for many years been utilised and administered by the Falkland Islands Government *effectively*, openly and... without any objection from the Republic of Argentina."[4]

The pre-eminence of effective display of State authority and its superiority when faced with a derelict legal title may also be a pertinent consideration with regard to the legal solution of the now century-old

[1] *Ibid.*, p. 839.
[2] *Ibid.*
[3] *PCIJ*, Series A/B, No. 53, pp. 45–46.
[4] *ICJ*, *Antarctica cases*, *Pleadings*, *Oral Arguments*, *Documents*, p. 9 (italics added); as regards the United Kingdom application against Chile, see *ibid.*, p. 49.

British Honduras-Guatemala Dispute. The origins of this dispute go back to 1859 when a Convention was signed between Great Britain and Guatemala fixing the boundaries between Guatemala and British Honduras (which territory is referred to by Guatemala as "Belize"). In the years 1939–1940 and again at the close of the Second World War Guatemala demanded the annulment of the 1859 Convention on the ground that Great Britain had not fulfilled her obligations under article 7 of the said Convention, under which the two parties were to co-operate in the construction of a road from Guatemala City to the Atlantic Coast. Guatemala further claimed that, as a consequence of the annulment of the Convention, sovereignty over the whole of British Honduras would revert to her. This contention was based on the assumption that the territory in question was Guatemalan territory up to the conclusion of the 1859 Convention and was ceded to Great Britain by virtue of that Convention. The basis of the Guatemalan assertion of sovereignty over what is now British Honduras, during the period leading up to the 1859 Convention, is the Latin-American concept of *uti possidetis*.[1]

In 1946 the United Kingdom offered to submit the dispute to the jurisdiction of the International Court of Justice,[2] but Guatemala, in her acceptance of the "Optional Clause," excluded "the dispute between England and Guatemala concerning the restoration of the territory of Belize, which the Government of Guatemala would... agree to submit to the judgment of the Court, if the case were decided *ex aequo et bono*...."[3]

A flurry of diplomatic exchanges and skirmishes has ensued ever since, but no legal proceedings have been instituted by either party since Guatemala's rejection of the British offer of 1946.

In a study published in 1953 Bloomfield maintains that, contrary to what is asserted by Guatemala, the *status quo ante* 1859 was not Guatemalan sovereignty, which Britain had never recognized, but that Britain herself had acquired by that date territorial rights, after Spain had tacitly abandoned her sovereignty over the area.[4] Thus, he considers the 1859 Convention as an act purely declaratory of a situation which already existed at that time. As to the application of the *uti possidetis* rule, the same writer points out that this principle, which is a rule inconsistent with general customary international law, is binding only on those who have expressly agreed to it; Great Britain, however, never

[1] For a more detailed discussion of this doctrine, see below, Appendix.
[2] *Cmd.* 6934 (1946).
[3] *ICJ Yearbook, 1946–1947*, pp. 219–220. (Italics in original).
[4] Bloomfield, *The British Honduras-Guatemala Dispute*, 1953, pp. 78–96.

entered any agreement in which the *uti possidetis* rule was made the test for the determination of the parties' rights.[1] He also quotes with approval Lawrence, who has pointed out that "long-continued possession of territory gives a good title to it when no other ground can be clearly shown, and even in cases where possession was originally acquired by illegal and wrongful acts."[2] Thus, one is tempted to share the view expressed by Bianchi that Guatemala has "a legally desperate case."[3]

The paramount significance of the effectiveness of a territorial situation, when contrasted with a purely abstract claim, was once more brought into the fore in the *Bahrein Islands Controversy* between Persia and Great Britain. Here the Iranian Government seems to have struck a somewhat discordant note in its appraisal of the weight of an abstract claim, maintaining that it should prevail in the teeth of an effective display of authority running counter to such a claim.

The early history of the Bahrein Islands is obscure, but they appear to have been inhabited from a very early time on account of their pearl fisheries.[4] When Portuguese power in the Persian Gulf started crumbling towards the turn of the 17th century, Persia revived her ancient claims over the islands in question, but was never able to exercise effective control over them, owing to the constant regional strifes between warring local sheikhs and chieftains. Great Britain made her appearance in this area shortly after the Napoleonic Wars and, through a series of agreements with the Sheikhs of Bahrein – culminating in a treaty concluded in 1892 – she brought the until then virtually independent islands under what practically amounted to British protection.

The serious flare-up between Great Britain and Persia in respect of these islands came in 1927 as a result of a treaty concluded in that year between Britain and Saudi Arabia in which the latter undertook, *inter alia*, to maintain friendly relations with Bahrein, on account of her "special treaty relations with His Britannic Majesty's Government."[5] This provision at once evoked a sharp Persian protest,[6] and in a second

[1] *Ibid.*, p. 94.
[2] *Ibid.*, p. 81; the quotation is from Lawrence, *The Principles of International Law*, 7th ed., 1923, p. 160.
[3] Bianchi, *Belize: The Controversy between Guatemala and Great Britain over the Territory of British Honduras in Central America*, 1959, p. 137; for a brief summary of the developments in this case in the years 1946–1960 see Waddell, 55 *AJIL* (1961), pp. 459–469.
[4] For the historical background of this controversy see Khadduri, "Iran's Claim to Sovereignty over Bahrayn," 45 *AJIL* (1951), p. 631, at pp. 632–644; see also Adamiyat, *Bahrein Islands*, 1955, p. 39 *et seq.*, containing a presentation of the Persian case.
[5] *Cmd.* 2951 (1927), p. 3.
[6] *League of Nations Official Journal*, 9th year, No. 5, May 1928, p. 605.

Note to Britain the whole Persian case seems to have been telescoped in the following words:

A territory belonging to a sovereign State cannot be lawfully detached so long as the right of ownership has not been transferred by this State to another State in virtue of an official act, in this case a treaty, or so long as its annexation by another State or its independence have not been officially recognised by the lawful owner of the territory.[1]

Sir Austen Chamberlain, the then British Foreign Secretary, in his reply challenged the Persian claims that Persia had ever possessed a valid legal title over Bahrein or that Britain had recognized such a title. The just-quoted Persian argument was met in the British Note with the following words:

The assertion that the consent of the dispossessed State is invariably required to validate a change of sovereignty is contradicted both by international practice and the fact of history.... *The effective establishment by the territory of its independence is the deciding factor in the question of international title*, and, in the case of Bahrein, His Majesty's Government regard as wholly untenable the proposition that effective possession and administration by the present ruling family for 145 years, during which these rulers have been independent of Persia, and during which no Persian authority has been exercised in their dominions, can be affected by the mere consideration that the Persian Government have not set their signature to a document formally recognising the fact of their independence.[2]

It would appear that the attitude taken up by Sir Austen, as expounded in the British Note, truly reflects the consensus of opinion on this point. The validity in international law of any Persian claims to Bahrein at the present time – assuming that Persia did, in fact, enjoy a title to the islands sometime in the past – is to be examined in the light of the considerations whether the various Persian protests were sufficient to deprive the factual situation prevailing in the islands of its "peaceful and uninterrupted" character and to keep alive the Persian claims. This question, however, touches upon the problem of the relevance of mere protest in the prevention of an historic title from maturing and its discussion has thus to be deferred to the section dealing *in extenso* with this problem.[3]

The problems relating to "effective occupation" arose in recent years with regard to the possibility of acquiring sovereignty over polar re-

[1] *Ibid.*, 9th year, No. 9, September 1928, p. 1360.
[2] *Ibid.*, 10th year, No. 5, May 1929, pp. 790–793, at p. 791. (Italics added).
[3] See below, section 44. For a more detailed investigation of the legal status of the Bahrein Islands, see Smith, *op. cit.*, vol. II, pp. 62–76.

gions, and, as has been shown by Waldock,[1] it is in this particular context that the relativity of the notion of "effectiveness" and its adaptation to the peculiar features of the territory involved can be best understood. Surveying doctrinal authorities on this point, Waldock explains that "effectiveness" was in the past identified with the actual settlement or use of territory and, because the polar regions were thought to be uninhabitable, they were also considered as being incapable of appropriation. Waldock rejects this argument – rightly, it is believed – on two grounds:

(a) The difficulty of establishing a permanent settlement on a given spot does not, by itself, prevent sovereignty being acquired over it. "It is scarcely less difficult," says Waldock, "to settle permanently in deserts like the Sahara or in mountain ranges such as the Himalayas, but no one has on that account denied that deserts or mountains may be the subject of sovereignty.... Barren and virtually uninhabitable lands [are] in law susceptible of occupation and therefore of sovereignty."[2]

(b) The relativity of the notion of "effectiveness" with regard to territorial situations is clearly emphasized in the second argument advanced by Waldock when he states that

> the view that polar regions are not susceptible of sovereignty was in fact based on the now-exploded theory that actual settlement or use of territory is essential to its effective occupation. That theory had behind it most respectable authorities.... But this theory has been decisively rejected by arbitral and judicial decisions of the present century.[3]

Waldock further maintains that "the requisites of effective occupation depend on the circumstances of the territory and ... settlement or local administration is not necessarily required in the case of uninhabited territory."[4] He cites in support of this contention, *inter alia*, passages from the *Legal Status of Eastern Greenland* case, from which it emerges that Denmark was held to have maintained her sovereignty over the disputed territory during long periods when no settlements existed there at all,[5] and the *Clipperton Island* case, where it was laid down that, in the case of an uninhabited territory, the mere arrival of the agents of the occupying State might amount to a taking of possession of the territory in question, even without the establishment of a local

[1] Waldock, "Disputed Sovereignty in the Falkland Islands Dependencies," 25 *BYIL* (1948), p. 311, at pp. 314–318.
[2] *Ibid.*, p. 315.
[3] *Ibid.*
[4] *Ibid.*, p. 317.
[5] *Ibid.*, p. 316, citing *PCIJ*, Series A/B, No. 53, pp. 45–46.

administration.[1] He sums up the matter by saying that regarding the present-day meaning of the notion of effectiveness "emphasis has shifted from the taking of physical possession of the land... to the manifestation and exercise of the functions of government over the territory.... The alleged impossibility of obtaining sovereignty by occupation of polar lands on the grounds of their uninhabitability is founded on a false legal premiss."[2]

These views of Waldock were expressed with regard to the problems relating to the occupation of the Falkland Islands Dependencies, which in turn are, so to speak, "superimposed" on the questions pertaining to the legal status of the Falkland Islands themselves. British sovereignty over these islands has been hotly contested by Argentina ever since her emergence as an independent nation in the 19th century. The Falkland Islands (in French "les Malouines"; in Spanish "las Ilas Malvinas") were discovered by the British towards the end of the 17th century. In 1765 a British settlement was established at Port Egmont in West Falkland (one of the two main islands of the group), following the foundation of a French colony in East Falkland the year before. East Falkland was handed over by the French in 1767 to the Spaniards. Subsequently, the title to the whole group was disputed between Great Britain and Spain.

The serious controversy regarding the islands originates in 1770 when a Spanish military unit forcibly captured Port Egmont. After lengthy negotiations the Spaniards in 1771 apologized and withdrew, and Port Egmont was duly restored. In 1774 the British garrison was withdrawn from the island, after having left behind an inscription stating that sovereignty over the islands was retained by Great Britain. For the following sixty years the islands seem to have been regarded in practice as no man's land.

In 1820 a vessel belonging to the Government of Buenos Aires (which had in the meantime seceded from the Spanish Crown) visited the islands and its commander took formal possession of them in the name of the Buenos Aires Government. No acts of occupation followed and no effective control was exercised there by the Buenos Aires authorities who confined themselves to the appointment of a governor of the Falklands. This official, however, never visited the islands.

An atmosphere of unreality surrounded these islands until they were

[1] *Ibid.*, quoting the *Clipperton Island* Award, as reproduced in English, 26 *AJIL* (1932), p. 390, at p. 394.
[2] *Ibid.*, p. 317.

re-occupied by the British in 1832. Indignant Buenos Aires protests soon followed, and Argentina has ever since challenged the British rights of sovereignty over this group of islands.

In analyzing the legal status of the Falkland Islands to-day, Smith takes the view that "in the eyes of modern international law the British title to these islands should be deemed to rest upon the re-occupation of 1832 rather than upon the dubious claims of sovereignty reserved by a leaden inscription in 1774."[1]

This assertion is warranted by the fact that British policy recognized, according to Smith, rights over territories only where such territories "*had been effectively occupied*."[2] Upon this principle, Smith goes on to say, there was a complete gap in the occupation of the islands in the period preceding British re-occupation and any Power, which established there effective authority, was therefore to be regarded as the territorial sovereign.[3]

It is impossible to lay down a general rule of universal applicability as to what acts amount to an effective display of State authority and what acts do not meet these requirements. The criterion of effective possession to be applied in a particular instance will in each case turn upon the facts and circumstances themselves. The main questions which will pose themselves in determining whether or not a State claiming a title to a given territory has in fact been in effective possession of that territory are as follows:

(a) Has the exercise of authority been continuous?
(b) Has authority been exercised "with the intention and will to act as sovereign?"
(c) Is there sufficient evidence of the manifestation of State authority in a manner appropriate in the circumstances?

It is now proposed to discuss in turn each of these problems and to examine in some detail the considerations determining the answers to each of the foregoing questions.

[1] Smith, *op. cit.*, vol. II, p. 62.

[2] *Ibid.*, p. 61. (Italics added).

[3] *Ibid.*, pp. 61–62; for a more detailed survey of this case, including some of the relevant documents exchanged between Great Britain, Spain and the Government of Buenos Aires, see *ibid.*, pp. 45–62. For the presentation of the case of Argentina see Goebel, *The Struggle for the Falkland Islands*, 1927, p. 411 *et seq.* See also Hayton, "The 'American' Antarctic," 50 *AJIL* (1956), p. 583 *et seq.*, and the authorities referred to at p. 583, n. 2, there. See also Jenks, "An International Regime for Antarctica?," *International Affairs* (1956), p. 414 *et seq.*, and the authorities cited at p. 414, n. 2, there.

34. *Effective display of State authority – The notion of continuity in respect of territorial situations*

The meaning of the requirement of continuity, which is one of the prerequisites for effective possession, has been explained by Verykios in the following words:

Cette condition signifie qu'il ne doit pas y avoir de lacunes dans l'exercice de la souveraineté territoriale.[1]

The author, however, qualifies the meaning of the term "lacune" in this context by stating that it "ne comprend pas tous les cas d'intermittence de la possession, car il existe des territoires qui ne sont pas susceptibles de possession continue; dans ces cas il suffit que l'exercice de la souveraineté territoriale soit régulier, malgré son intermittence."[2]

This passage seems to convey the idea that too much meaning should not be read into the requirement of continuity. It would appear that a "continuous" possession is not identical with a constant display of authority. It seems rather to indicate an exercise of authority in a manner which is appropriate in the light of the circumstances prevailing in the territory in question. The claimant State will not be called upon to prove a continuity in its possession going beyond what would have been normally expected elsewhere in similar circumstances. The real criterion for the continuity of possession is its *regularity*, i.e. its conformity with what is commonly regarded as regular practice in respect of the type of territory in question. Thus, a higher degree of continuity will be required for inhabited territories than for uninhabited ones; the standard of continuity applied to land territories will naturally be set higher than that applied to maritime areas. The test adopted in each case will consequently vary according to circumstances.

This principle has been succinctly stated by Judge Huber in the *Island of Palmas* case where he maintained:

Manifestations of territorial sovereignty assume... different forms, according to conditions of time and place. Although continuous in principle, sovereignty cannot be exercised... at every moment on every point of a territory. The intermittence and discontinuity compatible with the maintenance of the right necessarily differ according as inhabited or uninhabited regions are involved, or regions enclosed within territories in which sovereignty is incontestably displayed or again regions accessible from, for instance, the high seas.[3]

[1] Verykios, *op. cit.*, p. 82.
[2] *Ibid.*
[3] *UNRIAA*, vol. II, p. 840.

As further illustrations for his contention the arbitrator mentions the case where there is not in existence a conventional border-line of sufficient topographical precision, or if there are gaps in the frontiers otherwise established.[1]

Similarly, in the *Legal Status of Eastern Greenland* case the Permanent Court of International Justice held that

it is impossible to read the records of the decisions in cases as to territorial sovereignty without observing that in many cases the tribunal has been satisfied with very little in the way of the actual exercise of sovereign rights.... This is particularly true in the case of claims to sovereignty over areas in thinly populated or unsettled countries.[2]

From the foregoing and other pronouncements of international tribunals it seems to emerge that in those cases in which State authority cannot be exercised for one reason or another in the normal manner, namely, in a manner which is properly suited for inhabited territories having a fairly high density of population and being ruled by an effective administration, a rather high degree of leniency will be shown towards the claimant State. International law is most likely to content itself in these cases with lesser manifestations of sovereignty – intermittent in space and sporadic in time – which would not have been normally considered as sufficient to meet the requirements of continuity.[3]

In the *Island of Palmas* case Judge Huber was prepared to regard as "continuous" a possession which would not have been recognized as such in less remote and more densely populated areas of the globe. His readiness to dispense with a high degree of continuity was based on the realities prevailing on the Island of Palmas, taking into account its geographical isolation and its remoteness from the more populated and civilized parts of the world. The arbitrator commented on this aspect of the problem in the following words:

The acts of indirect or direct display of Netherlands sovereignty at Palmas (or Miangas), especially in the eighteenth and early nineteenth centuries are not numerous, and there are considerable gaps in the evidence of continuous display. But... manifestations of sovereignty over a small and distant island, inhabited only by natives, cannot be expected to be frequent.[4]

[1] *Ibid.*

[2] *PCIJ*, Series A/B, No. 53 p. 46; see also to the same effect the *Clipperton Island* case, *UNRIAA*, vol. II, p. 1110.

[3] Such lesser manifestations of State authority will suffice, however, only in the absence of competing territorial claims. For a detailed discussion of the problems relating to the assessment of the relative strength of competing claims, see below, chapter V, section 57.

[4] *UNRIAA*, vol. II, p. 867.

Likewise, in the *Legal Status of Eastern Greenland* case the Permanent Court of International Justice was faced with the question whether the display of authority by Denmark over Eastern Greenland was sufficiently continuous to warrant the conclusion that Denmark had exercised effective authority over that territory. Again, the Court conceived the notion of continuity as a relative one, varying from case to case, in accordance with the peculiar circumstances. The Court concluded that

> bearing in mind... the Arctic and inaccessible character of the uncolonized parts of the country, the King of Denmark and Norway displayed during the period from... 1721 up to 1814 his authority to an extent sufficient to give his country a valid claim to sovereignty.[1]

From the foregoing quotations it would appear that the term "continuity" coined to denote this requirement may be somewhat misleading, inasmuch as it is apt to indicate a need to prove an absolutely uninterrupted possession – both in space and in time. As has been shown, the test applied by international law is much less stringent. Reference to the term "regularity" may perhaps better express what is really understood when requiring a "continuity" of possession. "Regularity," by its very definition, differs from place to place and from time to time. A practice that may rightly be considered "regular" at a given place and time will not be necessarily viewed in the same light in different circumstances. "In accordance with this principle," says Waldock, "a display of sovereignty at irregular and comparatively long intervals was held sufficient... both in the *Island of Palmas* and *Eastern Greenland* cases."[2] Referring to the problem of continuity, as it poses itself with regard to polar regions, the same writer points out that "there is one special circumstance which affects the continuity of the display of sovereignty in the [polar] regions, namely, the seasonal nature of the access to the regions.... The facts that the regions are uninhabited and are susceptible only to very limited forms of human activity inevitably diminish the continuity to be expected in the exercise of sovereignty."[3]

The introduction of such vague and broad criteria may, no doubt, displease those primarily concerned with the doctrinal aspect of the matter. Such a course, nevertheless, appears to be the only practical one, because it takes into account the immense diversity of territorial situations and the varying intensity of State authority, which find their

[1] *PCIJ*, Series A/B, No. 53, pp. 50–51.
[2] Waldock, 25 *BYIL* (1948), p. 337. (Italics in original).
[3] *Ibid.*

justification in the particular circumstances conditioned by geography and time. The manner in which State authority will manifest itself will accordingly vary from place to place and from time to time. It is these manifestations of sovereignty to which attention has now to be drawn.

35. Effective display of State authority – Intention and will to act as sovereign

Earlier in this chapter passing reference was made to a passage in the judgment of the Permanent Court of International Justice in the *Legal Status of Eastern Greenland* case where the Court held that a claim to sovereignty based "merely upon continued display of authority, involves two elements each of which must be shown to exist: *the intention and will to act as sovereign, and some actual exercise or display of such authority.*"[1]

It is now proposed to focus attention on the italicized portion of the foregoing quotation and to make it the starting-point for an analysis of what is understood by "a will to act as sovereign" and by "some actual exercise or display of... authority."

The present section deals with the questions relating to the expressions of a State's will to act as sovereign, while the next one is devoted to the problems attendant on the actual display of State authority.

"The intention and will to act as sovereign" seems to mean, according to Waldock, "no more than that there must be positive evidence of the pretensions of the particular state to be the sovereign of the territory."[2] The usual way for States to display their intentions is by means of their domestic legislation. Acts of legislation – assuming different names and forms – give expression to a State's claim to a particular area, and indicate the extent of its pretensions. In fact, such assertions of a State's claims carry considerable weight in assessing the scope of its rights.

The conviction that State legislation is indicative of what a given State considers to be its rightful claim and reflects its will to act as sovereign over the area to which such act of legislation refers, is, apart from its being a rule of genuine common sense, a legal maxim of comparatively long standing.

Thus, in his well-known opinion of 1793, following the capture by the French of the British vessel *Grange* within the waters of Delaware Bay, Attorney-General Randolph of the United States, commenting

[1] *PCIJ*, Series A/B, No. 53, pp. 45–46. (Italics added).
[2] Waldock, 25 *BYIL* (1948), p. 334.

on the territorial status of the bay, took the view that it constituted in its entirety American territory. Among the considerations prompting him in this conclusion, Randolph mentioned the fact that

> under the... [British] and present governments the exclusive jurisdiction has been asserted; by the very first collection law of the United States, passed in 1789, the county of Cape May, which includes Cape May itself, and all the waters thereof, theretofore within the jurisdiction of the State of New Jersey, are comprehended in the district of Bridgetown.[1]

In *Stetson* v. *United States* the Court of Commissioners set up to deal with claims arising out of the American Civil War was confronted with the problem of the territoriality of Chesapeake Bay. This question arose as a consequence of the capture of the British vessel *Alleganean* by Confederate forces within the said bay. The Court held that Chesapeake Bay should be regarded American territory, justifying this conclusion, *inter alia*, by the fact that "the legislation of Congress has assumed Chesapeake Bay to be within the territorial limits of the United States."[2]

In the *Direct United States Cable Co.* v. *Anglo-American Telegraph Co.* the Judicial Committee of the Privy Council was called upon to pronounce on the territorial status of Conception Bay and found that it formed part of the territory of Newfoundland. Ranking high among the reasons given for this decision was the fact that

> the British Legislature has by Acts of Parliament declared it to be part of the British territory, and part of the country made subject to the Legislature of *Newfoundland*.[3]

The Judicial Committee of the Privy Council took the view that

> no stronger assertion of exclusive dominion... could well be framed.... This is an unequivocal assertion of the British Legislature of exclusive dominion over this bay as part of the British territory.[4]

A striking and illuminating illustration of this point is the considerable role which the Norwegian Decrees – from 1812 up to 1935 – played in the course of the deliberations in the *Fisheries* case, in evaluating the precise extent of Norway's exceptional rights over her coastal waters. Among the various manifestations of Norwegian sovereignty over certain maritime areas the Court mentioned the fact that "Norway has been in a position to argue that neither the promulgation of her delimitation Decrees in 1869 and in 1889, nor their application, gave rise to any opposition on

[1] Moore, *Digest of International Law*, vol. I, 1906, p. 738.
[2] Scott, *Cases on International Law*, 1922, p. 232, at p. 236.
[3] 2 (1877) *A.C.*, p. 394, at p. 420. (Italics in original).
[4] *Ibid.*, p. 421.

the part of foreign States."[1] Thus, the promulgation of these Decrees and their enforcement by Norway were considered by the Court as claear manifestations of sovereignty in the face of which other countries – wishing to dissociate themselves from the Norwegian claim – would have been expected to raise a clear and unequivocal protest. The promulgation and application of the Norwegian Decrees were therefore among the factors enabling the Court to infer a presumption of international acquiescence in Norway's exceptional claim.

The United Kingdom too relied in her applications in the *Antarctica* cases on numerous acts of legislation relating to the territories in question as one type of the manifestations of British sovereignty over these territories.[2] As a "convincing proof of the effectiveness of Great Britain's display and exercise of sovereignty" the applications mention the various acts of legislation promulgated by the Falkland Islands Government with a view to regulating whaling and sealing and conserving the fishing stocks in the area.[3]

It is clear, however, that, while acts of domestic legislation are indicative of a State's will and intention and are conclusive for its own national tribunals, the national pretensions finding expression in such enactments do not thereby acquire legal validity from the point of view of international law. Thus, in the *Fisheries* case the International Court of Justice, while giving full weight to the Norwegian Delimitation Decrees in appraising the legal validity of the Norwegian claims under international law, could not refrain from pointing out that

> the delimitation of sea areas... cannot be dependent merely upon the will of the coastal State as expressed in its municipal law. Although it is true that the act of delimitation is necessarily a unilateral act, because only the coastal State is competent to undertake it, the validity of the delimitation with regard to other States depends upon international law.[4]

The conclusion, according to which a State cannot simply invoke the provisions of its own domestic law as evidence for the validity under international law of an exceptional territorial claim – otherwise derogatory of the normally applicable rules of international law – is no more than the logical extension of the concept which postulates –

[1] *ICJ Reports*, 1951, p. 138; see also to the same effect Judge Hsu Mo's Separate Opinion where – though criticizing the Norwegian Rescripts prohibiting fishing by foreigners on the account of their lack of precision – he stresses the fact that "prohibition by the Norwegian Government of fishing by foreigners... is undoubtedly a kind of State action which militates in favour of Norway's claim of prescription." (*Ibid.*, at p. 157).

[2] *ICJ, Antarctica cases, Pleadings, Oral Arguments, Documents*, pp. 13, 16, 53 and 56.

[3] *Ibid.*, pp. 16 and 56.

[4] *ICJ Reports*, 1951, p. 132.

rightly, it is believed – that acts of national legislation have in international law no higher legal significance than any other facts from which the degree and intensity of the exercise of State authority by the claimant State can be inferred. The answer to the question whether or not such acts of municipal legislation provide sufficient evidence for the existence of a valid legal title under international law depends, of course, not on the nature of the acts of the national legislature, their contents and professed purposes, but solely on the rules governing international law itself.

This point appears to have been clearly stated in the award rendered in the *Guatemala-Honduras Boundary* Arbitration where the tribunal, headed by Chief Justice Hughes of the United States, held that, in assessing the weight of rival and conflicting territorial claims, "the Constitutions of ...new States... are of special importance."[1] The tribunal left, however, no room for doubt that it did not consider the unilateral acts and declarations of a State claiming territorial rights as having conclusive and binding legal validity from the point of view of international law. The tribunal regarded such unilateral declarations merely as assertions of national pretensions, the primary function of which – from the point of view of international law – is to invite the opposition of all those States who believe that their rights have been adversely affected by such unilateral acts or are likely to be infringed as their result. This section may therefore be fittingly closed with the relevant passage of the tribunal's award, which, it is submitted, correctly states the legal position on this point:

> While no State can acquire jurisdiction over territory in another State by mere declarations on its own behalf, it is equally true that... [the] assertions of authority by Guatemala... show clearly ...[her] understanding that this was her territory. These assertions invited opposition on the part of Honduras if they were believed to be unwarranted.[2]

36. Effective display of State authority – Manifestations of State sovereignty

While the legislative measures adopted by States – assuming a variety of names – usually provide the proof of the claimant State's intention to establish its authority over a given territory, such measures will, as a rule, not be regarded as adequate and sufficient manifestations of

[1] *UNRIAA*, vol. II, p. 1307, at p. 1325.
[2] *Ibid.*, p. 1327.

State sovereignty. This aim will be achieved either by applying and implementing the provisions of such legislative measures or by otherwise carrying out certain governmental functions which are usually exercised by State authorities and in a fashion in which the rightful sovereign would have exercised such authority. The manner in which such exercise of authority expresses itself, the frequency and intensity of the manifestations of State authority and the nature of the acts required as proof for the establishment of State authority vary according to the circumstances and the character of the territory in question. The generality and vagueness of this statement bear witness to the variety of territorial situations which renders the laying down of a more precise rule both impossible and impracticable.

In fact, there seems to exist a rather close relationship between the requirements of continuity and manifestation of State authority, inasmuch as the continuity of possession displays itself in manifestations of State authority. Thus, these two elements – though not interchangeable from the doctrinal point of view – are virtually interdependent and on occasions hardly distinguishable from one another. The amount and intensity of the manifestations of State authority required in respect of a given territory are in direct proportion to the degree and nature of the display of continuity required in that case. The stricter the requirements for the proof of continuity, the greater the need for concrete and numerous manifestations of State authority and *vice versa*. "Manifestations of territorial sovereignty," says Judge Huber in the *Island of Palmas* Award, "assume... different forms, according to conditions of time and place."[1] The nature of these manifestations of sovereignty required in each particular case cannot be laid down with reference to any general rule. Their character will be determined in each case by the characteristics of the territory in question. This, in fact, has been the course followed by international tribunals in assessing the adequacy of the acts of sovereignty relied upon by a State claiming a title to a disputed territory. The answer to the question what acts have been regarded by international tribunals as manifestations of State sovereignty is to be found through the perusal of the decisions rendered by these tribunals on the topic.

The present survey has no pretensions of completeness. It is meant rather as an illustration of the subject, indicating international legal practice on this matter. It is not intended to present an exhaustive list of acts of sovereignty (such attempt would in all likelihood be doomed

[1] *Ibid.*, p. 840.

to failure); all it endeavours to do is to submit a selection containing illustrations of various governmental acts that have come to be considered as sufficient manifestations of State sovereignty.

One of the most revealing decisions on this point is the judgment delivered by the International Court of Justice in the *Minquiers and Ecrehos* case,[1] where the Court elaborated at great length on this question, enumerating the manifestations of sovereignty which led it to the conclusion that the British claim to the disputed islets was the stronger one and that they should be awarded accordingly to the United Kingdom.

Among the manifestations of British sovereignty over the Ecrehos, the Court mentioned the institution in Jersey of criminal proceedings against Jerseymen charged with having committed criminal offences on the Ecrehos (the Court cited six instances of this kind during the period 1826–1921), concluding that "these facts show... that Jersey courts have exercised criminal jurisdiction in respect of the Ecrehos during nearly a hundred years."[2] Similarly, Jersey authorities had for centuries held inquests on corpses found on the Ecrehos.[3] In 1877 they had entered a fishing boat, belonging to a Jersey fisherman who lived permanently on the Ecrehos island, in the Jersey register of fishing boats, and Jersey customs officials paid occasional visits to the Ecrehos for the purpose of endorsing the licence of the boat until it was cancelled in 1882.[4] The Court also established that contracts of sale relating to real property on the Ecrehos had been registered in the public registry of deeds of Jersey island, after having been passed before the competent authorities of that island.[5] In 1884 Jersey customs authorities established a custom-house on the islet and in 1901 an official enumerator visited the island for the purpose of taking the census, thus including the said custom-house within the scope of the Jersey census enumerations.[6] Jersey authorities also carried out various works and constructions on

[1] *ICJ Reports*, 1953, p. 46 *et seq.*

[2] *Ibid.*, p. 65. In order to forestall the argument that the exercise of jurisdiction by Jersey Courts in respect of acts committed by Jerseymen at the Minquiers and Ecrehos did not warrant an assumption of *territorial* jurisdiction (jurisdiction *ratione soli*), but amounted merely to an assumption of *personal* jurisdiction (jurisdiction *ratione personae*), the United Kingdom submitted to the Court an affidavit of a former Solicitor-General and Attorney-General of Jersey, in which it was stated that "the Royal Court of Jersey has... no jurisdiction in the matter of a criminal offence committed outside the Bailiwick [of Jersey], even though that offence be committed by a British subject domiciled or ordinarily resident within the Bailiwick." (See *ICJ*, *Minquiers and Ecrehos case, Pleadings, Oral Arguments, Documents*, vol. I, p. 602, Annex A 153 to the United Kingdom Reply).

[3] *ICJ Reports*, 1953, p. 65.

[4] *Ibid.*

[5] *Ibid.*

[6] *Ibid.*, p. 66.

the islet, such as the construction of a slipway in 1895, a signal post in 1910 and the placing of a mooring buoy in 1939.[1] It was largely on these grounds that the Court reached the conclusion that "Jersey authorities have in several ways exercised ordinary local administration in respect of the Ecrehos during a long period of time."[2]

In upholding the United Kingdom's sovereignty over the Minquiers, the Court relied on evidence of a very similar nature. It is none the less noteworthy that the Court rejected one of the contentions made on behalf of the United Kingdom, invoking two judgments of the Royal Court of Jersey (of 1811 and 1817, respectively), relating to salvage services rendered by Jerseymen to two ships wrecked at the Minquiers. The Court's rejection of this contention was based on the fact that "it is not shown that the Royal Court of Jersey would have lacked jurisdiction if the salvage had taken place outside the territory of Jersey."[3]

On behalf of the French Government various acts, alleged to be governmental acts, were cited as constituting manifestations of French sovereignty over the Minquiers. Among these acts there are a hydrographical survey prepared by a French national in 1831,[4] a visit of the French Prime Minister and the Air Minister to the Minquiers in 1938 in order to inspect the buoying of the islet,[5] the erection by a Frenchman in 1939 of a house on one of the islets with a subsidy from the Mayor of Granville,[6] and certain French hydro-electric projects for the installation of tidal power plants in the region of the Minquiers islets.[7] It was further contended on behalf of France that since 1861 the French had assumed the sole charge of the lighting and buoying of the Minquiers, without having encountered any opposition from the United Kingdom for more than 75 years.[8] It was also asserted that in 1888 a French mission, appointed to carry out a hydrographic survey of the islets, erected provisional beacons on some of them in order to facilitate the survey.[9]

The Court, however, declined, to regard all these acts as manifestations of the exercise of French authority over the Minquiers, and contented itself with pointing out in a rather laconic manner that it "does not find that the facts, invoked by the French Government, are

[1] *Ibid.*
[2] *Ibid.*
[3] *Ibid.*, p. 69.
[4] *Ibid.*, p. 70.
[5] *Ibid.*
[6] *Ibid.*, pp. 70–71.
[7] *Ibid.*, p. 71.
[8] *Ibid.*, p. 70.
[9] *Ibid.*

sufficient to show that France has a valid title to the Minquiers.... Such acts can hardly be considered as sufficient evidence of the intention of that Government to act as sovereign over the islets; nor are those acts of such a character that they can be considered as involving a manifestation of State authority in respect of the islets."[1] It is a matter for regret that the Court did not deem it appropriate to enlarge further on the reasons prompting it in its decision on this point.

Judge Basdevant, in his Individual Opinion, while concurring in the operative part of the judgment which awarded the disputed islets to the United Kingdom, dissociated himself from some of the conclusions which had led the majority to decide in favour of the United Kingdom. He challenged the majority's view which regarded the census activities of the Jersey authorities on the Ecrehos and Minquiers as manifestations of British authority over the islets. In Judge Basdevant's opinion, "census operations extending to persons on the islets or to acts carried out there do not imply the exercise of a territorial competence."[2] He went on to say that "the same is true of rates imposed upon Jerseymen in Jersey, in respect of property belonging to them on the islets; there is nothing to prevent a State's taxation of its nationals in respect of property abroad or its compilation of statistics of facts occurring abroad."[3] Commenting on the majority's decision to take certain customs activities performed by Jersey authorities as yet another expression of display of sovereignty by the United Kingdom, Judge Basdevant stated that "it must not be forgotten that international practice recognizes or tolerates customs control carried out by a State outside its territorial waters."[4]

Judge Basdevant also voiced his reluctance to regard the assumption of jurisdiction by the United Kingdom in this case as amounting to the assumption of territorial jurisdiction, since the islets in question were, in his view, not more than emerged rocks on which there was no established authority, and the assumption of jurisdiction over them might therefore be easily construed as the extension of jurisdiction "just as if the wrong had been committed or the wreckage had been gathered on the high seas."[5] He found none the less for the United Kingdom on the ground that "there was, to the extent permitted by the character of these islets, greater and more continuous activity on the part of the

[1] *Ibid.*
[2] *Ibid.*, p. 82.
[3] *Ibid.*
[4] *Ibid.*
[5] *Ibid.* See on this point above, p. 119, note 2.

Jersey authorities,"[1] i.e. the British authorities displayed a more profound interest in the happenings in these islets. In this display of interest by the British, Judge Basdevant saw the confirmation of an intrinsically valid medieval title held by the British ever since the fourteenth century and it was this feudal title that was, in his view, the real basis for the British claims to the two islets.

The circumstances enumerated by the International Court of Justice in the *Minquiers and Ecrehos* case as manifestations of State authority bear a close resemblance to those referred to in the award rendered in 1909 by the Permanent Court of Arbitration in the *Grisbadarna* case. There, as will be recalled, a dispute arose between Norway and Sweden in respect of the Grisbadarna banks. Among the reasons given by the Court for assigning the Grisbadarna to Sweden, there were the factual considerations that "Sweden has performed various acts in the Grisbadarna region... as, for instance, the placing of beacons, the measurement of the sea, and the installation of a light-boat."[2] It is worth comparing these conclusions of the Permanent Court of Arbitration with the majority decision of the International Court of Justice in the *Minquiers and Ecrehos* case, where, as has been shown, the Court declined to accept the establishment of beacons by the French on the Minquiers and the conduct of a hydrographic survey by a French mission as evidence for the assertion of French sovereignty. The apparent contradiction between the two decisions might perhaps be resolved when bearing in mind that in the *Grisbadarna* case the Swedish manifestations of State authority met with no competing Norwegian measures of any kind, whereas in the *Minquiers and Ecrehos* case the French acts were heavily outweighed – both numerically and qualitatively – by rival British manifestations of authority.[3]

A further list of acts that may be regarded as manifestations of State authority can be found in the decision given by the Permanent Court of International Justice in the *Legal Status of Eastern Greenland* case, where the Court was confronted with a dispute between Denmark and Norway relating to the territorial sovereignty over Eastern Greenland. Among the manifestations of Danish sovereignty over that area – by reason of which the case was decided for Denmark – the Court referred to the granting in 1863 of a concession by the Danish Government to an Englishman. The concession was to run for 30 years and was to enable him

[1] *Ibid.*, p. 83.

[2] Scott, *Hague Court Reports*, 1st Series, 1916, p. 130; *UNRIAA*, vol. XI, p. 161.

[3] On the problems relating to the appraisal of the weight of rival claims in general, see below, chapter V, section 57.

to establish on the East coast of Greenland stations for the purpose of trading with natives, hunting, fishing or working any metalliferous or mineral-bearing mines.[1] Reference was also made to the concessions granted by the Danes for the erection of telegraph lines across the same area.[2]

Various manifestations of State authority have also been relied upon in support of the British claims to the Falkland Islands Dependencies. Among these manifestations of British State activity Waldock mentions the promulgation of different British ordinances regulating the whaling activities in the area and imposing royalties on them, as well as the enforcement of these regulations.[3] He also refers to the granting of various licences by the Falkland Islands Government to companies of different nationalities,[4] to the appointment by the British of a stipendiary magistrate for South Georgia and to the establishment of police, customs and post offices there.[5] Regarding the South Orkneys, he refers to the erection of a British meteorological station there and to seasonal visits made by administrative officers and in 1928 by the Governor himself.[6] As a further manifestation of State authority he also mentions extensive surveys made during the period 1927–1939 both of the South Shetlands and of Graham Land.[7]

It is not proposed to enlarge further on this point, since the number of instances that may be cited as manifestations of State authority is virtually legion. Attention is, however, drawn also to the decision delivered by the now-defunct Central American Court of Justice in the *Gulf of Fonseca* case,[8] and to the awards handed down by various arbitral tribunals in the *Island of Palmas* case,[9] in the *Clipperton Island* case,[10] in the *Guatemala-Honduras Boundary* Arbitration,[11] and in the *Colombian-Venezuelan Boundary* Arbitration,[12] all of which abound in valuable examples of acts that may be regarded as manifestations of State authority.

[1] *PCIJ*, Series A/B, No. 53, pp. 31–32.
[2] *Ibid.*, p. 53.
[3] Waldock, 25 *BYIL* (1948), pp. 327–329.
[4] *Ibid.*, p. 329.
[5] *Ibid.*
[6] *Ibid.*, p. 330.
[7] *Ibid.*, p. 331. For a list of various alleged manifestations of State activity in this region, see also the British applications in the *Antarctica* cases, *ICJ*, *Antarctica cases, Pleadings, Oral Arguments, Documents*, pp. 16–21 and pp. 56–61.
[8] 11 *AJIL* (1917), p. 674 *et seq.*
[9] *UNRIAA*, vol. II, p. 829 *et seq.*
[10] *Ibid.*, p. 1105 *et seq.*
[11] *Ibid.*, p. 1307 *et seq.*
[12] *Ibid.*, vol. I, p. 223 *et seq.*

37. *Effective display of State authority – Possession* à titre de souverain

Writers and international tribunals seised of the problems attendant on the acquisition of a territorial title are at one that the possession of the State purporting to have acquired such title must have been exercised *à titre de souverain.* The meaning of this principle is that the manifestations of State authority relied upon in support of the acquisition of a territorial title must be such as to imply a claim of sovereignty. Since in international law it is only the States and not private individuals who are endowed with the rights of sovereignty, it necessarily follows that the manifestations of State sovereignty relied upon in support of a territorial title must be the acts of the State, i.e. acts performed by persons who are in the service of the State or otherwise authorized to act on its behalf. Activities of private individuals acting on their own, however numerous and extensive, cannot confer on their States a title of sovereignty over the areas in which such activities were carried out. "The acquisition of sovereignty," says Waldock, "is a state act and if the act of a discoverer is to have any validity in international law it must be endorsed by the state; the *animus occupandi* ultimately must be that of the state, not of the individual. Accordingly, an annexation to have any effect must either have been carried out under a prior commission from the state or must have been adopted subsequently by the state – through express ratification."[1]

This principle – which is one of general application as regards the acquisition of a territorial title in international law – is of particular significance in the establishment of an historic title, the legal validity of which rests on the assumption that other States, affected by the formation of such a title, have acquiesced in the claimant State's rights. Such acquiescence – which is inferred from the exercise of sovereign rights by the claimant State without encountering opposition from other States – can, however, not be presumed unless the manifestations of authority emanate from the claimant State and can be imputed to it. Consequently, there can be no presumption of acquiescence without the existence of possession *à titre de souverain*; the requirement of the possession being *à titre de souverain* is therefore a prerequisite for the formation of an historic title.

While it appears to be generally accepted that no territorial title can be established without having fulfilled this requirement, criticism has been forthcoming from some quarters against this condition on the

[1] Waldock, 25 *BYIL* (1948), p. 323. (Italics in original).

ground that it is self-evident and therefore superfluous. Thus, Verykios describes the requirement of the possession being *à titre* de *souverain* as "absolument inutile car... il est évident que l'exercice de la souveraineté territoriale se fait à titre de souverain, autrement on ne l'appellerait pas ainsi."[1]

Admittedly, there is little that can be said against Verykios' line of argument from the doctrinal aspect; international practice, however, supplies ample evidence of the tendency of States to rely upon the activities performed by private individuals on their own as the basis for exceptional territorial rights. It is this tendency that justifies the consistency with which international lawyers have time and again insisted on the inclusion of this condition among the requirements laid down for the formation of an historic title. One needs only to mention the *Fisheries* case, where it was asserted on behalf of Norway that

les eaux litigieuses ont été placées sous l'autorité exclusive de la Norvège, et... l'exploitation des fonds de pêche qui s'y trouvent a été réservée aux populations côtières, soit sous la forme de propriété privée, soit sous celle de propriété collective, soit en vertu des interdictions de droit public prononcées par les pouvoirs compétents à l'égard des pêcheurs étrangers.[2]

The Norwegian assertion was met in the United Kingdom Reply with the following words, which, it is submitted, correctly state the legal position on this point:

The [Norwegian] Counter-Memorial... makes no distinction between individual acts of appropriation by fishermen or by parishes for their own benefit and acts of the Norwegian State asserting a claim to these areas as Norwegian territorial waters. Mere actions by individuals, unaccompanied by any Act of the State, could not of course confer upon Norway any rights under international law.[3]

And further:

Fishing by Norwegian fishermen in waters outside the generally recognized limits of maritime territory, even if proved from prehistoric times, is no evidence of, or basis for, Norwegian sovereignty over the waters concerned.[4]

The attitude of the United Kingdom on this point was summed up in the following words:

It is acts of State sovereignty, not acts of individuals, which may provide the foun dation for a title to territorial sovereignty.[5]

[1] Verykios, *op. cit.*, p. 75.
[2] *ICJ, Fisheries case, Pleadings, Oral Arguments, Documents*, vol. I, p. 572.
[3] *Ibid.*, vol. II, p. 318.
[4] *Ibid.*, p. 658.
[5] *Ibid.*

Faced with an impressive array of authorities relied upon by the United Kingdom in support of her contention, Norway deemed it appropriate to relinquish her former position on this question and in her Rejoinder she maintained that

sans doute des activités privées, qui s'exerceraient sans aucune intervention directe ou indirecte de l'Etat, n'auraient-elles pas d'influence sur la situation juridique de ce dernier. Mais il est fréquent que l'attitude de l'Etat se manifeste extérieurement à travers l'action de personnes privées.... Les activités privées des pêcheurs norvégiens qui avaient pour base et pour garantie le droit norvégien... constituent par conséquent des faits à retenir.[1]

One can hardly fail to notice the difference between the contentions contained in the Norwegian Counter-Memorial and Rejoinder, respectively. Whereas in the Counter-Memorial the acts of private individuals were invoked as one of the sources of Norway's exceptional claims, the Rejoinder is at pains to make it clear that such acts cannot form the basis of any legal rights of sovereignty and may be taken into account merely as evidence of the provisions of the domestic law, in pursuance of which they had been performed. There seems to be nothing basically wrong with this modified version of the Norwegian argument, which will be dealt with at some length further below.

In the majority judgment delivered in the *Fisheries* case, the International Court of Justice did not refer to this question, which was, however, taken up by the minority judges in their Separate and Dissenting Opinions. Both Judges Hsu Mo and McNair came out in no uncertain terms in what apparently is a clear and unmistakable refutation of the original Norwegian concept. Thus, Judge Hsu Mo stated:

In support of her historic title, Norway has relied on habitual fishing by the local people and prohibition of fishing by... foreigners. As far as the fishing activities of these coastal inhabitants are concerned, I need only point out that individuals, by undertaking enterprises on their own initiative, for their own benefit and without any delegation of authority by their Government, cannot confer sovereignty on the State, and this despite the passage of time and the absence of molestation by the people of other countries.[2]

Judge McNair gave expression to the same principle when he said:

[A]rule of law that appears to me to be relevant to the question of historic title is that some proof is usually required of the exercise of *State* jurisdiction, and that the independent activity of private individuals is of little value unless it can be shown that they

[1] *Ibid.*, vol. III, p. 451.
[2] *ICJ Reports*, 1951, p. 157.

have acted in pursuance of a licence or some other authority received from their Governments or that in some other way their Governments have asserted jurisdiction through them.[1]

While the activities of private individuals performed on their own cannot form the basis for any claims to a territorial title, such activities may, in certain circumstances, be construed as evidence of an already existing sovereignty. Thus, in the *Minquiers and Ecrehos* case, Counsel for the United Kingdom relied heavily on the fishing activities of Jersey fishermen from the disputed islets,[2] and this argument evoked strong criticism on the part of the French Agent on the ground that "le seul fait que des Jersais venaient jadis pêcher souvent aux Minquiers et aux Ecréhous... est sans pertinence aucune dans la présente affaire. Il s'agit de propriétés privées, par conséquent, ...d'une question entièrement étrangère au problème de souveraineté."[3] He also suggested "qu'il fallait distinguer entre les actes de pêches proprement dits... et les actes que nous appellerons pour plus de commodité les actes de souveraineté."[4] In what was apparently an attempt on the part of the United Kingdom to forestall the French contention, it was claimed in the United Kingdom Memorial that

for more than a hundred years Jersey fishermen, *with the support and encouragement of the Jersey authorities*, have regularly carried on fishing operations from the Ecréhous on the basis that they were British territory.[5]

The italicized portion of the above-quoted passage seems to indicate that, in the opinion of the United Kingdom, activities of the nature and on the scale of those carried out by the Jersey authorities could not have been undertaken unless British sovereignty had been established over the disputed islets. In fact, this is how the British argument was interpreted by Sir Gerald Fitzmaurice, who had acted as Counsel for the United Kingdom in the *Minquiers and Ecrehos* case. In an article published subsequently, he took the view that the activities of Jersey fishermen on the Minquiers and Ecrehos were invoked by the United Kingdom solely as evidence of the already existing British sovereignty, "since many of [the activities] were such as would not have been under-

[1] *Ibid.*, p. 184. (Italics added). As to further authorities on this point, see Johnson, 27 *BYIL* (1950), pp. 344–345.
[2] See e.g. *ICJ*, *Minquiers and Ecrehos case*, *Pleadings*, *Oral Arguments*, *Documents*, vol. II, pp. 157–159.
[3] *Ibid.*, p. 267.
[4] *Ibid.*, p. 397.
[5] *Ibid.*, vol. I, p. 110. (Italics added).

taken by these individuals if they had not thought British sovereignty existed."[1]

One can hardly fail to note the striking similarity of Sir Gerald's assertion to the argument advanced in the Norwegian Rejoinder in the *Fisheries* case, where it had been maintained by Norway that "si... une personne privée agit conformément à son droit national, ce qui apparaît dans les actes qu'elle accomplit, ce n'est pas seulement une volonté privée, c'est aussi l'ordre juridique étatique. Les activités privées des pêcheurs norvégiens qui avaient pour base et pour garantie le droit norvégien... constituent par conséquent des faits à retenir."[2]

In the judgment delivered by the International Court of Justice in the *Minquiers and Ecrehos* case, the long list enumerating the acts that were regarded by the Court as manifestations of British sovereignty over the disputed islets does not include the fishing activities of Jersey fishermen. Judge Carneiro, however, in his Individual Opinion, struck a rather surprising note when he stated

> that in certain cases, and in certain circumstances, the presence of private persons who are nationals of a given State may signify or entail occupation by that State.... Such individual actions are particularly important in respect of territories situated at the border of two countries which both claim sovereignty in that region.[3]

Judge Carneiro went on to say that British fishermen in the Minquiers and Ecrehos region have always been much more numerous than French fishermen and this fact was one of the reasons which led him to award the islets to the United Kingdom.

It is felt that Judge Carneiro's rather sweeping statement concerning the acquisition of State rights through the private activities of individuals does not accurately reflect the practice followed by international tribunals. From a closer perusal of his Individual Opinion it would appear that his attitude on this subject was clearly motivated by certain historical events in South America, where Brazil. for instance, had greatly increased her territory through persons who had crossed the borders in search of gold and emeralds and thereby acquired *uti possidetis* rights for their State.[4] It is at least debatable whether the views advocated by Judge Carneiro express more than a particular Latin-American concept on this point; this is particularly so in view of the fact that, in the opinion of many writers, the *uti possidetis* rule itself has

[1] Fitzmaurice. 30 *BYIL* (1953), p. 48, n. 3.
[2] *ICJ, Fisheries case, Pleadings, Oral Arguments, Documents*, vol. III, p. 451.
[3] *ICJ Reports*, 1953, pp. 104–105.
[4] *Ibid.*

not achieved in international law more than a regional status and cannot be regarded as a principle of general validity.[1]

It should be conceded, however, that the principle referred to by Judge Carneiro is of considerable importance in all those cases where the question of the acquisition of non-exclusive rights arises. Claims to sovereignty – whether over land territory or over maritime areas – are claims of an exclusive character. In addition to claims belonging to this category, there exist also claims aiming at the preservation of non-exclusive rights, habitually also referred to as "international servitudes."[2] Such claims to non-exclusive rights are usually raised in respect of maritime areas and it is their objective to safeguard some vested interest.

It is submitted that, in the acquisition of non-exclusive rights (e.g. the traditional right to exploit a given maritime area and to fish in it, without raising a claim of sovereignty), the activities of private individuals, even if acting on their own, may be of considerable legal significance, and a State may acquire such vested and non-exclusive rights in respect of a particular maritime area through the exercise of such rights on the part of its nationals.

Since, however, this problem arises primarily – if not exclusively – in respect of maritime areas, it will be dealt with further in the chapter devoted to an investigation of the specific aspects attendant on the acquisition of maritime historic rights.[3]

38. Acquiescence in the display of State authority – General

As will be recalled, the formation of an historic title is contingent upon the existence of two concomitant factors, both of which are required for its establishment:

(a) Effective display of State authority by the claimant State; and
(b) Acquiescence in such display of authority on the part of other States, affected or liable to be affected by the perfection of a new territorial title.

In the foregoing sections of this chapter the meaning and scope of the first requirement was examined; as has been shown, its function is to contribute towards raising the presumption of acquiescence, which, it

[1] On the meaning and scope of the *uti possidetis* rule in the sphere of international law, see below, Appendix.
[2] See above, chapter III, section 24.
[3] See below, chapter VI, section 73.

is submitted, ultimately sets the seal of legal validity on the historic claim.

Whereas the previous sections of this chapter were devoted to the requirements to be complied with by the claimant State, it is now proposed to focus attention on those aspects of the formation of an historic title which relate to the attitude of a State confronted with such an historic claim. For it turns primarily on the conduct and reaction – or lack of reaction – of the State likely to be affected by a claim deviating from the generally applicable rules of international law, when it has to be determined whether a claim – otherwise derogatory of the normally accepted norms of international law – will be allowed to ripen into a valid legal title.

The State affected by the exceptional territorial claim cannot, however, be expected to signify its attitude in respect of the new territorial situation unless it may be reasonably assumed that it has acquired knowledge – actual or constructive – of the new situation. Thus, the condition of notoriety of a territorial situation – at least *vis-à-vis* the affected State – cannot be dispensed with if a presumption of acquiescense is to be raised. For only the assumption of such knowledge on the part of the affected State can warrant the expectation of its coming out openly against the new territorial claim. The remedy resorted to by the States in order to signify their objection to a new state of affairs, and consequently to prevent a new title from maturing, is the device of diplomatic protest.

When faced with a dispute concerning the alleged formation of an historic title, international tribunals will therefore pose for themselves the following questions:

(a) Has protest been forthcoming against the purported infringement of the hitherto sovereign's rights?

(b) The reply to the first question being in the negative, would a State wishing to dissociate itself from the new territorial situation normally be expected to make its opposition known by lodging a formal protest with the claimant State?

Thus, the pre-eminence of the device of protest – or rather absence of protest – in the formation of an historic title becomes obvious. Indeed, the absence of protest may be regarded as the corner-stone of the doctrine of acquiescence.

The foregoing statement deserves, however, to be slightly qualified: the absence of protest is relevant in the formation of an historic title only in those cases in which protest would have been expected to be forthcoming, had the affected State really wished its objection to be made known. There are situations – and they will be dealt with further below – in which an inference of acquiescence cannot be justifiably drawn from the simple fact of absence of protest.

The following sections of this chapter will accordingly be devoted to a closer investigation of the meaning of the term "acquiescence," to an analysis of the problems relating to the notoriety of territorial situations and to an examination of the relevance of protest in the formation of an historic title.

39. Acquiescence in the display of State authority – The meaning of "acquiescence"

It would appear that the divergence of opinion regarding the process of formation of an historic title in international law may have arisen to a large extent because of the fact that the precise meaning of the term "acquiescence," the very pillar of historic rights, has not been free from controversy. In fact, writers and publicists seem to have espoused different concepts as to the exact meaning of this notion, and the pronouncements of international tribunals invoking this doctrine are also far from being unequivocal on this point.

The question constituting the main stumbling-block in this respect seems to be whether "acquiescence" properly so called should be confined merely to those cases where there is evidence of some *positive* acts indicating consent and capable of being construed as such, or whether it connotes exclusively a *passive* toleration on the part of a State faced with a situation which purportedly constitutes an encroachment upon its rights. In other words: is acquiescence a *positive* or *negative* concept?

The first assertion amounts to virtually equating the notion of acquiescence with the concept of express consent. This , in fact, is the view advocated by Fauchille, who conceives acquiescence as meaning positive consent.[1] Similarly, Ross, discussing the notion of consent in international law, maintains that "in all cases it is a condition that there should be real consent and not merely passivity in the face of inevitable facts."[2]

[1] Fauchille, *op. cit.*, vol. I, part II, p. 382; Fauchille quotes there with approval Perels in whose opinion "l'exercice unilatéral de prétendus droits, même quand il ne soulève pas les réclamations d'autres Etats,... ne peut jamais être opposé à ceux qui n'ont pas acquiescé expressément ou par des actes dont l'intention est évidente." (See Perels, *Manuel de droit maritime international*, French edition by Arendt, 1884, p. 44).

[2] Ross, *A Text-Book of International Law*, 1947, p. 244.

This idea of the meaning of acquiescence seems to have been conveyed as recently as 1951, and was contained in a French Note of April 7th of that year, delivered in reply to a United Kingdom request urging France to state her position as regards the unilateral extension of territorial waters beyond the generally accepted limits. In the French Note it was asserted that

> aucun Etat ne peut, par une déclaration unilatérale, étendre sa souveraineté sur la haute mer et rendre cette annexion opposable aux pays qui ont le droit d'invoquer le principe de la liberté des mers, tant que ces derniers ne l'auront pas formellement acceptée.[1]

Similarly, in the course of the voluminous correspondence that followed the outbreak of the dispute between Great Britain and Spain over the "*Cuban Cays*," Harding, the then Queen's Advocate, maintained that the attempt of Spain to rely on a Spanish Royal Order of July 8th, 1858, extending the limit of territorial waters, as a proof "that this limit has been conceded, merely because no Nation has 'reclaimed upon this point' (i.e. I presume because no Nation has formally protested against the order) is in my Opinion preposterous."[2]

It is felt that this approach not only amounts to an absolute denial of the role and function of acquiescence in international law, but that it rests, when applied in respect of historic titles, on a fundamental misunderstanding of the theory of historic rights. As has already been pointed out elsewhere, in cases where a State has expressly consented to a departure by another State from the normal rules of international law or to an exercise of rights derogatory of the normal rules, or has behaved in such a manner that its consent may be positively inferred from its attitude, there is no need whatsoever to invoke the theory of historic rights. This theory comes into play solely in those cases where "other States have neither consented expressly, nor, by their conduct, actively implied their consent, but have simply been *inactive*."[3] It is the function of this theory to supply "the necessary presumption of (tacit) acquiescence."[4]

It is therefore submitted that, when used in connection with the formation of an historic title, acquiescence should be interpreted as a

[1] The text of the French Note has been printed in *ICJ, Fisheries case, Pleadings, Oral Arguments, Documents*, vol. IV, p. 605.

[2] Opinion of November 11th, 1859, F.O. 83/2371, as reproduced in Smith, *op. cit.*, vol. II, pp. 228–231, at p. 230.

[3] Fitzmaurice, 30 *BYIL* (1953), p. 29. (Italics in original).

[4] *Ibid.*

purely negative concept, indicating "the inaction of a State which is faced with a situation constituting a threat to or infringement of its rights,... a silence or absence of protest in circumstances which generally call for positive reaction signifying an objection."[1] Mc Dougal and Burke also appear to advocate this more inclusive view on the nature of acquiescence when they maintain that

> the element of acquiescence should not be regarded technically: lack of protest by interested states..., the general assumptions of writers over a period of time, and the response of decision-makers both national and international would appear sufficient indication of concurrence with the coastal expectation to establish evidence of a community expectation.[2]

This concept is based on the assumption – which seems to be also a rule of common sense – that States will not look on idly and without any reaction whilst their alleged rights are being infringed and violated. The silence of the affected States in these circumstances cannot be regarded as devoid of any meaning, and from their conduct an inference of their acquiescence in the new situation may properly be drawn. It is common ground that long silence, without any valid reason, is equivalent to consent. This principle has found its clear expression in the maxims *qui tacet consentire videtur* and *qui ne dit mot consent.* According to Verykios, "l'interprétation la plus généralement admise est que celui qui se tait si longtemps et sans raison, consent à l'état de choses actuel; autrement il aurait protesté."[3]

The precise scope of this principle has been the subject of controversy. For some writers this rule has absolute validity,[4] whereas others maintain that it is only of relative scope.[5] It would, however, appear that silence *per se*, even if persisting for a long period of time, should not be credited with absolute validity unless the circumstances would have required and enabled anybody wishing to signify his disapproval to do so.

There may, however, arise circumstances in which silence will have to be construed as indicating objection to a given state of things. (*Qui tacet – negat*). In different circumstances silence will indicate neither

[1] MacGibbon, 30 *BYIL* (1953), p. 143. The Study on the *Juridical Regime of Historic Waters, Including Historic Bays,* prepared by the United Nations Secretariat for the 14th Session of the International Law Commission, comments on this "negative" concept of acquiescence in the following words: "If the proponents of the necessity of acquiescence really have in mind only the negative aspect, i.e. toleration on the part of the foreign States, it would be preferable to use the term 'toleration' which better expresses their thoughts." (U.N. Document A/CN. 4/143 of March 9th, 1962, *ILC Yearbook,* 14th session, 1962, vol. II, p. 16).

[2] McDougal and Burke, *The Public Order of the Oceans,* 1962, p. 340.

[3] Verykios, *op. cit.,* p. 26.

[4] E.g. Strupp, *Grundzüge des positiven Völkerrechts,* 1921, p. 96.

[5] E.g. Brüel, "La protestation en droit international," 3 *ASJG* (1932), p. 75.

consent nor objection, but merely indifference towards a newly-arisen situation. (*Qui tacet neque negat neque utique fatetur*). All the same, it is still true to say that in the majority of cases silence must be regarded as a tacit acceptance of a new practice by the State adversely affected by such practice. "Dans la plupart des cas," says Suy, "le silence équivaut à l'acceptation tacite par le destinataire d'une offre ou traduit sa résignation devant une violation ou une menace à l'encontre de ses droits. Cette résignation entraînerait la reconnaissance d'une nouvelle situation de fait comme licite et l'extinction pour l'espèce de ses propres droits ou, en tout cas, du droit à faire valoir ses propres droits."[1]

Thus, both the doctrine which denies any legal consequences flowing from mere silence and the concept which equates silence in all circumstances with consent seem to misrepresent the problem and, in the light of these conflicting opinions, the middle-of-the-road course suggested by Anzilotti is all the more commendable. "La simple manière de se comporter d'un Etat," says Anzilotti, "y compris, *dans des circonstances déterminées, même son seul silence*, ... peut signifier la volonté de reconnaître comme légitime un état de choses donné."[2] Similarly, Schwarzenberger has pointed out that acquiescence differs from recognition "in its mode of expression: *passive toleration*; for even implied recognition presupposes some acts which are capable of being interpreted as such."[3]

As is submitted elsewhere,[4] knowledge, or at least a presumption of knowledge, is essential if an inference of acquiescence is to be drawn. "Acquiescence," says Johnson, "is often implied, in the interests of international order, in cases where it does not genuinely exist; but without knowledge there can be no acquiescence at all."[5] On the other hand, if the State adversely affected by the new claim or situation can be shown to have acquired knowledge of such claim or situation, silence will be readily interpreted as acquiescence. The purpose of protest is, according to Schwarzenberger, "to exclude the interpretation of silence as either implied recognition or acquiescence and to reserve complete freedom of action to the protesting State."[6] According to the same writer, "silence is ambiguous. It is always a question of circumstances and specific rules of international law governing a particular subject or underlying the principle of good faith what the implications

[1] Suy, *Les actes juridiques unilatéraux en droit international public*, 1962, p. 61.
[2] Anzilotti, *op. cit.*, p. 348. (Italics added).
[3] Schwarzenberger, 87 *Hague Recueil* (1955), vol. I, p. 257. (Italics added).
[4] See below, section 40.
[5] Johnson, 27 *BYIL* (1950), p. 347; see also to the same effect Suy, *op. cit.*, p. 62 and the authorities cited there.
[6] Schwarzenberger, *loc. cit.*, p. 256.

of silence are."[1] Suy shares the same view when he asserts that the real meaning of silence "devra être établie dans chaque cas d'espèce selon les circonstances et les conditions dans lesquelles il se situe.... Le silence devra être interprété comme un consentement, chaque fois qu'on peut logiquement s'attendre à une protestation, ou encore, que la victime doit protester chaque fois que son silence pourrait être interprété comme un consentement ou comme une renonciation à ses droits ou une reconnaissance de ceux de la partie adverse."[2] Thus, the exact rule would appear to be, as Suy rightly maintains: *Qui tacet consentire videtur dum loqui potuit ac debuit.*[3]

This moderate approach, adapting itself to changing circumstances, is also borne out by international practice. Thus, for instance, in a Russian Memorandum to Great Britain concerning the *Alaska Dispute* between the two States, reference was made to Britain's failure to protest against certain Russian claims in the following words:

> La Russe était donc pleinement autorisée à profiter d'un consentement, qui, pour être tacite, n'en étoit pas moins solennel.[4]

In the *Fisheries* case the International Court of Justice invoked the same principle when it pointed out that

> for a period of more than sixty years the United Kingdom Government... in no way contested... [the Norwegian method of delimitation by straight baselines].... In respect of a situation which could only be strengthened with the passage of time, the United Kingdom Government refrained from formulating reservations.[5]

The relevance of protest in the establishment of a territorial title was again stressed by the Court in the case concerning *Right of Passage over Indian Territory*, where the Court said:

> The British found the Portuguese in occupation of the villages [under dispute] and exercising full and exclusive administrative authority over them. They accepted the situation as they found it and left the Portuguese in occupation of, and in exercise of exclusive authority over, the villages. The Portuguese held themselves out as sovereign over the villages. The British did not, as successors of the Marathas, themselves claim sovereignty, nor did they accord express recognition of Portuguese sovereignty, over them. The exclusive authority of the Portuguese over the villages *was never brought in question.* Thus Portuguese sovereignty over the villages was recognized by the British in fact and by implication and was subsequently tacitly recognized by India. *As a consequence the villages... acquired the character of Portuguese enclaves* within Indian territory.[6]

[1] *Ibid.*
[2] Suy, *op. cit.*, pp. 63–64.
[3] *Ibid.*, p. 64.
[4] Smith, *op. cit.*, vol. II, p. 5.
[5] *ICJ Reports*, 1951, pp. 138–139.
[6] *ICJ Reports*, 1960, p. 39. (Italics added).

Similarly, in the case concerning the *Arbitral Award made by the King of Spain on 23 December 1906*, the Court arrived at the conclusion that Nicaragua had in the past recognized the validity of that award and could not therefore challenge it. The Court's conclusion was based, *inter alia*, on "Nicaragua's failure to raise any question with regard to the validity of the Award for several years after the full terms of the Award had become known to it."[1]

More recently, the role and function of silence in the establishment of new territorial rights was again discussed at some length in the judgment delivered by the International Court of Justice in the *Temple of Preah Vihear* case.[2] There the Court was faced, *inter alia*, with the question whether Thailand's lack of reaction to the publication by the French authorities of various maps showing the disputed area of the Temple of Preah Vihear as falling within the domain of French Indo-China might be construed as acquiescence on her part in the French claims. (Cambodia, which instituted proceedings in this case, had been part of French Indo-China until 1953, when she attained her independence). The Court replied to this question in the following words:

> It is clear that the circumstances were such as called for some reaction, within a reasonable period, on the part of the Siamese authorities, if they wished to disagree with the map or had any serious question to raise in regard to it. They did not do so, either then or for many years, and thereby must be held to have acquiesced. *Qui tacet consentire videtur si loqui debuisset ac potuisset.*[3]

The Court also referred to "the most significant episode" of the visit paid to the Temple of Preah Vihear in 1930 by Prince Damrong, formerly Siamese Minister of the Interior, and at that time President of the Royal Institute of Siam, charged with duties in connection with the National Library and with archeological monuments. The visit was part of an archeological tour made by the Prince with the permission of the King of Siam and had, in the Court's view, a quasi-official character. When the Prince arrived at Preah Vihear, he was officially received by the French Resident for the adjoining Cambodian province, with the French flag flying. The Court commented on the legal implications of this episode in the following words:

> A clearer affirmation of title on the French Indo-Chinese side can scarcely be imagined. It demanded a reaction. Thailand did nothing.... Looking at the incident as a whole, it appears to have amounted to a tacit recognition by Siam of the sover-

[1] *Ibid.*, p. 213.
[2] *ICJ Reports*, 1962, p. 6 *et seq.*
[3] *Ibid.*, p. 23. (Italics in original). See also *ibid.*, pp. 27–31.

eignty of Cambodia (under French Protectorate) over Preah Vihear, *through a failure to react in any way, on an occasion that called for reaction* in order to affirm or preserve title in the face of an obvious rival claim.[1]

A similar note was struck by Sir Gerald Fitzmaurice in his Separate Opinion in the same case when he maintained:

I can place no other interpretation on Thailand's conduct, considered as a whole, than that she accepted this particular line [as drawn on the map] as representing the frontier in this region.... *Even negative conduct – that is to say, failure to act, react or speak, in circumstances where failure so to do must imply acquiescence or acceptance – is, in my opinion, quite sufficient for this purpose, if the facts are clear.*[2]

A somewhat different view was espoused by Judge Moreno Quintana, in his Dissenting Opinion in the same case, where he asserted that "silence has consequences in law only if the party concerned is under an obligation to make its voice heard in response to a given fact or situation."[3]

Judge Sir Percy Spender, in his Dissenting Opinion, did not basically challenge the majority view on the role of silence in the establishment of new territorial claims. However, he interpreted Siam's silence on various occasions in the past in a manner different from that indicated in the majority judgment. Thus, he held:

In determining what inferences may or should be drawn from Thailand's silence and absence of protest regard must, I believe, be had to the period of time when the events we are concerned with took place, to the region of the world to which they related, to the general political conditions existing in Asia at this period, to political and other activities of Western countries in Asia at the time and to the fact that of the two States concerned one was Asian, the other European. It would not, I think, be just to apply to the conduct of Siam in this period objective standards comparable to those which reasonably might today or might then have been applied to highly developed European States.[4]

It is, however, not difficult to visualize circumstances in which sheer silence maintained by a State is more likely to indicate its indifference than actual acquiescence. "Whether silence is to be interpreted as amounting to acquiescence" states one author, "depends primarily on the circumstances in which silence is observed."[5] This statement, while apparently summing up correctly the legal position, none the less introduces a dangerously subjective element into this sphere which renders

[1] *Ibid.*, pp. 30–31.
[2] *Ibid.*, p. 55. (Italics added).
[3] *Ibid.*, p. 70.
[4] *Ibid.*, p. 128.
[5] MacGibbon, 31 *BYIL* (1954), p. 170.

the evaluation of a situation allegedly warranting an inference of acquiescence a delicate task. At the same time it cannot be denied that there are, in fact, situations which do not readily lend themselves to an "objective" analysis. Silence may in some instances indicate the approval by a State of a certain situation, whereas such a conclusion may be ill-founded on other occasions. One certainly does not have to go as far as Vattel who suggested that acquiescence be not imputed to a State which sets forth "de justes raisons de son silence, comme l'impossibilité de parler, une crainte bien fondée."[1] Having regard to the harsh realities of international life, the admission of the pleas suggested by Vattel would indeed be tantamount to depriving international relations of the least chance of stability and certainty. The inadmissibility of these pleas, however, does not affect the fate of other pleas of substance which, if well-founded, serve to rebut the presumption of consent which might have otherwise been raised by a long and unexplained silence. Ranking high among these pleas is the plea of ignorance put forward by the affected State which maintains that it was not aware of the new situation that had arisen over a part of what it considers its own territory and that, as a result of its lack of knowledge, it cannot be presumed to have acquiesced in the new situation. This plea raises the problem of the notoriety of territorial situations and will be dealt with presently, while other pleas aiming at the rebuttal of the presumption of acquiescence will be touched upon at a later stage with reference to the relevance of protest in the formation of an historic title.[2]

40. *Notoriety of territorial situations*

If acquiescence is to be regarded as the legal basis for the formation of an historic title, then the State presumed to have acquiesced in the territorial situation giving rise to the historic claim must be shown to have acquired knowledge of that situation. In other words: the new territorial situation must have achieved a degree of notoriety or publicity, the existence of which is a prerequisite for the presumption of knowledge. "Publicity," says Johnson, "is essential because acquiescence is essential.... Acquiescence if often implied, in the interests of international order, in cases where it does not genuinely exist; but without knowledge there can be no acquiescence at all."[3] Only if the affected State's knowledge can be proved, or may be properly presumed, can

[1] Vattel, *op. cit.*, para. 144.
[2] See below, section 50.
[3] Johnson, 27 *BYIL* (1950), p. 347.

the State against which the adverse possession is meant to operate be expected to make known its objection to it.[1]

True, the very necessity of this requirement as one of the conditions for raising the presumption of acquiescence has been called in question by many an author, not because they deemed it superfluous or unnecessary, but because they took the view that a clandestine exercise of territorial possession was hardly conceivable on the international plane.[2] Thus, Verykios maintains that "on peut critiquer de même l'exigence de la publicité comme étant absolument inutile en droit international, où on ne peut concevoir une possession clandestine."[3] This argument seems to be founded on the situations prevailing on land territories which, in fact, have achieved a very high degree of notoriety. It overlooks at the same time the fact that this is by no means true in respect of maritime territorial situations where there exists the possibility "to acquire not only a piece of territory at the expense of another state but also a number of rights at the expense of the international community."[4] Moreover, as has been pointed out by Fauchille, there still exists the possibility of a clandestine adverse possession of land territory remaining for long unknown to the owner in the case of territories – the number of which is rapidly diminishing nowadays – which are either distant or of slight importance.[5]

International practice also requires the proof of knowledge as a prerequisite for the presumption of acquiescence. Thus, in the dispute between Great Britain and the United States relating to the *Title to Islands in Passamaquoddy Bay*, the United States Agent contended that "to form a rule of future action it was required that *it should... have been known and acknowledged*."[6]

In the *Alaskan Boundary* Dispute between the same parties the United States asserted that Britain's failure to protest ought to be construed as her acquiescence in the American exercise of authority over the disputed territory. This argument was met with the following reply on behalf of Great Britain:

[1] See to this effect Fauchille, *op. cit.*, p. 761.

[2] It may be perhaps argued that any clandestine possession would not fulfil the requirement of the possession being *à titre de souverain*, since it is not the practice of the State exercising its sovereign authority over a given territory to do so in a clandestine manner. Thus, the conditions of possession *à titre de souverain* and notoriety would be embraced under a single heading. However, as will be subsequently shown, there are circumstances in which a possession exercised in the normal manner and *à titre de souverain* may appear to have remained unknown to other States.

[3] Verykios, *op. cit.*, p. 75.

[4] Johnson, *loc. cit.*; see also to this effect de Visscher, *op. cit.*, pp. 200–201.

[5] Fauchille, *op. cit.*, p. 761.

[6] Moore, *International Adjudications (Modern Series)*, vol. VI, 1933, p. 95. (Italics added).

They say all these things were done and we never protested. Well, you cannot protest against a thing you have never heard of.[1]

And further:

How is Great Britain, on any ground of justice or fairness, to be affected with knowledge of such proceedings and acquiescence in them?... Surely at least we should have had some notice of it; and there is not even a shadow of pretence that we knew it.[2]

Similarly, the failure of Spain to challenge the rights of the Netherlands over the Island of Palmas was explained in the United States Memorandum by the fact that "the Spanish Government had no reason to suppose that the Netherlands Government claimed sovereignty over the island."[3]

Judge Huber in his award appears to have rejected the United States' submission on this point. He referred to the fact that the display of governmental functions over the island

has been open and public.... A clandestine exercise of State authority over an inhabited territory during a considerable length of time would seem to be impossible.[4]

The "open and public" character of the Netherlands' display of authority over the disputed island seems to have led the eminent arbitrator to the conclusion that Spain must have been aware of the situation prevailing there and consequently could not invoke a plea of ignorance in support of her claim.

The outcome of the Anglo-Norwegian dispute in the *Fisheries* case also turned to a very large extent on the same considerations. Both the majority and minority judges subjected the question of the validity of the Norwegian system of delimitation, *inter alia*, to the test of the notoriety of the system, and it was common ground between them that the Norwegian system could be held enforceable against the United Kingdom only if it could be proved that the United Kingdom had in fact acquired knowledge of this system and its methods of application. The differences of opinion which divided the Court in that case were not of a legal character; they were derived from different interpretations given to the same facts. The majority found that the application by Norway of the method of straight baselines had achieved a degree of notoriety and that Great Britain must have been aware of it. It was

[1] *Proceedings of the Alaskan Boundary Tribunal*, vol. VII, p. 531.
[2] *Ibid.*, p. 533.
[3] *Island of Palmas Arbitration: Memorandum of the United States of America*, p. 94.
[4] *UNRIAA*, vol. II, p. 868.

on this ground that the Court held the Norwegian system to be enforceable, in any case against the United Kingdom.[1] The minority judges, on the other hand, held that the Norwegian system was not made known to the world, that the United Kingdom was not aware of it, and that she could not be regarded as having acquiesced in it. Thus, Judge McNair said:

> ...I do not consider that the United Kingdom was aware... of the existence of a Norwegian system of long base-lines connecting outermost points, before this dispute began....[2]

And Judge Read followed suit by summing up the question in the following words:

> I cannot avoid reaching the conclusion that it has not been proved that the Norwegian System was made known to the world in time, and in such a manner that other nations, including the United Kingdom, knew about it....[3]

Similarly, in the *Antarctica* cases the United Kingdom stressed the fact that the British administration of the Falkland Islands Dependencies had been "utilised and administered... openly."[4]

It appears pertinent at this juncture to turn attention to some of the questions attendant on the principle of notoriety, the most important of which are the following:

(a) Is notification of the establishment of a new territorial situation a prerequisite for its achieving the required degree of notoriety and for the imputability of knowledge to the States adversely affected by its inception?
(b) To what extent may the concept of constructive knowledge be resorted to in cases where actual knowledge of the affected State cannot be proved?
(c) In what circumstances may a plea of excusable ignorance be raised?

It is these problems that will presently be dealt with in the following sections.

[1] *ICJ Reports*, 1951, p. 139, where the Court stated: "The notoriety of the facts, the general toleration of the international community, Great Britain's position in the North Sea, her own interest in the question, and her prolonged abstention would in any case warrant Norway's enforcement of her system against the United Kingdom."
[2] *Ibid.*, p. 180.
[3] *Ibid.*, p. 205. Both Judge McNair and Judge Read denied the existence of a "Norwegian system" in the disputed areas, but discussed the problem of notoriety on the assumption that such a system did, in fact, exist.
[4] *ICJ*, *Antarctica cases*, *Pleadings*, *Oral Arguments*, *Documents*, p. 9; see also to the same effect *ibid.*, p. 49.

41. Is notification a prerequisite of notoriety?

"Notification," says Oppenheim, "is the technical term for the communication to other States of certain facts and events of legal importance."[1] He further points out that a distinction must be drawn between voluntary and obligatory notification. In most cases notification takes place voluntarily, because "States cannot be considered subject to certain duties without knowledge of the facts and events which give rise to them."[2] Notification is, however, obligatory in cases where it has been expressly stipulated.[3] Apart from these cases there does not exist in international law any duty of formal notification. Notification, though, may undoubtedly have its salutary effects in so far as it precludes any affected State from claiming ignorance at a later stage. Thus, while its desirability cannot be called in question, the requirement of formal notification is not an obligatory rule of law, save where express provision has been made to this effect. Judge Huber seems to have stated correctly the legal position on this point when he asserted in his award in the *Island of Palmas* case that

> ...notification, like any other formal act, can only be the condition of legality as a consequence of an explicit rule of law. A rule of this kind adopted by the Powers in 1885 for the African continent does not apply *de plano* to other regions.[4]

It was on this ground that he dismissed the American contention that Spain could not have been attributed with a knowledge of the Netherlands' display of authority over the disputed island, owing to an absence of notification on her part to that effect. The arbitrator held that "an obligation for the Netherlands to notify to other Powers the establishment of suzerainty over the Sangi States or of the display of sovereignty in these territories did not exist."[5]

Similarly, in the *Clipperton Island* case, King Victor Emanuel III of Italy in his award rejected the Mexican argument that formal notification was a prerequisite for a lawful occupation and that France should not be recognized as the lawful occupant of Clipperton Island, because

[1] Oppenheim, *op. cit.*, p. 874; as to references for other definitions of "notification," see Suy, *op. cit.*, p. 82, notes 3 and 4.

[2] Oppenheim, *op. cit.*

[3] See e.g. Article 34 of the General Act of the Berlin Congo Conference of 1885, where it was laid down that the validity of any future occupation of African territories was contingent on its prior notification to the other Powers. For further examples of obligatory notification, see Suy, *op. cit.*, pp. 91–95.

[4] *UNRIAA*, vol. II, p. 868. (Italics in original).

[5] *Ibid.*

she had not notified other Powers of her occupation. The arbitrator dismissed this assertion in the following words:

La régularité de l'occupation française a aussi été mise en doute parce qu'elle n'a pas été notifiée aux autres Puissances. Mais il faut observer que l'obligation précise de cette notification a été stipulé par l'art. 34 de l'acte de Berlin..., qui... n'est pas appliquable au cas présent. Il y a lieu d'estimer que la notoriété donnée d'une façon quelconque à l'acte suffisait alors....[1]

For the sake of completeness it should be mentioned, however, that States have in the past tended to question other States' rights over certain territories on the ground that they had not been formally notified of such instances of occupation. Thus, in a Note delivered on August 10th, 1863, to Señor Tassara, the Spanish Minister in Washington, the then United States Secretary of State, Mr. Seward, maintained that the Spanish claim to a six-mile marginal belt of territorial waters off the coast of Cuba was not enforceable as against other States unless "it could be shown that on its being brought to their notice... [the United States] acquiesced in it, or that on its being brought to the notice of other powers it had been so widely conceded by them as to imply a general recognition of it by the maritime powers of the world."[2]

More recently, the French Government seems to have taken up the same line of argument when in a Note of April 7th, 1951, given in response to a United Kingdom request to state its attitude towards the unilateral extension by States of the generally accepted limits of territorial waters, it asserted that

le Gouvernement français n'a jamais reçu, par la voie diplomatique, notification des résolutions ou propositions adoptées, de 1945 à 1950, par le Mexique, le Chili, le Pérou, Costa-Rica et le Salvador, ayant pour effet de changer la limite de leurs eaux territoriales.[3]

It is submitted, however, that these isolated manifestations do not truly reflect the attitude taken up by international law on this topic and that they are heavily outweighed by those authorities which have dispensed with the condition of notification as one of the requirements

[1] *Ibid.*, p. 1110. In this case, though, the French consulate in Honolulu published in the local English paper "The Polynesian" of December 8th, 1858, the text of the French declaration of sovereignty over the island. From a perusal of the just-quoted passage of the award it emerges, however, that this publication was not regarded by the arbitrator as a formal notification, but merely as one of the acts through which the sovereignty of France over the island manifested itself in a manner appropriate to the circumstances prevailing there.

[2] The text of this Note has been printed in Moore's *Digest of International Law*, vol. I, 1906, pp. 709–712. The above-quoted passage is to be found at p. 710 there.

[3] The text of this Note has been reproduced in *ICJ*, *Fisheries case*, *Pleadings*, *Oral Arguments*, *Documents* vol. IV, p. 605.

for the legal validity of a territorial change. Moreover, it should be borne in mind that both the American and French Notes referred to above were concerned with maritime territorial claims; since maritime territorial situations, by their very nature, are less "notorious," owing to there being in general fewer opportunities of manifesting State authority, a requirement of notification as regards such claims may be perhaps more understandable, even if not justifiable, from the legal point of view. In an article commenting on the judgment rendered in the *Fisheries* case, Johnson makes the interesting observation that "States are often ignorant of each other's legislation in the matter of territorial waters. Even a maritime State, such as the United Kingdom, had no knowledge of some of the Decrees of other States put in as evidence by Norway during the proceedings [in the *Fisheries* case]."[1]

It may safely be maintained that an obligation for formal notification is not incumbent upon a State claiming an historic title and that its main value rests in the sphere of evidence, since it facilitates the proof of other States' knowledge of the territorial situation giving rise to the historic claim. According to Ross – who gives expression to the trend currently governing the field – "a formal *declaration of occupation* or notification is not required but of course is often to be recommended by way of proof."[2]

42. Constructive knowledge

The abandonment of the condition of formal notification necessarily leads to the adoption of the concept of constructive knowledge. In fact, more often than not, it is virtually impossible to prove a State's actual knowledge of a given territorial situation. Consequently, international law has to satisfy itself by resorting to the concept of constructive knowledge, thus substituting an inference based on the conduct of States and the general circumstances surrounding a situation for an express proof of actual knowledge.

There is little doubt that international law readily imputes such constructive knowledge to the States affected, or likely to be affected, by the acquisition of new territorial rights, provided the evidence – which is by its very nature of circumstantial character – unmistakably

[1] Johnson, "The Anglo-Norwegian Fisheries Case," 1 *ICLQ* (1952), p. 145, at p. 166, n. 34. This problem will be further elaborated in sections 42 and 43 below.

[2] Ross, *op. cit.*, p. 147. (Italics in original). See, however, Fauchille who maintains that "la notorieté d'une prise de possession ne saurait dispenser de sa notification: l'admettre serait ouvrir la porte aux abus et rendre possibles bien des conflits." (Fauchille, *op. cit.*, p. 739).

points in that direction and is not open to different interpretations. Perhaps the most striking example of the recognition of this principle in international law is the *Fisheries* case, where the Court attributed to the United Kingdom a constructive knowledge of the Norwegian system of straight baselines. The majority of the Court took the view that

> as a coastal State on the North Sea, greatly interested in the fisheries in this area, as a maritime Power traditionally concerned with the law of the sea and concerned particularly to defend the freedom of the seas, the United Kingdom *could not have been ignorant* of the Decree of 1869 which had at once provoked a request for explanation by the French Government.[1]

Thus, the Court, being unable to invoke the United Kingdom's actual knowledge of the system applied by Norway, contented itself with relying on her constructive knowledge of that system, which was inferred from a variety of circumstances indicating to the Court's satisfaction that the United Kingdom had, in fact, been aware of the Norwegian system. And it was because of their disagreement with the majority on this point that the dissenting judges reached a diametrically opposed legal conclusion. They too started from the same legal premises and posed the question whether the United Kingdom *ought to have been aware* of the Norwegian system. In fact, the greater part of Judge McNair's Dissenting Opinion is devoted to a searching analysis of the question "when, if at all, did the United Kingdom Government become aware of this system, or when *ought it to have become aware* but for its own neglect; in English legal terminology when did it receive actual or constructive notice of the system?"[2] Judge McNair took the view that the United Kingdom could not be attributed with either actual or constructive knowledge of the Norwegian system and this was one of the grounds for his final conclusion that Norway had not succeeded in proving her historic title.[3]

Similarly, Judge Read raised the question whether the Norwegian system "was made known to the world in such a manner that other nations, including the United Kingdom, knew about it or must be assumed to have had knowledge."[4] He also reached the conclusion that "it has not been proved that the Norwegian System was made known to the world in time, and in such a manner that other nations, in-

[1] *ICJ Reports*, 1951, p. 139. (Italics added).

[2] *Ibid.*, pp. 171–172. (Italics added).

[3] *Ibid.*, p. 180, where Judge McNair states: "I do not consider that the United Kingdom was aware, or ought but for default on her part to have become aware, of the Norwegian system of straight base-lines...."

[4] *Ibid.*, p. 194; see also to the same effect *ibid.* ,p. 199.

cluding the United Kingdom, knew about it or *must be assumed to have had constructive knowledge*."[1]

The concept of constructive knowledge had also been expressly referred to by Counsel for the United States in the course of the proceedings in the *Alaskan Boundary* Dispute. There it had been maintained on behalf of Great Britain that she had been completely unaware of the acts of authority performed by the United States in the disputed territory. To this plea of ignorance Counsel for the United States replied in the following words:

These acts were not done in the dark, but publicity was given to them. All Governments of this day – that is, first class Powers – are generally informed in regard to published public documents.... The Treaty of Purchase was the subject of lengthy debate in Congress in 1868, and it is a violent presumption to say that the British Minister at Washington had no knowledge of it. On the contrary we may safely assume that he had full knowledge, for being there, an alert and able Representative of his Government, you may be sure that nothing appeared in the official publications that did not pass under the eyes of his secretaries.[2]

It is rather revealing to contrast this statement, made in open court by a duly accredited representative of the United States, with a statement that had been made some forty years earlier by the American Secretary of State Mr. Seward in his Note to Señor Tassara, which has already been referred to above. In a manner which is hardly compatible with the basically correct view put forward by Counsel for the United States in the *Alaskan Boundary* Dispute, Mr. Seward in his Note had asserted that "nations do not equally study each other's statute books, and are not chargeable with notice of national pretensions resting upon foreign legislation."[3]

While the first part of Mr. Seward's statement is obviously correct, the conclusion to which it led him appears to be a *non sequitur*. It is certainly true to say that "nations do not equally study each other's statute books," but, as has been pointed out by Johnson, following the judgment in the *Fisheries* case, "ignorance as to another State's legislation on territorial waters, however excusable, can be fatal, and... States may neglect, at their own risk, to study each other's statute-books."[4] Mr. Seward's assertion is, it is felt, certainly out of tune with

[1] *Ibid.*, p. 205.

[2] *Proceedings of the Alaskan Boundary Tribunal*, vol. VII, p. 916.

[3] Moore, *Digest of International Law*, vol. I, 1906, p. 710.

[4] Johnson, 1 *ICLQ* (1952), p. 166. Johnson, though, criticizes the Court's judgment on this point on the ground that "it may be doubted if this interpretation of the law, emphasising, as it does, the duty of States to ferret out the details of each other's legislation and protest in the widest possible terms every time there is an implied threat to their rights, under penalty of losing these rights, will make for international harmony." (*Ibid.*)

the present practice adopted by international law and, according to one author, it is even doubtful whether it had any legal foundation at the time of its enunciation.[1]

The problem touched upon by Mr. Seward, raises, however, a much wider and more complex question: to what extent may a State be attributed with knowledge of another State's legislative acts? In other words: can a State rely on its unawareness of other States' domestic acts as the basis for a plea of excusable ignorance?

43. *The plea of excusable ignorance*

The plea of excusable ignorance of other States' official acts, has, on the whole, rarely been successful. It appears to be nowadays a generally accepted principle that the legislative and other public measures of a State, taken and applied in the ordinary manner, are presumed to be known to other States. This is particularly true of legislative acts having unmistakably implications reaching beyond the frontiers of the enacting State, which are therefore expected to be more closely scrutinized by other States. "In the case of legislation by a State in which it makes a claim of an international character, the legislation is itself the international act by which the State has declared its intention."[2]

Thus, in the *Fisheries* case, as will be recalled, the International Court of Justice, in assessing the legal validity of the exceptional Norwegian system of delimitation, took account of various Norwegian acts of legislation, Royal Rescripts and Decrees and made these legislative acts the starting-point for the presumption that the United Kingdom was aware, or at any rate ought to have been aware, of the Norwegian system of delimitation and of Norway's extensive claims.[3]

The question of the imputability of knowledge of another State's legislative activities was again raised in the *Anglo-Iranian Oil Company (Preliminary Objection)* case.[4] There the Court was seised of the problem of its jurisdiction. One of the arguments advanced there against the Court's jurisdiction was that the Iranian Imperial Declaration of October 2nd, 1930, and the law of June 14th, 1931 – whereby the

[1] MacGibbon, 31 *BYIL* (1954), p. 179. See, however, Waldock, in whose opinion "Secretary Seward's *dictum* that a state is not chargeable with notice of a claim expressed merely in municipal law and not brought to its attention seems to be correct in principle and reasonable in practice." (Waldock, 28 *BYIL* (1951), p. 166; italics in original).

[2] MacGibbon, *loc. cit.*, p. 180.

[3] *ICJ Reports*, 1951, pp. 134–137.

[4] *ICJ Reports*, 1952, p. 93 *et seq.*

Mejlis approved the Imperial Declaration in which Iran had adhered to the „Optional Clause" (Article 36 of the Statute) – were purely domestic instruments, were unknown to other Governments, were written only in the Persian language, and were not communicated to the League of Nations or to any other States. The Court, however, declined to accept this argument, since it was "unable to see why it should be prevented from taking this piece of evidence into consideration. The law was published in the Corpus of Iranian laws voted and ratified during the period from January 15th, 1931, to January 15th, 1933. It has thus been available for the examination of other governments during a period of about twenty years."[1] The Court therefore held that foreign Governments could not have been considered to have been unaware of this piece of Iranian domestic legislation.

It is worth noting that Judge Hackworth, in his Dissenting Opinion, strongly dissociated himself on this point from the majority view and declined to take into account the said Iranian law, because of its being "a unilateral act of a legislative body of which other nations had not been apprised. National courts may, as a matter of course, draw upon such acts for municipal purposes, but this Court must look upon the public declarations by States made for international purposes, and cannot resort to municipal legislative enactments to explain ambiguities in international acts."[2]

Similarly, Judge McNair, in his Individual Opinion, took the view that the Iranian domestic legislation "should be excluded from the consideration of the Court. Its admissibility in evidence is open to question, and its evidentiary value is slight."[3]

In spite of the above-quoted reservations made by two distinguished authorities on international law, it is felt that the weight of opinion seems to be in favour of the presumption that States are aware of each other's legislative acts. This presumption is, in fact, borne out in most cases by the realities and rests on the well-founded assumption that the diplomatic missions of the various States are in general eager to acquaint themselves with the legislative developments taking place in the countries to which they are accredited. Thus, this common-sense presumption is normally far from being fictitious.[4] This is the reason

[1] *Ibid.*, p. 107.
[2] *Ibid.*, pp. 136–137.
[3] *Ibid.*, p. 121.
[4] See, however, Johnson who maintains that "surprising as it may seem States are often ignorant of each other's legislation.... The United Kingdom had no knowledge of some of the Decrees of other States put in as evidence by Norway during the proceedings [in the *Fisheries* case]." (1 *ICLQ* (1952), p. 166, n. 34).

why international tribunals will rarely be persuaded of a State's ignorance of other States' domestic legislative activities. The onus of satisfying a tribunal in this matter is a heavy one, "commensurate with the sense of responsibility and vigilance traditionally displayed by States in defence of their rights."[1]

The hypersensitiveness of States as to every actual or imaginary threat to their rights is well illustrated by their readiness to oppose even territorial "map claims," i.e. territorial claims which are reflected in maps printed by the authority or under the auspices of the claimant State. Thus, in a letter dated August 2nd, 1887, written by Lord Salisbury to the British Minister in Lisbon, exception was taken to some Portuguese maps contained in Portuguese White Books.[2] Honduras, likewise, protested against the "incorporation" of Swan Island by the United States in an official United States map.[3] In a Russian Memorandum delivered to the Duke of Wellington in respect of the *Alaska Dispute* between Russia and Great Britain it was pointed out that

> depuis près d'un siècle, des établissements Russes ont pris... une extension progressive, qui, dès l'année 1799 les avoit fait parvenir jusqu'au 55 parallèle, comme le porte la première charte de la Compagnie Russe-Américaine, charte qui a reçu dans le temps une publicité officielle, et qui n'a motivé aucune protestation de la part de l'Angleterre.[4]

Thus, Russia's rights were based, *inter alia*, on Great Britain's refraining from voicing any opposition against the Russian "map claims." This assertion was most emphatically challenged by the United Kingdom in the course of the *Alaskan Boundary* Dispute. Counsel for Great Britain vigorously denied that it was the practice of States to keep a vigilant watch over the maps published by the civilized nations, and by the efflux of time to become bound by what these maps indicate.[5]

More recently, various Chinese maps showing parts of Indian territory as being under Chinese sovereignty have evoked strong protest on the part of the Indian authorities. In a Note presented on September 10th, 1959, in Peking, the Indian Government expressed its regret "that large areas of Indian territory should continue to be shown on official Chinese maps as part of China.... It is most extraordinary that the Government of China have not found time during the past ten years to withdraw these faulty maps. The continued circulation of these

[1] MacGibbon, 31 *BYIL* (1954), p. 181.
[2] The text of this letter is reproduced in Smith, *op. cit.*, vol. II, p. 5.
[3] *Foreign Relations of the United States, 1935*, 1953, vol. IV, pp. 750–752.
[4] Smith, *op. cit.*, vol, II, p. 5.
[5] *Proceedings of the Alaskan Boundary Tribunal*, vol. VII, p. 528.

maps is a standing threat to India's integrity and evidence of unfriendliness towards India...."[1] These Chinese maps, as published by the Indian Government on September 29th, 1959,[2] show big inroads into Indian territory, mainly in the north-east of the country. On September 15th, 1959, Mr. Jigme Dorji, the Prime Minister of Bhutan, protested against Chinese map infringements of his country's territory which affected an area of approximately 200 square miles.[3]

Similarly, on December 8th, 1960, it was reported from Bonn that the West German Foreign Ministry had complained to The Times Publishing Company because of a map in Volume III of *The Times Atlas of the World* in which the Oder-Neisse line is shown as Germany's eastern frontier. It was reported that Herr von Brentano, the then Foreign Minister, answering a question in the Bundestag, complained that "the German frontier which was still 'valid in international law' was marked by a 'barely visible dotted violet line,' described in the key at the foot of the page as 'boundary of Poland, 1939.'"[4] The West German Foreign Ministry had made representations to The Times Publishing Company against "these false statements."[5]

These recent instances of protests lodged against "map claims" seem to indicate that States do, in fact, "keep a vigilant watch over the maps published by the civilized nations," contrary to what had been asserted on behalf of Great Britain in the course of the deliberations in the *Alaskan Boundary* Dispute. On the whole, it seems to emerge that States will be imputed with knowledge of each other's domestic legislative activities and other acts done under their authority, and that the plea of ignorance will be accepted only in the most exceptional circumstances. States desirous of reserving their rights will therefore be well advised to follow with a substantial amount of self-interested awareness the official acts of other States and to raise an objection to them – through the legitimate means recognized by international law – should they feel that their rights have been affected, or are likely to be affected, by such acts.

The need for such vigilance has been well illustrated in the judgment delivered by the International Court of Justice in the *Temple of Preah Vihear* case. There, it will be recalled, Cambodia relied on various maps in support of her claim to territorial sovereignty over the Temple area.

[1] Quoted after *Keesing's Contemporary Archives* vol. XII, 1959–1960, p. 17118.
[2] *The Times* of September 30th, 1959.
[3] *The Times* of September 16th, 1959.
[4] *The Times* of December 8th, 1960.
[5] *Ibid.*

Thailand, on the other hand, contended that the boundary line indicated on those maps, printed and published in 1907 by a French cartographical firm, as the final stage of the delimitation works carried out by a Mixed French-Siamese Commission, departed from the boundary line agreed upon between the parties to the boundary treaty concluded in 1904.

The Court confirmed the boundary line, as drawn on the 1907 maps, holding that

> the publication and communication of the... maps referred to... was something of an occasion.... The maps were given wide publicity in all technically interested quarters by being also communicated to the leading geographical societies in important countries, and... to the Siamese legations accredited to the British, German, Russian and United States Governments; and to all the members of the Mixed Commission, French and Siamese.... It is clear that the circumstances were such as called for some reaction, within a reasonable period, on the part of the Siamese authorities, if they wished to disagree with the map or had any serious question in regard to it. They did not do so, either then or for many years, and thereby must be held to have acquiesced.[1]

The Court went on to say that

> there were also indications on the face of the map sheet which required a reaction if the Siamese authorities had any reason to contend that the map did not represent the outcome of the work of delimitation.... The Siamese authorities by their conduct acknowledged the receipt, and recognized the character, of these maps.[2]

Objections against territorial claims – whether "map claims" or other types of claims – will usually be raised in the form of a formal protest. The relevance of this remedy to the prevention of an historic title from maturing, as well as the relevance of the absence of protest to the formation of an historic title, will be considered in the following sections.

[1] *ICJ Reports*, 1962, pp. 22–23.

[2] *Ibid.*, pp. 23–24. See, however, Judge Moreno Quintana's Dissenting Opinion, where he asserts that "a well- established rule... states that, when there is a discrepancy concerning a frontier delimitation between the text of a treaty and maps, it is the text and not the maps which is final." (*Ibid.*, p. 70). Judge Moreno Quintana cites in support of his contention a provision to this effect embodied in Article 29 of the Treaty of Versailles of June 28th, 1919, which he regards as "a well-established rule of international law." (*Ibid.*). It is doubted, however, whether such a general rule does, in fact, exist in international law. It would appear that the provisions of Article 29 of the Treaty of Versailles were specifically inserted precisely because the signatories did not believe that the existence of such a general rule could be presumed.

For an appraisal of the judgment rendered by the International Court of Justice in the *Temple of Preah Vihear* case, see Verzijl, 9 *NTIR* (1962), pp. 229–263; see also Johnson, in 11 *ICLQ* (1962), pp. 1183–1204; see also Weissberg, "Maps as Evidence in International Boundary Disputes: a Reappraisal," 57 *AJIL* (1963), pp. 781–803; see also Rosenne, "La Cour Internationale de Justice en 1962," 67 *RGDIP* (1963), pp. 754–777.

44. *The relevance of protest to the formation of an historic title*

The relevance of protest – or rather absence of protest – to the formation of an historic title is not far to seek. As will be recalled, the existence of an historic title in international law depends on the proof of continuous and peaceful possession. "Peacefulness" in this context is understood as meaning other States' acquiescence in a certain situation giving rise to territorial claims.[1] It is therefore only too obvious that the question as to whether the States affected, or likely to be affected, by the formation of such exceptional rights raised any objection against the new territorial situation is of crucial importance. Thus, the lodging of a diplomatic protest is of overriding legal significance in determining whether a State has taken all the necessary and adequate measures to prevent an historic title from maturing.[2] Because acquiescence is instrumental in the establishment of an historic title, it is only proper to investigate at some length one of the main devices by means of which the States wishing to dissociate themselves from a new and unwelcome territorial situation are expected to signify their objection.

It is the function of protest to rebut the presumption of acquiescence which might have been otherwise inferred from the circumstances, viewed as a whole. This is why doctrine and practice alike have consistently maintained that protest is necessary for the preservation of the rights of the protesting State and for the prevention of another State's exceptional rights from maturing, in circumstances where a failure to protest would amount to acquiescence. Thus, Brüel asserts that "toujours facultative, la protestation n'est juridiquement nécessaire que dans le cas où le silence équivaudrait à un assentiment tacite".[3]

The device of protest fulfils, in fact, a twofold purpose. In the first instance, the lack of protest on the part of other States may be interpreted as meaning that the States refraining from formulating reser-

[1] "Peacefulness" is not intended to denote the positive attitude of the local population and its approval of the territorial sovereign. From the point of view of international law, the attitude of the local population and the degree of its support of the internal regime is immaterial. Thus, when referring to "peacefulness," international tribunals are concerned with the attitude of other States towards the alleged territorial sovereign. This point was clearly brought out by Judge Huber in the *Island of Palmas* case, where he explicitly stated that "the continuous and peaceful display of territorial sovereignty (*peaceful in relation to other States*) is as good as a title." (*UNRIAA*, vol. II, p. 839; italics added).

[2] Protest, though, has lost ever since the end of World War I much of its former significance as a bar to the emergence of a new territorial title; see on this in more detail section 47 below.

[3] Brüel, 3 *ASJG* (1932), p. 89.

vations have accepted the situation as being in conformity with the existing law. In addition to this – and from the point of view of the formation of historic rights this aspect appears to be the decisive one – "absence of protest may... in itself become a source of legal right inasmuch as it is related to... estoppel or prescription."[1] Protest is, according to Lauterpacht, "an essential requirement of stability... [which] prevents states from playing fast and loose with situations affecting others."[2] The same author also points out that the relevance of the failure to protest is particularly conspicuous in the international sphere where "the normal avenues for ascertaining disputed rights through the compulsory jurisdiction of tribunals are not always available."[3]

Verdross defines protest as "a declaration challenging the legality of a given state of things. Since, however, mere silence does not amount to recognition, the raising of a protest is rendered necessary in those cases only in which a *prise de position* is warranted by the existing situation."[4]

The consensus of writers on this point is well reflected in international practice where the lack of protest is frequently resorted to as the proof of acquiescence. Thus, in the course of the proceedings in the *Alaskan Boundary* Dispute, Counsel for the United States contended that, had Britain believed her rights to be menaced, she would have protested rather than "permit a claim of this sort to pass unchallenged and grow into a right, or at least something by which a right can be perfected."[5]

Similarly, in the Printed Argument submitted by Venezuela in the *Venezuela-British Guiana Boundary* Arbitration, it was pointed out that "no holding by force, against the protest of the State whose territory has been seized, will ever ripen into a title by prescription.... There is no tribunal to which an injured State can appeal to recover the territory of which it has been deprived by force. Its maintained protest has the... effect to arrest the maturing of her title...."[6]

Commenting on the legal status of the Falkland Islands Dependencies, Waldock points out, in support of the British claim, that the Letters Patent issued formally in 1908, declaring the territories in question to

[1] Lauterpacht, "Sovereignty over Submarine Areas," 27 *BYIL* (1950), p. 376 *et seq.*, at p. 395.

[2] *Ibid.*, p. 396.

[3] *Ibid.* See to the same effect Verykios, *op. cit.*, p. 99; see also Hyde, *op. cit.*, vol. I, p. 387, and Gidel, *op. cit.*, vol. III, p. 634.

[4] Verdross, *Völkerrecht*, 4th edition, 1959, p. 99, where the author states: "Der Protest besteht aus einer Erklärung, welche die Rechtmässigkeit einer bestimmten Sachlage bestreitet. Da aber das blosse Stillschweigen noch keine Anerkennung bedeutet, ist die Erhebung eines Protestes nur nötig, wenn nach der Sachlage eine Stellungnahme erwartet werden kann."

[5] *Proceedings of the Alaskan Boundary Tribunal*, vol. VII, p. 868.

[6] *Cmd.* 9501 (1899), p. 45.

be Dependencies of the Falkland Islands, "evoked no protest from any other state."[1]

Likewise, the absence of any protests on the part of Argentina and Chile against various British manifestations of sovereignty was invoked by the United Kingdom as a proof of these countries' recognition of British authority over the Falkland Islands Dependencies. Thus, it was claimed that

> Argentina made no protests... against the issue of the British Letters Patent of 1917. Nor did she make any protests or reservations against the promulgation of British Laws for the Dependencies, nor against the applications of those laws to... [an] Argentine company.... These facts establish beyond any question that... Argentina recognised British sovereignty over the Dependencies.[2]

The purpose of diplomatic protest was stated by the Agent for the United Kingdom in his oral pleadings in the *Fisheries* case as being a registration of the fact that the protesting States "have not acquiesced and to prevent a prescriptive claim being built up against them."[3]

In the *Minquiers and Ecrehos* case Counsel for the United Kingdom observed that in general protest records "the opinion of the protesting country that the act protested against is invalid and is not acquiesced in."[4]

In the award rendered in the *Chamizal* Arbitration between the United States of America and Mexico, the Commissioners rejected the American claim that the United States had acquired a title by possession to the Chamizal tract, since they found that "the Mexican Government had done all that could be reasonably required of it by way of protest against the alleged [American] encroachment."[5]

Thus, the absence of protest may be regarded as the corner-stone of the doctrine of acquiescence. It rests on the assumption that States will not remain silent when faced with a situation likely to affect adversely their rights, if there is the slightest justification for any objection on their part. "Governments are not prone to understate their claims," says Judge McNair in his Dissenting Opinion in the *Fisheries* case.[6] They will usually give air to their grievances by the formulation and dispatch of a protest, the purpose of which is to build up an almost instinctive defence mechanism designed to vitiate any possible inter-

[1] Waldock, 25 *BYIL* (1948), p. 328.

[2] *ICJ, Antarctica cases, Pleadings, Oral Arguments, Documents*, p. 23. Similar considerations were relied upon regarding the presumed recognition by Chile of United Kingdom rights in the area in question. (*Ibid.*, pp. 63–64).

[3] *ICJ, Fisheries case, Pleadings, Oral Arguments, Documents*, vol. IV, pp. 375–376.

[4] *ICJ, Minquiers and Ecrehos case, Pleadings, Oral Arguments, Documents*, vol. II, p. 171.

[5] *UNRIAA*, vol. XI, p. 329; 5 *AJIL* (1911), p. 807.

[6] *ICJ Reports*, 1951, p. 162.

pretation of silence as acquiescence. Thus, protest may be considered as the remedy resorted to by international law in order to prevent the excessive application of the principle *qui tacet consentire videtur*, and the scope of the principle reflected in this maxim is buttressed by what Verykios terms "le mouvement instinctif de la protestation."[1]

In order to fulfil its role in the prevention of an historic title from maturing, a protest must comply with various requirements. The conditions for the validity of a protest will therefore be discussed presently.

45. *The conditions for the validity of a protest*

(a) The origins of the protest

Protest has been defined by Oppenheim as "a formal communication from one State to another that it objects to an act performed, or contemplated, by the latter."[2] The governmental origin of the protest – a requirement that has been clearly brought out in this definition – has found widespread support among writers who have devoted more than cursory attention to this problem.[3] It is common ground among these writers that a protest, designed to serve the purpose of preservation of rights and of rebutting any presumption of acquiescence in certain acts or situations, should emanate from, or on behalf of, the State whose rights are purported to be safeguarded thereby. A protest, which has not emanated from official and duly authorized sources and which has not been given at least subsequent ratification, may turn out to have been lodged in vain. This principle was emphatically relied upon by the United States in the course of the *Alaskan Boundary* Dispute. During the proceedings in that case Great Britain referred to the so-called "Dawson letter" of 1888, which, she alleged, gave notice to the United States of the Canadian claims. The United States, however, declined to attach any significance to this letter on the ground that it would have been "a most remarkable procedure... for a Government to waive the usual channels of diplomatic communication on matters of great import, and to entrust the advancement of a contention... to be made by an unaccredited person."[4]

[1] Verykios, *op. cit.*, p. 27.
[2] Oppenheim, *op. cit.*, p. 874.
[3] E.g. Brüel, *loc. cit.*, pp. 81-82; see also Rousseau, *Principes généraux du droit international public*, 1944, vol. I, p. 144; see also Anzilotti, *op. cit.*, p. 349.
[4] *Proceedings of the Alaskan Boundary Tribunal, United States Senate Documents*, No. 162, 58th Congress, 2nd session (1904), vol. V, p. 183.

(b) The formality of the protest

Although a protest may be lodged orally,[1] it is in the interest of the protesting State to respect the condition of formality and to reduce its protest into writing. By placing their protest on written record, the protesting States considerably diminish the risk of impairing their efficiency or of causing any deficiency in form. These risks are the result of the fact that "the impermanence of the spoken word renders oral protests liable to the twin dangers of distortion and oblivion."[2] Governments wishing to signify their objection to a certain act or situation will therefore be well advised to make full use of the advantages of a written protest in order to safeguard both its form and substance. International practice provides ample proof that Governments are aware of these advantages. Thus, the British Foreign Secretary Canning, in a dispatch dated December 8th, 1824, explaining the reasons for Great Britain's protest against the Russian pretensions to dominion over vast areas of the Pacific, stated that the Russian Ukase of 1821, in which these pretensions had been raised for the first time, "could not continue longer unrepealed without compelling us to take some measure of public and effectual remonstrance against it.... [A] private disavowal of a published claim is no security against the revival of that claim."[3]

(c) The nature and contents of the protest

Protests are expected to indicate clearly the wrongs against which they are directed. States have been insistent that their position should not be affected by mere rumours and possible future eventualities. A diplomatic protest will usually indicate the reasons which prompted its initiators to believe that the acts which it is directed against run counter to the generally accepted rules of international law. Some States – and this practice has been consistently followed by the United States of America – would explicitly add that they reserve their rights as regards the point in issue. In view of the fact that it is the essence of a protest and its very purpose to preserve such rights, this express stipulation appears to be superfluous. As a matter of course, the rights in the defence of which a protest is made must, in fact, pertain to the protesting State, and a protest made in order to safeguard another State's rights will normally be devoid of any legal effect.

[1] According to Brüel, the protest "peut être formulée verbalement ou par écrit ou encore par des acts 'concluants'...." (Brüel, *loc. cit.*, p. 83).

[2] MacGibbon, 30 *BYIL* (1953), p. 295.

[3] *Behring Sea Arbitration, British Case, Cmd.* 6918 (1893), p. 46.

(d) The purpose of the protest

The purpose of the protest has already been dealt with above at some length. Its aim is to make it known that the protesting State does not recognize the validity of the acts against which the protest is directed, does not condone them and does not acquiesce in the situation created, or likely to be brought about, by such acts. In Martens' view protests are designed "pour empêcher que des actes qu'on prévoit ne pouvoir éviter ne soient interprétés comme faisant preuve de consentement."[1] Rousseau states that "la protestation est une déclaration de la volonté de ne pas reconnaître comme légitime une prétention donnée, une conduite donnée, un état de choses donné."[2] Adopting the same line of thought, Sir Edward Grey, indicating the motive of the British protest against the *Panama Canal Act* of 1912, explained that the British Government "were unwilling to give ground for an assertion that their silence had been taken for consent."[3] The British Foreign Secretary Canning, likewise, resorted to a similar reasoning when he stressed, in a dispatch relating to the Russian Ukase of 1821, that

> we have seen in the course of this negotiation that the Russian claim... rests in fact on no other ground than the presumed acquiescence of the nations of Europe.... It becomes us to be exceedingly careful that we do not, by a similar neglect on the present occasion, allow a similar presumption to be raised as to an acquiescence in the Ukase of 1821.[4]

46. *Anticipatory protest*

It is generally agreed that States should not, as a rule, protest prior to the actual occurrence of the wrong alleged to have been done to them, i.e. before the objectionable measure has been enforced against them or their nationals. However, there seems to be no express obligation to refrain from such a course of action at an earlier stage. Thus, States are known to have protested on the conclusion of treaties which they considered as likely to infringe their rights,[5] or even earlier, i.e. at the time when they acquired knowledge that the conclusion of such treaties was being contemplated. Similarly, States have also protested against legislative measures of other States – whatever their

[1] Martens, *Précis du droit des gens moderne de l'Europe* (revised edition of 1858), vol. I, p. 202.

[2] Rousseau, *op. cit.*, vol. I, p. 149; see also to the same effect Vattel, *op. cit.*, para. 145; see also Fauchille, *op. cit.*, p. 760 and Strupp, *Eléments du droit international public*, 2nd edition, vol. I, 1930, p. 260.

[3] *Foreign Relations of the United States, 1912*, 1919, p. 470.

[4] *Cmd.* 6918 (1893), p. 46.

[5] For authorities on this point see McNair, *Law of Treaties*, 1961, pp. 547–549; see also MacGibbon, 30 *BYIL* (1953), p. 299, n. 3.

names may be – which, if enforced, would, in the protesting State's opinion, prejudice its rights.[1] Instances are also known where States protested against contemplated legislative measures of other States, pending their promulgation or during their enforcement.[2]

The practice of States on this topic was accurately summed up in the course of the proceedings in the *Fisheries* case, when the Agent for the United Kingdom stressed that

> Governments do often protest against decrees... even when they have not yet been enforced against their nationals.[3]

After citing various instances in which protests were lodged against acts of domestic legislation – prior to their enforcement – Counsel for the United Kingdom gave the reasons for making such anticipatory protests in the following words:

> Sometimes a protest is made at once against a decree because of the potential threat of enforcement against the protesting State's own vessels;... Sometimes a protest is made at once simply to place on record objection to the claim and to reserve the rights of the protesting State;... Sometimes a protest is made at once in the hope of modifying the views of the... [other] State.[4]

The relevance of protest as a vital factor in the assessment of other States' attitude towards an act of domestic legislation was also clearly borne out in the pleadings of Bourquin who – on behalf of Norway – observed that there had been an absence of protest on the part of the international community against the Norwegian Decree of 1935. Bourquin commented on this lack of objection in the following words:

[1] Having regard to the views put forward in sections 42 and 43 above, where it was suggested that States are normally imputed with knowledge of each other's legislation, the lodging of protests at such an early stage would be expected to be the rule rather than the exception to it. The hesitancy of States on this point is explained by the fact that the delivery of protests is usually construed by the recipient State as an act of unfriendliness on the part of the protesting State and is therefore the subject of much pondering, especially if the chances of any practical result are slight. Moreover, the transfer of a latent international dispute into the limelight of international publicity frequently has the effect of driving the rival State into an entrenched position of marked intransigence and thus creates an atmosphere of mounting tension which is not favourable for the settlement of disputes. States will therefore normally postpone the delivery of protests as long as possible. These considerations of statesmanlike wisdom and practical expediency were recently voiced by the Lord Privy Seal of the day in the House of Commons. Asked by Mr. William Yates, M.P., why he did not "send a strong Note" to Portugal because of her recent policies in Angola, Mr. Edward Heath replied: "...When one is dealing with other countries and trying to influence their policy, sending strong Notes is not necessarily the way to do it." (*Hansard* (Commons) of June 28th, 1961, vol. 643, col. 446).

[2] For references on this point see MacGibbon, *ibid.*, p. 301.

[3] *ICJ*, *Fisheries case*, *Pleadings*, *Oral Arguments*, *Documents*, vol. IV, p. 375.

[4] *Ibid.*, pp. 396–397.

Si... [les autres nations] avaient cru que le décret de 1935 portait attente à leurs droits, il est probable qu'elles seraient intervenues. Or, aucune d'elles n'a manifesté une véritable opposition.[1]

Bourquin equally registered the fact that the United Kingdom had, on previous instances, lodged protests with various Governments against the promulgation of laws which she had regarded as objectionable, and that these protests had been made prior to the enforcement of the laws against British nationals or vessels and had been aimed at the mere existence of these laws. Referring to the protests made against the unilateral extension of territorial waters by means of domestic legislation, Bourquin observed:

La protestation porte sur les dispositions mêmes qui ont été édictées par ces Etats pour délimiter leurs mers adjacentes.... Mais l'objet de la protestation, c'est la délimitation elle-même, et ce ne sont pas du tout des actes d'éxécution qui auraient été accomplis sur la base de cette délimitation. Il n'y en a pas eu.[2]

In fact, the most conspicuous number of "anticipatory protests" has been forthcoming in respect of domestic legislation – taking sometimes the form of proclamations or decrees – purporting to extend by way of unilateral legislation the width of the area of marginal waters over which States claim sovereignty. Such unilateral pretensions regarding the extension of territorial waters have frequently met with the opposition of other States and have evoked numerous protests – even prior to their enforcement.[3]

47. Protest as a bar to the acquisition of an historic title

The question has been frequently raised whether protest in itself can constitute a bar to the growth of an historic title. The authorities on this point do not appear to be unamimous. There are indications to the effect that simple protest was regarded in some instances as a sufficient means for the prevention of an historic title from coming into being. Thus, Audinet would maintain that a weak State might remain passive not because it acquiesced in the situation which appeared to be detrimental to its interests, but "parce qu'il ne sera pas à même de soutenir, au besoin, ses réclamations par les armes."[4]

Later authorities, however, and particularly authors writing after

[1] *Ibid.*, p. 234.
[2] *Ibid.*, p. 241.
[3] For a detailed list of such protests, see MacGibbon, *loc. cit.*, pp. 303–4.
[4] Audinet, *loc. cit.*, p. 322; see to the same effect, Suy, *op. cit.*, p. 78.

the advent in 1919 of a permanent international machinery for the judicial settlement of international disputes, seem to have displayed a more cautious and reserved attitude on this point. From a perusal of these authorities it seems to emerge that a single and simple protest – which is not followed up by further action – cannot be regarded now as an adequate remedy for preventing indefinitely an historic title from maturing. Protest, according to the prevailing trend, will be sufficient only in those cases where the circumstances were such that it constituted the only feasible method for the assertion by a State of its rights.[1]

Protests alone will, however, not suffice in those cases – to which their overwhelming majority nowadays belongs – where the protesting State could reasonably be expected to take further steps in order to prove its seriousness, its good faith and its sincere intention to oppose the alleged encroachments upon its rights.[2] Among such measures one might mention acts such as the severance of diplomatic relations, measures of retorsion, and the reference of the dispute to the United Nations or to the International Court of Justice.

The diminishing importance of protest as an obstacle to the acquisition of an historic title and its reduction to the status of a mere temporary bar, to be followed up by additional and more effective means, is warranted by the establishment in 1919 of the Permanent Court of International Justice and subsequently, in 1945, of the International Court of Justice. According to Johnson, "the advent of this new machinery for settling international disputes has largely altered the role of protest.... The result is that the diplomatic protest is of reduced significance."[3]

[1] The role of protest as a bar to the acquisition of State rights was also discussed – in a somewhat different context – by the International Law Commission, when it dealt with the draft articles relating to the continental shelf. At the fifth session of the Commission, its Secretary, Mr. Liang, raised the question whether, "in view of the protests directed against... [the various national shelf proclamations] by other governments... those declarations reflected the practice of States.... The most that could be claimed was that they indicated a tendency." (*ILC Yearbook*, 5th session 1953, vol. I, p. 86). Sir Hersch Lauterpacht, referring to this argument, did not basically challenge the role of protests in general in preventing the emergence of a practice, but confined himself to stating that "the protests entered by governments against the proclamations expressed opposition, not to the claim that the continental shelf appertained to a certain coastal State, but to claims of rights over the superincumbent seas, which was a very different matter." (*Ibid.*, p. 88).

[2] Thus, says Suy: "...la protestation diplomatique ne constitue plus qu'un moyen initial pour arrêter temporairement la prescription. Si elle reste isolée, si elle n'est pas suivi d'autres actes unilatéraux par lesquels le sujet de droit dont ils émanent manifeste sa volonté de ne pas reçonnaître un état de fait illicite et de sauvegarder ses droits, la protestation ne peut avoir qu'un effet limité voire pas d'effet du tout." (Suy, *op. cit.*, pp. 75–76).

[3] Johnson, 27 *BYIL* (1950), p. 346.

However, this tendency has been partly offset by the conclusion of the General Treaty for the Renunciation of War, in conjunction with the provisions of Article 2 (4) of the Charter of the United Nations, which severely restricted the possibility of using force, or threatening the use of it, in international relations. The outcome of this development is that international tribunals can no longer insist, in addition to protest, on evidence of a readiness to support the protest by force or show of force.

In an article published in 1960, Kunz has pointed out that "the complete prohibition of the use of military force as a sanction by single states, without collective and effective sanctions for enforcing international law in general, has left states, against which violations of international law not constituting an armed attack have been committed, sometimes without any adequate remedy.... These states, it is true, may protest; but it is certain that a protest or even repeated protests, if they remain without effect, do not preserve the rights of the protesting states indefinitely."[1]

The changing climate of international judicial opinion as regards the role of protest in preventing the acquisition of an historic title can readily be appraised by contrasting decisions rendered by international tribunals before 1919 and after that date, respectively.

In the award delivered in 1911 in the *Chamizal* Arbitration, the Commissioners observed that Mexico had, in fact, succeeded in preventing the United States from perfecting a territorial title to the Chamizal tract, by consistently protesting against repeated American encroachments on the said territory. The Commissioners felt that Mexico "had done all that could be reasonably required of it *by way of protest* against the alleged encroachment."[2]

Dismissing the suggestion, according to which Mexico should have followed up her protests by more drastical steps, the Commissioners took the view that "however much the Mexicans may have desired to take physical possession of the district [of El Chamizal], the result of any attempt to do so would have provoked scenes of violence and the Republic of Mexico cannot be blamed for resorting to the milder forms of protest contained in its diplomatic correspondence."[3]

[1] Kunz, "Sanctions in International Law," 54 *AJIL* (1960), p. 324, at p. 340.
[2] *UNRIAA*, vol. XI, p. 329; 5 *AJIL* (1911), p. 807. (Italics added).
[3] *Ibid.* A similar note was struck in the Printed Argument submitted by Venezuela in the course of the proceedings in the *Venezuela-British Guiana Boundary* Arbitration, where it was stated that "Venezuela's claims and her protests against alleged British usurpation have been constant and emphatic, and have been enforced by all the means practicable for a weak

The award rendered in the *Chamizal* Arbitration case was invoked by France in the course of her pleadings in the *Minquiers and Ecrehos* case. The French contention was that sporadic French protests against various manifestations of British sovereignty over the disputed islets were sufficient and adequate means to keep alive the alleged French rights over the Minquiers and Ecrehos. Judge Carneiro in his Individual Opinion dismissed this French argument in the following words:

> The French Government has referred to the arbitral award in the Chamizal case.... This award was made in 1911 and relates to facts in the period 1848–1895. At that time there was no international court.... But such a tribunal has now been created and has existed for many years. Why did France not at least propose that the dispute should be referred to this tribunal, as England has done, after more than half a century of intermittent and fruitless discussion? The failure to make such a proposal deprives the claim of much of its force; it may even render it obsolete.... I consider that the action of the Court might easily be restricted or even nullified if disputes were allowed to be prolonged indefinitely without good reason and if an attempt were not made to obtain the Court's decisive intervention but preference was given to mere periodical and ineffectual 'paper' protests. This state of affairs would be incompatible with the régime under which the rights of each State would be specified and guaranteed.[1]

Thus, doctrine and practice alike seem to support the view that ever since 1919, having regard to the availability of permanent international tribunals, a mere protest appears to amount to no more than a temporary bar to the formation of historic rights.

In order to preserve alleged rights, protests must be followed up by some evidence of positive initiative intended to bring about the settlement of the dispute in question, by utilizing all proper and available means which are recognized by international law for this purpose. These means will usually comprise the active prosecution of the objection through diplomatic negotiations, the arrangement of some kind of *modus vivendi*, or the seeking of a solution by enquiry, mediation or conciliation. The dispute may also be referred to the United Nations

power to employ in its dealings with a strong one, even to the rupture of diplomatic relations." (See *Cmd.* 9501 (1899), p. 29).

[1] *ICJ Reports*, 1953, pp. 107-108. The same view was also clearly reflected in the United Kingdom Reply in the *Fisheries* case, where it was asserted that "a diplomatic protest is by itself effective to manifest the objection of the protesting State and *for a certain period* reserve its rights.... A State which contents itself with paper protests and does not use the available means of pressing its objections may after a certain lapse of time be debarred from further questioning what has become part of the established legal order" (*ICJ, Fisheries case, Pleadings, Oral Arguments, Documents*, vol. II, p. 654; italics added). For further authorities to the same effect see *ICJ, Fisheries case, Pleadings, Oral Arguments, Documents*, vol. II, p. 656 and p. 678; see also the Reply of the United Kingdom in the *Corfu Channel* case, *ICJ, Corfu Channel* case, *Pleadings, Oral Arguments, Documents*, vol. II, p. 277; see also the United Kingdom Reply in the *Minquiers and Ecrehos* case, *ICJ, Minquiers and Ecrehos case, Pleadings, Oral Arguments, Documents*, vol. I, p. 554.

General Assembly or to the Security Council, in accordance with the provisions contained in Chapter VI, Articles 33-37, of the United Nations Charter, laying down the rules for the pacific settlement of disputes.

All the attempts for the settlement of the dispute on the diplomatic and political level having failed, the matter may be referred to international arbitration or to the International Court of Justice.

If both parties to the dispute are signatories to the "Optional Clause" (Article 36(2) of the Statute of the International Court of Justice), or to any treaty which makes adjudication before the Court compulsory for them (in accordance with the provisions of Article 36(1) of the Statute), proceedings may be instituted by unilateral application. Where, however, the parties, or one of them, have not submitted to the Court's compulsory jurisdiction, such proceedings will normally be instituted by a special agreement (*compromis*).

There exists also the basis for a unilateral arraignment of a State before the Court in cases where the respondent is not subject to the Court's jurisdiction, neither by virtue of the "Optional Clause," nor of any other treaty provision, nor of any special agreement. In such cases the respondent will be entitled to accept, or reject, the jurisdiction of the Court after the proceedings have formally been instituted, in accordance with the provisions of Article 40(1) of the Statute of the Court.[1]

There are, however, certain situations in which the general trend of the constantly diminishing significance of diplomatic protest has been – if not outweighed – at least slowed down by a wide range of exceptional circumstances, some of which would appear to deserve further consideration. As has been pointed out by Lauterpacht – rightly, it is believed – protest is still the only appropriate, and consequently an adequate, course of action in all those cases "where the normal avenues for ascertaining disputed rights through the compulsory jurisdiction of tribunals

[1] See in this connection the *Antarctica* cases, where the United Kingdom unilaterally instituted proceedings against Argentina and Chile. (*ICJ, Antarctica cases, Pleadings, Oral Arguments, Documents*, pp. 35–37 and pp. 72–74). Both Argentina and Chile having rejected the British offer for the judicial settlement of these disputes, contained in the United Kingdom applications, the International Court of Justice duly declared its lack of jurisdiction on this matter. (See *ICJ Reports*, 1956, pp. 12–17). There is little doubt indeed that the United Kingdom had, in fact, anticipated the rejection by Argentina and Chile of the British offer for the judicial settlement of the Antarctica disputes; there is good reason to believe that the British applications were filed solely with a view to obviating any future Argentinian and Chilean claims based on an alleged British acquiescence in the Argentinian and Chilean territorial pretensions over certain regions of the Antarctic. For a more detailed analysis of the legal implications of Article 40 (1) of the Statute of the Court, see Rosenne, *The International Court of Justice*, 1957, pp. 258 and 295–296.

are not... available."[1] Lauterpacht apparently alludes to those cases in which States, which are not bound by any commitment of obligatory judicial or arbitral settlement, refuse to submit voluntarily to international adjudication. As a further instance in which protest may be regarded as a proper and sufficient way of objection to any exceptional claims or pretensions, Lauterpacht mentions the case where a legislative or administrative measure was adopted in the form of a proclamation of intention and assertion of a right, without being followed up by any actual attempt of enforcing such assertion by the application of the law in question. Lauterpacht expresses the view that "until an injury has actually occurred, it is probable that no judicial remedy will lie."[2] Similar considerations will apply to those cases in which the remedy of appealing to a political agency, such as the United Nations, is not available, because, according to its constitution, "the controversy is of not sufficient importance in terms of preservation of international peace to warrant action... in relation to the subject-matter of the dispute."[3]

In such cases a protest, which was promptly presented and subsequently maintained, would suffice to reserve the rights of the protesting State, at least until an attempt is made to enforce the legislation. This appears to have been the situation envisaged by Counsel for the United Kingdom in the course of the oral arguments in the *Minquiers and Ecrehos* case, when he remarked that the type of action taken by the protesting State ought to be related to the type of acts against which objection has been raised and that sometimes a mere protest might be adequate to nullify claims of minor significance.[4]

The same argument had been advanced by the Agent for the United Kingdom in the *Fisheries* case, where he had suggested that

> the decree made by a State is only one aspect of the matter. The other and equally important aspect is the attitude of other States towards the decree and in particular... to its enforcement against their nationals or vessels.... The paper protest is at least as important as the paper decree.... For the Court, as evidence of the practice of States,... protests are every bit as valuable evidence as the text of... [a] decree.[5]

Likewise, a protest will be held to be sufficient in situations of recent origin; in cases where the consolidating time factor is lacking, protest may be regarded as a sufficient and proper means for the preservation of the rights of the protesting State. Bourquin, pleading on behalf of

[1] Lauterpacht, 27 *BYIL* (1950), p. 396.
[2] *Ibid.*
[3] *Ibid.*
[4] *ICJ, Minquiers and Ecrehos case, Pleadings, Oral Arguments, Documents*, vol. II, p. 367.
[5] *ICJ, Fisheries case, Pleadings, Oral Arguments, Documents*, vol. IV, pp. 37–38.

Norway in the *Fisheries* case, seems to have given expression to this train of thought when he stated that

> nous sommes... d'accord avec le Gouvernement britannique pour admettre que, si une prétention nouvelle est formulée par un Etat, cette prétention n'est pas opposable à un autre Etat qui, dès le début et d'une manière non équivoque, y aurait fait opposition. Une opposition, même isolée, suffirait en pareil cas, pour préserver les droits de l'opposant, parce qu'il s'agit d'une prétention nouvelle et sur laquelle, par conséquent, l'action du temps n'a pas encore pu produire ses effets.[1]

Subject to the foregoing qualifications, protest alone will, as a rule, not be sufficient to constitute a bar for the perfection of an historic title unless it is followed up and supported by other appropriate and available remedies which are aimed at preventing such title from coming into being.

It is felt that this analysis may fittingly be closed with a passage written by Verykios in 1934, where the author seems to have summed up the legal position on this point in a manner which still holds good after the lapse of three decades. Commenting on the significance of protest in the assertion of rights by States, Verykios wrote:

> Mais une protestation pure et simple par voie diplomatique suffit-elle à interrompre la prescription? En principe oui, mais il faut pour cela que la protestation sera suivie d'une contestation et d'un règlement de la question; sinon on a vu qu'un Etat pourra protester indéfiniment, s'il le fait sans résultat il ne pourra pas interrompre l'effet du temps.[2]

48. The repetition of protest

A question frequently arising in this connection is whether the repetition of a protest may be considered as an appropriate measure to prevent the perfection of an historic title, thus taking the place of other remedies which have been enumerated above. In MacGibbon's view, "scant regard will be paid to the isolated protest of a State which takes no further action to combat continued infringements of its rights."[3] He further asserts that "increased weight will be attached to the cumulative effect of protests which have been persistently reiterated."[4] The reason given for this assertion is that "failure to supplement the initial expression of disapproval will not unreasonably give rise to the presumption either that... opposition could not be supported by any show of legal right, or that, even if able to protest on the basis of a claim of

[1] *Ibid.*, p. 308.
[2] Verykios, *op. cit.*, p. 101.
[3] MacGibbon, 30 *BYIL* (1953), p. 310.
[4] *Ibid.*, n. 1.

right,... [the State affected] was for some reason indifferent to the outcome."[1]

No doubt, a protest will lose much of its force and value once it is not supported by any other action at the time when the practice, against which the original protest was lodged, is being repeated. While it is generally admitted that a protest is *necessary* to constitute a temporary bar to the perfection of an historic title, this by no means indicates that such protest – even if repeated – will be *sufficient* to keep alive indefinitely the alleged rights of the protesting State.

Considerable doubt also persists as to the precise length of time during which the effectiveness of a protest lasts. The matter is of course without complications whenever a subsequent recognition of the claim, against which objection was raised, is forthcoming, as "les effets de la protestation cessent si l'Etat reconnaît les prétensions ou les faits contre lesquels il avait protesté."[2] The solution of this problem is, however, much more complex in those cases – and they are the typical cases of establishing an historic title – where no express recognition has been forthcoming, but acquiescence has to be inferred from all the surrounding circumstances. Thus, the question has to be left open and must be dealt with specifically in each case, having regard to its particular circumstances.

It is, however, worth noting that, in the course of the oral proceedings in the *Fisheries* case, it was suggested on behalf of Norway that the oral protest of the German Government against the Norwegian Decree of 1935, purporting to extend Norwegian territorial waters as a result of the enforcement of the Norwegian method of delimitation by baselines, was devoid of any probative value, because "cette communication est restée sans effet et elle n'a été suivie d'aucune autre démarche. Après avoir fait ce geste, le Gouvernement allemand s'est abstenu d'en tirer la moindre conséquence."[3]

In an earlier stage of the proceedings it had been pointed out in the Norwegian Rejoinder that the French protest of 1870 against the principles contained in the Norwegian Decree of 1869, relating to the application of the "Norwegian system," could not be regarded as a bar to the formation of exceptional rights by Norway, since France did not further prosecute her objection and the matter was allowed to drop.[4]

The Court in its judgment, while not pronouncing explicitly on

[1] *Ibid.*
[2] Anzilotti, *op. cit.*, p. 349.
[3] *ICJ, Fisheries case, Pleadings, Oral Arguments, Documents,* vol. IV, p. 234.
[4] *Ibid.*, vol. III, pp. 481–484.

this question, seems to have upheld by implication the Norwegian contention, since it concluded that the Norwegian system "was consistently applied by [the] Norwegian authorities and... *it encountered no opposition on the part of other States*."[1]

Thus, this issue may be summed up by stating that a single diplomatic protest will not of itself prevent indefinitely the formation of an historic title unless it is followed up by more effective measures of contestation. Protests which will not be supported in this manner will, as a rule, lose their force.

49. *The relevance of the protest of a single State*

It is felt that at this juncture reference ought to be made to the question of the effect of the protest of a single State on the formation of an historic title. This question is of negligible importance as long as one is faced with claims relating to an historic title to land territory, since the number of States affected, or likely to be affected, by such a claim is relatively small; it gains, however, considerably in significance when related to questions attendant upon the acquisition of a maritime historic title, since such a title – being acquired at the expense of the international community as a whole – is a matter for all of its member – States. The question therefore arises whether a protest, emanating from one State or from a small number of States, in circumstances where the rights of the international community as such are at stake, may be regarded as a sufficient measure to prevent the acquisition of a maritime historic title, in spite of the silence observed by the majority of States.

In approaching this problem, a proper distinction must be drawn between two basically different situations:

(i) the protest is made against a practice or a situation which has at this stage already become part and parcel of the international legal order;

(ii) the protesting State wishes to signify its objection to a *new* practice or situation while such practice or situation are still in their formative period and prior to their having become binding rules of international law.

It would appear that the protest of a single State will not be deemed sufficient to invalidate and nullify a practice which has been repeatedly resorted to, and acquiesced in, by other States to such an extent that "the conviction is generally prevalent that that practice has become part of

[1] *ICJ Reports*, 1951, pp. 136–137. (Italics added).

the established legal order."[1] A State which has limited its objections to the raising of protests – without utilizing other available means – will have lost, in the face of international acquiescence, those rights which its protests are intended to preserve.

If, however, a State has vigorously and unambiguously opposed a new practice or situation from its inception and from the moment this practice or situation – otherwise derogatory to the prevailing international legal order – were taking shape, supporting and fortifying its initial objection by all other means and measures legally available on the international plane, then it can be hardly presumed that such a State will forfeit its rights merely as a result of other States' inactivity in the face of a new situation. In such circumstances the presumption of acquiescence, on which the acquisition of an historic title depends, will be rebutted by the facts themselves pointing towards the protesting State's lack of acquiescence in the new situation.

This fundamental distinction seems to account for the divergence of opinion which arose in the *Fisheries* case as to the relevance of the protest of a single State. Throughout the proceedings there seems to have persisted a disagreement between the parties to the dispute as to the legal effects of such a protest. Both parties to the dispute were at one in conceding that a State which has acquired certain rights will not lose them as a result of a change that has occurred in the appropriate rules of international law, provided that the State in question has unambiguously dissociated itself from the new rule from its period of gestation and initiation. However, Great Britain and Norway parted company once they were faced with the question of the acquisition of maritime historic rights. The United Kingdom maintained that any historic title must be regarded as an exception, derogatory to the generally accepted rules of international law, and will only be recognized if it can be proved that this exceptional claim has met with the tacit approval of other States. According to the United Kingdom Reply in the *Fisheries* case, "the protest of a single State... is effective to prevent the establishment of a... title precisely to the extent that the State takes all necessary and reasonable steps to prosecute all available means of redressing the infringement of its rights."[2]

The Norwegian Rejoinder does not basically challenge this concept, but expounds a somewhat different notion of historic titles. In Norway's view, historic titles are not a departure from an otherwise applicable

[1] MacGibbon, 30 *BYIL* (1953), p. 317.
[2] *ICJ, Fisheries case, Pleadings, Oral Arguments, Documents*, vol. II, p. 654.

norm of international law; it is rather the generally accepted rules of international law that should be regarded as a deviation from formerly binding rules of international law. Historic titles are in fact, in the view of the Norwegian Government, the remainders of an earlier legal regime governing the seas, and their validity has not to be based on any modern mode of *acquisition.* They derive their validity from the fact that these rights, although exceptional nowadays, were from time immemorial belonging to the claimant States and have never been relinquished by them. In the words of the Norwegian Rejoinder itself:

Le Gouvernement norvégien ne croit pas nécessaire de discuter la question de savoir dans quelle mesure des parties de haute mer peuvent être incorporées au territoire maritime de l'Etat en vertu d'un titre historique, parce que la question ne se pose pas en l'espèce. Elle ne se poserait que si les règles générales que le Gouvernement britannique prétend applicables à la délimitation du territoire maritime étaient réellement en vigueur. Or, le Gouvernement norvégien a démontré qu'elles ne le sont pas; qu'elles n'ont jamais acquis la consistance de règles coutumières; et qu'elles ne sont certainement pas opposables à la Norvège, celle-ci s'étant toujours refusée, d'une manière non équivoque, à abandonner son système traditionnel pour se soumettre aux règles en question.[1]

However, it is at least debatable whether a single State's constant and unambiguous protest against a novel practice can render this practice invalid indefinitely in respect of the protesting State, in spite of the acceptance of such practice by the rest of the international community. The United Kingdom appears to have been at one with Norway on this point in the *Fisheries* case and asserted that a State signifying its unmistakable disapproval of a new practice from the time of its inception may thereby be left unaffected by the emergence of the new rule and its incorporation into the international legal order. In his pleadings before the International Court of Justice in the course of the oral proceedings in the *Fisheries* case, the then Attorney-General, Sir Frank Soskice, agreed that "a State with established rights does not lose its rights by reason of a change in the customary law, if it has unambiguously and persistently manifested its dissent from the new customary law."[2] It is, however, more controversial whether such an exceptional title is valid *erga omnes*, or only against States which have either expressly assented to, or at least tacitly acquiesced in, it.

Nor can protests coming from different States always be put on the

[1] *Ibid.*, vol. III, pp. 461–462; see also to the same effect *ibid.*, at pp. 442–443.

[2] *Ibid.*, vol. IV, p. 136. See, however, Gidel who maintains that "une seule contestation émanant d'un seul Etat ne saurait infirmer un usage." (Gidel, *op. cit.*, vol. III, p. 634).

same plane. It will be unrealistic to attach the same weight to a protest emanating from a remote country, which is not directly affected by the practice against which the protest is directed, as to a protest lodged by a State which in fact bears the brunt of the departure from the normally applicable rules of international law. Gidel seems to echo these considerations when he argues that

> les contestations ne peuvent... être placées toutes sur le même plan, sans distinction de leur nature, de la situation géographique ou autre de l'Etat dont elles émanent.[1]

Thus, in Gidel's view, which on this point truly reflects the general consensus of opinion, protests should be distinguished according to their nature and the geographical situation of the protesting State in relation to the disputed area. The geographical propinquity of the protesting State, its interests in the area to which the protest makes reference, its position within the international community, these and other factors are of considerable significance in determining what weight should be attached to a protest made by that State. Each protest must be viewed against the background of the situation which gave rise to it and having regard to the specific circumstances of each case. No rigid rule can be laid down in this respect. To illustrate this point, it may be suggested that a protest raised by the main maritime Powers of the world will be sufficient to prevent a new maritime practice from being recognized as a rule of international law, even though the numerical majority of the maritime States may have given their assent to this practice. Conversely, the acquiescence of these comparatively few main maritime Powers may set the seal of legal validity on a new maritime practice, although this practice may have met with the opposition of a considerable number of other States, whose part, however, in shaping the patterns of international maritime behaviour is inferior to that of the great seagoing nations.

50. *Lack of protest does not always indicate acquiescence*

In one of the foregoing sections reference was made to the plea of excusable ignorance, and it was submitted that, in those cases where it can be proved that a genuine and justifiable ignorance was the reason for the absence of objection on the part of the State adversely

[1] Gidel, *op. cit.*

affected by the new practice, the mere fact of silence could not be regarded as proof of acquiescence.[1]

For the sake of completeness it should be added at this stage that there exist other circumstances also in which such inference of acquiescence, based on mere silence, would be improper and unjustified. This applies to all those cases where the settlement of the question in dispute has been expressly and deliberately left open by the contesting parties with a view to preserving their original rights pending their search for a final settlement. This point was clearly brought out in the Dissenting Opinion delivered by Judge Read in the *Fisheries* case, when he pointed out that the 1912 Report of the Norwegian Royal Commission, appointed to investigate the problems relating to Norwegian maritime territorial limits, was meant to constitute a draft *modus vivendi* to be enforced pending the negotiations with Great Britain. Judge Read expressed the view that

> by its very nature, a *modus vivendi* implies the reservation and preservation of the legal positions of both Parties to the controversy. ...I think that the British Government was justified in regarding all aspects of the negotiations... as covered by the basic reservation. The omission to make a specific reservation or objection at this stage cannot possibly be treated as proof of acquiescence in or acceptance of the Norwegian system.[2]

Judge Read's words seem to indicate that, in circumstances where it can be proved that the parties had in fact reserved their rights, the silence of one of them pending a permanent settlement of the dispute cannot be held out against it as amounting to acquiescence in the other party's alleged rights and cannot adversely affect the rights which it had hitherto claimed to exercise as of right.

The same principle seems to underlie also the judgment given by the International Court of Justice in the case concerning the *Rights of United States Nationals in Morocco*, where the Court found that the lack of objection by Morocco to the exercise by the United States of consular jurisdiction over a period of many years could not be regarded as a tacit consent or recognition of the United States' right to do so, because during the relevant period negotiations were going on between the parties with a view to renouncing, amongst other matters, the exceptional capitulatory rights exercised by the United States.[3]

Likewise, in the British Argument in the *Alaskan Boundary* Dispute

[1] See above, section 43.

[2] *ICJ Reports*, 1951, p. 203. (Italics in original).

[3] *ICJ Reports*, 1952, pp. 200–201. See, however, the Dissenting Opinion of four of the judges, in which France's silence was construed as her acquiescence in the American rights.

it was asserted that "it was impossible to say that anything that was done so long as this question remained open ... could come within any possible doctrine of acquiescence."[1]

Apart from such exceptional circumstances, however, it will be proper and permissible to draw an inference of acquiescence from a State's silence, when faced with a situation that imperatively calls for reaction on the part of any State wishing to signify its objection to a new practice or situation.

51. The geographical element in the formation of an historic title

There is little doubt that geographical considerations determine to a very large extent the question whether or not certain acts performed over a given territory may properly be regarded as adequate manifestations of territorial sovereignty over that territory. As will be recalled, the degree of effectiveness displayed by a State discharging its sovereign authority over a given territory varies from case to case according to circumstances, and one of the primary considerations to be taken into account is, no doubt, the geographical factor and the specific geographical character of the area to which an exceptional claim is being laid.

There exists, however, in international law a trend which conceives the "geographical factor" in the formation of an historic title as a concept of much wider scope. It is alleged by the supporters of this concept that, in the growth of an historic title, the geographical factor assumes an independent role, and it is asserted by them that a unique geographical situation, displaying exceptional geographical features, is in itself a sufficient ground for claiming an historic title, regardless of whether or not there exists any evidence of the claimant State having manifested its purported sovereignty in any manner.

It is therefore proposed to turn now to a closer investigation of the function of the geographical factor in the formation of an historic title and to an examination of the question whether a peculiar and exceptional territorial configuration, real or imaginary, can in itself give rise to exceptional territorial rights which would not have otherwise existed.

The acuteness of this problem became evident in the course of the deliberations in the *Fisheries* case. There Norway appears to have

[1] *Proceedings of the Alaskan Boundary Tribunal,* vol. VII, p. 715.

asserted that geographical considerations *per se* – in conjunction with political, economic and security considerations or without them – can sufficiently warrant the establishment of an historic title, irrespective of the existence of any manifestations of the claimant State's sovereignty and of other States' acquiescence in such claims. It was thus contended in the Norwegian Counter-Memorial in the *Fisheries* case that the Norwegian method of delimiting territorial waters was not an arbitrary innovation of Norway, but constituted a natural consequence of the peculiar and unique geographical configuration of the Norwegian coast, which was described in the Counter-Memorial in the following words:

> Il serait difficile de trouver dans le monde entier une région où l'interpénétration de la mer et de la terre fût plus étroite et plus inextricable. Le dessin tourmenté de la bordure continentale et du 'skjaergaard', la multitude des îles, des îlots, des récifs qui parsèment la mer adjacente, donnent à cet ensemble une unité qu'on ne pourrait juridiquement briser qu'en fermant les yeux à la réalité.[1]

For these reasons the Norwegian Counter-Memorial maintained that

> la géographie fait de ces eaux l'accessoire de la terre, les rattache au domaine de la Norvège, les soumet logiquement à la souverainaté du pays.[2]

Here clearly geography was invoked as the source and legal basis of an exceptional territorial title and it was contended that geography as such sufficed for the formation of an historic title.

The Norwegian concept was vigorously challenged in the United Kingdom's Reply, in which the accuracy of both the factual and legal arguments contained in the Norwegian Counter-Memorial was called in question. The United Kingdom Government did not basically contest the relevance of geographical considerations in determining the territorial rights of States. Nor did it dispute the fact that the peculiar geographical configuration of the Norwegian coast entitled Norway to treat substantial areas of sea adjacent to her coast as internal waters, in view of the generally accepted principle that an unusual configuration of the land (e.g. a continuous line of land enclosing the sea, or a line consisting of broken island fringes creating the same effect) may bring bodies of water within the territory of a State. The United Kingdom went as far as to concede that "these particular configurations are relevant in determining whether or not a Norwegian title to areas beyond the limits allowed under the general

[1] *ICJ*, *Fisheries case*, *Pleadings*, *Oral Arguments*, *Documents*, vol. I, p. 571.
[2] *Ibid.*

rules has been established as an exceptional territorial title."[1] Exception was, however, taken to the Norwegian contention, according to which a particular geographical configuration will of itself be sufficient to serve as the basis and legal foundation of an historic title, irrespective of any manifestations of authority by the claimant State and other States' acquiescence in such an exceptional claim. The scope and function of the geographical factor, in the United Kingdom's submission, is not to *found* an historic title, but to strengthen, alongside other considerations of equal importance, the presumption of other States' acquiescence in such an exceptional claim. Thus, the geographical factor also is relevant precisely to the extent to which an inference of such acquiescence may be drawn from it. The more unusual and peculiar the geographical configuration – the stronger the presumption of such an acquiescence. In the words of the United Kingdom Reply:

An exceptional title can only be founded on the acquiescence of other States and it is where the configuration of the land tends to enclose areas of sea that the acquiescence of other States in a larger claim may more readily be inferred from the absence of any reaction to the claim.[2]

The Court in its judgment did refer to the unusual geographical configuration of the Norwegian coast as one of the reasons prompting it to decide the case in favour of Norway. It is, however, not clear what exactly was the role assigned by the Court to the geographical factor in the formation of an historic title and how heavily it weighed with the Court in arriving at its final conclusions. The Court commented on the geographical peculiarities of the Norwegian coast in the following words:

Another fundamental consideration, of particular importance in this case, is the more or less close relationship existing between certain sea areas and the land formations which divide or surround them. The real question raised in the choice of base-lines is in effect whether certain areas lying within these lines are sufficiently closely linked to the land domain to be subject to the regime of internal waters. This idea, which is at the basis of the determination of the rules relating to bays, should be liberally applied in the case of a coast, the geographical configuration of which is as unusual as that of Norway.[3]

From the above-quoted passage of the Court's judgment it seems to emerge that the Court relied upon the geographical factor as only *one*

[1] *Ibid.*, vol. II, p. 660.
[2] *Ibid.*
[3] *ICJ Reports*, 1951, p. 133.

of the considerations meant to strengthen the presumption of acquiescence on the part of other States in Norway's exceptional claim. This becomes abundantly clear in view of the fact that, in a later passage of the judgment, the Court poses the question – which is the really decisive one from the legal point of view – "whether the application of the Norwegian system encountered any opposition from foreign States."[1] It is not unreasonable to assume that the Court would not have proceeded to the investigation of this matter had it adopted the Norwegian contention, according to which the geographical configuration in itself – without other States' acquiescence – might suffice for the acquisition of an historic title.

Thus, it may safely be maintained that geographical considerations – alongside a variety of other considerations – may influence other States' attitude in determining whether and to what extent they ought to acquiesce in an exceptional claim; however, it is not the particular geographical configuration *per se*, but the acquiescence of other States, that sets the seal of legal validity on such a claim.

No excessive significance should therefore be attached to the geographical factor in assessing the value of claims put up by different States. In the nature of things, States tend to overemphasize the uniqueness of their geographical configuration in order to justify exceptional claims going beyond the generally accepted rules of international law. A striking illustration of this tendency is the line of argument adopted by Norway in the *Fisheries* case, which has already been referred to in this section; throughout her pleadings Norway endeavoured to create the impression that the geographical configuration of the Norwegian coast was unique to such an extent that the generally applicable rules relating to the delimitation of territorial waters could not be invoked in respect of the Norwegian coast, which, owing to its alleged peculiarities, merited the peculiar "Norwegian system" of delimitation. As has already been shown above, the majority judgment of the Court did not justify the Norwegian method by relying on the exceptional geographical configuration of the Norwegian coast, but preferred to rely on the acquiescence and toleration of the international community. The Norwegian line of argument did, however, evoke the vigorous opposition of the two dissenting judges, both of whom had some unusually strong words for the rejection of the Norwegian contention. Judge McNair expressed the view that

[1] *Ibid.*, p. 138.

Norway has no monopoly of indentations or even of skerries.... There are many countries in the world possessing areas of heavily indented coast-line.... The coast of Canada is heavily indented in almost every part. Nearly the whole of the west coast of Scotland and much of the west coast of Northern Ireland is heavily indented and bears much resemblance to the Norwegian coast.[1]

Judge Read in his Dissenting Opinion echoes the same view, adding a warning which, it is felt, is well worth being reproduced here word for word:

There could be no greater danger to the structure of international law than to disregard the general rules of positive law and to base a decision on the real or imaginary exceptional character or uniqueness of the case under consideration.[2]

The geographical factor in the formation of an historic title should not be confounded with the concept of contiguity which, in the not too distant past, used to be regarded as a valid title to territory. The doctrine of contiguity was usually invoked with regard to islands close to the shores of the mainland; the littoral State would in such cases assert that the islands too formed part of its territory by virtue of their geographical proximity. The theory of contiguity has also been invoked on occasions to support territorial claims over groups of islands which – so the argument runs – comprise one unit and the fate of the main island or islands of such a group should therefore determine that of the rest.

The concept of acquiring a territorial title by means of geographical contiguity has, however, been discarded in recent times. Judge Huber, in the *Island of Palmas* Arbitration, categorically denied the existence of such a rule in contemporary international law, stating that

it is impossible to show the existence of a rule of positive international law to the effect that islands situated outside territorial waters should belong to a State from the mere fact that its territory forms the *terra firma* (nearest continent or island of considerable size). Not only would it seem that there are no precedents sufficiently frequent and sufficiently precise in their bearing to establish such a rule of international law, but the alleged principle itself is by its very nature so uncertain and contested that even Governments of the same State have on different occasions maintained contradictory opinions as to its soundness. ... This principle... is... lacking in precision and would in its application lead to arbitrary results.[3]

Commenting further on the question of contiguity with regard to groups of islands (or archipelagoes), Judge Huber pointed out that, while the act of first taking possession can hardly extend to every

[1] *Ibid.*, p. 169.
[2] *Ibid.*, p. 193.
[3] *UNRIAA*, vol. II, pp. 854–855. (Italics in original).

portion of territory, the display of sovereignty as a continuous and prolonged manifestation must make itself felt through the whole territory, and the exercise of authority over certain portions would of itself not warrant a claim to the whole territory on the basis of contiguity.[1]

In rejecting the American claim, which was founded, *inter alia*, on a title arising out of contiguity, the arbitrator held that "the title of contiguity, understood as a basis of territorial sovereignty, has no foundation in international law."[2]

In a paper read in 1950 before the Grotius Society, Waldock took the view that these doctrines of contiguity, continuity or unity of territory "were seen to be merely pretexts for attempts to preempt the sovereignty of large areas which the States concerned were not yet in a position to acquire by effective occupation. ... Geographical proximity and other geographical considerations certainly have some relevance in determining the precise limits covered by an effective occupation. ... But contiguity is not a title."[3]

52. *The role of "legitimate interests" in the formation of an historic title*

Closely resembling the concept which attaches primary importance to the geographical element in the formation of an historic title is the doctrine of "legitimate interests" (or "vital interests"). According to this theory, the "legitimate" interests of the claimant State should be reckoned as a sufficient basis for the acquisition of an exceptional territorial title. The supporters of this concept assert that a State may acquire a valid title to territory solely on the ground that the acquisition of such exceptional territorial rights is deemed essential by the claimant State for safeguarding its legitimate interests. Here again, as in the case of exceptional territorial claims based on an allegedly unique and unusual geographical configuration, one is faced with the difficulty that it will invariably be the claimant State itself which will

[1] *Ibid.*, p. 855.

[2] *Ibid.*, p. 869. As to the application to this notion to the doctrine of the continental shelf, see below, chapter VI, section 75.

[3] Waldock, "The Legal Basis of Claims to the Continental Shelf," in *Grotius Transactions*, vol. 36 (1950), p. 115, at p. 120. As to the application of this principle to the "sector claims" relating to the territories bordering on Polar districts, see Waldock, 25 *BYIL* (1948), pp. 337–346, where this writer asserts that, inasmuch as these claims are based on notions of "proximity" or "contiguity," they have no validity in law, because "proximity has been not... a legal principle independent of effective occupation but... a fact indicating the extent of an effective occupation." (*Ibid.*, p. 344). For a discussion of the meaning of the concept of contiguity see also Jennings, *op. cit.*, pp. 74–76.

determine – unilaterally and arbitrarily – the nature and extent of its "legitimate" interests. This situation is, of course, symptomatic of the present structure of international society and of the immense diversity of international situations, which render the laying down of universally applicable standards in this field a formidable and virtually insurmountable task. It is not denied that the recognized interests of a State, its paramount interests in the field of economy, national defence etc., do in fact play – and rightly so – an important role in the considerations of other States who are confronted with the question whether or not to recognize an exceptional territorial claim, raised by a member of the international society. But, as in the case of the geographical factor, here again, it is not the "legitimate interests" *per se*, as interpreted by the claimant State, but the *recognition* of these interests by other States and their acquiescence in the exceptional claim that sanction and validate such a claim from the legal viewpoint.

The close relationship existing between the geographical factor and the "legitimate interests" springs from the fact that it is usually a particular geographical configuration which lies at the root of particular State interests, such as the interests of national economy and self-defence. A State with an unusual geographical configuration like that of Norway will find more easily an attentive ear when it asserts that, because of its traditional dependence on fishing as the main source of livelihood for a fairly high percentage of its population, its primordial interests may be adversely affected by the application to its coasts of the general rules of customary international law regulating the regime of territorial waters.

Similarly, a State, the territory of which encloses a bay almost completely, as is the case with Chesapeake Bay, which is almost entirely surrounded by United States territory, will in all likelihood have the approval of foreign States in its assertion that its interests may be severely prejudiced by treating such a bay as part of the high seas.

It is, however, one thing to claim that "legitimate interests" of themselves can sanction an exceptional territorial claim going beyond what is generally accepted to be international law; it is quite a different thing to maintain that "legitimate interests" may and should be taken into account in assessing the validity of a State's exceptional claim, not as the legal basis for such an exceptional claim, but as evidence for the degree of recognition that such a claim has been granted by the international community. For it is the acceptance of such claims by the members of the international society that transforms a mere national pretension into an historic title valid under international law.

A conspicuous body of States – among which the countries of the Latin American continent are prominent – have in recent decades advanced the claim that "vital" interests should be regarded as a sufficient ground for the recognition by the international community of exceptional territorial claims, in derogation of the normally applicable rules of international law. This phenomenon is explained by the fact that these comparatively "new" States – most of which came into existence only in the nineteenth century – cannot invoke history – or, in other words, a practice sanctioned by the passage of time – in support of their exceptional territorial claims. Consequently, these States find themselves at a disadvantage when compared with the "old" European States, which are usually capable of tracing back their political history for many centuries. McDougal and Burke, discussing the problem of State claims to "vital bays," rightly point out that

> the historic bay concept has always been connected with past events. By defenition it had no reference at all to emerging needs and aspirations.... It is for this reason that some states and commentators have suggested a category of "vital bays" by which new claims would be... honored, much as is the case of historic assertion. The point urged in these suggestions, of course, is that the factors which led to the claims protected by the historic bays concept continue to operate and that new claims ought to be permitted as in the past.[1]

The South American concept, assigning to "vital" interests a major role in the formation of an historic title, was already foreshadowed in the Dissenting Opinion of Drago in the *North Atlantic Fisheries* Arbitration of 1910 between Great Britain and the United States, where he observed that certain bays "undoubtedly belong to the littoral country,... when such country has asserted its sovereignty over them, and particular circumstances such as geographical configuration, immemorial usage and *above all, the requirements of self-defense*, justify such a pretension."[2]

This passage from Judge Drago's Dissenting Opinion, and in particular the italicized portion thereof, have been frequently referred to as indicating a recognition on his part of the "vital interests" of the claimant State as the legal basis for an historic title. It would appear, however, that a closer perusal of Judge Drago's words does not warrant

[1] McDougal and Burke, *op. cit.*, pp. 358–359.

[2] *UNRIAA*, vol. XI, p. 206; Scott, *Hague Court Reports*, 1st series, 1916, pp. 199–200. (Italics added).

such a sweeping conclusion, since he apparently did not consider the interests of self-defence of themselves as justifying an exceptional title, although he was prepared to accord to them, among the factors intrumental in the shaping of an historic title, a place ranking higher than geographical configuration or immemorial usage. What the supporters of the theory of "legitimate interests" are only too apt to overlook is the fact that, according to Drago, such "vital interests" have any value only in conjunction with the assertion of sovereignty by the claimant State, which in the long run would prove impossible without the acquiescence of other States.

That Drago had no intention of challenging the necessity of other States' acquiescence in an exceptional claim, as a condition and prerequisite for such claim to develop and ripen into an exceptional right, clearly emerges from an article written by him in 1912, where he commented on the *North Atlantic Fisheries* Arbitration of 1910. There Drago elaborated on the concept of historic bays, defining them as "une catégorie spéciale et distincte, dont la propriété appartient aux pays qui les entourent."[1] He further maintained that the littoral States "lorsqu'ils ont procédé à l'affirmation de leur souveraineté, en acquièrent la possession et les incorporent à leur domaine, *du consentement des autres nations.*"[2]

Thus, it is evident that, according to Drago too, the positive attitude of other States towards the building up of an exceptional title cannot be dispensed with. This, however, has not prevented certain South American jurists from carrying the idea further and from insisting on the self-determined "vital necessity" of a State being recognized as a sufficient ground for the acquisition of an exceptional territorial title. In a paper read before the 31st Conference of the International Law Association held in Buenos Aires in 1922, Captain Segundo Storni (the then Director of the Buenos Aires Naval Academy) maintained that the right of the littoral State to a marginal belt of water, over which it was entitled to exercise rights of jurisdiction, was founded on the vital needs of the State, which he enumerated as being as follows:

(a) Les nécessités de la défense;
(b) Les nécessités et les obligations de la neutralité;
(c) Les nécessités de la surveillance, de la police, du balisage, du dragage, de la conservation des canaux, etc.[3]

[1] 19 *RGDIP* (1912), p. 5, at p. 37.
[2] *Ibid.* (Italics added).
[3] International Law Association, *Report of the 31st Conference*, Buenos Aires, 1922, vol. II, p. 95.

Turning to the question of historic waters, Captain Storni suggested that estuaries, bays, gulfs and parts of the marginal sea in general be treated as being within the territorial waters of the littoral State, if "un usage continu et séculaire aura consacré sa juridiction, ou qui, dans le cas où les précédents n'existeraient pas, seraient d'une nécessité inéluctable."[1]

Captain Storni also took the view that this suggestion properly fitted into "la doctrine des 'baies historiques' selon la manière dont cet ancien principe fut formulé par le docteur Drago,"[2] and that it was capable of meeting the requirements of "les nations nouvelles (américaines par exemple) dont beaucoup parmi elles possèdent des côtes étendues, encore peu peuplées, et chez lesquelles on ne peut présenter les antécédents d'un domaine séculaire comme chez les nations qui compte mille années d'existence ou davantage."[3]

However, as has already been shown, Drago's Dissenting Opinion – if properly interpreted – does not lend itself to Captain Storni's concept of historic titles. Notwithstanding this fact, the concept of "vital interests" was further canvassed by some States at the 1930 Hague Codification Conference. During the discussion, which took place in the Second Committee of the Conference on Basis of Discussions No. 8, Senhor Magalhães, representing Portugal, suggested that the definition of historic bays should be worded in such a manner as to include bays which are recognized as being absolutely necessary for the State in question to guarantee its defence and neutrality and to ensure the navigation and maritime police services.[4] In support of his proposal, Senhor Magalhães argued that

> if certain States have essential needs, I consider that those needs are as worthy of respect as usage itself, or even more so. Needs are imposed by modern social conditions, and if we respect age-long and immemorial usage which is the outcome of the needs experienced by States in long past times, why should we not respect the needs which modern life, with all its improvements and its demands imposes upon States?[5]

[1] *Ibid.*, p. 98. The definition of what Captain Storni considered as "nécessité" has been quoted above.

[2] *Ibid.*

[3] *Ibid.*, pp. 98–99. See to the same effect McDougal and Burke, *op. cit.*, pp. 340–341, where the authors state: "The most difficult problem concerning historic title to bays arises because of the emergence of new states, having no past as independent political entities and therefore presumably unable to escape the confines of allegedly restrictive rules concerning bays by relying on historic title, as have the older states.... States having particular needs should be permitted to create, under certain conditions, larger areas of internal waters than are generally needed by others and should not be forced to rely on an escape valve, not easily open to them in the form of historic title."

[4] *Ser. L.o.N.P.* 1930, V. 16, p. 107.

[5] *Ibid.*, p. 106.

This argument of Senhor Magalhães – which concisely summarizes the attitude taken up by the supporters of the "legitimate interests" concept – appears to be fallacious, inasmuch as it tends to overlook the cardinal feature of the historic title, namely, the fact that it is not historicity or the time element as such that lends to such a title the seal of legal validity, but that such title rests rather on the element of other States' recognition of the exceptional claim. True, this recognition usually takes the form of tacit acquiescence, as evidenced by the passage of time. But the Portuguese argument certainly misrepresents the concept of historic titles in international law when it attaches to the time element more than probative value. Such being the legal construction of the historic title, it may readily be admitted that the consent of other States to the acquisition of an exceptional territorial title may be the outcome of a variety of considerations, among which one may mention the conviction of the international community that the security or economic interests of a given State justify acquiescence in such a claim. In such circumstances an historic title may come into being, even if the period of time during which it developed cannot be measured in centuries or even decades, thus depriving the historic title of the historic element properly so called. But the manner in which this concept has been described by Senhor Magalhães virtually amounts to the complete rejection of the notion of historic titles and the substitution for it of what may properly be termed "vital titles." The adoption of such a principle and its introduction into international law would only increase the already prevailing chaotic conditions in this field of law, and would, in fact, be tantamount to creating a state of things where every State would be authorized to determine in an arbitrary manner what should be regarded as its "vital interests." It would thus enable the State in question to fix unilaterally the territorial limits of its sovereignty. The practical results of such an approach are not far to seek. Gidel, commenting on this aspect of the problem, issued a clear and unequivocal warning when, referring to the notion of "vital bays," as distinct from "historic bays" proper, he said:

> Ce seraient des prétentions arbitraires ... qui seraient fondées purement et simplement sur des besoins ou des intérêts de l'Etat riverain, susceptibles d'être invoquées par d'autres Etats riverains de côtes d'une configuration géographique ou hydrographique différente.[1]

Writing in 1952, Bourquin expressed the view that, if the territoriality of a bay is to be determined in the light of all the circum-

[1] Gidel, *op. cit.*, vol. III, p. 635.

stances which surround it, then clearly the vital interests of the coastal State must also be taken into account.[1] He admitted, however, that Captain Storni's concept, as understood and interpreted by the Portuguese Government during the Hague Codification Conference, suffered from a considerable oversimplification of the issues involved, since it raised one of the factors, which are likely to determine the territorial status of a given body of water, above all other factors, thus unduly ignoring various other elements, which should also be reckoned with in establishing the legal status of a given maritime area. He went on to say that "vital interests," however widely and liberally interpreted, had no place in the theory of "historic titles," since, if it is solely the vital interests of the claimant State on which an exceptional territorial title rests, then the historic element, which, as the term itself indicates, is the very pillar of the historic title, will be lacking altogether.[2]

This approach by Bourquin is not entirely compatible with the attitude he had taken up a short time before the publication of his article, while pleading on behalf of Norway in the *Fisheries* case. There he had suggested that the regime applied to territorial waters ought to be "réaliste, qu'elle respecte les besoins légitimes des Etats et la diversité des situations particulières."[3] Sir Frank Soskice, in his statement on behalf of the United Kingdom, challenged the Norwegian contention – rightly, it is believed – by pointing out that "if a State has the right to fix its maritime territory by reference to what it conceives to be its legitimate interest and there is no other test of the legitimacy of these interests, why should the historic nature of a claim have any special importance?"[4]

It is certainly a matter for regret that the Court in its judgment did not indicate in a clear-cut manner which of the two conflicting concepts it favoured. On the one hand, there are to be found in the judgment passages which *prima facie* appear to approve of the Norwegian contention. Thus, for instance, the Court held:

> In these barren regions [of Norway] the inhabitants of the coastal zone derive their livelihood essentially from fishing.[5]

[1] Bourquin, "Les baies historiques," *Mélanges Sauser-Hall*, 1952, p. 38 *et seq.*, at p. 51.

[2] *Ibid.* See to the same effect McDougal and Burke, *op cit.*, p. 359, where they assert that "it is not intended... to discuss the concept of historic bays as if it were useful for recognizing claims based upon the alleged 'vital interests' of the coastal state rather than upon the passage of time."

[3] *ICJ, Fisheries case, Pleadings, Oral Arguments, Documents*, vol. IV, p. 512.

[4] *Ibid.*, p. 122.

[5] *ICJ Reports*, 1951, p. 128.

And again:

There is one consideration not to be overlooked ...: that of certain economic interests peculiar to a region, the reality and importance of which are clearly evidenced by long usage.[1]

On the other hand, in summing up the legal considerations which prompted it to decide the case in favour of Norway, the Court did not mention at all the unusual circumstances referred to by Norway, but placed particular emphasis on the toleration by foreign States of the Norwegian practice, without any formal challenge or protest.[2]

Thus, it would appear that the Court's reference to the peculiar economic interests of the local population is but one of the considerations which were taken into account by the Court in assessing Norway's claim. It is also worth noting that, in evaluating the scope of the economic factor in the formation of Norway's exceptional rights, the Court deemed it appropriate to add that these economic interests "are clearly evidenced by long usage,"[3] a pronouncement virtually amounting to introducing the element of acquiescence in disguise, since it is mainly through the efflux of time that acquiescence normally finds its expression.

Whereas the wording of the majority judgment is on this point somewhat nebulous, Judge McNair, in his Dissenting Opinion, made no bones of his opposition to the Norwegian concept. In the strongest possible terms he dissociated himself from the proposition which invoked Norway's economic interests as justifying, from the legal point of view, the Norwegian system of delimitation. Judge McNair observed that he was wholly unable to reconcile the Norwegian Decree of 1935 with the notion of territorial waters prevailing in international law. He explained this conclusion, *inter alia*, by the fact that

the delimitation of territorial waters by the Decree of 1935 is inspired, amongst other factors, by the policy of protecting the economic and other social interests of the coastal State,[4]

these being factors which, in his opinion, could not be taken into account in international law in delimiting territorial waters.

The *Fisheries* case, which, no doubt, constitutes one of the leading cases in international jurisprudence, is, however, by no means the first decision in which an international tribunal was prepared to

[1] *Ibid.*, p. 133.
[2] *Ibid.*, pp. 138–139.
[3] *Ibid.*, p. 133.
[4] *Ibid.*, p. 171.

consider the peculiar economic interests of a littoral State, in assessing its claim to an exceptional title which would not accrue to it without a departure from general international law. Thus, in the *North Atlantic Fisheries* Arbitration between Great Britain and the United States the tribunal, defining the term "bay," remarked that such a definition should take into account

all the individual circumstances which for any one of the different bays are to be appreciated, ... *the possibility and the necessity of its being defended by the State in whose territory it is indented; the special value which it has for the industry of the inhabitants of its shores;* ... and other circumstances not possible to enumerate in general.[1]

Similarly, in the *Gulf of Fonseca* case the now-defunct Central American Court of Justice laid down the rule that

in order to fix the international legal status of the Gulf of Fonseca it is necessary to specify the characteristics proper thereto from the threefold point of view of history, geography and the vital interests of the surrounding States.[2]

Among the factors to which the Court explicitly referred as evidence for the existence of such vital interests of the littoral States, there may be mentioned the construction of a railway by Honduras, destined to develop the rich and extensive regions of the country and to promote the inter-oceanic traffic, a railroad under the control of El Salvador, a project concerning the prolongation of the Chinandega railroad to a point on the Real Estuary on the Gulf of Fonseca, and the establishment of a free port decreed by the Salvadorean Government on Meanguera Island. The Court also pointed out that the Gulf of Fonseca was surrounded by extensive departments of the three riparian States, was destined to play an important role in their commercial, industrial and agricultural development, and must therefore be regarded as their lifeline of imports and exports.[3] Having regard to the geographical configuration of the gulf, the Court remarked that its strategic situation was so advantageous that "the riparian States can defend their great interests therein and provide for the defence of their independence and sovereignty."[4]

True, the Court fully recognized the "vital interests" of the riparian States in assessing the legal status of the gulf; at the same time it must, however, be borne in mind that the Court deduced the legal validity of the alleged exceptional status of the gulf from the fact that "a

[1] *UNRIAA*, vol. XI, p. 199; Scott, *Hague Court Reports*, 1st series, 1916, p. 187. (Italics added).

[2] 11 *AJIL* (1917), p. 700.

[3] *Ibid.*, pp. 704–705.

[4] *Ibid.*, p. 705.

secular possession such as that of the Gulf [of Fonseca] could only have been maintained by the acquiescence of the family of nations."[1]

The decisions of international tribunals referred to above appear to have in common a readiness to take into account the affected States' particular interests and needs, as far as these needs have been (at least tacitly) recognized by the international community. There is, however, no indication whatsoever that the tribunals faced with this problem ever regarded the "vital interests" of the claimant States as justifying in themselves an exceptional claim and as the legal basis for the formation of an exceptional territorial title. It is only through the interdependence and combination of a great variety of factors, historic, geographic, economic, strategic etc. – that the acquiescence of foreign Powers in such an exceptional claim may reasonably be inferred. It is this legal presumption – always open to rebuttal – on which the legal validity of an exceptional title rests.

Thus, the "vital interests" of the claimant State assume the role of one of the contributory evidentiary elements in the establishment of an historic title. The probative value of the "legitimate interests," as displayed in the practice of States, is of considerable scope indeed. This is clearly evidenced in that passage of the judgment delivered by the International Court of Justice in the *Fisheries* case, where the Court, with reference to the baselines drawn across the Lopphavet, observed that

> the historical data produced in support of... [the Norwegian] contention ... lend some weight to the idea of the survival of traditional rights reserved to the inhabitants... over fishing grounds.[2]

The Court held that "such rights, founded on the vital needs of the population and attested by very ancient and peaceful usage, may legitimately be taken into account in drawing a line which, moreover, appears to the Court to have been kept within the bounds of what is moderate and reasonable."[3]

It is therefore evident that the "vital needs" *per se* would not have been regarded by the Court as a sufficient justification for the application of the Norwegian method of delimitation, had it not been "attested by a very ancient and peaceful usage," i.e. the acquiescence of the international community. It has therefore been rightly observed that "a country could not, merely by reason of the alleged economic

[1] *Ibid.*, p. 700.
[2] *ICJ Reports*, 1951, p. 142.
[3] *Ibid.*

needs of some part of its population, put forward a *legal* claim to delimit its waters in a manner not otherwise permitted by international law."[1] The invocation of the "vital needs" of a given State as the root of its legal rights would inevitably lead to the abandonment of any objective legal criterion as the basis for legal rights, a danger of which Judge McNair, in his Dissenting Opinion in the *Fisheries* case, warned in the following words:

> In my opinion the manipulation of the limits of territorial waters for the purpose of protecting economic and other social interests has no justification in law; ... the approbation of such a practice would have a dangerous tendency in that it would encourage States to adopt a subjective appreciation of their rights instead of conforming to a common international standard.[2]

It would be only proper to add that, according to a classification made by Sir Gerald Fitzmaurice, vital needs and exceptional necessities, while not constituting in themselves the source of any legal right, may none the less have a threefold effect:

Firstly, they serve as "evidence of a genuine need on the part of a State to depart from, or to be recognized as entitled to, a special application of the normal rule, ... the basis on which other States can condone such departure or special application."[3] The exceptional territorial title that will eventually emerge will, however, be based not on the State's exceptional needs, but on its having succeeded in building up an exceptional title, in accordance with the applicable rules of international law.

Secondly, they are "the basis of a change in the law..., the factual basis of, or motive for, a new practice which the generality of States will come to regard themselves as entitled, and bound, to observe; thus leading to the development of a new rule of customary law."[4] Sir Gerald points out that, seen from this aspect also, it is not the exceptional circumstances as such that lend legal validity to such a claim, but it is rather the new rule, if and when it has emerged, that constitutes the basis of the newly acquired exceptional right.

Thirdly, exceptional circumstances may also provide evidence of reasonableness. International tribunals are prone to attach a good deal of importance to the question whether a given conduct or course

[1] Fitzmaurice, 31 *BYIL* (1954), p. 402. (Italics in original).
[2] *ICJ Reports*, 1951, p. 169. See, however, Judge Alvarez' Individual Opinion, where he observed that "in fixing the breadth of its territorial sea, the State must indicate the reasons, geographic, economic, etc., which provide the justification therefor." (*Ibid.*, p. 150).
[3] Fitzmaurice, 92 *Hague Recueil* (1957), vol. II, p. 115.
[4] *Ibid.*, p. 116.

of action may be regarded as reasonable. "In such cases, the existence of special interests or particular circumstances of, for instance, an economic, social or geographical character may well affect ... the reasonableness of the action taken."[1] Sir Gerald draws attention to the conclusion reached by the International Court of Justice in the *Fisheries* case, according to which, having regard to the exceptional configuration of the Norwegian coast, the manner in which Norway delimited her territorial waters was not unreasonable.[2] Thus, the question of the validity of the Norwegian claim turned to a large extent on the reasonableness of the Norwegian measures, which, in the first place, depended heavily on the exceptional geographical configuration of the Norwegian coast.[3]

The matter may fittingly be summed up by saying that economic considerations and exceptional circumstances in general cannot of themselves constitute the basis of any legal right, but they have at the same time a decisive importance in evaluating the question as to whether or not an exceptional title came into existence. Thus, their value rests completely in the sphere of evidence and they cannot endow a State with a new substantive right.

53. *The role of the time element in the formation of an historic title*

It was submitted elsewhere[4] that the role and primary function of the time factor in the formation of an exceptional territorial title in international law is to raise a presumption of acceptance of the new and exceptional situation on the part of the affected States. The efflux of time, it was asserted, is necessary because the circumstances from which such an acceptance might be inferred – and to the detailed analysis of which the present chapter has been devoted – cannot arise unless a certain period of time had elapsed. The passage of time, coupled with an absence of protest on the part of the States affected, or likely to be affected, by the exceptional claim, serve to strengthen this presumption of acquiescence underlying the historic title.

Having regard to the manifold aspects of the manifestations of an historic claim, as described above in detail, it now becomes abundantly clear that what is usually referred to as the "historic element" or "time factor" in the establishment of an historic title is no more than the

[1] *Ibid.*

[2] *ICJ Reports*, 1951, pp. 133 and 142.

[3] The adoption of the test of reasonableness has met with the criticism of Waldock on account of its subjectiveness. (See Waldock, 28 *BYIL* (1951), p. 150).

[4] See above, section 22.

sum total of all those considerations which form the components of an historic claim and its contributory factors, all of which would in themselves be rather meaningless if they were not sanctioned by the efflux of time. It is the main function of the time element in the formation of an historic title to provide the framework necessary for the *consolidation* of these diverse and manifold factors, in proportion to their intensity and frequency. "Long usage" – the emphasis being now on the qualifying adjective "long" – is therefore the concise expression of the sum total of interests and relations, the existence of which entitle the international lawyer to raise a presumption that an exceptional territorial title has indeed come into being. According to de Visscher, it is these interests and relations – varied as they are from case to case – and not the mere efflux of time – immaterial in itself in international law – which are taken into account when considering the question whether or not such an historic title has been consolidated.[1] De Visscher's concept of the role and function of an historic title appears to have been influenced by a well-known and much-quoted passage of the judgment delivered by the International Court of Justice in the *Fisheries* case, where the Court seems to have alluded to the theory which conceives the "historic title" as the product of an "historical consolidation." Commenting on the emergence of a Norwegian maritime historic title, the Court observed, *inter alia*, that the Norwegian system of fixing the baselines of Norway's territorial sea had acquired legal validity owing to "an *historical consolidation* which would make it enforceable as against all States."[2]

From the passage in which the above-quoted portion occurs, it emerges that Norway's "historical consolidation" of an exceptional territorial title is based on her effective application of a well-defined and uniform system, in the face of which other States did not raise any objection. Thus, "historical consolidation" embraces both the manifestations of sovereignty by the claimant State and a tacit acquiescence on the part of the international community. The qualifying adjective "historical" clearly brings out the function of the time factor in the process of the consolidation of an exceptional title. It relegates history to the rank of a probative element, thus incorporating this factor among the various considerations which come into play in the establishment of an historic title.

In an article published in 1955, Johnson dwelt upon some of the

[1] De Visscher, *op. cit.*, p. 200.
[2] *ICJ Reports*, 1951, p. 138. (Italics added).

advantages that might be derived from the introduction of the notion of consolidation and its adoption as a starting-point for a better understanding of the theory of historic titles. One of the cardinal virtues of this notion is, he asserts, that, in addition to its being concerned with the mode of *acquiring* a title to territory, it displays interest also in the manner in which such a title has been *maintained*. The notion of consolidation, he claims, takes account of the fact that the maintenance of a valid legal title is a process of complex character, frequently spread over a long period of time. By employing the notion of "historical consolidation," he goes on to say, it would be possible "to present the law relating to territory on a new basis ... [which] would stress the close relation between the *acquisition* and the *maintenance* of titles,"[1] thus avoiding "the ambiguities surrounding the present doctrine of acquisitive prescription."[2] By introducing the term "consolidation," the historical aspect of the process and its primary dependence on a great and multiple variety of factors – the operation of which is made possible only within the framework of time – is more clearly brought into light.

Although the term "consolidation" does not occur in the award rendered in the *Island of Palmas* Arbitration, it may safely be assumed that the decision rendered by Judge Huber in that case practically rested on that concept and that the function of time was merely subsidiary in that it enabled the combined operation of all those factors, which in their entirety justified an inference of acquiescence on the part of Spain in the Netherlands' exceptional claim. Thus, for instance, the arbitrator asserts that, if the alleged title to territory is not based on one of the commonly accepted titles, like cession, conquest, occupation etc., but is based merely on the fact of display of actual sovereignty, "it cannot be sufficient to establish the title by which territorial sovereignty was validly acquired at a certain moment; it must also be shown that the territorial sovereignty has continued to exist."[3] Then follows the well-known phrase in which the arbitrator held that "continuous and peaceful display of territorial sovereignty ... is as good as a title."[4]

This statement, which has since been recognized as an authentic presentation of the state of affairs prevailing in international law,

[1] Johnson, "Consolidation as a Root of Title in International Law," *Cam bridge Law Journa* (1955), p. 215 *et seq.*, at p. 225. (Italics in original).
[2] *Ibid.*
[3] *UNRIAA*, vol. II, p. 839.
[4] *Ibid.*

would, however, be completely deprived of any meaning if the efflux of a rather considerable period of time – varying, of course, according to circumstances – were not to be presupposed. For continuity and peacefulness – these very corner-stones of an historic title – can manifest themselves only through the operation, and within the framework, of time. The length of time required for the formation of an historic title is thus relevant precisely to the extent to which it helps to enhance the presumption of continuity (or effectiveness) and peacefulness (or acquiescence).

The requirement for the effective *maintenance* of an already acquired title – as distinct from its effective *acquisition* – has sometimes met with disapproval on the ground that it is liable to create instability and uncertainty in the international sphere, since "every state would constantly be under the necessity of examining its title to each portion of its territory in order to determine whether a change in the law had necessitated, as it were, a reacquisition. If such a principle were applied to private law and private titles, the result would be chaos. Title insurance would be an impossibility."[1]

Thus, in the cases where the States affected by the practice alleged to have created certain exceptional rights have neither expressly nor by their conduct implied any recognition or consent of such a practice, it is only the historic element, or time factor, which supplies the necessary presumption of passive acquiescence arising out of the practice in question. This presumption is based on the effective manifestation of such practice for a period of time, the length of which is sufficient to raise an inference of acquiescence, provided that no objection to this practice has been forthcoming.

Thus, the time factor is in itself completely irrelevant from the legal point of view and neither creates nor determines any substantive legal rights. It is at the same time of immense evidentiary value, making up for the lack of evidence of recognition by the affected States of the practice in question. It is the time element which most forcefully raises the presumption of acquiescence, to be inferred from an alleged exercise of authority by the claimant State, in the face of which the adversely affected State refrained from formulating the objection which would have been reasonably expected from it, had it wished to signify its disapproval of the new practice.

The legal basis for the validation of an exceptional right remains, however, neither the exercise of authority, nor the efflux of time, but

[1] Jessup, "The Palmas Island Arbitration," 22 *AJIL* (1928), p. 735 *et seq.*, at p. 740.

the acquiescence of the affected States. Such acquiescence is inferred from the general circumstances surrounding the new territorial situation, which consolidate the new exceptional right and imbue it with legal validity.

This indeed seems to be the meaning of the above-quoted passage of the judgment rendered by the International Court of Justice in the *Fisheries* case, where the Court held that the promulgation by Norway of the various Decrees relating to the delimitation of her territorial waters, and the application without any opposition of these rules of delimitation for a period of over sixty years, should be considered "the basis of an historical consolidation" of the Norwegian system. The role assigned to the time factor in the formation of an historic right is perhaps even more clearly emphasized in another passage of the judgment where the Court observed that "in respect of a situation which could only be *strengthened by the passage of time*, the United Kingdom Government refrained from formulating reservations."[1]

It is worth mentioning that Judge McNair in his Dissenting Opinion, though disagreeing with the majority as to its final conclusions, approached the problems attendant upon the acquisition of an historic title from a similar angle when he stated that, in his opinion, the Government of the United Kingdom were not aware of the application by Norway of the "Norwegian system" of delimitation "before this dispute began in 1906 or 1908 or 1911."[2] It is evident that, in challenging the existence of Norway's exceptional rights, Judge McNair took into account the relative brevity of the period during which, in his opinion, the Norwegian pretensions persisted.

The matter may be summed up by saying that the passage of an appreciable period of time is necessary for the building up of historic rights, because "if the essential role of the historic element is to supply an inference of acquiescence on the part of other States, arising from their inactivity coupled with the passage of time – then time must be allowed to pass."[3]

[1] *ICJ Reports*, 1951, p. 139. (Italics added).
[2] *Ibid.*, p. 180.
[3] Fitzmaurice, 30 *BYIL* (1953), p. 30.

CHAPTER V

MISCELLANEOUS PROBLEMS OF INTERPRETATION AND EVIDENCE RELATING TO THE ACQUISITION OF AN HISTORIC TITLE

54. *General*

In one of the previous chapters[1] it has been submitted that the notion of acquiescence – being one of the main devices employed in the development of customary international law – underlies the process of formation of historic titles. In another chapter[2] the elements from which such acquiescence may be inferred were investigated at some length.

The present chapter is devoted to some general problems of interpretation and evidence relating to the acquisition of an historic title.

First problem

Historic claims being founded, by their very nature, on distant events of the past, it may well happen that the allegedly acquired rights of a State claiming such an exceptional title were created under a legal regime greatly differing from the international law of our days. Thus, the question of the role of intertemporal law in the formation of an historic title has to be faced and dealt with.

Second problem

Since historic claims built up by States usually rely on a variety of acts, omissions, events and patterns of behaviour which have been spread over long periods of time – sometimes centuries – it is essential to fix the "final date," or, in other words, the date after which no further proof will be admissible and no happenings will be taken into account in the evaluation of the contesting States' respective rights. This brings us up against the problem of the "critical date" in general, and with regard to territorial disputes, in particular.

[1] See above, chapter III.
[2] See above, chapter IV.

Third problem

The typical territorial dispute being a controversy between two litigants, each of whom will normally adduce a good deal of evidence in support of his claim, the tribunal faced with such a dispute will have to determine which of the rival claims is to prevail. This will be done by resorting to the method of comparing the relative weight of the competing territorial claims, and the method of assessing such claims will accordingly be dealt with in one of the following sections.

The remaining sections of this chapter are devoted to the investigation of the following topics:

(a) The problems relating to the onus of proof of an historic title (i.e. on which of the parties is it incumbent to discharge the burden of proof in a case in which an historic claim is raised).

(b) The strict geographical interpretation of an historic claim. This principle means that an historic claim – even if recognized – should be given the narrowest possible construction. In fact, this is no more than the logical extension of the concept of acquiescence which implies that no State can be presumed to have acquiesced in any situation or claim unless its alleged consent can be unmistakably shown and proved.

The present chapter will thus deal with the problems of intertemporal law, the critical date, the assessment of the relative worth of two competing territorial claims, the onus of proving an historic title and the strict geographical interpretation to be given to an historic claim.

55. *The application of intertemporal law in the interpretation of an historic title*

The problem of "the temporal conflict of laws"[1] is a general problem facing jurisprudence, both on the national and international level. It is a rule generally recognized by civilized nations that in principle no retroactive application should be given to any legal norm. This rule found its expression as early as 440 A.D. in an order issued by Emperor Theodosius, and was restated in the Justinian Code in the following words:

> Leges et constitutiones futuris certum est dare formam negotiis, non ad facta praeterita revocari, nisi nominatim et de praeterito tempore adhuc pendentibus negotiis cautum sit.[2]

[1] This is the expression used by Verzijl, 1 *NTIR* (1953–1954), p. 265, n. 1.
[2] C. 1, 14, 7 (440).

The principle embodied in this rule has also found acceptance in Canon Law and gained later almost universal currency among civilized nations.[1]

The requirement for the non-retroactivity of laws is particularly insisted upon in the field of criminal law and found its clear formulation in the maxim *nullum crimen sine lege* or *nulla poena sine lege*.

The precise meaning of the principle of non-retroactivity of laws is not free from doubt. In a paper read before the Grotius Society in 1955, Woodhouse rightly pointed out that "laws cannot be said to operate on past events in the same way as they operate on future events. ... It is of course impossible to change past events."[2] He asserted at the same time that

> though a law cannot change past facts it can *alter the rules applicable* to those facts. Moreover, a law can go further and ... declare that these rules are changed as from some date in the past, i.e. those responsible for the law enforcement are directed to ignore the rules previously governing past events and to pretend or assume that other rules governed.[3]

Thus, Woodhouse appears to regard as "retrospective" a law which affects vested rights and he cites to this effect an utterance by Buckley L. J. in *Batt* v. *Metropolitan Water Board*, where his Lordship took the view that

> the operation of a statute is correctly said to be retrospective when it enacts that something which was not the law at a date anterior to its passing shall be treated as having been the law at that date.[4]

Seen in this light, the principle of the non-retroactivity of laws transcends the limits of a rule of interpretation properly so called and becomes a rule of substantive law; it implies at the same time the requirement for a *contemporaneo expositio* of any given norm of law.

The impact of this rule in the sphere of international law is not far to seek: owing to the relative brevity of time that has elapsed since the emergence of modern international law, coupled with the relative longevity of international persons, the international lawyer is likely to be called upon to state his views with regard to the present-day validity of juridical facts which were undoubtedly valid in law at the

[1] For a detailed survey of the States which follow the principle of non-retroactivity of laws see Baade, "Intertemporales Völkerrecht," 7 *Jahrbuch für internationales Recht* (1956), p. 229, at pp. 230-231.

[2] Woodhouse, "The Principle of Retroactivity in International Law," *Grotius Transactions*, vol. 41 (1955), p. 69, at p. 76.

[3] *Ibid.*, p. 78. (Italics added).

[4] [1911] 2 *K.B.*, p. 970.

period of their inception, but which may be devoid of any legal meaning according to the legal concepts prevailing in contemporary international law. This is particularly true of the acquisition of historic titles, the origins of which are frequently uncertain and the acquisition of which was, more often than not, governed by rules which have since been abrogated or modified by international society.

It is only in recent years that specific attention has been given to this problem in the sphere of international law. The reason for the dearth of learned authority on this subject is most probably the still overwhelmingly customary character of international law. The majority of the scholarly treatises and dissertations relating to the problems attendant on the principle of non-retroactivity of laws in the domestic sphere may rightly be regarded as a side-product of the great codificatory movements of the nineteenth century, which involved in most cases the introduction of new legal norms, abrogating the older ones. By contrast, changes in customary law take place in what may be termed an "unconscious" manner. As has been stated by Anzilotti, in customary law

> il s'agit d'une formation lente, souvent quasi inconsciente, par le moyen de laquelle de simples normes de la coutume voient s'ajouter peu à peu à elles cette *opinio iuris* qui les transforme en normes juridiques; généralement nous constatons l'existence d'une coutume, mais nous sommes bien difficilement à même de dire quand elle a commencé d'exister.[1]

Customary law is mainly judge-made law and is therefore dependent to a very large extent on legal precedent. But, as has been observed by Blackstone,

> this rule admits of exception, where the former determination is most evidently contrary to reason; much more if it be contrary to the Divine Law. But even in such cases the subsequent judges do not pretend to make a new law, but to vindicate the old one from misrepresentation. For if it be found that the former decision is manifestly absurd or unjust, it is declared, not that such a sentence was *bad law*, but that it was *not law*; that is, that it is not the established custom of the realm, as has been erroneously determined.[2]

This "classical" concept of Common Law explains the difficulty in tracing the changes and evolutions which do, in fact, take place within the framework of customary law. The judge, who to all intents and purposes assumes the function of a law-maker, does not in theory

[1] Anzilotti, *op. cit.*, p. 93. (Italics in original).
[2] Blackstone, *Commentaries on the Law of England*, 7th edition, 1775, vol. I, pp. 69–70. (Italics in original).

create law; he merely *declares* and applies it. And, since in theory no changes take place in such a law, the problem of the temporal conflict of laws is rendered superfluous. Needless to say that practice does not bear out theory on this point and that customary law also undergoes a constant process of change and development, with the aid of various legal devices specially designed for this purpose, such as the well-known device of "distinguishing." Notwithstanding this fact, it is true to say that in most cases it will be virtually impossible to fix the exact moment at which such an alleged change took place, since in all probability the change will have occurred gradually and will have been spread over a long period of time. This difficulty, inherent in the very structure of customary law, does not, however, detract from the fact that in those cases where it can reasonably be ascertained that a change did in fact take place – regardless of the exact moment of such a change – the rule of non-retroactivity of laws will equally apply to customary rules of law.

Lauterpacht adopts the principle of the non-retroactivity of laws for international law on the ground that "it is a general principle of law that legislation, unless it specially provides to the contrary or unless irresistible considerations of justice so require, is not retro-active. This is not a principle confined to the field of criminal law."[1] He further states that "non-retroactivity is a general principle of interpretation. ... It is a principle which may be overridden by the clearly expressed will of the legislator or, in extreme cases, by judicial construction intent upon avoiding a result patently inconsistent with justice."[2]

Kelsen, on the other hand, maintains, that "no positive norm restricting the temporal validity of general international law exists. It is vain to object that international law has appeared in the course of time, that formerly there were periods when international law did not yet exist. This is without importance, for the norms of international law can also have retroactive effect."[3] He does, however, admit that "in the course of time, general international law has undergone certain changes, that norms of general international law which were valid at an earlier time, have ceased to be valid or have been modified. A legal relation implying duties of one state and corresponding rights of

[1] Lauterpacht, "Nationality of Denationalized persons," *Jewish Yearbook of International Law* (1948), p. 164, at p. 168.

[2] *Ibid.*, pp. 170–171. See also Lauterpacht, *The Function of Law in the International Community*, 1933, pp. 283–285.

[3] Kelsen, *Principles of International Law*, 1952, p. 95.

another state is to be judged by that international law under which the legal relation has been established...."[1]

International tribunals faced with problems attendant upon the application and recognition of norms of international law, which have no longer validity under the currently prevailing concepts of international law, have, in fact, recognized the existence of this principle of non-retroactivity in the field of international law.

In the well-known *Grisbadarna* Arbitration the Permanent Court of Arbitration was called upon the decide in a dispute between Norway and Sweden. The origins of that dispute go back to the 17th century, when Norway and Sweden formed a united kingdom. In accordance with the peace treaty of Roskilde, concluded in 1658 between Denmark and Sweden, Denmark ceded to Sweden the area known as the Bohuslän territory. Towards the end of the 19th century it became apparent that the Grisbadarna banks, which bordered on this territory, were rich in lobster. As a consequence a dispute arose between Norway and Sweden as to the precise demarcation of the border along the Grisbadarna banks. In 1908 this controversy was submitted by the parties for judicial settlement and the Permanent Court of Arbitration was called upon to decide whether the maritime boundary between the two countries had been fixed, in whole or in part, by the boundary treaty concluded in 1661, i.e. 3 years after the conclusion of the Treaty of Roskilde, and if not – to fix this boundary in conformity with the principles of international law. In its award of October 23rd, 1909, the tribunal found that the boundary line had indeed not been fixed by the 1661 treaty beyond a certain point and that a portion of it was uncertain. The arbitrators thereupon proceeded to fix the boundary and in doing so applied the principles which were in force at the time when the original treaty was concluded, and which would have been applied by Norway and Sweden during the 17th century. Turning to the question of fixing the precise boundary-line dividing the two countries, the tribunal held that

> in order to ascertain which may have been the automatic dividing line of 1658 [when the territory was ceded by Denmark] we must have recourse to the principles of law *in force at that time*.[2]

The tribunal declined to apply either the "median line" or the "*thalweg*" methods of demarcation, since neither of these methods

[1] *Ibid.*. See also Guggenheim, *Traité de droit international public*, vol. I, 1953, pp. 111–112.
[2] Scott, *Hague Court Reports*, 1st series, 1916, p. 121, at p. 127; *UNRIAA*, vol. XI, p. 159. (Italics added).

had achieved a degree of validity in international law in the 17th century. In the tribunal's own words:

The rule of drawing a median line midway between the inhabited lands does not find sufficient support in the law of nations in force in the seventeenth century; ... It is the same way with the rule of the *thalweg* or the most important channel, inasmuch as the documents invoked for the purpose do not demonstrate that this rule was followed in the present case.[1]

The tribunal therefore decided to follow the "general direction of the coast" rule, explaining this decision by the fact that

we shall be acting much more in accord with the ideas of the seventeenth century and with the notions of law prevailing at that time if we admit that the automatic division of the territory in question must have taken place according to the general direction of the land territory of which the maritime territory constituted an appurtenance, and if we consequently apply this same rule at the present time in order to arrive at a just and lawful determination of the boundary.[2]

Thus, the tribunal applied the "general direction of the coast" principle on the assumption that this principle – while no longer valid in modern international law – must be preferred in this case to the currently prevailing concepts of demarcation (median line, *thalweg*), because it was the "general direction of the coast" principle, and not the other methods referred to, that was in force at the time when the disputing parties had acquired their original rights.

Incidentally, this assumption of the tribunal may be regarded as having been reversed – though in a different context – some forty years later by the International Court of Justice in the *Fisheries* case where the majority of the Court adhered to the principle that "the belt of territorial waters must follow the general direction of the coast."[3] This passage of the Court's judgment may properly be considered as having effected a sort of revival of the ancient principle which, in the view of the tribunal in the *Grisbadarna* case, had lost its validity in modern international law.[4]

It is worth noting at the same time that, while considerations relating to the temporal sphere of validity of laws were pleaded at some length by the parties to the *Fisheries* case,[5] the Court appears to have evaded this issue in its judgment and apparently endeavoured

[1] Scott, *op. cit.*, p. 129; *UNRIAA*, vol. XI, p. 160. (Italics in original).
[2] Scott, *op. cit.*, p. 129; *UNRIAA*, vol. XI, p. 160.
[3] *ICJ Reports*, 1951, p. 129.
[4] This dictum of the Court has evoked criticism in many quarters; see e.g. Waldock, "The Anglo-Norwegian Fisheries Case," 28 *BYIL* (1951), p. 114, at p. 148; see also Johnson, "The Anglo-Norwegian Fisheries Case," 1 *ICLQ* (1952), p. 145, at pp. 161–163.
[5] See e.g. *ICJ*, *Fisheries case*, *Pleadings*, *Oral Arguments*, *Documents*, vol. I, pp. 342 *et seq*; vol. II, pp. 652–655.

to give the impression that the problems attendant upon the application of intertemporal law were not really relevant in resolving this controversy. It would appear that the only reference there which may be taken as an endorsement of the principle of non-retroactivity of laws is that passage of the judgment where the Court, discussing Norway's title to the whole of the Lopphavet, pointed out that at the end of the 17th century the King of Norway had granted to Lt. Commander Erich Lorch an exclusive privilege to fish and hunt whales in the Lopphavet.[1] The Court found that these privileges included "all fishing banks from which land was visible, the range of vision being, as is recognized by the United Kingdom Government, the principle of delimitation in force at that time."[2]

In the course of the pleadings in the *Fisheries* case, as well as in the *Minquiers and Ecrehos* case which was heard two years afterwards, the parties to these disputes relied heavily on, and referred frequently to, the arbitral award rendered by Judge Huber in the *Island of Palmas* Arbitration some quarter of a century earlier. In fact, Judge Huber's decision may rightly be regarded as the leading case in international law on this topic. It was in this award that the arbitrator explicitly invoked the doctrine of intertemporal law in determining the legal validity of a territorial title acquired under a legal regime which has since given place to another. As will be recalled, the United States contended that, since Spain had acquired an original title to that island by means of discovery, she, by virtue of her being the successor to Spain, must be deemed to be the territorial sovereign over the Island of Palmas (or Miangas). Discovery was, in fact, recognized as one of the roots of a territorial title by international law in force in the 17th century (when the island was first discovered by Europeans), but no valid territorial title can be based on mere discovery, according to the concepts prevailing in contemporary international law.

The Netherlands accordingly challenged the United States' claim, relying on a title subsequently acquired by way of effective possession. The arbitrator was thus called upon to decide what legal significance international law of the 20th century was prepared to attach to a title based on discovery. The arbitrator commented on this aspect of the problem in the following words:

It is admitted by both sides that international law underwent profound modifications between the end of the Middle-Ages and the end of the nineteenth century,

[1] *ICJ Reports*, 1951, p. 142.
[2] *Ibid.*

as regards the rights of discovery and acquisition of uninhabited regions or regions inhabited by savages or semi-civilised peoples. Both Parties are also agreed that a juridical fact must be appreciated *in the light of the law contemporary with it,* and not of the law in force at the time when a dispute in regard to it arises or falls to be settled. The effect of discovery by Spain is therefore to be determined by the rules of international law in force in the first half of the sixteenth century.[1]

At this juncture, however, the arbitrator parted company with the United States' Argument by introducing the all-important distinction between the *acquisition* of a territorial title and its *maintenance.* While the validity of the original act of acquisition is determined in the light of the rules in force at the moment of the acquisition, the questions relating to the maintenance of such a title are viewed, according to the arbitrator, by the rules "required by the evolution of law." The arbitrator formulated this distinction in the following terms:

As regards the question which of different legal systems prevailing at successive periods is to be applied in a particular case (the so-called intertemporal law), a distinction must be made between the *creation* of rights and the *existence* of rights. The same principle which subjects the act creative of a right to the law in force at the time the right arises, demands that the existence of the right, in other words, its continued manifestation, shall follow the conditions required by the evolution of law.[2]

The arbitrator went on to say that international law in the 19th century "laid down the principle that occupation, to constitute a claim to territorial sovereignty, must be effective."[3] It seemed therefore incompatible with this rule of positive law "that there should be regions which are neither under the effective sovereignty of a State, nor without a master, but which are reserved for the exclusive influence of one State, in virtue solely of a title of acquisition which is no longer recognized by existing law, even if such a title ever conferred territorial sovereignty."[4]

It necessarily followed, in the arbitrator's view, that the United States could not rely on a title based merely on simple discovery. He doubted, moreover, whether international law ever regarded discovery as more than an "inchoate title," which, in order to constitute a perfect and valid territorial title, must be followed up within a reasonable period by the effective occupation of the region alleged to have been discovered. "This principle," said the arbitrator, "must be applied in the present case, for the reasons given above, in regard to the rules

[1] *UNRIAA*, vol. II, p. 845. (Italics added).
[2] *Ibid.* (Italics added).
[3] *Ibid.*, p. 846.
[4] *Ibid.*

determining which of successive legal systems is to be applied (the so-called intertemporal law)."[1] The arbitrator concluded that "an inchoate title [based on discovery] could not prevail over the continuous and peaceful display of authority by another State,"[2] and accordingly rejected the United States' claim.

Thus, the arbitrator appears to have required only for the *acquisition* of a territorial title the application of the rules in force at the time when such acquisition is alleged to have taken place, while the question whether or not such a title has been subsequently maintained must be viewed, in his opinion, in the light of the legal principles in force at later periods.

The first proposition of Judge Huber was unanimously accepted as an accurate presentation of the legal situation; his second proposition, however, met with considerable opposition on the ground that the principle enunciated therein might create a situation where no State would know for certain if a title originally acquired by it was still valid in international law. According to Jessup, who is among those emphatically challenging the views expounded by Judge Huber on this point, "every state would constantly be under the necessity of examining its title to each portion of its territory in order to determine whether a change in the law had necessitated, as it were, a reacquisition .... The result would be chaos."[3]

It would appear, however, that Judge Huber's award does not necessarily entail the far-reaching consequences ascribed to it by Jessup. All it means is that, if a State is in effective possession of a territory to which another State has laid a claim based on a purely abstract right, unaccompanied by any concrete act or manifestation of authority, then, in the light of the rules of contemporary international law, the State in effective possession will be deemed to have a superior title; this will be so because in modern international law an abstract title without effective possession cannot prevail over a constant and effective manifestation of authority.[4]

[1] *Ibid.*

[2] *Ibid.*

[3] Jessup, "The Palmas Island Arbitration," 22 *AJIL* (1928), p. 735, at p. 740. See also to the same effect Versfelt, *The Miangas Arbitration*, 1933, pp. 14–16. Cf. also Jennings, *op. cit.*, pp. 30–31.

[4] This aspect of the problem will be gone into more extensively in the section discussing the relative strength of competing territorial claims (below, section 57); see to this effect Johnson, *Cambridge Law Journal* (1955), pp. 224–225, and Baade, *loc. cit.*, p. 242. This second aspect of the application of intertemporal law is unlikely to be the source of any injustice because, as has been pointed out by Roche, "intertemporal law has never been applied where a change in the law has come about in a short time, as when there is an international con-

This, in fact, was the interpretation given to Judge Huber's award by both parties to the *Minquiers and Ecrehos* case, in which the problem of the temporal conflict of laws was again brought to the fore. There the International Court of Justice was seised of a dispute concerning two islets to which both the United Kingdom and France claimed an original title going back to the Middle Ages. Both parties invoked in support of their claims what they understood to have been the rules in force at the time when their alleged rights had taken shape. Thus, Sir Lionel Heald for the United Kingdom in his oral argument stated that "not only must claims to sovereignty based on medieval feudal law be examined in the light of that law, but also ... any such claims, if put forward as still valid to-day, must be examined in the light of international law *as it has developed during the intervening centuries* and, in particular, in the light of what international law, as it now stands, requires in order to constitute a title to territory."[1]

Similarly, Gros, on behalf of France, observed that "un titre doit être apprécié selon les conceptions et les règles en vigueur à l'époque où il est né."[2] He further pointed out that "un fait juridique doit être apprécié à la lumière du droit qui lui est contemporain et non à celle du droit en vigueur au moment où le différend s'élève ou est réglé."[3] Giving his interpretation of the *Island of Palmas* case, Gros contended that it clearly emerged from the award in that case that "lorsque disparaît le système juridique en vertu duquel le titre a été valablement créé, ce droit ne peut plus être maintenu dans le système juridique nouveau, à moins qu'il ne se conforme aux conditions exigées par ce dernier."[4] The application of such a rule was, in Gros' opinion, vital in the interests of adapting international law to changing circumstances and realities, "parce qu'elle exige que le titre ancien se conforme aux conditions du droit nouveau et évite aussi de prolonger à l'infini, isolé de tout le reste du milieu juridique contemporain, un droit acquis sous l'empire d'un ordre juridique aujourd'hui périmé."[5]

Thus, the parties seem to have been at one as to the applicability of

vention. Generally speaking, therefore, the intertemporal law will apply in cases where international customary law has changed gradually over the years. In which case, the change of the rule of law will usually be the result of the combined practice of many states." (Roche, *The Minquiers and Ecrehos Case*, 1959, p. 83).

[1] *ICJ, Minquiers and Ecrehos case, Pleadings, Oral Arguments, Documents*, vol. II, p. 53. (Italics added).

[2] *Ibid.*, p. 206.

[3] *Ibid.*, p. 375.

[4] *Ibid.*

[5] *Ibid.*

the rules of intertemporal law in international law, as regards the acquisition of a territorial title.

The Court in its judgment appears to have associated itself with the opinions voiced by the parties holding that

> even if the Kings of France did have an original... title ... in respect of the Channel Islands, such a title must have lapsed as a consequence of the events of the year 1204 and following years. Such an alleged original ... title of the Kings of France in respect of the Channel Islands could to-day produce no legal effect, unless it had been replaced by another title valid according to the law of the time of replacement.[1]

Thus, the Court, following the rules laid down in the *Island of Palmas* Award, decided that the maintenance of a territorial title – in contradistinction to its acquisition – was to be determined not by the law in force at the period of the acquisition of the title, but by the legal principles as they evolved through the periods during which such authority is purported to have been exercised.[2]

In a paper read before the Grotius Society in 1954, Wade expressed the view that in the *Minquiers and Ecrehos* case "the court missed an opportunity of contributing a precedent to international law on the working of the inter-temporal law doctrine."[3] In his opinion, the Court "could only have taken up the neutral attitude which it did to this material because it had at its disposal more cogent evidence of the ownership of the islets."[4] This statement, however, is hardly compatible with a further observation made by Wade that "the court was prepared to interpret two Charters of the early 13th century granting land in one of the groups, and also to interpret a record of litigation in the early 14th century which confirmed the effect of these grants."[5] Had the Court really declined to apply the rules of intertemporal law, as is asserted by Wade, the interpretation of these medieval documents must indeed appear to be irrelevant. As Wade himself points out, the Court could have declined "to decide the issue of ancient title at all

[1] *ICJ Reports*, 1953, p. 47, at p. 56; see also pp. 60–62. For a further instance of the application of intertemporal law, see Judge Moreno Quintana's Dissenting Opinion in the *Temple of Preah Vihear* case, *ICJ Reports*, 1962, p. 67.

[2] There has been some argument as to whether the examination of feudal law by the Court should be interpreted as an application of this law by the Court or not. Verzijl seems to hold the view that the Court in fact applied feudal law in this case (*loc. cit.*, p. 362). Roche, on the other hand, thinks that the Court's practice in this case merely amounts to "ascertaining as a fact the content of another system of law." (Roche, *op. cit.*, p. 81, n. 5).

[3] Wade, "The Minquiers and Ecréhous Case," *Grotius Transactions*, vol. 40 (1954), p. 97, at p. 101.

[4] *Ibid.* A similar view is taken by Roche, *op. cit.*, p. 85.

[5] *Ibid.*

and have based its decision on the exercise of authority in modern times."[1]

Both the *Island of Palmas* case and the *Minquiers and Ecrehos* case have clearly demonstrated the difficulties attendant upon the application on the international level of frequently contradictory rules of customary law. These difficulties are derived from the fact that, owing to the unique process of evolution which characterizes customary law, it will be virtually impossible to ascertain at what date a given rule of customary law lapsed and at what time another rule of law took its place.

In this connection it is worth mentioning another case – this time a case decided by a national court of law – in which the United States Supreme Court came up against this stumbling-block of the temporal conflict of laws. In *New Jersey* v. *Delaware*[2] the Court dealt with a boundary dispute between two neighbouring states of the Union and was called upon to fix the boundary between them. The dividing line between the states of New Jersey and Delaware is first Delaware River and then Delaware Bay. The state of Delaware claimed that the boundary should follow the geographical median line, while New Jersey relied upon the *thalweg* principle.

The Court observed on this point that

> up to the time when New Jersey and Delaware became independent states, the title to the soil under the waters below the circle was still in the Crown of England. When independence was achieved, the precepts to be obeyed in the division of the waters were those of international law ... [which] today divides the river boundaries between states by the middle of the main channel, when there is one, and not by the geographical centre, half way between the banks. ... The underlying rationale of the doctrine of the Thalweg is one of equality and justice.[3]

The Court could not, however, establish beyond any doubt the exact date at which the *thalweg* principle found admission into positive international law. While this principle was certainly "*in the making*" during the latter part of the 18th century, it did not achieve at that time supremacy among "the conflicting methods of division ... contending for... mastery."[4] The application of the *thalweg* principle was none the less warranted in this case, in the Court's opinion, by the fact that

> in 1783, when the Revolutionary War was over, Delaware and New Jersey began with a clean slate. There was no treaty or convention fixing the boundary between

[1] *Ibid.*
[2] 291 U.S. (1934), p. 361 *et seq.*
[3] *Ibid.*, pp. 378–380.
[4] *Ibid.*, p. 383.

them. There was no possessory act nor other act of dominion to give to the boundary ... a practical location, or to establish a prescriptive right. In these circumstances, the capacity of the law to develop and apply a formula consonant with justice and with the political and social needs of the international legal system is not lessened by the fact that at the creation of the boundary the formula of the Thalweg had only a germinal existence. The gap is not so great that adjudication may not fill it.[1]

This passage affords a good illustration of the rather widespread – but usually less pronounced – tendency to apply retroactively a new rule of customary rule, under the pretext that at the time to which it is being applied it was at least "taking shape." It should be noted, however, that in the given case the Court's inclination to apply a rule which it considered as just and reasonable was considerably facilitated by the concession made by Counsel for Delaware who "[made] no point that the result is to be affected by difference of time."[2]

It may also be mentioned that in article III of the Agreement between Great Britain and the United States of Venezuela respecting the settlement by arbitration of the *Venezuelan-British Guiana Boundary* Dispute, the contracting parties stipulated that the arbitral tribunal "shall investigate and ascertain the extent of the territories belonging to, or that might lawfully be claimed by, the United Netherlands or by the Kingdom of Spain respectively *at the time of the acquisition* by Great Britain of the Colony of British Guiana."[3]

In the arbitral award of October 3rd, 1899, the tribunal reproduced verbatim these terms of reference and stressed that it "investigated and ascertained the extent of the territories belonging to or that might lawfully be claimed by the United Netherlands or by the Kingdom of Spain respectively at the time of the acquisition by Great Britain of the Colony of British Guiana."[4]

The examples referred to above seem to indicate that, notwithstanding the doctrinal dearth of authority on this subject, the introduction of the rules of intertemporal law into the field of international

[1] *Ibid.*

[2] *Ibid.*, p. 384.

[3] 89 *BFSP*, pp. 57–65, at p. 59. (Italics added). It should be added, however, that the scope of this provision was somewhat restricted by the stipulation made in article IV (a) of the same treaty where it was laid down that "adverse holding or prescription during a period of fifty years shall make a good title." (*Ibid.*, p. 60).

[4] 92 *BFSP*, pp. 160–162, at p. 161; the award is also reproduced in La Fontaine, *Pasicrisie internationale*, 1902, pp. 556–557. Further instances for the application of intertemporal law in State practice may be found in the express stipulation to this effect inserted in the Protocol signed at Washington on May 28th, 1884, by the United States and Haiti, submitting for arbitration the Dispute relating to *Pelletier and Lazare* (see Moore, *International Arbitrations*, vol. V, p. 4768), and in the decision rendered by Pope Leo XIII in 1885, in the *Caroline Islands* case between Germany and Spain (76 *BFSP*, p. 293).

law constitutes the well-recognized practice and flows from a genuine necessity to ensure a certain degree of stability for an existing state of things. Were the operation of these rules on the international plane called in question, this would almost certainly lead to the invalidation of the majority of the territorial titles on which the rights of States at present rest, as most States rely on titles which are no longer valid in present day international law, though they were undoubtedly recognized as good titles at the time of their acquisition. At the same time, the application of this principle is not intended to form an obstacle to the development of international law and to its being brought into line with the prevailing and evolving concepts of a more refined legal system. Thus, a balance has to be struck between the seemingly conflicting needs of stability and adaptability. In the view of Gros, as expressed in his oral argument in the *Minquiers and Ecrehos* case, the distinction between the law applicable to the acquisition of a new right and that applicable to its maintenace – which has been gone into above – reconciles "les deux exigences fondamentales du droit: la sécurité et l'adaptation. La sécurité, parce qu'elle évite de rendre caducs de droits acquis valablement sous l'empire du système juridique ancien; l'adaptation, parce qu'elle exige que le titre ancien se conforme aux conditions du droit nouveau...."[1]

The twofold aspect of the application of intertemporal law seems to meet both requirements. The first principle, namely, the principle that facts must be judged in the light of the law contemporaneous with their creation, is aimed at upholding the interests of stability and security in international relations; the second principle, i.e. the principle that rights validly acquired under the law in force at the time of their acquisition will lose their validity unless they are maintained in accordance with the changes brought about by the development of international law, is intended to meet the requirements of the adaptation of the law to the changing international scene. While it is essential to recognize the fundamental difference between these two aspects of intertemporal law, it is equally vital to realize that neither of the concomitant factors of intertemporal law can be invoked in isolation, disregarding the other. All the same, the first principle seems to have been generally accepted, while the second is still hotly contested. Nevertheless, in spite of the criticism levelled against recourse being had to the second principle – to which criticism reference has been made above – it can hardly be doubted, in view of the judicial

[1] *ICJ, Minquiers and Ecrehos case, Pleadings, Oral Arguments, Documents,* vol. II, p. 375.

decisions referred to in this section, that this principle too has gained acceptance in the sphere of international law.

In order to achieve a reconciliation between these two aspects of intertemporal law, which are frequently present in territorial disputes, it is vital that a certain date be fixed which will serve as the starting-point for the investigation of the rival claims and for a decision as to which of the competing claims is to prevail. The fixing of such a "critical date" is indeed decisive for the outcome of a dispute of this kind; for it follows that acts performed after the "critical date" will normally be held as devoid of any legal significance. This is why it is felt that the following sections of this chapter should be devoted to a more thorough analysis of the problems pertaining to the fixing of the "critical date" and to the method of assessment of the relative strength of competing claims.

56. The selection of the "critical date"

International disputes relating to territorial claims are frequently a matter for protracted negotiations and lengthy discussion and procrastination. Frequently such disputes will be dragged on for decades or even for centuries and their settlement will be reached long after the dispute first arose. Thus, it is easy to understand that a tribunal confronted with a controversy of this kind will have to determine at what time the dispute must be presumed to have arisen. Such a decision is rendered necessary for two main reasons:

(a) by fixing the date at which the dispute is presumed to have begun, the tribunal, in fact, determines what rules of law should govern the problems relating to the acquisition of the territorial title, in accordance with the rules of intertemporal law, which were dealt with in the previous section;

(b) by fixing this date, the tribunal automatically excludes any subsequent acts performed by either of the litigant parties with a view to upsetting the *status quo* existing at the time of the outbreak of the dispute, and taking advantage of such improvements in its position.

Thus, it is of the utmost importance in each of these territorial disputes to fix the date at which the dispute arose, or, to use the specific term employed for this purpose: to fix the "critical date."[1] The "critical date" has rightly been defined by one writer as "the date after

[1] On the problems of the "critical date" in general see Goldie, "The Critical Date," 12 *ICLQ* (1963), pp, 1251–1284. For a discussion of this problem with regard to territorial disputes, see *ibid.*, pp. 1252–1267.

which the acts or omissions of the parties cannot affect the legal situation."[1] It is an assumption of law that at a certain moment in the past the situation which gave rise to the dispute between two rival parties became, so to speak, "frozen." It is the situation that prevailed at that given moment which serves as the legal criterion and yardstick by which the merits of the conflicting parties' alleged rights are being measured. Any subsequent change or modification, as a result of the parties' acts or omissions, will be deemed irrelevant from the legal point of view and will be unable to improve, impair or alter in any way the rights of the parties.

Some international treaties contain express provisions fixing the date or event which is to govern the legal position in a certain case and which constitutes the "critical date" in the case in question.

This result of the "freezing" of a territorial situation was effected in the provisions of article IV of the 1959 Antarctic Treaty which stipulates that there shall be no "renunciation by any Contracting Party of previously asserted rights of or claims to territorial sovereignty in the Antarctica" and that "no acts or activities taking place while the present Treaty is in force shall constitute a basis for asserting, supporting or denying a claim to territorial sovereignty... or create any rights of sovereignty. ... No new claim... shall be asserted while the present Treaty is in force."[2]

While the notion of the "critical date" seems to have always been implicit in territorial disputes, the term itself appears to have originated comparatively recently, namely, in the award given by Judge Huber in the *Island of Palmas* case, where the distinguished arbitrator referred to the Treaty of Paris as to the "critical moment" in that case,[3] and went on to say:

> the question arises whether sovereignty ... existed at the critical date, i.e. the moment of conclusion and coming into force of the Treaty of Paris.[4]

[1] Johnson, "The Minquiers and Ecrehos Case," 3 *ICLQ* (1954), p. 189, at p. 208. The same writer defined in an article written in 1950 the critical date as "the date after which the actions of the parties cannot affect the legal situation." (See Johnson, 27 *BYIL* (1950), p. 342, n. 4). Another definition given by Roche is: "the date after which the actions of the parties may no longer affect the issue; the titles of the parties having to be determined according to the legal situation existing at that date." (Roche, *op. cit.*, at p. 88). For other possible definitions, see Fitzmaurice, 32 *BYIL* (1955–56), p. 20, n. 2.

[2] Article IV of the Antarctic Treaty of December 1st, 1959, printed in *Cmnd.* 913 (1959), and in 9 *ICLQ* (1960), p. 475. For the history of the different national claims to the Antarctic regions and the various stages leading up to the conclusion of the treaty, for its critical appraisal, as well as for references to the relevant literature, see Hanessian, "The Antarctic Treaty, 1959," 9 *ICLQ* (1960), p. 436 *et seq.*

[3] *UNRIAA*, vol. II, p. 843; see also *ibid.*, p. 866.

[4] *Ibid.*, p. 845. See also the *Legal Status of Eastern Greenland* case where the Court stated that

Now, it is evident that the "critical date" cannot be chosen arbitrarily since, if this were allowed, it would be tantamount to deciding the case before going into its merits. The selection and fixing of the "critical date" being of primordial importance and entailing most serious legal consequences, it must accordingly be done in conformity with the accepted legal principles on this point.

In his oral argument before the International Court of Justice in the *Minquiers and Ecrehos* case, Sir Gerald Fitzmaurice, Counsel for the United Kingdom, stressed the fact that "the whole point, the whole *raison d'être*, of the critical date rule is, in effect, that time is deemed to stop at that date. Nothing that happens afterwards can operate to change the situation that then existed. Whatever that situation was, it is deemed in law still to exist; and the rights of the parties are governed by it."[1]

In an article published in 1957 Sir Gerald gave a list of possible criteria for determining the critical date. In his view, the following are the main possibilities for the selection of the critical date:

(i) the date of the commencement of the dispute;
(ii) the date ... when the challenging or plaintiff State first makes a definite claim to the territory;
(iii) the date ... when the dispute 'crystallized' into a definite issue between the parties as to territorial sovereignty;
(iv) the date when one of the parties ... takes active steps to initiate a procedure for the settlement of the dispute, such as negotiations, conciliation, mediation ... or other means falling short of arbitration or judicial settlement;
(v) the date on which any of these procedures [mentioned in (iv) above] is actually resorted to and employed;
(vi) the date on which, all else failing, the matter is proposed to be or is referred to arbitration or judicial settlement.[2]

Sir Gerald himself describes these rather speculative remarks as being tentative and breaking new ground,[3] and it is therefore felt that the principles underlying the rules, according to which the critical date is selected, can be best ascertained by investigating some of the more important judicial decisions in which this question arose. Here again, perhaps the most revealing decision is the arbitral award of

"the date at which... Danish sovereignty must have existed in order to render the Norwegian occupation invalid is the date at which the occupation took place, viz., July 10th, 1931." (*PCIJ*, Series A/B, No. 53, p. 45). The Court went on to say that "the critical date is July 10th, 1931." (*Ibid.*)

[1] *ICJ*, *Minquiers and Ecrehos case*, *Pleadings*, *Oral Arguments*, *Documents*, vol. II, p. 64. (Italics in original).

[2] Fitzmaurice, 32 *BYIL* (1955–56), pp. 23–24.

[3] *Ibid.*, p. 20.

Judge Huber in the *Island of Palmas* case. With his characteristic lucidity and clarity of style the eminent Swiss international lawyer and former President of the Permanent Court of International Justice set out to discuss this problem. He found that the critical date in that case was the year 1898, this being the date on which Spain had transferred her rights over the Philippine archipelago to the United States. Basing himself on the well-known maxim *nemo dare potest quod non habet*, the arbitrator took the view that it had been at that moment that the Treaty had "focused" the dispute and had formed the basis for the determination of the critical date. In the arbitrator's own words:

> The essential point is therefore whether the Island of Palmas (or Miangas) at the moment of the conclusion and coming into force of the Treaty of Paris formed a part of the Spanish or Netherlands territory.[1]

It is significant that Judge Huber fixed the critical date at 1898 and not, for instance, at 1648, the date of the conclusion of the Treaty of Münster, which, in the arbitrator's own words, was "the earliest Treaty... to define the relations between Spain and the Netherlands in the regions in question."[2] Thus, it can readily be seen that the critical date is not the date at which a dispute is "born," but rather the date at which it is "focused." It was only in 1898 that the issue originated whether the purported transfer of the title to the Island of Palmas from Spain to the United States under the Treaty of Paris was valid or not. The arbitrator quoted to this effect a letter written in 1900 by the United States Secretary of State to the Spanish Minister in Washington where this point was explicitly made in the following words:

> This Government must ... hold that the only competent and equitable test of fact by which the title to a disputed cession ... may be determined is simply this: 'Was it Spain's *to give*? If valid title belonged to Spain, it passed; if Spain had no valid title, she could convey none.'[3]

Judge Huber's insistence on the selection of 1898 as the critical date is explained by the fact that the dispute as to the sovereignty in that case turned on a distinct event, i.e. the coming into force of the Treaty

[1] *UNRIAA*, vol. II, p. 843.

[2] *Ibid.*, pp. 844–845. In 1648, though, there did not arise any dispute between the parties to the Treaty of Münster regarding the Island of Palmas. Seen in retrospect, however, that date may be regarded as the date of the "birth" of the dispute, giving rise to the *facts* which underlay the later dispute.

[3] *Ibid.*, p. 842. (Italics added).

of Paris. In other cases the determination of a territorial dispute may turn upon the validity or otherwise of a law or decree proclaiming sovereignty, such law or decree being promulgated by one of the parties to the dispute and being challenged by the other. In such cases the point in issue is the validity of the law or decree relied upon from the viewpoint of international law, and the critical date will accordingly be fixed as the date of the promulgation of such law or decree. In territorial disputes of this kind the selection of the critical date is more or less obvious, or, to use the term employed by Sir Gerald Fitzmaurice, we are dealing with "self-evident critical dates."[1]

This point was made abundantly clear in the *Legal Status of Eastern Greenland* case where the Permanent Court of International Justice had to pronounce on the validity, as against Denmark, of a Norwegian Royal Decree of July 10th, 1931, in which Norway had proclaimed her sovereignty over Eastern Greenland. The Court held that the Royal Decree was, in effect, the matter "which gave rise to the ... dispute,"[2] from which statement it followed that

> the date at which such Danish sovereignty must have existed in order to render the Norwegian occupation invalid is the date at which the occupation took place, viz., July 10th, 1931.[3]

Here again, the Court did not select as the critical date the period at which the dispute was "born." The dispute between the two countries in all probability "began" as early as 1814, when the Union between them came to an end. There was also ample evidence that from 1921 onwards Norway openly challenged Denmark's rights over Eastern Greenland. Yet, the Court selected July 1931 as the critical date, because it was on that date that happened the concrete event which "focused" the dispute.[4]

Both in the *Island of Palmas* Arbitration and in the *Legal Status of Eastern Greenland* case the critical date was determined with reference

[1] 22 *BYIL* (1955–56), p. 22.

[2] *PCIJ*, Series A/B, N. 53, p. 26.

[3] *Ibid.*, p. 45.

[4] The selection of the critical date in this case has met with criticism by Roche on the ground that the Court should have fixed 1921 as the critical date in view of the fact that Norway's acts after that date were performed, in her own admission, for the purpose of improving her position during the forthcoming legal proceedings. Roche holds the view that the Court's decision was due largely to the fact that Denmark herself did not formulate her case before the Court in such a way as to make it depend on the position as it stood in 1921, in order to preclude Norway from invoking any subsequent acts. He reaches the conclusion that "the critical date may depend on the will of one party so long as the other does not object. If the other party does object, it falls to the Court to decide what shall be the critical date." (Roche, *op. cit.*, p. 95).

to a treaty or proclamation which made it relatively easy to ascertain the precise moment at which the dispute arose. This task is, however, rendered less straightforward in those cases in which one cannot point at any instrument or event which can "focus" the dispute and form the basis for the determination of the critical date. The difficulties attendant upon the fixing of the critical date in such cases are vividly illustrated by the pleadings of the parties on this point in the *Minquiers and Ecrehos* case. It will not be too bold to assert that this case virtually revolved around the determination of the critical date, it being apparently understood by both parties that if the events of the last hundred years were to be taken into account, then the United Kingdom title must prevail. This conclusion was the result of the fact that during the past century or so the manifestations of British authority over the two disputed islets were far more numerous than those of the French and it was therefore hardly surprising that, in the written arguments submitted on behalf of France, the critical date was set back as far as 1839, in the belief that the further this date could be put back, the stronger was the chance for the French case to succeed. The year 1839 was chosen by the French Government on the ground that in that same year a Fishery Convention was signed between the litigant parties whereby they defined and regulated the limits within which the general right of fishing was to be reserved thenceforth for the subjects of Great Britain and France, respectively. According to the provisions of article 3 of the said Convention, the Minquiers and Ecrehos formed part of an area within which common or joint fishery rights were established.[1] It was contended on behalf of France that any acts performed subsequent to the conclusion of that Treaty were irrelevant to the issues before the Court, because the dispute in this case had arisen at the moment of the conclusion of the Convention and the situation which had existed at that date must be presumed to have prevailed ever since.[2]

This contention was refuted by the United Kingdom Reply for a variety of reasons, and it was argued, *inter alia*, that the Minquiers and Ecrehos had never come under article 3 of the 1839 Convention, because they had already been under British sovereignty at that time.[3] Against this arbitrary selection of a somewhat artificial critical date,

[1] For the text of the Convention see Annex A 27 to the United Kingdom Memorial, *ICJ, Minquiers and Ecrehos case, Pleadings, Oral Arguments, Documents*, vol. I, pp. 179–186. The text of article 3 may be found at p. 183 there.

[2] *Ibid.*, pp. 720–723.

[3] *Ibid.*, p. 447.

the United Kingdom maintained throughout the proceedings that the real critical date in this case was the year 1950, the date on which the dispute "*crystallized*," i.e. was submitted by the parties for adjudication by the Court. As far as can be established, this notion of "crystallization" as a criterion for the selection of the critical date was first introduced by the United Kingdom in this case and had never been resorted to before. According to Sir Gerald Fitzmaurice, Counsel for the United Kingdom in that case, who pleaded before the International Court of Justice for the adoption of this test, a dispute crystallizes into a concrete issue at the moment when

> the Parties are no longer negotiating, or protesting, or attempting to persuade one another. They have taken up position and are standing on their respective rights, and when that occurs, the claims of the Parties must obviously be adjudged according to the facts as they stand at that moment. ...[1]

The notion of crystallization was invoked again shortly afterwards in the United Kingdom applications in the *Antarctica* cases where it was asserted that the acts of the parties after 1926, in the case of the South Orkneys, and after 1937, in the case of the South Shetlands and Graham Land, were of limited juridical relevance, because "the dispute crystallised when Argentina first asserted her claims, namely in or about 1926 in the case of the South Orkneys, and in or about 1937 in the case of the other two territories; and according to well-established principles of law, it is at the date of crystallisation that the rights of the Parties are to be adjudged."[2]

Roche takes the view that this conception of the "crystallization" of an issue "bears a considerable resemblance to the situation which is often required by treaty, that the possibility of settlement by diplomatic negotiations should have been exhausted before the submission of a dispute to a judicial authority."[3]

The precise meaning of this notion has been described at some length by Sir Gerald in the course of his oral argument in the *Minquiers and Ecrehos* case and it appears well worth-while to enlarge further on his thesis on this point. In his view, the basis for the determination of the critical date would be "the position existing on the date on which the differences of opinion that have arisen between the

[1] *Ibid.*, vol. II, p. 68.

[2] *ICJ, Antarctica cases, Pleadings, Oral Arguments, Documents*, p. 32; see to the same effect *ibid.*, p. 70, where the notion of "crystallization" was further resorted to in the application instituting proceedings against Chile. The date of the crystallization of the dispute with Chile was given as 1940.

[3] Roche, *op. cit.*, pp. 96–97.

Parties have crystallized into a concrete issue giving rise to a formal dispute."[1] He suggests that the preliminary period preceding most disputes, during which there are diplomatic exchanges, protests, or even negotiations – a period the length of which varies according to circumstances – be not taken into account in the determination of the critical date, because at that time the parties have not yet taken up any final position. In Sir Gerald's view,

> in the ordinary course of events and assuming that once a concrete issue has arisen between two countries, they decide to settle it by international adjudication, the critical date would be the date on which they agreed to submit the dispute to a tribunal.[2]

Counsel for the United Kingdom was, however, at pains to point out that, since the selection of the critical date serves an equitable purpose, namely, to ensure that the dispute be determined on the basis that seems most just and equitable, there may arise cases in which the critical date will have to be fixed at a date other than the date on which the dispute was submitted by the parties for adjudication. He therefore pointed out that one of the main objects of the fixing of the critical date being to prevent one of the parties from unilaterally improving its position by means of taking some steps after the issue has been definitely joined, it would be contrary to the professed aims of doing justice to the real merits of each country's case to stick indiscriminately to the date of the submission of the dispute for adjudication as the test for the determination of the critical date. Such a course would obviously be unjust in cases where one of the parties at first evades a settlement, rejects the suggestion to go to arbitration, and then proceeds to take various steps to improve its position. If such a party eventually expresses its willingness to submit the dispute for a judicial settlement, it would surely be unfair to the other party, which has all along been willing to accept arbitration, to make the date of the eventual submission to a tribunal the critical date. Sir Gerald suggested that in such cases it would be more in consonance with the general notions of justice that the day on which arbitration was first proposed be fixed as the critical date.

While warning against putting the critical date too late, Sir Gerald had equal misgivings as regards putting it too early. He felt – rightly, it is believed – that such a course might unduly favour the party "which has put forward a claim in a general way, but has not pursued

[1] *ICJ, Minquiers and Ecrehos case, Pleadings, Oral Arguments, Documents,* vol. II, pp. 8–69.
[2] *Ibid.,* pp. 68–69.

it, or has only pursued it in a desultory or intermittent way, without attempting to bring the matter to a head, or to prosecute its claim by seeking international adjudication."[1] This would "place a premium on the making of paper claims which the country concerned need not then follow up or insist upon,"[2] and it would enable such a State to "freeze" the legal position by the mere raising of a claim, thus depriving any subsequent acts performed by the other party from any legal significance.

Sir Gerald's analysis of the problems relating to the critical date represents, it is felt, the correct and proper approach to this delicate and at the same time decisive question for the acquisition of a territorial title in general, and of an historic title in particular. This is why it was deemed appropriate to recapitulate his views on this subject at some length. It is certainly a matter for regret that the Court in its judgment showed some reluctance in expressing its views on this question. There is, however, little doubt that the Court rejected outright the French submission to regard the 1839 Convention as the critical date, by pointing out that

> at the date of the Convention of 1839, no dispute as to the sovereignty over the Ecrehos and Minquiers groups had yet arisen. The Parties had for a considerable time been in disagreement with regard to the exclusive right to fish oysters, but they did not link that question to the question of sovereignty over the Ecrehos and the Minquiers. In such circumstances there is no reason why the conclusion of that Convention should have any effect on the question of allowing or ruling out evidence relating to sovereignty.[3]

Following the same line of argument, Judge Levi Carneiro, in his Individual Opinion, pointed to the contradiction inherent in the French contention which tried to fix the critical date in the year 1839 and at the same time did not fail to consider acts subsequent to 1839 and to invoke them in support of its case.[4]

Thus, the Court clearly declined to associate itself with the French proposition without, however, stating in an unequivocal manner what it considered to be the critical date in this case. A closer perusal of the Court's judgment does, however, indicate that the Court, without expressly claiming to do so, fixed the years 1886 and 1888 as the critical dates as regards the Ecrehos and Minquiers, respectively. This

[1] *Ibid.*, p. 69.
[2] *Ibid.*
[3] *ICJ Reports*, 1953, p. 59.
[4] *Ibid.*, p. 106.

seems to emerge from that passage of the judgment in which the Court states that

a dispute as to sovereignty over the groups did not arise before the years 1886 and 1888, when France for the first time claimed sovereignty over the Ecrehos and the Minquiers respectively.[1]

The Court's judgment seems to have attached to the notion of "crystallization" a meaning somewhat different from that assigned to it by the United Kingdom. The Court, in fact, fixed the critical date at the time at which the French Government had made a definite claim to sovereignty in respect of each of the disputed islets. Thus, the critical date appears to be the date of the *origin* of the dispute rather than its crystallization. While setting back the critical dates to the years 1886 and 1888, the Court at the same time declared that it was prepared to take account of various acts which had been performed after the critical dates, explaining this decision by the "special circumstances of the case." In the Court's own words:

In view of the special circumstances of the present case, subsequent acts should also be considered by the Court, unless the measure in question was taken with a view to improving the legal position of the Party concerned. In many respects activity in regard to these groups had developed gradually long before the dispute as to sovereignty arose, and it has since continued without interruption and *in a similar manner*. In such circumstances there would be no justification for ruling out all events which during this continued development occurred after the years 1886 and 1888 respectively.[2]

This conclusion may strike one at first sight as rather odd, because, as will be recalled, the very purpose of fixing the critical date is to *exclude* any subsequent activities from being taken into account.[3] The Court in this case, after determining the critical dates as being in 1886 and 1888, did, in fact, refer to acts and events which occurred as recently as 1950.[4] True, the Court left no doubt that the acts

[1] *Ibid.*, p. 59.

[2] *Ibid.*, pp. 59–60. (Italics added).

[3] In the United Kingdom application against Argentina in the *Antarctica* cases this point was explicitly made when it was alleged that all acts performed by the Argentine Government subsequent to what the United Kingdom regarded as the dates of crystallization in these cases "were clearly undertaken, not as a genuine manifestation of an existing title, but with a view to trying to create one and in order to improve Argentina's legal position. They are not, therefore, to be taken into consideration." (*ICJ, Antarctica cases, Pleadings, Oral Arguments, Documents*, p. 32). As regards various acts performed by Chile, see to the same effect, *ibid.*, p. 70.

[4] See e.g. *ICJ Reports*, 1953 p. 65, where the Court relied on inquests held in Jersey on corpses found at the Ecrehos in 1948 and on rating schedules of 1950 relating to the Ecrehos kept by the Jersey authorities. As to the Minquiers, the Court invoked various works and constructions carried out by the Jersey authorities as late as 1933, and rating schedules of 1950 (*Ibid.*, p. 69).

following the commencement of the dispute in 1886 and 1888 were not regarded as constituting further stages in the emergence of the critical date, *prior* to its coming into being, but rather as acts *subsequent* to its coming into existence. Still, the passage of the judgment just quoted does seem to contradict the definition of the critical date given in this section,[1] where it was asserted that the function of the critical date was to "freeze" the legal situation as it existed on that date and to exclude from the scope of legal consideration any events which occurred after that moment. This apparent contradiction resolves itself when one bears in mind that, although evidence of acts occurring after the critical date cannot be adduced directly in proof of a title, it may at the same time be admissible indirectly because of the light it throws on events occurring before the critical date or on the position as it stood at that date. Thus, the function of these subsequent acts is not to supply evidence required for the proof of a title, but rather to serve as a means of interpreting a title or situation as it existed on the critical date. As was pointed out by Sir Gerald Fitzmaurice in the course of his oral argument in the *Minquiers and Ecrehos* case, the principle involved on this point is analogous to the "principle of subsequent practice" with regard to the interpretation of treaties. "Just as the subsequent practice of parties to a treaty, in relation to it, cannot alter the meaning of the treaty, but may yet be evidence of what that meaning is, or what the parties had in mind in concluding it, so equally events occurring after the critical date in a dispute about territory cannot operate to *alter* the position as it stood at that date, but may nevertheless be evidence of, and throw light on, what the position was."[2]

This, in fact, was the line adopted by Judge Huber in the *Island of Palmas* Arbitration. As will be recalled, the arbitrator selected the year 1898 as the critical date in that case; this, however, did not prevent him from referring to a subsequent visit of the American General Leonard Wood to the island in 1906, which he described as "the first entry into contact by the American authorities with the island."[3] The arbitrator regarded this event as the "*origin of the dispute*"[4] between the United States and the Netherlands, as distinct from

[1] See above, p. 209, n. 1.

[2] *ICJ, Minquiers and Ecrehos case, Pleadings, Oral Arguments, Documents,* vol. II, p. 94. (Italics in original). For a more detailed analysis of the "principle of subsequent practice" and for further authorities in support of the admissibility of such practice as a principle of treaty interpretation, see Fitzmaurice, 28 *BYIL* (1951), p. 9 and pp. 20–22.

[3] *UNRIAA*, vol. II, p. 836.

[4] *Ibid.* (Italics in original).

the "critical moment," which he fixed as being the year 1898. The term "origin of the dispute" is warranted by the fact that it was this visit which sparked off the legal controversy between the parties, leading ultimately to the conclusion of an arbitration agreement in 1925.

It therefore appears that the "critical date" and the "origin of the dispute" are not identical and interchangeable terms. What is more: contrary to what may perhaps be reasonably assumed, the "origin of the dispute" may on occasions be later than the "critical date." Judge Huber made it, however, quite plain that the events which had taken place between the critical moment and the origin of the dispute "cannot in themselves serve to indicate the legal situation of the island at the critical moment when the cession of the Philippines by Spain took place. They are however indirectly of certain interest, owing to the light they might throw on the period immediately preceding."[1] The arbitrator illustrates this by pointing out that "there is no essential difference between the relations between the Dutch authorities and the Island of Palmas (or Miangas) before and after the Treaty of Paris. There cannot therefore be any question of ruling out the events of the period 1899–1906 as possibly being influenced by the existence of the said Treaty."[2]

The International Court of Justice appears to have followed suit on this point in the *Minquiers and Ecrehos* case, when it ruled that acts subsequent to the critical date might be taken account of, provided these acts were *not* performed with a view to *improving the legal position* of one of the parties to the detriment of the other, and on the condition that they merely constituted a *continuation* of an already accepted practice, carried out *in a similar manner* as before.[3]

The same course was also followed by Judge Basdevant, in his Individual Opinion in the same case.[4]

More recently, reference was again made to this principle by Sir Gerald Fitzmaurice in his Separate Opinion in the *Temple of Preah Vihear* case, in the following words:

> It is a general principle of law, which has been applied in many contexts, that a party's attitude, state of mind or intentions at a later date can be regarded as good evidence – in relation to the same or closely connected matter – of his attitude, state of mind or intentions at an earlier date also; provided of course that there is

[1] *Ibid.*, p. 866.
[2] *Ibid.*
[3] *ICJ Reports*, 1953, pp. 59–60.
[4] *Ibid.*, p. 83.

no direct evidence rebutting the presumption thus raised. Similarly – and very important in cases affecting territorial sovereignty – the existence of a state of fact, or of a situation, at a later date may furnish good presumptive evidence of its existence at an earlier date also, even where the later situation or state of affairs has in other respects to be excluded from consideration.[1]

It is believed that the soundness of this approach is well borne out by the realities of international life, because normally sovereignty over territory is not something that springs up overnight. It is a lengthy process which is usually going on constantly for some time. If the critical date is fixed in a given case and it is also established that for a number of years afterwards one of the contestants has been exercising governmental authority over the disputed territory, displaying the normal signs of effective and regular State control, then this stability and regularity of State control will in itself strongly militate in favour of the presumption that the State now in effective control was also in control for some time before, including, in all likelihood, the critical date itself.[2]

It is, however, worth noting that under no circumstances will it be permissible to invoke in support of a claim to a territorial title acts which have taken place after the dispute has been narrowed into a concrete issue. In most cases this will mean that all acts performed by the parties, or by either of them, subsequent to the conclusion of an agreement to submit the outstanding issues to a judicial settlement, will be excluded by the tribunal called upon to settle such a dispute from among the facts to be taken into account in determining the rights of the parties. The "origin of the dispute" will not always coincide with the conclusion of the treaty for the judicial settlement of the dispute. It signifies rather the first in a series of events which ultimately result in the submission of the dispute for judicial settlement.

This rule is founded on the assumption that it is the duty of the parties to preserve a *status quo* after the submission of their dispute for

[1] *ICJ Reports*, 1962, p. 61.

[2] The foregoing statement should not be taken as an endorsement of a principle which would found a State's sovereignty on a purely abstract presumption, raised by the fact that the territory in question was under the authority of that State at two different dates, from which it would follow that, in the absence of any evidence to the contrary, this State must be presumed to have also been in possession of that territory in the intervening period. The adoption of such a principle was, in fact, emphatically rejected by Judge Huber in the *Island of Palmas* Award when he stated that "the admission of the existence of ... sovereignty [at two given periods]... would not lead... to the conclusion that, unless the contrary is proved, there is a presumption for the existence of sovereignty in the meantime.... No presumptions of this kind are to be applied in international arbitrations." (*UNRIAA*, vol. II, p. 864). See also to the same effect the judgment rendered in the *Minquiers and Ecrehos* case, *ICJ Reports*, 1953, p. 55.

judicial decision and that any action taken by them afterwards must be assumed as being aimed at upsetting the balance existing between them at the time of the conclusion of the agreement. This rule was invoked by Judge Huber in the *Island of Palmas* case when, referring to acts which had occurred after the "origin of the dispute," he said:

> As regards the 20th century it is to be observed that events subsequent to 1906 must in any case be ruled out, in accordance both with the general principles of arbitral procedure between States and with the understanding arrived at between the Parties. ...[1]

Here the arbitrator fixed as the "final date" the year 1906 and not 1925 – in which year the arbitration treaty was concluded – because it was the events of 1906 – notably the visit of General Wood in Palmas – that set in train the chain of events which ultimately led to the conclusion of the arbitration agreement some 19 years later.

Similarly, in the *Minquiers and Ecrehos* case the Court, though fixing the years 1886 and 1888 as the critical dates, was prepared at the same time to take into account events up to the conclusion in 1950 of the Special Agreement between the parties.

In no case, however, will acts performed *after* the reference of a dispute to arbitration or to judicial settlement be taken cognizance of in appraising the rights of the parties to the dispute. This principle was perhaps most succinctly enunciated by the Permanent Court of International Justice in the case concerning the *Legal Status of the South-Eastern Territory of Greenland*.[2] There the Court dealt with a territorial dispute that had arisen between Norway and Denmark. Norway asked the Court to order interim measures whereby Denmark would be instructed to abstain in the disputed territory from any coercive measures directed against Norwegian nationals.[3] The Norwegian request was motivated, amongst other things, by the fear that certain acts performed by the Danes after the institution of the proceedings might affect the rights of the parties.

The Court, however, while recognizing that "the object of the measures of interim protection ... is to preserve the respective rights of the Parties pending the decision of the Court, in so far ... as the damage threatening these rights would be irreparable in fact or in

[1] *UNRIAA*, vol. II, p. 866.
[2] Order of August 3rd, 1932, *PCIJ*, Series A/B, No. 48, p. 13.
[3] *Ibid.*, p. 14.

law,"[1] dismissed the Norwegian request because, after the institution of proceedings,

no act on the part of the ... [Governments of Denmark and Norway] in the territory in question can have any effect whatever as regards the legal situation which the Court is called upon to define.[2]

57. The relative strength of competing claims

The selection of the critical date in any given dispute – whatever this date may be – does not mean of course that the situation as it exists at that particular moment will in itself determine the rights of the parties, regardless of what happened before. The typical territorial dispute will normally have been in existence for a long period at the time when the critical date emerges. During this period both contestants may have exercised certain governmental functions in the disputed territory and may have manifested in one way or another their willingness to lay a valid territorial claim to it. This is the normal state of things in most cases where a title to land territory is disputed and is not altogether unlikely to be the case even when the dispute revolves around the acquisition of a maritime historic title.[3] As has been pointed out elsewhere, in disputes of this kind the issue is not whether the territory in question is *res nullius* or in the possession of one of the parties to the conflict; the real issue is *which* of the parties has acquired sovereignty over the disputed territory. The party claiming sovereignty in such disputes will not base it on a title by occupation of a formerly ownerless territory; it will invoke a title founded either on adverse holding or on a long-standing (so-called "immemorial") possession, the origins of which it is impossible to trace.

International tribunals faced with such a type of territorial dispute will approach it on the assumption that the issue may turn not so much on the intrinsic value of the acts or claims of the rival parties, as on their relative worth when looked upon as being in competition with one another. In theory, a situation can be conceived in which neither of the contestants has put forward a sufficiently strong and well-founded claim based on abstract rights; it will then fall to the tribunal faced with such competing claims to establish, to quote Sir Gerald Fitzmau-

[1] *Ibid.*, p. 20.
[2] *Ibid.*, p. 23.
[3] See e.g. the *Grisbadarna* Arbitration where both Sweden and Norway claimed to have acquired a title to the disputed banks by virtue, *inter alia*, of their alleged exercise of authority over them.

rice, that "these grounds are *less* insufficient in the one case than in the other, and therefore can afford a basis for a finding of sovereignty."[1] It could equally happen that both parties put forward claims which, if taken separately and in isolation, would perhaps suffice to give each of them a valid title, but, when confronted with each other, the tribunal called upon to determine the issue will have to decide which of the contestants has made out a *better* or *superior* title.

The concept, according to which the tribunal will consider "the general weight of the claim" of each party rather than the situation prevailing at the critical date alone, makes it necessary to view each country's claim as a whole. It would clearly be contrary to this "weight of the claim" concept, if the claims were to be examined stage by stage, drawing comparisons of the strength of the competing parties' claims at successive periods. Accordingly, Judge Huber in the *Island of Palmas* case, in assessing the respective rights and claims of the United States and of the Netherlands, did not go back to the earliest date mentioned in that case (i.e. the period of the Thirty Years' War). Nor did he compare the titles of the competing parties at that date or at any successive moment. He declined, likewise, to adopt the critical date as the starting-point for his examination from which he would go backwards, comparing the titles of the contestants at various previous dates. In neither of these ways would a broad legal comparison of the two competing titles have been feasible. Instead, Judge Huber followed a method which considered each of the two competing titles as a whole and as an entity. This method was described by Sir Lionel Heald in his oral argument in the *Minquiers and Ecrehos* case in the following words:

> Instead of working purely chronologically, either forwards or backwards, [Judge Huber] studied and analyzed first the one title by itself, and the other by itself, then the first again, comparing the two titles not in terms of the moment, but in respect of their legal weight, taken as a whole over the whole period.[2]

There is little doubt that Sir Lionel did, in fact, correctly interpret the general tenor of this award which was summarized by the arbitrator himself as follows:

> The conditions of acquisition of sovereignty by the Netherlands are therefore to be considered as fulfilled. It remains now to be seen whether the United States as successors of Spain are in a position to bring forward an equivalent or stronger title. This is to be answered in the negative.[3]

[1] Fitzmaurice, 32 *BYIL* (1955–56), p. 35. (Italics added).
[2] *ICJ, Minquiers and Ecrehos case, Pleadings, Oral Arguments, Documents*, vol. II, p. 49.
[3] *UNRIAA*, vol. II p. 868.

The arbitrator therefore concluded:

The Netherlands title of sovereignty, acquired by continuous and peaceful display of State authority during a long period of time going probably back beyond the year 1700, ... holds good.[1]

Roche makes the point that Judge Huber may have felt all the more entitled to use the "relative strength" method of assessment, because he took the view that, due to the dearth of specific evidence relating to the Island of Palmas, the parties must have foreseen such an approach to this problem.[2] This statement is, in fact, borne out by the following passage of the award:

The possibility for the Arbitrator to found his decision on the relative strength of the titles invoked on either side must have been envisaged by the Parties ..., because it was to be foreseen that the evidence produced as regards sovereignty over a territory in the circumstances of the island in dispute might prove not to be sufficient to lead to a clear conclusion as to the existence of sovereignty.[3]

The same idea was conveyed perhaps even more clearly by the Permanent Court of International Justice in the *Legal Status of Eastern Greenland* case, where the Court commented on the problem of the relative strength of competing territorial claims in the following words:

Another circumstance which must be taken into account by any tribunal which has to adjudicate upon a claim to sovereignty over a particular territory, is the extent to which the sovereignty is also claimed by some other Power. In most of the cases involving claims to territorial sovereignty which have come before an international tribunal, there have been two competing claims to sovereignty and the tribunal has had to decide which of the two is the stronger.[4]

Thus, in this case too, the Permanent Court of International Justice seems to have upheld the view that a tribunal faced with a territorial dispute based on two competing claims will examine these titles not piecemeal, but as a whole, by comparing them over the entire material period.[5]

In the *Minquiers and Ecrehos* case, the United Kingdom relied heavily on this concept of the relative strength of competing claims and it was argued on her behalf that "it would be unsound to embark on any historical comparison of the strength of the two countries' claims at

[1] *Ibid.*, p. 869.
[2] Roche, *op. cit.*, p. 67, n. 6.
[3] *UNRIAA*, vol. II, p. 869.
[4] *PCIJ*, Series A/B, No. 53, p. 46.
[5] See, however, Roche, who asserts that this case "indicates a tendency to favour the 'period to period' method." (Roche, *op. cit.*, p. 66).

successive periods of time."[1] Counsel for the United Kingdom suggested that "the right method is to take each country's claim as a whole and as it stands now, and then to decide which is the weightier."[2]

The Court in its judgment appears to have resorted to the method laid down by Judge Huber in the *Island of Palmas* case and followed in the *Legal Status of Eastern Greenland* case, thus upholding the United Kingdom contentions on this point. It examined separately the grounds of title alleged by each of the parties in respect of each of the disputed islets and then compared the relative weight of the competing claims.[3] With reference to the Ecrehos, the Court concluded:

The Court, being now called upon to appraise the relative strength of the opposing claims to sovereignty over the Ecrehos in the light of the facts considered above, finds that ... the sovereignty over the Ecrehos belongs to the United Kingdom.[4]

With reference to the Minquiers, the Court did not pronounce itself in so many words; it is, however, clear from the perusal of those pages of the judgment devoted to the analysis of the evidence produced by the parties concerning the Minquiers that it followed precisely the same method in this case also.[5]

Since the strength and weight of a territorial claim of this type is to be assessed in the light of the strength of the competing claim, it is only too obvious that the objective is not to ascertain whether one of the contestants has acquired an absolute title, but rather which party has acquired a *superior* title. The essential issue in this kind of case "is not so much 'What has each party done?', but 'Which has done the most?'"[6] It clearly follows that acts or omissions which would be regarded as a sufficient proof of title in the absence of a rival claim will have to be considered in a different light altogether once there is a competing claim in existence. To quote Sir Gerald Fitzmaurice:

Acts that will be sufficient, or, conversely, neglects that will be immaterial, in the

[1] *ICJ, Minquiers and Ecrehos case, Pleadings, Oral Arguments, Documents*, vol. II, p. 46.

[2] *Ibid.* Wade, who was one of the United Kingdom Counsel in that case, expressed the same idea when he maintained that "in deciding between two competing claims to territory, each country's claim and grounds of claim should be considered as a whole, and the decision should be in favour of the country whose claim is the weightier." (*Ibid.*, p. 96).

[3] Prefacing its analysis of the rival claims to the Ecrehos, the Court said: "The Court will now consider the claims of both parties to sovereignty over the *Ecrehos* and begin with the evidence produced by the United Kingdom Government." (See *ICJ Reports*, 1953, p. 60). The same phrasing also occurs literally as regards the Minquiers. (*Ibid.*, p. 67).

[4] *Ibid.*, p. 67.

[5] *Ibid.*, pp. 67–72.

[6] *ICJ, Minquiers and Ecrehos case, Pleadings, Oral Arguments, Documents*, vol. II, p. 57. (Oral argument of Sir Lionel Heald).

face of a low degree of counter-activity, will not be so if that counter-activity is high.[1]

This statement has, in fact, far-reaching consequences inasmuch as the degree of *continuity* of possession required for the establishment of a valid title will turn to a very large extent on the existence or otherwise of a competing territorial claim.[2]

On this point, again, guidance may be sought in some of the major decisions rendered in recent decades by international tribunals called upon to pronounce on territorial disputes. The general principle underlying the considerations of international tribunals in such cases appears to have been formulated by the Permanent Court of International Justice in the *Legal Status of Eastern Greenland* case, where the Court observed:

It is impossible to read the records of the decisions in cases as to territorial sovereignty without observing that in many cases the tribunal has been satisfied with very little in the way of the actual exercise of sovereign rights, provided that the other State could not make out a superior claim. This is particularly true in the case of claims to sovereignty over areas in thinly populated or unsettled countries.[3]

The Court had obviously in the back of its mind the award rendered shortly before in the *Clipperton Island* case. There, as will be recalled, France had displayed no governmental functions with regard to the disputed territory for about forty years, since first taking possession of the island in 1858. In 1897 Mexico raised a claim to the island. But, since no other State had claimed or maintained authority over the island in the intervening period, France's original act of taking possession was considered as still valid in international law. King Victor Emanuel III, the sole arbitrator in that case, took the view that in "les cas ordinaires" the taking of possession itself – indicating *animus occupandi* – must be followed up by the ocupant by "une organisation capable de faire respecter ses droits."[4] He stressed, however, that

il peut y avoir aussi des cas où il n'est pas nécessaire de recourir à ce moyen. C'est ainsi que, si un territoire, par le fait qu'il était complètement inhabité, *est, dès le premier moment où l'Etat occupant y fait son apparition, à la disposition absolue et incontestée de cet Etat,* la prise de possession doit être considérée, à partir de ce moment, comme accomplie et l'occupation est achevée par cela même.[5]

[1] Fitzmaurice, 32 *BYIL* (1955–56), p. 64.
[2] For a more detailed discussion of the notion of "continuity" with reference to the acquisition of an historic title, see above chapter IV, section 34.
[3] *PCIJ*, Series A/B, No. 53, p. 46.
[4] *UNRIAA*, vol. II, p. 1105, at p. 1110.
[5] *Ibid.* (Italics added).

The italicized portion of the above-quoted passage seems to warrant the conclusion reached by Fitzmaurice that "any subsequent or intervening manifestation of sovereignty by another State – unless immediately reacted against (as France reacted against Mexico's intervention) – would have been detrimental to the French claim still to be sovereign at the date of the Mexican assertion of claim, unless it had been offset by some concrete activity on the part of France over and above her initial *prise de possession*."[1] According to Waldock, there is, however, little doubt that the inactivity of France "would surely have been fatal to her claim in the face of an intervening exercise of sovereignty by another state."[2]

The *Legal Status of Eastern Greenland* case presented some analogous features and the Court did not miss the opportunity to state that

> up to 1931 there was no claim by any Power other than Denmark to the sovereignty over Greenland. Indeed, up till 1921, no Power disputed the Danish claim to sovereignty.[3]

It is in the light of this finding that one should read the Court's statement that "in many cases the tribunal has been satisfied with very little in the way of actual exercise of sovereign rights."[4] This statement of the general rule is, however, subject to the all-important qualification: "provided that the other State could not make out a superior claim."[5]

In this connection it is worth-while considering the Court's approach to the problem whether the rights of Denmark could have been maintained even during certain periods when there was no shadow of Danish authority over Greenland. It appears pertinent to interpose at this juncture that some time after 1380 – this being the date at which the Danish and Norwegian Crowns were joined – the Norse settlements, which had before existed in Greenland, disappeared and

> during the first two centuries or so after the settlements perished, there seems to have been no intercourse with Greenland and knowledge of it diminished; but the

[1] Fitzmaurice, 32 *BYIL* (1955–56), pp. 65–66. (Italics in original).

[2] Waldock, 25 *BYIL* (1948), p. 325. Nevertheless, this appears to be one of those instances in which the "period to period" method was employed. This may be explained by the fact that "here the facts were comparatively simple" (Roche, *op. cit.*, p. 65), as well as by the brevity of the period relevant to the dispute which was spread over less than 40 years. Thus, the arbitrator found it convenient to consider the relative merits of the parties' cases in 1858, when France first claimed the island, and then in 1897, when Mexico first reacted to the French assertion of sovereignty. (For a more detailed analysis of the implications of the *Clipperton Island* case on this point see Roche, *op. cit.*, pp. 65–66).

[3] *PCIJ*, Series A/B, No. 53, p. 46.

[4] *Ibid.*

[5] *Ibid.* For an appraisal of the Court's judgment on this point, see Lauterpacht, *The Development of International Law by the International Court*, 1958, pp. 240–241.

tradition of the King's rights lived on, ... [and] the King considered that in his dealings with Greenland he was dealing with a country with respect to which he had a special position superior to that of any other Power.[1]

Of course, this conviction of the King would not have been sufficient in itself to preserve any title for Denmark and the Court was the first to recognize this fact by saying:

That the King's claims amounted merely to pretensions is clear, for he had no permanent contact with the country, he was exercising no authority there.[2]

That this absence of exercise of authority on the part of Denmark did not prove fatal to her rights, is warranted solely by the fact that

the claims [of Denmark] ... were not disputed. No other Power was putting forward any claim to territorial sovereignty in Greenland, and *in the absence of any competing claim* the King's pretensions to be the sovereign of Greenland subsisted.[3]

It seems quite clear that the Court would have found that the original title of Denmark had been lost by the inactivity which had lasted for about two centuries, were it not for the absence of a competing claim actively maintained at the time. Commenting on the Court's judgment, Waldock makes the point that the Court "did not dispense altogether with state activity; it only recognized that state activity may be slight when the territory is uninhabited and *when there is no competing state activity*."[4] It is therefore hardly surprising that in his argument in the *Minquiers and Ecrehos* case, Counsel for the United Kingdom asserted that the State activities referred to by France as indicating the display of authority on her part over the disputed islets might have perhaps sufficed in the absence of a competing claim and of competing State activities, but could not be regarded as sufficient for the upkeep of a title in the face of rival claims and activities. Citing in his support the *Legal Status of Eastern Greenland* case, Counsel for the United Kingdom maintained:

It is just conceivable that, supposing France to have had an original title to the Minquiers and Ecréhous, this might have simply continued even without any concrete display of State authority, *provided France had been alone in the field*. ... But *with an actively competing claim in the field*, over the whole period, any *such original rights were bound to suffer extinction* unless supported by effective possession and control, and by the active exercise of State authority.[5]

[1] *Ibid.*, p. 47.
[2] *Ibid.*, p. 48.
[3] *Ibid.* (Italics added).
[4] Waldock, *loc. cit.*, p. 325. (Italics in original).
[5] *ICJ, Minquiers and Ecrehos case, Pleadings, Oral Arguments, Documents*, vol. II, p. 57. (Italics added).

The Court in its judgment seems to have approved of this approach, for, after enumerating the various activities performed by the contesting parties in respect of the islets, it concluded, with reference to the Minquiers, that

> the Court does not find that the facts, invoked by the French Government, are sufficient to show that France has a valid title to the Minquiers.[1]

It may safely be assumed that this conclusion was warranted to a very large extent by the superior manifestation of British authority over the Minquiers, and the French claim would have probably been upheld in the absence of such competing activities.

58. The burden of proving an historic title

The question of the burden of proof is, of course, a general problem of law. At first sight it might appear that this procedural question has no real bearing on the eventual outcome of a legal dispute and is little more than indulging in legalistic niceties and minutiae. Such a view, may, however, prove frequently both deceptive and illusionary. The annals of legal history provide ample illustration of cases in which the ultimate decision was a direct result of the rules of evidence, and parties are known to have lost their cases solely because they have not succeeded in discharging the burden of proof resting on them. It may therefore be readily seen that the questions attendant on the onus of proof are of direct relevance in the establishment of an historic title.

In the sphere of domestic law the problems pertaining to the onus of proof are not fraught with particular difficulties. In civil law this duty is normally incumbent on the plaintiff. *Actori incumbit probatio.* Similarly, in criminal proceedings the burden of proof is laid on the shoulders of the prosecution.

In exceptional circumstances – explicitly enumerated by the law itself – the onus of proof may rest on the other side. This usually happens in those cases where the law infers certain presumptions as being the logical outcome of given situations, and, once the claimant has invoked in his favour such a presumption, the burden of proof shifts to the rival side. Likewise, certain legal systems establish such legal presumptions in favour of the applicant whose claim is based on a negative fact, the proof of which is incomparably more difficult than that of a positive allegation.

[1] *ICJ Reports*, 1953, p. 71.

Apart from these relatively few departures, however, it may be taken as sound law that the burden of proof rests on the shoulders of the party which has set in motion the wheels of the legal machinery. It then becomes the duty of this party to make out a *prima facie* case, proving all those facts which are relevant to, and material for, the success of its claims. Then, and only then, will the burden of proof shift to the other side, which, in turn, if willing to refute and thwart the charges levelled against it, will be called upon to prove all the facts on which its alleged case rests.

In international law there do not appear to exist elaborate rules as to the burden of proof. The reason for this obvious drawback is thought to be the fact that "the parties before international tribunals, and also international judges, often come from states whose municipal law on the subject varies considerably."[1] Another reason given is that in many cases the parties to international disputes have the same standing and there is neither plaintiff nor defendant.[2] International law is no doubt influenced on this point by the fact that a fair proportion of cases is started by *compromis*. If more use were made of the "Optional Clause" procedure, the position might be perhaps different.

As far as the problem of the onus of proof is concerned, international law follows, broadly speaking, the same rules as domestic law. It is incumbent on each party to prove the facts alleged by it, and to bring forth evidence in support of its legal arguments. Thus, it is first for the applicant State (if there is such) to prove the facts on which its action relies and to establish a *prima facie* case; the opposing State will then proceed to prove those facts which, in its view, defeat the applicant State's case.

As has been stressed before, the process of evidence normally involves merely the proof of facts. It is admitted that, as on the national legal level, international law does not require the parties to supply evidence as to the state of law and as to the contents of the rules of law applicable in each given case;[3] international tribunals are presumed to have judicial notice of the general rules of international law. The age-old maxim *jura novit curia* finds application in the field of international law too. This statement, however, must be read *cum grano salis*. It is, as has been stated before, the *general* rules of inter-

[1] Roche, *op. cit.*, p. 129.
[2] *Ibid.*
[3] This rule, though, has its exceptions on the national level where, as is well known, foreign law is regarded as a question of fact, which has to be proved with the aid of expert witnesses.

national law that are within the knowledge of an international tribunal. "There is no burden of proof," said Sir Eric Beckett in the course of his statement in the *Fisheries* case, "so far as the general rules of international law are concerned and ... the maxim *jura novit curia* applies to everything that is part of the general rules of international law."[1] Historic titles, however, do not constitute the *rule*; they are, as has been submitted in a previous chapter, a deviation and departure from the general rules of customary international law and, being basically founded on adverse holding, they find their legal justification in the fact that the State or States faced with such an exceptional claim have acquiesced in a situation which is contrary to, and derogatory of, the normally applicable rules of international law. "It is where a State relies upon something special to itself, such as a prescriptive or historic title or treaty right, that the burden of proof arises."[2]

Having reached this stage, it will be more easily understood why the parties to the *Fisheries* case should have devoted so much space and energy to what at first sight may appear as a futile academic discussion, namely, the problem whether the regime of historic waters is part of the general international maritime regime, as was contended on behalf of Norway, or whether, as was asserted by the United Kingdom, "historic waters" form an exception, because it is their function to accord to a body of water a legal status which would not have normally accrued to it under the applicable rules of international law. This seemingly superfluous discussion between the parties was indeed only a preliminary "jockeying for position" – to use the words of Waldock in his oral reply in the *Fisheries* case[3] – for what was really involved in this controversy was the question: does the United Kingdom have to prove that Norway has *not* acquired any exceptional rights beyond her marginal belt of territorial waters, as measured according to the commonly accepted and employed methods of delimitation, or is it imcumbent on Norway to prove that, owing to some exceptional circumstances, she has acquired an exceptional right of delimiting her territorial waters by resorting to the "Norwegian method" of delimitation, which entails a considerable increase in the width of her territorial waters?

The practical importance of this question has been also pointed out

[1] *ICJ, Fisheries case, Pleadings, Oral Arguments, Documents,* vol. IV, p. 33. (Italics in original).
[2] *Ibid.*
[3] *Ibid.*, p. 394.

in the Study on the *Juridical Regime of Historic Waters, Including Historic Bays*, prepared by the United Nations Secretariat for the 14th Session of the International Law Commission, in the following words:

> Whether or not the régime of 'historic waters' is an exceptional régime may seem to be an academic question. In reality, it is of practical importance with respect to the question of what is needed to establish title to such waters. If the right to 'historic waters' is an exceptional title which cannot be based on the general rules of international law or which even may be said to abrogate these rules in a particular case, it is obvious that the requirements with respect to proof of such title will be rigorous. The reasons for accepting the title must be pursuasive; for how could one otherwise justify the disregarding of the general rule in a particular case?[1]

It is submitted that, owing to the exceptional character of an historic claim and its deviation from the general rules of customary law, the burden of proof in such cases falls on the State which claims such a title in its favour to prove all those facts which, in its opinion, support the exceptional claim, irrespective of whether the legal proceedings had been instituted by the party alleging such a title or by a party denying the acquisition by its opponent of an historic title. A State raising a claim to rights and titles which would not normally accrue to it under international law must obviously be prepared to prove that it has, in fact, acquired such rights or titles. Such a course of action will undoubtedly better meet the requirements of both reason and justice than a demand postulating that it is on the State relying on the normal rules to justify its reliance on them. The acceptance of the contention, according to which the burden of proof invariably lies on the applicant, would, in fact, create a serious anomaly in that the application of the general rules of international law would depend on the accident whether the State relying on these rules happens to be the applicant or whether the action was filed by the State which claims exemption from them. "The decision [of the Court]," asserted Sir Eric Beckett in his opening statement in the *Fisheries* case, "in a case which turns on the general rules of international law and which is inevitably a precedent of the greatest importance for the whole world, cannot turn on the accident whether the United Kingdom happens to have brought the case as plaintiff or whether Norway has. ... The Court's conclusions on the general rules of international law will not depend in any way on whether Norway or the United Kingdom is the applicant State."[2]

[1] U.N. Document A/CN. 4/143 of March 9th, 1962, *ILC Yearbook*, 14th session, 1962, vol. II, p. 7.

[2] *ICJ, Fisheries case, Pleadings, Oral Arguments, Documents*, vol. IV, pp. 33–34.

Norway, in her written Rejoinder, did not basically challenge the correctness of this proposition, recognizing in principle that "celui qui invoque un fait ou un droit exceptionnel a l'obligation de l'établir, sous peine de voir sa prétention écartée."[1] At the same time she maintained that

> quand il s'agit d'une règle coutumière faisant partie du droit international commun, on peut raisonnablement soutenir que ... les éléments d'appréciation sur lesquels la Cour appuie sa conviction ne sont plus nécessairement limités à ceux qui ont été produits devant elle par la partie chargée du fardeau de la preuve.[2]

Norway attempted, however, to escape the logical conclusions of these apparently correct statements by asserting that her alleged historic right to apply the Norwegian method of delimitation by straight baselines, connecting the outermost points of the *skjaergaard*, did not constitute an exception, since the generally applicable rule of following the physical line of the coast had not achieved the degree of a general rule of customary international law. The Norwegian method, Norway maintained, was the original method of delimitation recognized by maritime international law and other methods of delimitation – and in particular the coast-line method advocated by the United Kingdom and generally applied by the littoral States of the world – being comparative "late-comers" on the stage of international law, could not be regarded as ranking higher in the hierarchy of the binding rules of international law. Norway also charged the United Kingdom with misunderstanding the true nature and purpose of the rules governing the legal regime of the seas and the delimitation of the maritime territorial domain of the littoral State. In Norway's opinion "ces règles, en effet, n'ont pas pour objet *d'attribuer* à l'Etat côtier les compétences qu'il exerce sur la mer voisine de ses côtes, de donner un *fondement juridique* à sa souveraineté. Elles ont pour objet de limiter et de *restreindre* le champ de cette souveraineté."[3] Thus, in the opinion of Norway, it is not the national pretensions of the various littoral States that encroach upon the principle of the freedom of the high seas, but it is rather the principle of the freedom of the high seas that encroaches on the original rights of the littoral States to be regarded as the sovereigns

[1] *Ibid.*, vol. III, p. 285.
[2] *Ibid.*
[3] *Ibid.*, vol. III, p. 287. (Italics in original). In another passage of the Counter-Memorial Norway maintained that the sea areas landwards to the Norwegian-drawn baselines "ni juridiquement, ni historiquement,... n'ont jamais fait partie de la mer libre. Elles ont toujours été norvégiennes et ne représentent même que le résidu d'un domaine plus vaste, qui s'est contracté au profit de la communauté des Etats." (*Ibid.*, vol. III, p. 442).

over wide portions of the sea areas adjacent to their land territories.[1]

It would appear, however, that this concept of the nature of the maritime historic title and its "incorporation" into the general international legal practice, as being in *conformity* with the normal rules of law and not a *departure* from them, is borne out neither by doctrine nor by practice, both of which seem to have upheld the traditional view that the role of an historic title is to validate an intrinsically invalid claim and not merely to confirm an already existing title. It necessarily follows that the historic claim being regarded as an exception to, and derogation of, the general rule – sanctioned only by the acquiescence of the State or States adversely affected by the new practice or situation – the burden of proof rests on the State claiming for itself such an exceptional title, irrespective of whether it happens to be the plaintiff or not. "En ce qui concerne le fardeau de la preuve," says Gidel, in discussing the onus of proof attendant on the proof of a maritime historic title, "il pèse sur l'Etat qui prétend attribuer à des espaces maritimes proches de ses côtes le caractère, qu'ils n'auraient pas normalement, d'eaux intèrieures. C'est l'Etat riverain qui est le demandeur dans cette sorte de procès. Ses prétentions tendent à un empiètement sur la haute mer: le principe de la liberté de la haute mer, qui demeure la base essentielle de tout le droit international public maritime, ne permet pas de faire peser le fardeau de la preuve sur les Etats, au détriment desquels la haute mer sera réduite par l'attribution de certaines eaux en propre à l'Etat qui les réclame comme telles."[2]

Similarly, Colombos maintains that the rules fixing the normal breadth of territorial waters in bays are subject to the exception that

> on historic or prescriptive grounds ... the territorial State is entitled to claim a wider belt of marginal waters, provided that *it can produce evidence* ... that its claim has been accepted, expressly or tacitly, by the great majority of other nations.[3]

Both Gidel and Colombos merely follow in this respect the principles which seem to emerge from Basis of Discussions No. 8, drafted by the Preparatory Committee of the 1930 Hague Codification Conference. The Preparatory Committee, appointed under a resolution

[1] See to this effect the Norwegian Counter-Memorial where it is asserted that "historiquement... ce n'est pas généralement la souveraineté de l'Etat qui s'est étendue au détriment de la haute mer, mais bien la haute mer qui s'est développée en absorbant des espaces soumis jusque-là à l'autorité de l'Etat." (*Ibid.*, pp. 444–445).

[2] Gidel, *op. cit.*, vol. III, p. 632.

[3] Colombos, *op. cit.*, pp. 164–165. (Italics added).

adopted by the Council of the League of Nations on September 28th, 1928, had at an earlier stage of its deliberations examined the replies of the Governments to its request for information on questions relating to the agenda of the proposed conference. Basis of Discussions No. 8 prepared by this Committee reads as follows:

The belt of territorial waters shall be measured from a straight line drawn across the entrance of a bay, whatever its breadth may be, if by usage the bay is subject to the exclusive authority of the coastal State; *the onus of proving such usage is upon the coastal State.*[1]

True, the Hague Codification Conference proved abortive and its deliberations came to nought; it is, however, worth noting that, although Basis of Discussions No. 8 underwent some criticism in the Second Committee of the Conference, it was not seriously questioned by anybody that the burden of proof as regards the establishment of a special claim rested on the coastal State. Moreover, it may be added that the only Government which, in its reply to the request of the Preparatory Committee, expressly referred to the question of the burden of proof was the Government of Germany which stated that

as regards 'historic bays,' it would seem right in principle *to require the coastal State making such a claim* in respect of bays exceeding six nautical miles in width *to prove* that the bay has acquired the status of 'inland waters' of the coastal State through long usage generally recognised by other States.[2]

As has been stated before, the question of the burden of proof of an historic title was canvassed at great length in the *Fisheries* case. It is therefore a matter for sincere regret that once more the Court did not make full use of the opportunity to pronounce unambiguously on an important question of law which had been raised before it. It is perhaps true to say that the Court might have deemed it superfluous to go into this problem, since it did not consider Norway's alleged rights over certain maritime areas as being of an "historic" character properly so called. The Court seems to have rejected the United Kingdom contention, according to which Norwegian sovereignty over the waters in dispute would constitute an exception, historic titles justifying situations which would otherwise be in conflict with international law. The Court held that, as regards bays "the ten-mile rule has not acquired the authority of a general rule of international law,"[3] and

[1] *Ser. L.o.N.P.* 1929, V. 2, p. 45. (Italics added).
[2] *Ibid.*, p. 111. (Italics added).
[3] *ICJ Reports*, 1951, p. 131.

that consequently any deviation from this alleged rule did not constitute an exception. Similarly, the Court rejected the United Kingdom claim that baselines drawn between various points must be limited to a maximum length of ten miles, pointing out that no such rule existed in international law and that the Norwegian method did not form an exception to such an alleged rule, but rather "the application of general international law to a specific case."[1]

It is therefore submitted with some diffidence that the majority judgment of the Court did not find in favour of Norway on "historic" grounds, in the meaning which this term has generally acquired in doctrine and practice.[2] Support for this view is lent by the fact that Judge Hackworth, while concurring in the operative part of the majority judgment, dissociated himself from its motives, emphasizing that he did so for the reason that "he considers that the Norwegian Government has proved the existence of an historic title to the disputed areas of water."[3]

Those of the judges, however, who dealt with the problem of the acquisition of an historic title, namely, Judges Hsu Mo, McNair and Read, stressed the need for the claimant State to prove its alleged historic title. Thus, Judge McNair quoted with approval Lord Stowell in the *Twee Gebroeders* case where it had been stated that the general presumption was against the existence of such rights and that an historic title "is a matter to be established, on the part of those claiming under it, in the same manner as all other legal demands are to be substantiated, by clear and competent evidence."[4]

Judge Read expressly voiced the opinion that, as regards the acquisition of any "historic rights" by Norway, "the burden is upon Norway to prove [the relevant] facts"[5] and after a searching analysis of the history of the case, he reached the conclusion that "it has not been proved that the Norwegian System was made known to the world in time, and in such a manner that other nations, including the United Kingdom, knew about it or must be assumed to have had constructive knowledge."[6]

Judge Hsu Mo, likewise, in his Separate Opinion appears to have required from Norway to prove her alleged historic title and it is be-

[1] *Ibid.*
[2] Cf. McDougal and Burke, *op. cit.*, p. 365.
[3] *ICJ Reports*, 1951, p. 144.
[4] (1801) 3 *Christopher Robinson's Admiralty Report*, p. 336, at p. 339; this case is cited in *ICJ Reports*, 1951, pp. 183–184.
[5] *ICJ Reports*, 1951, p. 194.
[6] *Ibid.*, p. 205.

cause Norway did not put forward legally sound evidence in support of her historic claims, that Judge Hsu Mo dismissed the Norwegian historic claims as regards the Svaerholthavet and Lopphavet.[1]

An important contribution to international law on this topic was, however, made in the judgment delivered by the International Court of Justice in the *Minquiers and Ecrehos* case. There France claimed an original title to the disputed islets, alleging that it was the United Kingdom's turn to prove that Britain had acquired a good title, displacing the French one. This contention was explained on the ground that "en cas de doute, le droit doit être présumé en faveur de la République française qui a succédé à la souveraineté des anciens rois de France."[2]

To this contention the United Kingdom replied that, even if France had proved her ancient title – and on this point also the United Kingdom entertained doubts – it would not suffice for France to rely on such an ancient title, without adducing positive proof of a good and valid title. The United Kingdom cited in support of her argument Judge Huber's award in the *Island of Palmas* case, where it had been laid down that there was no presumption of continuity of territorial titles.[3]

The Court appears to have endorsed the United Kingdom assertion on this point, holding that

> such an alleged original feudal title of the Kings of France in respect of the Channel Islands could to-day produce no legal effect, unless it had been replaced by another title valid according to the law of the time of replacement. *It is for the French Government to establish that it was so replaced.*[4]

The question of the burden of proof was further dealt with recently by the International Court of Justice in its judgment delivered in the *Temple of Preah Vihear* case, where the Court held:

> As concerns the burden of proof, it must be pointed out that though, from the formal standpoint, Cambodia is the plaintiff, having instituted the proceedings, Thailand also is a claimant because of the claim which was presented by her in the second Submission of the Counter-Memorial and which relates to the sovereignty over the same piece of territory. Both Cambodia and Thailand base their respective claims on a series of facts and contentions which are asserted or put forward by one Party on the other. *The burden of proof in respect of these will of course lie on the Party asserting or putting them forward.*[5]

[1] *Ibid.*, p. 157.
[2] *ICJ, Minquiers and Ecrehos case, Pleadings, Oral Arguments, Documents*, vol. I, p. 383.
[3] *Ibid.*, vol. II, p. 53–54.
[4] *ICJ Reports*, 1953, p. 56. (Italics added).
[5] *ICJ Reports*, 1962, pp. 15–16. (Italics added).

Thus, the matter may be summed up by saying that, owing to the exceptional nature of the historic claim itself and as a direct consequence of the departure from the general rules of international law inherent in the acceptance of such a claim, the general rules governing the onus of proof also undergo some modification. Contrary to the maxim *actori incumbit probatio*, according to which the onus of proof will always fall on the applicant who will be expected to furnish the evidence necessary to make out a *prima facie* case, the onus of proving an historic claim will invariably fall on the State relying on such a claim and invoking an historic title in its support, irrespective of whether or not the legal proceedings in such a case were instituted by the State claiming an historic title.[1]

59. Strict geographical interpretation of an historic title

Since an historic title is acquired as a result of an encroachment upon the rights previously acquired by another State, or the community of States, and develops through a process of adverse holding, it necessarily follows that any claim of this kind must be given the strictest possible geographical interpretation. If historic titles are exceptions to the general rules of customary international law – as it is submitted they are – then it is only reasonable to restrict the scope of such exceptions to the bare minimum justified by the clearest evidence. Such a restrictive interpretation as regards the extent of the area acquired by means of an historic title is indeed imperative, because it constitutes one of the most vital safeguards for the proper manipulation of the device of acquiescence. MacGibbon formulates this idea in the following words:

[1] A somewhat different view on this point has been adopted in the Study on the *Juridical Regime of Historic Waters, Including Historic Bays*, prepared by the United Nations Secretariat for the 14th Session of the International Law Commission. (*ILC Yearbook*, 14th session, 1962, vol. II, p. 1 *et seq.*). It is claimed there that "the general statement that the burden of proof is on the State claiming historic title to a maritime area, is not of much value.... The elements of the title have evidently to be proved to the satisfaction of the arbitrator, otherwise he will not accept the title.... It would be unnecessary, and possibly misleading, to include in a regulation of the regime of 'historic waters' a general statement regarding the burden of proof. It would seem preferable to leave that question to be solved by the procedural rules which may be applicable in a particular case." (*Ibid.*, pp. 22–23). It is noteworthy that the *Memorandum on Historic Bays* prepared by the United Nations Secretariat for the first Geneva Conference on the Law of the Sea (U.N. Document A/CONF. 13/1, *United Nations Conference on the Law of the Sea, Official Records*, vol. I, *Preparatory Documents*, p. 1, at pp. 31–34) had confined itself to mentioning the various doctrinal and judicial views regarding the question of the burden of proof in respect of "historic waters," without expressing any opinion on the merits of those views.

The purpose of insisting on circumspection in inferring the consent of a State from its inaction is to ensure that such acquiescence corresponds accurately with the implied intention of the acquiescing State, and to limit the benefits of acquiescence to claims which have been formulated in such a way that the acquiescing State has or ought to have knowledge of them.[1]

Thus, in the arbitration between Great Britain and Venezuela respecting the *Venezuelan-British Guiana Boundary* Dispute, the United Kingdom maintained that the potential capacity of a State's expansion should be taken into account only in cases of acquiring titles by occupation (i.e. taking possession of *res nullius*), while in cases involving adverse possession and the infringement of the rights of a previous possessor, the rights of the newcomer should be interpreted strictly and should apply only to the territory effectively held by it.[2] (Venezuela, in turn, contended that when a territory is vacant, the entrant State may enter it as for the whole territory, but when the entry is adverse, only the territory effectively held will be acquired thereby).[3]

It was on similar grounds that the minority judges in the *Fisheries* case rejected some of the Norwegian claims. Judge Hsu Mo, discussing in his Separate Opinion the Norwegian claim for the acquisition of an historic title to the Lopphavet and Svaerholthavet, pointed out that

the Rescripts on which [Norway] has relied contain one fatal defect: the lack of precision. For they fail to show any precise and well-defined areas of water, in which prohibition [of fishing by foreigners] was intended to apply and was actually enforced. And *precision is vital to any prescriptive claim* to areas of water which might otherwise be high seas.[4]

Judge McNair in his Dissenting Opinion refuted the Norwegian contention, according to which the lack of protest on the part of Great Britain against the Norwegian Decrees of 1869 and 1889 ought to have been considered as her consent of the "Norwegian method" of delimitation in general. Judge McNair held that acquiescence might have been imputed to Great Britain solely as regards the localities which were explicitly covered by these Decrees and that Britain could not have been expected to have acquiesced in any claim going beyond these territories. In Judge McNair's own words:

The question ... arises whether the two Decrees of 1869 and 1889, affecting a total length of maritime frontier of about 83 miles, and connecting islands but not headlands of the mainland, ought to have been regarded by foreign States when they

[1] MacGibbon, 31 *BYIL* (1954), p. 169.
[2] See *British-Venezuelan Boundary Dispute*, The British Case, 1898, pp. 149–150.
[3] See *British-Venezuelan Boundary Dispute*, The Venezuelan Case, 1898, p. 228.
[4] *ICJ Reports*, 1951, p. 157. (Italics added).

became aware of them, or ought but for default on their part to have become aware, as notice that Norway had adopted a peculiar *system* of delimiting her maritime territory, which, in course of time, would be described as having been from the outset of universal application throughout the whole coast line amounting ... to about 3,400 kilometres (about 1,830 sea-miles), or whether these Decrees could properly be regarded as regulating a purely local, and primarily domestic, situation. I do not see how these two Decrees can be said to have notified to the United Kingdom the existence of straight base-lines applicable to the whole coast.[1]

And Judge Read followed suit by saying:

I am unable to conclude that the British Government, or, indeed, any other foreign government except France, had any reason to believe that a Norwegian System had come into being in 1869–1889, or that these Decrees were anything more than local *ad hoc* measures.[2]

It is a matter for regret that, in contradistinction to the unequivocal and sound legal approach of the minority judges, the majority of the Court seems to have obscured this issue by contenting itself with the rather ambiguous statement that

the United Kingdom could not have been ignorant of the Decree of 1869 which had at once provoked a request for the explanations by the French Government. Nor, knowing of it, could it have been under any misapprehension as to the significance of its terms, which clearly described it as constituting the application of a system. The same observation applies *a fortiori* to the Decree of 1889 relating to the delimitation of Romsdal and Nordmöre which must have appeared to the United Kingdom as a reiterated manifestation of the Norwegian practice.[3]

The matter may be concluded by saying that when a title to territory is based on adverse possession, more stringent and less liberal criteria will be applied as to the extent of the area covered by such possession than would be the case with a claim founded on occupation.

[1] *ICJ Reports*, 1951, p. 177. (Italics in original).
[2] *Ibid.*, p. 200.
[3] *Ibid.*, p. 139. (Italics in original). For a critical evaluation of the majority decision on his point see Fitzmaurice, 30 *BYIL* (1953), pp. 33–42.

CHAPTER VI

JURIDICAL ASPECTS SPECIFICALLY RELATED TO THE FORMATION OF MARITIME HISTORIC TITLES

60. General

The present chapter deals with those aspects of the acquisition of an historic title which relate specifically to the acquisition of historic rights over maritime areas. The inclusion in this study of a chapter devoted solely to the problems attendant on the establishment of maritime historic rights seems to be warranted for several reasons.

First, since the high seas cannot be appropriated by any single State and all member-States of the international community enjoy equal rights over them, a maritime historic title has to be acquired, as a rule, at the expense of the entire community of States, whereas an historic title to land territory is normally acquired at the expense of only one other State.

Secondly, the doctrine of historic titles in general has, in fact, evolved from the theory of historic bays and thus has its roots in the sphere of the law of the sea.

Thirdly – and this is merely a logical consequence of the reason just mentioned – the majority of writers dealing with historic titles have been preoccupied in the past with the problem as it posed itself with regard to maritime areas.

Fourthly and lastly, in contradistinction to historic titles to land territories, historic claims falling short of full sovereignty feature prominently in the sphere of maritime historic rights and constitute a fair proportion of these claims. This pre-eminence of non-exclusive historic rights in the field of the law of the sea also merits special attention.

Thus, the present chapter will be devoted to an examination of the impact of the principle of the freedom of the high seas on the formation of a maritime historic title, to the problems relating to "international acquiescence," to a brief study of the specific manifestations of State authority over maritime areas, to an analysis of the various aspects of the doctrine of historic waters in general, and historic bays in particular, and to a discussion of the juridical status of historic waters.

A special section then deals with the problems pertaining to the acquisition of non-exclusive historic rights, with special reference to traditional rights of fishing (sometimes also referred to as "historic rights in reverse").

Finally, there follow two sections in which the relevance of the theory of historic titles with regard to the continental shelf and sedentary fisheries, respectively, is more closely examined.

There has been ample reference in previous chapters to judicial decisions and State practice regarding maritime historic claims, inasmuch as such decisions and practice are indicative of legal aspects common to all historic titles, whether claimed over land territories or maritime areas. The purpose of the present chapter, however, is to concentrate merely on those aspects of the formation of an historic title which affect the acquisition of such a title to maritime areas.

61. The impact of the principle of the freedom of the high seas on the formation of maritime historic rights

"Le principe de la liberté de la haute mer ... demeure la base essentielle de tout le droit international public maritime."[1] These words of Gidel, indisputably one of the foremost contemporary authorities on the international law of the sea, clearly state the principle on which rests the whole edifice of modern maritime international law.

An historical analysis of the evolution of this commonly accepted principle of our days would clearly go beyond the scope of this chapter. Suffice it to say here that the emergence of this rule went by no means unchallenged and that the concept of *mare liberum*, as propounded and put forward by Grotius, met with the doctrinal opposition of Selden, who was a supporter of the theory of *mare clausum*. There is good reason to believe that the respective attitudes taken up by these two scholars, and later by their disciples and followers, were largely influenced by the national pretensions and other vested interests of their countries. Whatever the reason for their divergence of opinion as to the precise legal status of the high seas, it is an undeniable fact that, since the days of Grotius, the principle of the freedom of the high seas found an ever wider currency and that, after a gradual evolution, it gained the upper hand towards the beginning of the nineteenth

[1] Gidel, *op. cit.*, vol. III, p. 632.

century, when it crystallized into a universally accepted principle of international law.[1]

Reference to the open sea as an area which is "free" to all by no means suggests that the sea is *territorium nullius*. Indeed, such a construction might lead to the inevitable conclusion that the seas are open to appropriation by the first occupant, just as any *terra nullius* is open to occupation. Such a course would, no doubt, bring about the very situation which was meant to be avoided by the invocation of the principle of the freedom of the high seas, namely, the raising of national pretensions over certain bodies of water beyond the limits recognized in international law. It would thus defeat the very purpose for which the doctrine of *mare liberum* was introduced into international law.

In fairness to those who regard the high seas as *res nullius*, it should be added, however, that they interpret the meaning of this term, when related to maritime areas, in an entirely different manner. According to Gidel, they employ this term to indicate their view that

> la haute mer est un espace qui ne relève actuellement comme tel, qui ne peut pas relever comme tel, de l'ordre juridique d'aucun Etat particulier.... Pour exprimer ....[cette proposition], on dit: la haute mer est *res nullius*.[2]

This expression, however, is most likely to mislead the student, for the reasons given above. Its choice must therefore be regarded as highly unfortunate, because, as Gidel points out, the idea which is meant to be conveyed is the very opposite to that which is normally attached to the term *res nullius*. What is really intended to be expressed by resorting to this term is the fact that the sea *cannot* be occupied by anyone. Thus, this concept seems to be better covered by the expression: *res quae nullius domini esse potest*.[3]

Thus, in order to avoid confusion arising from the use of a somewhat misleading terminology, it would appear that the terms *res communis* or *res extra commercium* are better suited to give a precise notion of what is meant by the freedom of the high seas. *Res communis* implies that the high seas have to be looked upon as a property over which the whole of the community of nations has joint ownership.[4] The supporters of the theory of *res extra commercium* wish to indicate that

[1] For a more extensive historical survey of the evolution of this cardinal principle of modern maritime international law see Gidel, *op. cit.*, vol. I, pp. 123–212.

[2] *Ibid.*, p. 213. (Italics in original).

[3] *Ibid.*, p. 214; by contrast, *res nullius* is defined in Roman law as *res nullius cedit primo occupanti*.

[4] For a critical analysis of this concept see Gidel, *op. cit.*, vol. I, p. 215. On the problem of the juridical nature of the high seas in general, see also Bierzanek, "La nature juridique de la haute mer," 65 *RGDIP* (1961), p. 233.

the seas are to be regarded as a property which is not subject to the normal processes of property transfer and which, consequently, cannot be acquired by any of the members constituting the family of nations.[1]

But whatever course one is tempted to adopt, the question of proper terminology – however important in itself – is only of secondary significance in this respect, because the results flowing from the recognition of the principle of the freedom of the high seas are well understood. The principle implies, to use again the words of Gidel, that

> l'idée, qui domine le droit de la mer est l'idée de la liberté de l'utilisation licite et normale des espaces maritimes; toute restriction inutile à cette liberté doit être évitée.[2]

It follows that there is, as it were, a presumption of law that the waters of the sea are free and that any pretensions of sovereignty over a certain body of water, going beyond what is admittedly the maritime appurtenance of the littoral State, constitute exceptions to this rule which have to be justified by a special rule recognized in international law.

It is as well to stress this point from the outset, because in recent years the attempt has been made to conceive a different interpretation of this cardinal and fundamental principle of maritime international law. As will be recalled, in the *Fisheries* case Norway challenged the idea of the supremacy of the principle of the freedom of the seas, maintaining that this principle was only *one* among many notions, the application of which was vital for the enforcement of modern maritime international law. It was contended on behalf of Norway that the principle never achieved the degree of a basic principle of the international law of the sea. The triumph of this rule was confined, in Norway's view, solely to those areas of water which had not been submitted before to the exclusive authority of any State. The principle, however – so ran the Norwegian argument – could not be resorted to for the purpose of narrowing and restricting any national pretensions,

[1] Thus, says Grotius: "The sea is included among those things which are not articles of commerce, that is to say, the things that cannot become part of anyone's private domain. Hence it follows..., that no part of the sea may be regarded as pertaining to the domain of any given nation." (Grotius, *De Jure Praedae Commentarius,* Scott's ed., vol. I, 1950, p. 236). Similarly, Oppenheim maintains that "the term 'freedom of the open sea' indicates the rule of the Law of Nations that the open sea is not, and never can be, under the sovereignty of any State whatever. Since... the open sea can never be under the sovereignty of any State, no State has a right to acquire parts of the open sea through occupation." (Oppenheim, *op. cit.*, p. 589). See also Schwarzenberger, 87 *Hague Recueil* (1955), vol. I, p. 367.

[2] Gidel, *op. cit.*, vol. III, p. 674; as to the various connotations given to this principle in the past, see Gidel, *op. cit.*, vol. I, pp. 125–126.

however unreasonable they may seem in the light of modern international law. In Norway's view, the two conflicting and rival concepts of the freedom of the high seas and the national pretensions of the coastal State over wide portions of the sea adjacent to its territory are on the same legal footing and "on commettrait une erreur si l'on prétendait établir entre elles une sorte de hiérarchie."[1] Norway also vigorously denied the concept put forward in the United Kingdom Memorial, according to which there is a presumption of law that waters of the sea are free and that any claim to sovereignty over a given area of water has to be justified as an exception recognized in international law. In the United Kingdom Memorial it had been submitted that "a presumption of law arises that any given area of sea which is not within the inland or territorial waters of a State under the general rules of international law, forms part of the high seas."[2] Norway took strong exception to this view, arguing that "ce n'est pas la souveraineté de l'Etat qui a empiété sur la haute mer. C'est la mer libre qui a refoulé la souveraineté de l'Etat."[3]

This seemingly meaningless legalistic quibble has, as will readily be

[1] *ICJ, Fisheries case, Pleadings, Oral Arguments, Documents,* vol. I, p. 344.

Among the foremost exponents of this approach one might mention Bourquin who, it will be recalled, acted as Counsel for Norway in the *Fisheries* case. In his article "Les baies historiques," published in *Mélanges Georges Sauser-Hall*, 1952, pp. 38–51, Bourquin has come out strongly in favour of the view that the theory of "historic bays" cannot be regarded as an exception to, and a departure from, the general customary rules of maritime international law, since there do not exist elaborate general rules regarding the delimitation of bays and other maritime areas. The study on the *Juridical Regime of Historic Waters, Including Historic Bays*, prepared by the United Nations Secretariat, seems to have given preference, although couched in cautious terms, to these rather isolated views of Bourquin. Thus, it is maintained there:

> There seem to be certain difficulties inherent in the view that title to "historic waters" is an exception to the general rules of international law... and that such title therefore must be based on some form of acquiescence on the part of the other States.... The general rules in this field from which the régime of "historic waters" would be an exception could only be customary rules. This means that both the general rules and the title to "historic waters" would be based on usage. Why then should the latter be considered as exceptional and also inferior with regard to its validity, so that the acquiescence of other States would be necessary to validate the title?... The so-called general rules would... be "general" in the sense only that they would be more generally applicable than the "exceptional" title to "historic waters".... A distinction between "general" and "exceptional" in this case would be wholly arbitrary.... It may be even doubted whether there exist at present any general customary rules regarding the delimitation of the maritime domain of States. (U.N. Document A/CN.4/143 of March 9th, 1962, *ILC Yearbook*, 14th session, 1962, vol. II, p. 10).

[2] *ICJ, Fisheries case, Pleadings, Oral Arguments, Documents,* vol. I, p. 95.

[3] *Ibid.*, p. 345. This statement deviates to some extent from the Norwegian contention that "il est... inexact d'interpréter la situation juridique présente comme impliquant une subordination du principe de souveraineté (valable pour la mer territoriale) au principe de non-souveraineté (valable pour la haute mer).... Les deux principes sont *juridiquemant égaux.* C'est leur *conciliation* – et non *la subordination de l'un à l'autre* – qui donne la clef du droit international moderne de la mer." (*Ibid.*, vol. III. p. 265; italics in original).

admitted, far-reaching legal implications which have already been alluded to in the section dealing with the problems of evidence pertaining to the establishment of an historic title.[1] There is, however, little doubt, that the Norwegian concept, though it may historically be correct as far as the emergence of the rule of the freedom of the high seas is concerned, runs counter to the generally accepted view on this point, as upheld by doctrine and practice alike. Thus, says Calvo:

Au fond ..., toutes les questions que nous avons discutées plus haut se rattachent directement ou aboutissent forcément à un seul et même principe fondamental, celui de la liberté des mers.[2]

The principle of the freedom of the high seas was also given expression by Phillimore in the following words:

The reason of the thing, the preponderance of authority and the practice of nations have decided, that the main ocean, inasmuch as it is the necessary highway of all nations and is from its nature incapable of being continuously possessed, cannot be the property of any one State.[3]

In the well-known *Lotus* case the principle of the freedom of the high seas was defined as "the absence of any territorial sovereignty upon the high seas."[4] More recently, Judge Read, in his Dissenting Opinion in the *Fisheries* case, made a forceful statement in support of this overriding principle of modern maritime international law when he maintained:

No question of *res nullius* or annexation arises in the case of the sea. All nations enjoy all rights and all privileges in and over all of the sea beyond the limit of territorial waters. It follows that the power of a coastal State to mark out its maritime domain cannot be used so as to encroach on the high seas and impair these rights and privileges. Its power is limited to the marking out of areas already subject to its sovereignty.[5]

It was because of this clash of the Norwegian claims with the principle of the freedom of the high seas that Judge Read considered the

[1] See above, section 58.

[2] Calvo, *Le droit international théorique et pratique*, 5th edition, 1896, vol. I, section 384; see also Gidel, *op. cit.*, vol. III, p. 674; see also Schwarzenberger, 87 *Hague Recueil* (1955), vol. I, pp. 358–371, where the author elevates this principle to the rank of one of the seven fundamental principles of international law.

[3] Phillimore, *op. cit.*, vol. I, section 172; Perels sums up the matter by saying that "rights of property or sovereignty over the sea neither exist nor can they be acquired." In the original German: "Ein Eigentums-, oder Hoheitsrecht am Meere existiert weder, noch kann ein solches erworben werden." (Perels, *Das internationale öffentliche Seerecht*, 1903, p. 16).

[4] *PCIJ*, Series A, No. 10, p. 25.

[5] *ICJ Reports*, 1951, p. 190. (Italics in original).

"Norwegian system" to be contrary to international law, an idea which was also reflected in the following words of Judge McNair:

I consider that the delimitation of territorial waters made by the Norwegian Decree of 1935 [marking out the straight baselines applied by Norway] is in conflict with international law, and that its effect will be to injure the principle of the freedom of the high seas and to encourage further encroachments upon the high seas by coastal States.[1]

More recently still this principle was once more reaffirmed by the 1958 Geneva Conference on the Law of the Sea. Article 2 of the *Convention on the High Seas* proclaims, *inter alia*, that "the high seas being open to all nations, no State may validly purport to subject any part of them to its sovereignty."[2] Here the idea of the high seas being incapable of appropriation is clearly enunciated.

It has been deemed fit to dwell at some length on this fundamental principle of maritime international law, not for its own sake and without any pretension to exhaust the topic,[3] but because it was felt that by stressing and reiterating this basic principle, the problem of the so-called "maritime historic rights" might be seen in its true perspective. Maritime historic rights – or "historic waters" as they are frequently called – are, to employ the definition given by the International Court of Justice in the *Fisheries* case, "waters which are treated as internal waters but which would not have that character were it not for the existence of an historic title."[4] In other words: historic waters are waters which would normally have been regarded as forming part of the high seas, were it not for some exceptional reasons, owing to which they are accorded an exceptional status. If the existence of such exceptional and unusual circumstances can be proved, the claimant State will be entitled to the recognition of certain rights which go beyond the normally accepted maritime rights of littoral States.

As will be seen below, such exceptional claims may amount either to claims of full sovereignty and exclusive rights over the "historic waters" (claims which involve the right to treat such waters as if they formed part of the claimant State's internal waters or territorial waters), or to more limited claims relating to the exercise of certain rights over the waters in question, such as the right of fishing, without at the same time involving a claim of full and unlimited sovereignty. Both categories of

[1] *Ibid.*, p. 185.
[2] *Cmnd.*, 584 (1959), p. 27.
[3] Gidel, in his monumental work on the law of the sea, devotes to this question about 90 pages. (See above, p. 243, n. 1.)
[4] *ICJ Reports*, 1951, p. 130.

such rights may justly be termed "historic rights." It would appear, however, that only the first kind of historic rights relates to "historic waters" properly so called, whereas the second deals with what may be termed "non-exclusive historic rights," in the sense that they do not imply a claim of full sovereignty.

Both forms of maritime historic rights will be dealt with under separate headings further below. However, it cannot be overemphasized that both categories of maritime historic rights – in other words, all maritime historic rights – share one all-important and never-to-be-forgotten attribute. This is that they are normally established at the expense, and to the detriment, of the community of nations as a whole. They do not therefore affect solely the rights of one State or another, but are intended to encroach upon the rights which would normally accrue to the entire international community. In this respect maritime historic titles differ sharply from historic titles to land territories, which, as will be recalled, usually affect only two States, namely, the claimant State and the State which considers itself affected by such a claim. It is this fundamental divergence of maritime historic rights, as compared with "ordinary" historic rights, that seems to justify the insertion of a special chapter devoted entirely to the legal aspects attendant upon the creation and upkeep of maritime historic rights.

As has been stated elsewhere, the basic principles relating to terrestrial and maritime historic rights are identical; however, it remains true that in the majority of instances in which historic claims are put forward by different States, the areas involved are various bodies of *water* and not land territories. Thus, it is hardly astonishing that the problems of historic rights have been expounded mainly by writers who have devoted more than cursory attention to the international law of the sea. It is primarily they who deserve credit for having introduced some measure of clarity and lucidity into this confused field of international law.

The distinctive legal status of the high seas and the fact that they form the common and inalienable property of the international community, and not of a single State or even a group of States, lies at the root of the particular process through which maritime historic rights are created. In fact, this exceptional status of the high seas affects the acquisition of maritime historic rights in at least three ways:

(a) The legal basis of historic rights in general is, as will be recalled, the concept of acquiescence, which means that the State whose rights have been encroached upon, or are likely to be infringed, by an historic claim has, by its conduct, acquiesced in such an exceptional claim. As long as historic claims are put forward in respect of land areas, the controversy will normally affect only two States, notably, the claimant State and the State affected by such a claim. As regards maritime historic rights, however, the claimant State will find itself faced with the international community at large whose rights are inevitably subject to restriction, if the maritime historic claim of a particular State is to prevail. The importance of this distinction is obvious: since the purported maritime historic rights infringe the rights of the international community, the exceptional claim can be sanctioned only through *international acquiescence*, i.e. acquiescence given not by a single State, but rather acquiescence of such a representative body of States as may be regarded as truly reflecting international recognition of an otherwise illegal situation. This aspect of the acquisition of maritime historic titles will further be enlarged upon in the next section.

(b) In view of the fact that sovereignty over maritime territories is exercised by States in a manner which differs considerably from the manifestations of authority over land areas, it necessarily follows that the requirements for the formation of a maritime historic right (that is to say, the manifestations of State authority from which a presumption of acquiescence may be inferred) should also differ to some extent from those usually enumerated when dealing with the establishment of historic rights over land areas. The notions of effectiveness, continuity, notoriety, possession *à titre de souverain*, etc., when applied to maritime territorial situations, assume a meaning which is somewhat different from that normally attached to these notions. This aspect of the problem will also be dealt with further in the section in which the various manifestations of sovereignty over maritime areas are investigated. (See section 63 below).

(c) The fact that the high seas form the joint property of international society and thus are not open to acquisition by a single State, as would be the case with an ownerless piece of land territory, has another far-reaching consequence. This consequence is that maritime historic rights can never be acquired merely by means of occupation of a hitherto ownerless territory. Instead, the claim to a maritime historic title must be based on the adverse holding by the claimant. In other words, the claimant State must be able to assert successfully that it built up its title by depriving the community of States of a right which had formerly belonged to it.

Thus, in this last respect too, the acquisition of a maritime historic title differs from the establishment of an historic title over land territory. The latter, as will be recalled, may be acquired in different ways. Among them there is the so-called "immemorial possession" which, in effect, means that, as the origins of the claimant State's pretensions to the territory in question cannot be traced, the situation prevailing at present is deemed to have always existed and is therefore presumed to be in conformity with legal requirements. Such a presumption may be raised as regards territorial situations which have prevailed for a very considerable length of time. The modern international law of the sea, however, took its final shape only at the beginning of the nineteenth century, and it would appear that maritime historic claims put forward by different States can be recognized to-day only if the claimant State is in a position to prove that it asserted its authority over the allegedly historic waters since the emergence of the relevant rules of the modern international law of the sea and with the acquiescence of the international community. It may safely be maintained that a claim resting solely on extensive medieval pretensions, which may have been valid as long as a different legal regime prevailed over the high seas, will not be deemed as sufficient to uphold maritime historic claims and to validate them in accordance with the law in force at present. When the new international law of the sea took its final shape with the undisputed triumph of the *mare liberum* doctrine, each State was deemed to have been under the obligation, as it were, to *reacquire* its rights beyond those parts of the maritime territory which were conceded by the new regime to form the marginal belt of the coastal State. Such a "reacquisition" of rights could only be made at the expense of the international community at large.

These distinctive features of the maritime historic claim do, in fact, considerably increase the already grave legal problems surrounding the acquisition of an historic title in general.

The following sections are intended to throw some light on the questions related to acquiescence – with regard to the acquisition of a maritime historic title – and to the manifestations of authority from which such acquiescence may be inferred.

62. *What is international acquiescence?*

In contradistinction to the "ordinary" historic claim, where the acquiescence of the single State affected by the raising of such a claim will suffice to validate an intrinsically invalid title, a maritime historic claim will only be sanctioned through the acquiescence of the international community. Since a maritime historic claim is likely to affect the entire community of States, it will be open to each of the member-States making up the international community to lodge a protest against such an extensive claim and take whatever measures it sees fit to prevent such a title from maturing. (With respect to land territories the right to protest against, and to oppose the building up of, an historic title accrues, as will be recalled, only to the States directly affected by such a claim.)

In examining the problem whether the international community may be presumed to have acquiesced in the establishment of some historic claim raised by a given State in respect of a given body of water, one faces again the question of the "generality of practice," which has been dealt with in chapter II above.[1] As has been pointed out there, this general problem of customary international law cannot be solved in a clear-cut manner. In the opinion of Sørensen, what is required is not a unanimity of practice, but a practice followed by the great majority of nations.[2] This rather vague formulation of the requirements necessary for the establishment of a new customary rule of international law does, however, bring out clearly one fundamental point, namely, that "*generality* of practice" should not be confounded with "*universality* of practice." The adoption of such stringent and rigid a criterion for the emergence of new rules of customary international law would, no doubt, paralyse the progress of international law and render its development virtually impossible. One tends to lend whole-hearted support to Kunz when he maintains that the practice in question "must be 'general,' not universal."[3] At the same time, however, he is at pains to point out that, by dispensing with the requirement for a unanimous and universal acceptance of the new rule by the international community, the door has by no means been thrown open to the adoption of a "majority test." To quote again Kunz:

> A mere majority of states is not enough. The practice must have been applied by the overwhelming majority of states which hitherto had an opportunity of applying it.[4]

Thus, Kunz enunciates an important principle, namely, that it is not a mere "arithmetical majority" of States that is required for the creation

[1] See above, chapter II, section 18.
[2] Sørensen, *op. cit.*, p. 102.
[3] Kunz, 47 *AJIL* (1953), p. 666.
[4] *Ibid.*

of a new customary rule, but rather what may perhaps be best termed a "functional majority" of the States affected, or likely to be affected, by the emergence of the new rule. Such a "functional majority" may sometimes involve a great number of States. On other occasions, however, it may well happen that the number of States directly affected by the creation of a new rule may be extremely small.

The application of the "functional majority" test may be of considerable help in the sphere of maritime historic rights. As has rightly been pointed out by Gidel, the acts or omissions of various States cannot always be put on the same level.[1] For instance, the presumed acquiescence of Afghanistan (which is a land-locked country anyway) in a practice which has allegedly sprung up off the coast of Denmark can hardly be equated with the acquiescence given to the same practice by Sweden which, being one of Denmark's neighbours and a maritime Power herself, is likely to be affected in a much more direct and acute manner by the emergence of such a practice.

It is not proposed here to lay down a rule which would confirm, by examining the number or the identity of the States which have given their assent to the establishment of a purported maritime historic right, whether or not a new and exceptional maritime historic right has come into existence. Nor would the laying down of such a rule appear to be feasible or practicable. One cannot lose sight of the fact that the number of the member-States of the international community undergoes constant and rapid changes, which is one more reason for denying any resort to such a mechanical device as the adoption of the "arithmetical majority" test. This surely is not a heartening conclusion for the academic lawyer who would undoubtedly welcome a fixed and easily ascertainable rule of law. However, the chaotic conditions which still characterize international relations do not permit of the adoption of such rules. International law, being unable to lose touch with international realities, must, in the course of shaping its norms, take due account of frequently harsh facts. It certainly cannot overlook the present-day structure of the international society, which – in respect of the creation of maritime historic rights – has the consequence that, in any given case in which a claim to maritime historic rights is raised, it will be necessary to investigate whether the new and exceptional practice has been applied by "the overwhelming majority of states which hitherto had an opportunity of applying it."[2] The test applied is

[1] Gidel, *op. cit.*, vol. III, p. 634.
[2] Kunz, *loc. cit.*, p. 666.

not a *quantitative*, but rather a *qualitative* one. This argument was expressly referred to in the United Kingdom pleadings in the *Fisheries* case when, for instance, it was contended in the Reply that "the Court's freedom to appreciate all the circumstances alleged to establish a customary rule also extends to appreciating the relative significance of the quantity of its acceptance as law by other States."[1]

Closely related to the question of the number of States which must acquiesce in the creation of a maritime historic title is the problem of protest against a practice derogatory of the normal rules of law. In other words: how many States ought to protest to prevent such a title from maturing? And can all the protests be put on the same level, irrespective of the status of the various protesting States among the maritime Powers of the world and regardless of their interests in the area in question?

It may safely be assumed that a protest emanating from a single State will not prevent indefinitely a new – and in itself unlawful – practice from coming into existence, provided such a practice, otherwise derogatory of the commonly accepted rules of international law, has met with the assent of the international community. It is, however, impossible to state how many States are supposed to protest in order to show that an allegedly new rule of law is no rule at all. The impossibility of laying down a rule on this point either was clearly recognized by various writers of international law. Thus, Gidel maintains that

> il paraît impossible d'exiger ni que la reconnaissance ... soit rigoureusement 'universelle' ni qu'elle soit expresse. Une seule contestation émanant d'un seul Etat ne saurait infirmer un usage; les contestations ne peuvent d'autre part être placées toutes sur le même plan, sans distinction de leur nature, de la situation géographique ou autre de l'Etat dont elles émanent.[2]

It appears that one cannot go beyond vague statements like the one just quoted. This also becomes clear when one reads a similar statement made by Johnson on this point, where he asserts that

> it is not possible to lay down a general rule stating how many states must protest and how strongly they must protest in order to prevent the growth of a prescriptive claim over areas of the high seas, but at least the governing principle is clear – there must be 'a general recognition of it by the maritime Powers of the world.'[3]

This writer too did not find it possible to specify more precisely what is meant by the presumably intentionally vague phrase "the general

[1] *ICJ, Fisheries case, Pleadings, Oral Arguments, Documents*, vol. II, p. 427.
[2] Gidel, *op. cit.*, vol. III, p. 634.
[3] Johnson. 27 *BYIL* (1950), p. 351.

recognition... by the maritime Powers of the world." One may, however, assume that the rules normally applicable to the growth of any new customary rule of international law will also apply to the growth of maritime historic rights. If the standards set by international law fall short of those to which one has become accustomed in municipal law, this is surely a sad reflection on the standard reached by international law at the present time. But a denial of the practicability of these rules, when applied to the regime of historic waters, on account of these obvious shortcomings, would be no more justified than a refusal to recognize the need to apply any norms of customary international law, owing to the indisputable deficiencies which at present beset the machinery of customary international law.[1]

Finally, it should be pointed out that, with regard to the establishment of maritime historic titles too, as is the case with historic titles in general, the time factor is of no direct legal relevance. It is, however, through the passage of time that a presumption of acquiescence is inferred and it is with the further efflux of time that such a presumption is strengthened. But – and this point too cannot be overemphasized – it is not the passage of time that sets the seal of legal validity on an otherwise invalid claim. The time factor is relevant here – as in any other historic claim – precisely to the extent that an inference of acquiescence may be drawn from it.

63. *Manifestations of State authority over maritime areas*

The requirements which have been enumerated above as being prerequisites for the establishment of an historic title in general[2] undergo some modifications, when applied to maritime historic titles, in order to adapt them to the peculiar character of the maritime domain of States and to the manner in which State authority is being exercised over such territories. It will readily be understood that such notions as "effectiveness," "continuity," "notoriety," assume, with regard to maritime areas, a meaning different from that normally attached to them when referring to land territories. As will be recalled, the prerequisite for raising a presumption of acquiescence in a given territorial situation is the effective display of authority by the State claiming for itself the benefits of such a situation, such authority being displayed in

[1] For a more detailed discussion of the impact of a single State's protest on the prevention of the formation of an historic title, see above, chapter IV, section 49.

[2] See above, chapter IV.

a manner appropriate to the nature of the territory in question. Now, "effectiveness" assumes various forms under various circumstances. What may be regarded as "effective" when referring to a remote and isolated district, may be considered as "ineffective" when applied to a densely populated area. Similarly, measures which might prove insufficient as proof of manifestations of State authority over terrestrial areas, might be considered as meeting the requirements of "effectiveness" with regard to maritime territory, where no "effective" control, in the usual sense, can be exercised.

Here again, no rules can be laid down as to what may be regarded as "effective," "continuous," "notorious," etc. in maritime territorial situations. The ultimate decision in such cases will invariably rest with the tribunal called upon to pronounce in a legal controversy in which a maritime historic right is claimed. The tribunal, in turn, will decide the case having regard to the peculiar circumstances and facts of the case. Any recourse to preconceived and abstract notions of law will be of no avail.[1]

It is certainly not a matter of pure coincidence that the theories of the "effectiveness" of territorial situations and of the freedom of the high seas crystallized contemporaneously, both being the products of the earlier part of the nineteenth century. Once the notion of "effective control" was insisted upon as the main – if not sole – criterion for the recognition of the sovereign rights of a State over a given area, it became virtually impossible to support the national pretensions to wide portions of the high seas over which the exercise of national sovereignty was inconceivable to all intents and purposes. So the notion of "effectiveness" is one more factor which militates in favour of limiting national pretensions over maritime territories, thus restricting them to those areas which – owing to peculiar and unusual circumstances, arising mainly from an unusual geographical configuration and a consequently close link with the coastal State's land domain – may properly be regarded as having come under the effective control of the claimant State. It is therefore hardly surprising that the theory of "historic waters" has been applied mainly with regard to certain bays over which the littoral States do, in actual fact, exercise much the same functions as any State does in its internal waters. Moreover, the theory of "historic waters" in general is in reality merely a later doctrinal

[1] The meaning of the concept of effectiveness, when applied to maritime areas, has been discussed by Bouchez in his article "The Concept of Effectiveness as Applied to Territorial Sovereignty over Sea-Areas, Air Space and Outer Space," published in 9 *NTIR* (1962), p. 150, at pp. 160–174.

extension of the concept of "historic bays," as will be shown in the next section. It is therefore mostly through cases relating to bays, claimed on historic grounds as belonging to the coastal State's maritime domain, that the various possible manifestations of authority over maritime areas can be ascertained.

Both municipal and international case law afford an opportunity to establish on what grounds historic claims to various bays have been recognized in the past. As will be presently shown, the considerations relied upon by the parties to disputes regarding the legal status of certain bays, to justify the incorporation of such bays in the national domain of the claimant State, form a mixture of geographical, economical, strategical and historical elements. The common feature of all these claims seems to be the belief that a special relationship exists between the water area concerned and the land territory enclosing it. According to this concept, the maritime area is a dependency of the land territory, by which it is controlled and dominated, and the coastal State is entitled to exercise over it much the same authority and acts of sovereignty as it does or would do over its internal waters (like lakes and rivers). The legality of such an historic claim is to be measured, in the words of Jessup, "not by the size of the area affected, but by the definitiveness and duration of the assertion and the acquiescence of foreign powers."[1]

In its award rendered in the *North Atlantic Fisheries* Arbitration, the tribunal made several remarks regarding the conditions required for justifying the territoriality of bays in general, and it would appear that the considerations enumerated there, at a time when geometrical or arithmetical criteria for defining bays had not yet been established, still hold good to-day with regard to historic bays, the territoriality of which cannot be determined – by their very nature – by geometrical or similar tests. Giving its definition of the term "bay" in general, the tribunal said:

> The interpretation [of the term 'bay'] must take into account all the individual circumstances which for any of the different bays are to be appreciated, the relation of its width to the length of penetration inland, the possibility and the necessity of its being defended by the State in whose territory it is indented; the special value which it has for the industry of the inhabitants of its shores; the distance which it is secluded from the highways of nations on the open sea and other circumstances not possible to enumerate in general.[2]

As will readily be seen, the tribunal referred to elements of geography ("width and length of penetration"), national security ("the possibility

[1] Jessup, *The Law of Territorial Waters and Maritime Jurisdiction*, 1927, p. 382.
[2] *UNRIAA*, vol. XI, p. 199; Scott, *Hague Court Reports*, 1st series, 1916, p. 187.

and the necessity of its being defended"), economy ("the special value... for the industry"), and to what can be regarded as the maritime interests of the international community in general ("the distance by which it is secluded from the highways of nations on the open sea"). The tribunal was at the same time careful enough to indicate that this list of considerations was by no means exhaustive and that in appropriate circumstances many other reasons might also be taken into account as additional grounds justifying an historic claim.

While the *North Atlantic Fisheries* Arbitration Award did not refer to "historic bays" in particular, this was explicitly done by the now-defunct Central American Court of Justice in the *Gulf of Fonseca* case. There the Court expressly stated that it had determined the juridical status of the gulf "from a threefold point of view of history, geography and the vital interests of the surrounding States."[1]

As regards the historical element – or time factor – involved, the Court found that Spain, and subsequently the Federal Republic of Central America, and later the three successor States of Nicaragua, Honduras and El Salvador,

> notoriously affirmed their peaceful ownership and possession in the Gulf ... and ... have performed acts and enacted laws having to do with the national security, the observance of health and with fiscal regulations.[2]

Thus, the Court expressly referred to what was called in a previous chapter the manifestations of State authority, which, as was submitted there, are a prerequisite for a presumption of acquiescence in an historic claim, such acquiescence being the legal basis for the acquisition of an historic title. It is noteworthy that the Court attached paramount importance to the fact that the riparian States legislated for the gulf in question, and what is even more important: they *enforced* the relevant legislative measures.

The relevance of the concept of acquiescence, as underlying the acquisition of the littoral States' title to the Gulf of Fonseca, becomes abundantly clear in another passage of the judgment where the Court said:

> A secular possession such as that of the Gulf [of Fonseca] could only have been maintained by the acquiescence of the family of nations; and in the case here at issue it is not that the *consensus gentium* is deduced from a merely passive attitude on the part of the nations, because the diplomatic history of certain Powers shows that for more than half a century they have been seeking to establish rights of their own

[1] 11 *AJIL* (1917), p. 700.
[2] *Ibid.*, pp. 700-701.

in the Gulf for purposes of commercial policy, but always on the basis of respect for the ownership and possession which the States have maintained by virtue of their sovereign authority.[1]

The Court went on to elaborate on various economic considerations which were also taken into account in fixing the juridical status of the gulf, and mentioned in particular the following:

(1) A projected railway-line started by Honduras, the terminal of which was to be located near the coast of the gulf;

(2) A railroad under the control of El Salvador starting at the gulf;

(3) A projected prolongation of a railroad connecting the Real Estuary in the Gulf of Fonseca with the interior of Nicaragua.[2]

Turning from the enumeration of the particular economic interests of each of the three riparian States, the Court alluded to their joint economic interests in the ownership of the gulf. On this point the Court had the following to say:

The Gulf is surrounded by various and extensive departments of the riparian countries. These are of great importance because they are destined to great commercial, industrial and agricultural development; their products, like those of the departments in the interior of those States, must be exported by way of the Gulf of Fonseca and through that Gulf must also come the increasing importations.[3]

Dealing with the question of the geographical configuration of the gulf which facilitated the exercise of effective authority over it by the coastal States, the Court remarked that

the configuration and other conditions of the Gulf facilitate the enforcement of fiscal laws and regulations and guarantee the full collection of imposts against frauds against the fiscal laws.[4]

Lastly, the Court also referred to the strategical aspect – this too being largely the outcome of the geographical shape of the gulf – and pointed out that

the strategic situation of the Gulf and its islands is so advantageous that the riparian States can defend their great interests therein and provide for the defense of their independence and sovereignty.[5]

It was the combined strength and the cumulative effect of all the above-mentioned considerations which caused the Court to reach its conclusions as to the historic character of the riparian States' rights.

[1] *Ibid.* (Italics in original).
[2] *Ibid.*, p. 704.
[3] *Ibid.*, p. 704–705.
[4] *Ibid.*, p. 705.
[5] *Ibid.*

However, these considerations in themselves – indispensable as they are for the establishment of an historic title – could not have been deemed sufficient for the acquisition of such a title, had it not been for the fact that in the circumstances of the case they – in their entirety – warranted a presumption of acquiescence in the historic claim of the riparian States on the part of the international community. This is clearly brought out in the Court's conclusions where it is observed that the above-mentioned circumstances "combine all the characteristics or conditions that the text writers on international law, the international law institutes and precedents have prescribed as essential to territorial waters, to wit, secular or immemorial possession accompanied by *animo domini* both peaceful and continuous and by *acquiescence on the part of other nations*."[1]

It would therefore appear that the geographical factor, as well as the economic considerations and the elements of national defence and other vital interests of the coastal State, are relevant in the establishment of an historic title to the extent that they indicate the degree of consent accorded to historic claims by the nations affected by such national pretensions; in the case of a maritime historic claim, "the nations affected" are the entire international community.

While the ultimate conclusion reached by the Court as regards the juridical status of the Gulf of Fonseca is believed to be erroneous, for the reasons given further below,[2] the various considerations enumerated by the Court as being instrumental in the acquisition of a maritime historic title are certainly correct. In fact, this enumeration is the most exhaustive list that has been given by any international tribunal in respect of the motives underlying and justifying a maritime historic claim.[3]

In advancing various national claims to historic rights over certain bays, the claimant States have usually stressed one aspect or another of these motives. Thus, in his opinion relating to the juridical status of Delaware Bay, Attorney-General Randolph of the United States dwelt mainly on the geographical aspect, pointing out that the whole bay was bounded by United States territory, and that "the Delaware does

[1] *Ibid.* (First italics in original, second added).

[2] See below, section 72.

[3] Another valuable illustration for what has been regarded as manifestation of State authority over maritime areas is to be found in the *Grisbadarna* Arbitration Award where the tribunal mentioned among the various acts, through which Swedish sovereignty over the banks in question was displayed, the placing of beacons, the measurement of the sea and the installation of a light-boat. (Scott, *Hague Court Reports*, 1st series, 1916. p. 130; *UNRIAA*, vol. XI, p. 161).

not lead from the sea to the dominions of any foreign nation."[1] He also referred to the various American assertions, as expressed and enforced in different acts of legislation, and to the interests of security of the United States.

The elements of configuration, defensibility and the degree of assertion of sovereignty were relied upon by the Judical Committee of the Privy Council in the *Direct United States Cable Co.* v. *The Anglo-American Telegraph Co.* in deciding the territorial status of Conception Bay.[2]

It is fitting at this juncture to indicate that the so-called "vital interests" of the coastal State, taken in isolation, do not appear to have been recognized in the past as a sufficient ground for the acquisition of an historic title, and were relied upon only *in conjunction* with all the other considerations which, through their combination, warrant the inference of an international acquiescence.[3] Thus, the concept of acquiring an historic title to a given area on purely "vital" grounds, i.e. by reason of the subjective interests of the claimant State, as conceived by that State itself, is just as unjustified on the maritime plane as it is in general, with the sole difference that if "vital grounds" form the basis of a maritime historic claim – affecting as it normally does a great number of nations – this doctrine is even more unlikely to be accepted than in respect of "ordinary" historic claims. In rejecting claims to "vital" bays, based solely on the real or imaginary needs of the coastal State, Gidel observes:

> Ce seraient des prétentions arbitraires... qui seraient fondées purement et simplement sur des besoins ou des intérêts de l'Etat riverain....[4]

Thus, the interests of the coastal State will be taken into account – alongside other pertinent factors – to the extent that they are clearly evidenced by a long usage and recognized, either expressly or tacitly, by the family of nations.

In a previous chapter the various manifestations of State authority

[1] Moore, *Digest of International Law*, vol. 1, 1906, p. 735. See also the decision of the Second Court of Commissioners of Alabama Claims in the *Alleganean* case, where Chesapeake Bay was treated as an historic bay of the United States on similar grounds. (Moore, *International Arbitrations*, vol. IV, pp. 4332–4341).

[2] 2 (1877) *A.C.*, p. 394 *et seq.*

[3] The role of the "legitimate interests" of the claimant State in the establishment of an historic title was dealt with at some length above, in chapter IV, section 52, and the views submitted there as regards the acquisition of an historic title in general hold good also in respect of the acquisition of a maritime historic title.

[4] Gidel, *op. cit.*, vol. III, p. 635. See to the same effect Bourquin *loc. cit.*, p. 51. See, however, the contrary opinion expressed by Senhor Magalhães, the Portuguese delegate to the 1930 Hague Codification Conference, where he invoked such considerations of "vital interests" as justifying an historic claim. (*Ser. L.o.N.P.*, 1930, V. 16, p. 106).

over a given territory were considered at some length.[1] In summing up this section it may be said that the same requirements also apply, *mutatis mutandis*, to maritime areas. Certain adjustments are rendered necessary by the fact that State authority over maritime areas is normally exercised in a more sporadic and isolated manner than over terrestrial areas. The principle, however, remains the same: the claimant State will be required to prove such a degree of effective display of State authority as would normally be expected from a State in possession of a similar body of water under similar circumstances.

Normally, the assertion of State sovereignty over maritime areas will express itself by the exclusion from the water areas in question of all foreign vessels and their subjection to the domestic legislation of the coastal State. Other manifestations of State authority and assertions of State sovereignty will, however, be also taken into account. To quote Gidel:

> En ce qui concerne la nature de ces actes d'appropriation, il est difficile d'en préciser rigoureusement le caractère: l'exclusion de ces parages des navires étrangers, leur soumission à des règles émanant de l'Etat riverain et dépassant le domaine habituel de la réglementation édictée dans l'intérêt de la navigation serait évidemment des actes pleinement démonstratifs de la volonté de l'Etat. Il serait trop rigoureux de n'admettre que ceux-là.[2]

Similarly, McDougal and Burke maintain that

> control of fisheries, imposition of administrative regulations upon foreign vessels, legislative enactments, and local judicial decisions affecting foreign vessels all may serve to indicate the local belief that the bay is a part of state territory.[3]

64. Historic waters - Historic bays in general

The term "historic waters" is applied nowadays in respect of maritime areas in general, with reference to bodies of water which – in spite of their being situated beyond the normal limits of a State's maritime domain – are treated as if they were part of the maritime appurtenance of the littoral State. Thus, this term denotes all waters which, owing to an unusual geographical configuration, combined with overriding economic interests, strategical factors etc., are subjected to the riparian State's authority, in derogation of the normally applicable rules of international law.

[1] See above, chapter IV, section 36.
[2] Gidel, *op. cit.*, vol. III, p. 633.
[3] McDougal and Burke, *op. cit.*, p. 340.

While, from the legal point of view, the theory of "historic bays" forms only one aspect of the more general doctrine of "historic waters," it is none the less true to say that historically and chronologically this latter doctrine evolved from the more limited concept of "historic bays" and is, in fact, merely an extension of this concept which was already frequently resorted to in the last century. This fact is hardly surprising, bearing in mind that a great number of bays display a close link and intimate relationship with the countries washing their shores and thus comply with the requirements usually enumerated for the establishment of a maritime historic title.

The fact that maritime historic claims have been laid in the past mainly with regard to bays has been commented upon in the Study on the *Juridical Regime of Historic Waters, Including Historic Bays*, prepared by the United Nations Secretariat for the 14th Session of the International Law Commission, in the following words:

If the term 'historic bays' has been used more frequently than 'historic waters,' this is mainly due to the fact that claims on an historic basis have been made more often with respect to what was called or considered to be bays than regarding other waters. In principle ... [this theory] applies also to other maritime areas than bays.... In the *Fisheries* case between the United Kingdom and Norway, both parties agreed that the theory of 'historic waters' was not limited to bays.[1]

It is therefore felt that a closer perusal of the problems surrounding historic bays might afford a welcome opportunity for a better understanding of the problems attendant on historic waters in general. Furthermore, the greater part of the literature that has been devoted to the problems of maritime historic titles deals more specifically with historic bays.

Consequently, the present section, as well as sections 65 and 66, are devoted to a discussion of the theory of historic bays. Sections 67–69 deal with historic waters other than historic bays.

The origins of the theory of historic bays go back to the nineteenth century when the modern concept of the freedom of the high seas emerged as the paramount rule of modern maritime international law. It thus became necessary to fix the precise boundary between the high seas – over which all States were deemed to enjoy a sort of common ownership – and the maritime appurtenances of the littoral States – over which the coastal States were exercising all or a part of the rights of sovereignty. For obvious reasons many littoral countries were keen on

[1] See U.N. Document A/CN. 4/143 of March 9th, 1962, *ILC Yearbook*, 14th session, 1962, vol. II, p. 6. (Italics added).

extending the limits of their jurisdiction as far as possible and were looking for a legally valid pretext for the extension of their jurisdiction beyond the almost universally accepted three-mile limit. The geographical situation of certain bays, the close link between them and the States by whose land territories they are enclosed, the defensibility of their entrances by the coastal States, their economic interests, all these and other factors combined to make the bays the suitable object for the introduction of a theory which was destined to grant to the littoral States rights going beyond the normally applicable rules of international law. The riparian States' main purpose was to advance the starting-line of the territorial sea further seawards, towards the opening of the bay. The result would be twofold:

(a) Parts of the sea, which would otherwise have been considered as territorial waters, would become internal waters of the littoral State;

(b) Through the extension of the internal waters, the territorial waters were to be measured from various points further seawards, thus carrying the marginal belt of the littoral State into parts of what would normally have been considered as the open sea.

Before going further into the legal problems pertaining to historic bays, it would appear pertinent to deal briefly with the definition of "bays" in general.

Article 7, paragraph 2, of the 1958 Geneva *Convention on the Territorial Sea and the Contiguous Zone* (hereinafter referred to as the "*Territorial Sea Convention*") defines a bay, *for the purposes of the article*, as

> a well-marked indentation whose penetration is in such proportion to the width of its mouth as to contain landlocked waters and constitute more than a mere curvature of the coast. An indentation shall not, however, be regarded as a bay unless its area is as large as, or larger than, that of the semi-circle whose diameter is a line drawn across the mouth of that indentation.[1]

This definition has removed an important stumbling-block in international law. Up to 1958 there does not seem to have been any commonly accepted definition of the term "bay." The pleadings of the parties to the *Fisheries* case serve as a good illustration of the confusion that had pervaded this subject; there considerable space and energy were devoted to an effort to formulate such a definition,[2] relying on various authorities who had tackled that problem before. Some authors went even as far as to distinguish between "bays" – an expression reserved for

[1] *Cmnd.* 584 (1959), p. 21.

[2] See e.g. *ICJ, Fisheries case, Pleadings, Oral Arguments, Documents,* vol. I, pp. 422–425; see also *ibid.*, vol. II, pp. 467–472.

smaller identations – and "gulfs" – a term which was meant to denote only larger indentations.[1] Such a distinction, however, is borne out neither by law nor by practice[2] and the terms appear to be interchangeable.

The term "historic bays" is designed to define all "those areas of water the legal status of which differs – with the consent of other States – from what it ought to have been according to the generally recognized rules of law."[3] Gidel, while giving this definition, criticizes it at the same time on the ground that the word "historic" in this context is inappropriate. It is not the bays, he asserts, that have a "history," for there is no bay without its history. The States advancing "historic claims" over certain bays mean to indicate thereby that, owing to some peculiar circumstances, they are entitled to "*historic rights*" over a given bay.[4]

It used to be common ground that the principle of historic bays did not have to be invoked in all those cases where the width of the entrance of the bay was less than six miles (that is to say, less than twice the commonly accepted breadth of territorial waters), provided that the bay was engulfed by one and the same State.[5] These bays are territorrial, even without resorting to the doctrine of historic bays. Says Oppenheim:

> Such gulfs and bays as are enclosed by the land of one and the same littoral State, and have an entrance from the sea not more than six miles wide, are certainly territorial.[6]

The problem of historic bays arises, accordingly, solely with regard to bays, the entrance of which exceeds twice the width of territorial waters.[7]

Various criteria have been suggested in the past with a view to setting an upper limit to the width of the entrance of bays which might be regarded – on historic grounds – as territorial bays of the littoral States.[8] The strictest of these suggestions – amounting virtually to an

[1] See e.g. Colombos, in whose view "bays which penetrate deep into the land are called gulfs." (Colombos, *op. cit.*, p. 162).

[2] Thus, the area known as Hudson Bay comprises a vast body of water, whereas the Gulf of St. Tropez is one of the small bays.

[3] This is the English translation of the definition given by Gidel, which in the original French is as follows: "L'expression 'baies historiques'... désigne les espaces maritimes dont le statut juridique n'est pas, du consentement des autres Etats, celui qu'il devrait être aux termes des règles généralement admises." (Gidel, *op. cit.*, vol. III, p. 623).

[4] *Ibid.*

[5] As to historic claims raised in respect of "multinational" bays, see below, section 65.

[6] Oppenheim, *op. cit.*, p. 505.

[7] In view of the lack of general agreement as to the breadth of the territorial sea, any reference to an arithmetical definition on this point is avoided.

[8] The term "territorial bays" is used in this study to denote bays or gulfs, the waters of which are regarded as *internal* waters of the coastal State. The choice of this term might perhaps look somewhat unfortunate, for it is likely to lend itself to the misleading impression

absolute negation of the theory of historic bays – was advanced by Lord Fitzmaurice, when he declared in the House of Lords on February 21st, 1907, on behalf of His Majesty's Government, that only bays, the entrance of which does not exceed six miles, were to be regarded as territorial bays and that no exceptions to that rule could be recognized.[1] Different writers pleaded for a ten-mile test,[2] and, as has been pointed out by Oppenheim, "the practice of several States, such as Germany, Belgium and Holland, accords with this opinion."[3] The practice of other States, however, goes much beyond this limit. In the *Memorandum on Historic Bays* prepared by the United Nations Secretariat for the First Geneva Conference on the Law of the Sea[4] there appears a list of various bays claimed by the littoral States as territorial bays on historic grounds although their entrances by far exceed the width of ten miles. Among these bays one might mention the Bay of Cancale with an entrance of 17 miles (claimed by France as a territorial bay),[5] and the Bays of Chaleur (16 miles entrance)[6] and Miramichi (14 miles entrance)[7] which are both regarded by Canada as territorial bays. The

that the waters of the bay are *territorial* waters, rather than *internal* waters. It should be borne in mind, however, that the more or less clear-cut distinction between internal waters and territorial waters is of comparatively recent origin and appears to have crystallized only in the course of the 1930 Hague Codification Conference. Prior to that Conference doctrine and practice alike do not seem to have taken due account of the distinction existing between these two categories of water. (See Gidel, *op. cit.*, vol. I, pp. 44–62). The term "territorial bay" had already gained widespread currency in the nineteenth century. Rivier, for example, writing in 1896, asserted that "territorial gulfs are governed by the principles of law which also govern internal seas.... The littoral sea begins where the territorial gulf ends." (Rivier, *Principes du droit des gens*, 1896, vol. I, p. 154, as translated from the French in the U.N. *Memorandum on Historic Bays, United Nations Conference on the Law of the Sea, Official Records*, vol. I, *Preparatory Documents*, U.N. Doc. A/CONF. 13/1, p. 17).

[1] *Hansard* (Lords), 4th Series, vol. 169, col. 989.

[2] See e.g. Cavaré, *Le droit international public positif*, 1951, vol. II, p. 512. See also Brierly, *The Law of Nations*, 5th ed. 1955, p. 172. These views were advanced prior to the 1958 Geneva Conference on the Law of the Sea. Cf. however, Cavaré, *op. cit.*, 2nd rev. ed., vol. II, 1962, p. 682; and Brierly, *op. cit.*, 6th ed. (edited by Waldock), 1963, pp. 197–198.

[3] Oppenheim, *op. cit.*, p. 506.

[4] *United Nations Conference on the Law of the Sea, Official Records*, vol. I, *Preparatory Documents*, U.N. Doc. A/CONF. 13/1.

[5] See the French Reply to the questionnaire submitted to various Governments by the Preparatory Committee of the 1930 Hague Codification Conference, as reported in *Ser. L.o.N.P.*, 1929, V. 2, p. 160.

[6] See *Mowat* v. *McFee* (1880), *Reports of the Supreme Court of Canada*, vol. 5, p. 66, where the Supreme Court of Canada held that the bay was in its entirety "within the present boundaries of the Provinces of Quebec and New Brunswick and within the Dominion of Canada." This finding was upheld by the Permanent Court of Arbitration in the *North Atlantic Fisheries* Arbitration (see *UNRIAA*, vol. XI, p. 199, and Scott, *Hague Court Reports*, 1st series, 1916, p. 189), and also found acceptance in the Treaty concluded between the United States and Great Britain on July 20th, 1912 (see *Treaties and Conventions between the United States and other Powers*, 1910–1923, vol. III, p. 2632).

[7] See Annex 64 to the Norwegian Counter-Memorial in the *Fisheries* case (*ICJ, Fisheries case, Pleadings, Oral Arguments, Documents*, vol. II, p. 271), where an extract of the British Argument in the *North Atlantic Fisheries* Arbitration has been reproduced. In that extract

most extreme example in this respect is perhaps that of Hudson Bay, with an entrance of 50 miles and embracing 580,000 square miles, which is claimed by Canada as part of her territory.[1]

Thus, the width of the entrance of a bay does not seem to be, in itself, of direct relevance in the establishment of an historic title by the littoral State. The only bearing this consideration seems to have on the acquisition of an historic title lies in the fact that an excessively wide entrance strongly militates against the presumption that the bay in question is sufficiently closely linked with the land domain of the coastal State and correspondingly weakens any inference of the littoral State being capable of exercising effective control over the bay in question. If, however, it can be proved that the coastal State did, in fact, exercise such authority and control over the bay and a reasonable inference of international acquiescence in that practice can be drawn, then the excessive width of a bay's entrance will not prevent its being recognized as an historic bay.

Meanwhile, the problem of historic bays in general seems to have lost much of its former significance and acuteness in view of the adoption by the 1958 Geneva Conference on the Law of the Sea of article 7, paragraph 4, of the *Territorial Sea Convention.* This article reads as follows:

> If the distance between the low-water marks of the natural entrance points of a bay does not exceed *twenty-four miles*, a closing line may be drawn between these two low-water marks, and the waters enclosed thereby shall be considered as internal waters.[2]

reference is made to various acts of legislation in which the territoriality of Miramichi Bay was asserted.

[1] See e.g. Johnston, 15 *BYIL* (1934), pp. 1–20. See also Strohl, *The International Law of Bays*, 1963, pp. 233–250.

A more detailed list of maritime areas which have been claimed, on historic grounds, as territorial waters of the littoral States, can be found in the *Memorandum on Historic Bays*, prepared by the United Nations Secretariat for the 1958 Geneva Conference on the Law of the Sea (U.N. Doc. A/CONF. 13/1, pp. 3–10). The Memorandum lists maritime historic claims put forward by about twenty States. It is believed, however, that the number of States which lay claim, on historic grounds, to various maritime areas is far greater. No agreed list of "historic waters" is in existence. In the course of the preparatory work for the 1930 Hague Codification Conference, Schücking, Rapporteur of the Sub-committee dealing with problems connected with the law of the territorial sea, suggested the establishment of an International Waters Office which would register rights possessed by the riparian States outside the proposed fixed zone of their territorial seas, including rights to "historic waters." He also suggested that application for the registration of such rights should be made within a given time limit and that such applications could be opposed within a fixed time limit. (See *L.o.N.* Doc. C. 196. M. 70. 1927. V, pp. 38–41 and 58). The idea of an International Waters Office was later dropped by the Rapporteur. (*Ibid.*, p. 72). In the Study on the *Juridical Regime of Historic Waters, Including Historic Bays*, prepared by the United Nations Secretariat, doubts have been voiced as to the practicability of such an arrangement which "might provoke a number of unnecessary disputes as States would be tempted, in order to be on the safe side, to overstate both their claims and their objections." (U.N. Doc. A/CN. 4/143 of March 9th, 1962, *ILC Yearbook*, 14th session, 1962, vol. II, p. 24.)

[2] *Cmnd.* 584 (1959), p. 21. (Italics added).

The provision contained in this article appears to represent a concession made to the countries favouring throughout the deliberations of the Conference the recognition of a twelve-mile limit for the breadth of the territorial sea, twenty-four miles being twice the suggested width of the marginal belt. The adoption of the twenty-four mile limit departed from the original proposal by the International Law Commission of a twenty-five mile limit,[1] which was later reduced – following an amendment put forward by Sir Gerald Fitzmaurice – to fifteen miles.[2] The First Committee of the 1958 Geneva Conference on the Law of the Sea reversed, however, this proposal and recommended, by a majority of four votes, the adoption of a twenty-four mile limit.[3] This recommendation was carried by the plenary by 49 votes to 19, with 9 abstentions.[4]

One might therefore whole-heartedly subscribe to the assertion made by McDougal and Burke that

> the notion of 'historic bays' may now have, in view of the decision of the 1958 Conference to provide that the baseline in bays may extend to twenty-four miles, considerably less significance than was formerly attributed to it.... In fact practically none of the most frequently cited illustrations of historic bays have openings as wide as twenty-four miles.... If the [Territorial Sea Convention] is regarded as expressing a general consensus upon permissible length of the baseline, then clearly the major function of historic bays has largely disappeared. If the 1958 Convention is not widely ratified or otherwise accepted, and is not generally considered to express community consensus, then of course the idea of historic bay may still possess some viability and attract more than academic interest.[5]

As a logical extension of the provision contained in article 7, paragraph 4, paragraph 5 of the same article stipulates that

> where the distance between the low-water marks of the natural entrance points of a bay exceeds twenty-four miles, a straight baseline of twenty-four miles shall be drawn within the bay in such a manner as to enclose the maximum area of water that is possible with a line of that length.[6]

The meaning of this stipulation is that in those cases in which the entrance of a bay exceeds twenty-four miles, a straight baseline will be drawn at a point nearest to the entrance where the opposing coasts are not more than twenty-four miles apart, so as to confer on all the

[1] *ILC Yearbook*, 7th session, 1955, vol. II, p. 36.
[2] *ILC Yearbook*, 8th session, 1956, vol. I, p. 197.
[3] *United Nations Conference on the Law of the Sea, Official Records*, vol. III, *First Committee*, p. 146.
[4] *Ibid.*, vol. II, *Plenary Meetings*, p. 63.
[5] McDougal and Burke, *op. cit.*, pp. 357–358.
[6] *Cmnd.* 584 (1959), p. 21.

waters from the baseline landwards the status of internal waters.

This provision – carried by the plenary meeting of the Conference by 47 votes to 19, with 8 abstentions[1] – further reduces the practical significance of the theory of historic waters as regards its application to bays, because it transforms into internal waters all those parts of the bays landwards to the baselines, the length of which does not exceed twenty-four miles, even though their entrance may be wider than twenty-four miles. (The *Territorial Sea Convention* came into force on September 10th, 1964, one month after the deposit of the twenty-second instrument of ratification,[2] the *Convention on the High Seas* and the *Convention on the Continental Shelf* having earlier come into force.)[3] The considerable number of States who voted in favour of article 7, and particularly the proportion of those who voted for its adoption, as compared with those who opposed it (article 7, as a whole, was approved by 63 votes to 6, with 5 abstentions), certainly reflects the general mood of the international society and a consensus of opinion prevailing among the States of the world, and this general consensus must surely be reckoned with as expressing also the views of those States who associated themselves with the article in question, even if they have not yet formally become parties to the *Territorial Sea Convention.*

While the provisions contained in article 7 are likely to eliminate many problems relating to the juridical status of a great number of hitherto "historic" bays, they certainly do not dispose of the problem altogether. The Conference was the first to recognize this fact, to which recognition it gave a twofold expression:

(a) Article 7, paragraph 6, of the *Territorial Sea Convention* stipulates that "the foregoing provisions shall not apply to so-called 'historic' bays,"[4] thus expressly excluding the problem of the remaining "historic bays" from the scope of the Convention's provisions;

(b) The Conference also adopted a joint Indian-Panamanian draft resolution, submitted by the First Committee, in which the United

[1] *United Nations Conference on the Law of the Sea, Official Records*, vol. II, p. 63.

[2] The provisions relating to the signature and ratification by the various States are laid down in articles 25–29 of the *Territorial Sea Convention.* (Similar provisions may be found in the remaining three Conventions).

By mid-September 1964 the Convention had been signed by 44 States and had been ratified by 23 States.

[3] The *Convention on the High Seas* came into force on September 30th, 1962. By mid-September 1964 it had been signed by 49 States (29 ratifications). The *Convention on the Continental Shelf* came into force on June 10th, 1964. By mid-September 1964 it had been signed by 46 States (24 ratifications). The *Convention on Fishing and Conservation of the Living Resources of the High Seas* has not yet come into force. By mid-September 1964 it had been signed by 37 States, but had received by then only 17 ratifications.

[4] *Cmnd.* 584 (1959), p. 21.

Nations General Assembly was requested "to arrange for the study of the juridical régime of historic waters, including historic bays, and for the communication of the results of such study to all States Members of the United Nations."[1]

Following the adoption of this resolution, the Sixth Committee of the United Nations General Assembly, on December 4th, 1959, unanimously recommended to the General Assembly the adoption of a resolution which requested the International Law Commission "as soon as it considers it advisable, to undertake the study of the question of the juridical régime of historic waters, including historic bays, and to make such recommendations regarding the matter as the Commission deems appropriate."[2] On December 7th, 1959, the General Assembly unanimously adopted this draft resolution.[3]

For the sake of completeness it must be added, however, that article 7 of the *Territorial Sea Convention*, in its entirety, refers solely to bays "the coasts of which belong to a single State."[4] This introductory remark of the article raises an important problem, namely, the question whether an historic claim may be asserted in respect of a "multinational" bay, that is to say, a bay which is enclosed by the territories of more than one littoral State.

65. Can multinational bays be claimed as historic bays?

As to the "historicity" of bays which are enclosed by more than one littoral State, doctrine and practice alike seem, on the whole, to uphold the view that such bays are incapable of acquiring the status of historic bays and cannot be appropriated by the littoral States or any of them, irrespective of the width of their entrances or other geographic, economic or strategic considerations. Thus, the Swiss-Belgian writer Rivier stated as early as 1896:

> Where there are several coastal States, the gulf is an open sea regardless of the width at the entrance.[5]

And Oppenheim seems to echo this view when he maintains that

> as a rule, all gulfs and bays enclosed by the land of more than one littoral State,

[1] *Ibid.*, p. 50.
[2] *United Nations, General Assembly, Official Records, 14th Session*, 1959, *Sixth Committee*, p. 241. For the text of the draft resolution see Document A/4333, para. 11.
[3] *Resolution 1453 (XIV)*, adopted at the 847th plenary meeting, December 7th, 1959.
[4] *Cmnd.* 584 (1959), p. 21.
[5] Rivier, *op. cit.*, pp. 154–155. Quoted after U.N. Doc. A/CONF. 13/1, p. 17.

however narrow their entrance may be, are non-territorial. They are parts of the open sea, the marginal belt inside the gulfs and bays excepted. They can never be appropriated.[1]

To understand the reason why multinational bays are generally regarded as being incapable of acquiring the status of historic bays, it is as well to remember that one of the main motives usually advanced in support of an historic claim to a bay is that the bay in question "does not lead from the sea to the dominions of any foreign nation."[2] This argument was resorted to by the Second Court of Commissioners of Alabama Claims in the *Alleganean* case, where the arbitral tribunal had to pronounce on the territorial status of Chesapeake Bay and found that it constituted United States internal waters. Amongst the reasons given by the tribunal for this finding was the fact that the bay

is entirely encompassed about by... [United States] territory.... It cannot become an international commercial highway; it is not and cannot be made a roadway from one nation to another.[3]

Thus, it becomes evident that one of the major considerations which permit a given bay to be turned into an historic bay is the fact that by its incorporation into the national domain of the littoral State no harm is done, or is likely to be done, to another State and that the rights of such a State are not affected thereby. It is, however, abundantly clear that these considerations do not hold good in those cases where the shores of a bay are possessed by more than one littoral State. In such cases it can hardly be maintained that the bay "is not and cannot be made a roadway from one nation to another." This seems to account to a very large extent for the fact that multinational bays have generally come to be regarded as parts of the open sea, except the marginal belt to which each of the littoral States is entitled in accordance with the general rules of international law.[4] This consideration, which seems to

[1] Oppenheim, *op. cit.*, p. 508.

[2] See Attorney-General Randolph's opinion as regards the juridical status of Delaware Bay, in connection with the naval incident of 1793 between the British vessel *The Grange* and the French vessel *L'Embuscade*. (Moore, *Digest of International Law*, vol. I, 1906, pp. 735–739).

[3] Moore, *International Arbitrations*, vol. IV, pp. 4332–4341, at p. 4339.

[4] In some narrow bays the marginal belts of the various coastal States are likely to overlap. The solution in such cases would be usually an agreement between the parties concerned, failing which article 12, paragraph 1, of the *Territorial Sea Convention* provides that the territorial seas of the participants should not extend beyond the median line every point of which is equidistant from the nearest points on the baselines from which the breadth of the territorial seas of each of the States is measured. (*Cmnd.* 584 (1959), p. 22). The paragraph adds, however, that these general provisions shall not apply "where it is necessary, by reason of historic title or other special circumstances, to delimit the territorial seas of the two States in a way which is at variance with this provision." (*Ibid.*)

be implicit in all those cases where multinational bays are involved, was given explicit recognition in an arbitration case which arose as a consequence of the seizure in 1843 of the United States vessel *Washington* by a British vessel within the Bay of Fundy. Umpire Bates rejected the British contention, according to which the bay was British domain, and explained his decision, *inter alia*, by the fact that

one of the headlands of the Bay of Fundy is in the United States, and ships bound to Passaquamoddy must sail through a large space of it.[1]

Commenting on this decision, Dana took the view that

the real ground [for this decision] was that one of the assumed headlands belonged to the United States and it was necessary to pass the headland in order to get to one of the ports of the United States.[2]

Fauchille appears to take the same view when he asserts that

la sentence arbitrale ... relative à la baie de Fundy a considéré que cette baie était une mer libre ... surtout parce que *ses côtes n'appartenaient pas tous au même Etat.*[3]

The only instance in which a claim to historic rights over a multinational bay seems to have been recognized by an international tribunal appears to be the *Gulf of Fonseca* case.[4] As has already been pointed out above, this gulf is bounded by the territories of Nicaragua, Honduras and El Salvador.[5] Its entrance is nineteen and a half miles wide. By a treaty concluded in 1914 between the United States of America and Nicaragua (the Bryan-Chamorro Treaty), the United States were granted for a period of 99 years certain rights in portions of Nicaraguan territory bordering on the Gulf of Fonseca, as well as rights concerning the construction of an inter-oceanic canal. The validity of this treaty was disputed by El Salvador which instituted proceedings against Nicaragua before the Central American Court of Justice. On behalf of El Salvador it was contented that Nicaragua was not entitled to grant any rights to the United States in the Gulf of Fonseca, since the Gulf constituted, on historical grounds, the common property of the three riparian countries.

In its judgment of March 9th, 1917, the Court upheld the contentions of El Salvador and unanimously held that the gulf was "a historic bay

[1] Moore, *International Arbitrations*, vol. IV, 1898, p. 4344.

[2] Quoted by Phillimore, *op. cit.*, vol. I, pp. 287–289.

[3] Fauchille, *op. cit.*, vol. I, part II, p. 384. (Italics added).

[4] Reported in 11 *AJIL* (1917), p. 674 *et seq.*

[5] During the period from 1522 down to 1821 the gulf formed part of the royal patrimony of the Crown of Castille. From 1821 down to 1839 it was part of the Federal Republic of Central America. This Republic was dissolved in 1839 and the three successor States of Nicaragua, Honduras and El Salvador took its place.

possessed of the characteristics of a closed sea."[1] The Court then proceeded to enumerate the considerations which led it to this conclusion and found, by a majority vote, that

the three riparian States of El Salvador, Honduras and Nicaragua are ... recognized as coöwners of [the gulf's waters], except as to the littoral marine league which is the exclusive property of each.[2]

The *Gulf of Fonseca* case, however, rather than conforming with the rules of international law, seems to be a deviation from them. This apparently isolated case of the recognition of a multinational bay as an historic bay has come ever since under severe fire from doctrinal sources and, as far as can be ascertained, has not been followed since by any other tribunal. Gidel considers this decision as "une anomalie tout à fait notable dans le système logique des baies historiques."[3]

More recently the question of the "historicity" of a multinational bay arose once more with regard to the Gulf of Aqaba, which has been claimed by the various Arab States as forming part of "regional Arab waters." According to this view, the gulf in its entirety constitutes a "closed Arab gulf" and consequently its waters are to be regarded as "Arab territorial waters."[4] It has also been contended by Saudi Arabia that the gulf "is of the category of historical gulfs that fall outside the sphere of international law,"[5] on the ground that it forms "the historical route to the holy places in Mecca. Pilgrims from different Muslim countries have been streaming through the Gulf, year after year, for fourteen centuries. Ever since, the Gulf has been an exclusively Arab route under Arab sovereignty."[6]

The Gulf of Aqaba – with an approximately six-mile entrance – is about ninety-six miles long and its breadth at no point exceeds fifteen miles. The islands of Tiran and Sanafir, in the approach of the Gulf, reduce the navigable routes at the entrance of the gulf to two narrow passages of a few hundred yards each.[7] In approximately 700 A.D. the

[1] 11 *AJIL* (1917), p. 716.

[2] *Ibid.*

[3] Gidel, *op. cit.*, vol. III, p. 627. He also calls the judgment rendered in this case "un accident qui ne saurait en altérer la ligne." (*Ibid.*)

[4] See e.g. the official statement of the Saudi Arabian Government as published on March 17th, 1957, in the Mecca daily *Al-Bilad al-Saudiyah*, as cited in an article by Charles B. Selak Jr. on "A Consideration of the Legal Status of the Gulf of Aqaba," 52 *AJIL* (1958), p. 660 *et seq.*, at p. 676.

[5] *United Nations, General Assembly, Official Records, 12th Session*, 1957, *Plenary Meetings*, p. 233.

[6] *Ibid.*

[7] For the geographical and hydrographical details relating to the gulf, see *United Nations Conference on the Law of the Sea, Official Records*, vol. I, *Preparatory Documents*, U.N. Document A/CONF. 13/15, pp. 208–209.

gulf came under Arab domination as a result of the conquest of the entire area by the Arabs. In 1517 the Turks conquered the whole district surrounding the gulf and until the end of the First World War it formed an integral part of the Ottoman Empire. At present, the gulf washes the shores of four States: the United Arab Republic (a coastline of about 100 miles), Saudi Arabia (a coastline of about 100 miles), the Hashemite Kingdom of Jordan (a three-and-a-half-mile coastline) and Israel (a six-mile coastline). The first two States possess the shores overlooking the entrance of the gulf, while each of the latter two possesses a small coastal strip at the head of the gulf.

When the status of the gulf was discussed during the twelfth session of the United Nations General Assembly, the representative of Saudi Arabia, Mr. Shukairy, claimed that

> the Gulf of Aqaba is a national inland waterway, subject to absolute Arab sovereignty. The geographical location of the Gulf is conclusive proof of its national character.... Thus, by its configuration the Gulf is in the nature of a *mare clausum* which does not belong to the class of international waterways. ... The Gulf is so narrow that the territorial areas of the littoral States are bound to overlap. ... The Gulf of Aqaba is of the category of historical gulfs that fall outside the sphere of international law. ... Israel ... has no right to any part of the Gulf. ... The area under Israel is nothing but military control without sovereignty whatsoever.[1]

It is difficult to conceive how this last assertion, namely, that Israel has no sovereignty over any part of the gulf's coastline, but only military control – an assertion which in itself is at least dubious – can in any way advance the historic claim put forward by the Saudi Arabian delegate. Even without the presence of Israel, the gulf would still be enclosed by three different States. These States have, in fact, some important features in common, notably, that the majority of their subjects are of the Arab racial stock, speak the same language and adhere to the Moslem faith. These common features, however, do not appear to be of any *legal* relevance, since international law – being a law of *nations* and not of religious creeds, languages or races – recognizes as its subjects *States* and not religions, races or linguistic groups. Thus, it is difficult to follow the line of argument adopted by the Saudi Arabian representative when he stresses the allegedly strong historical link existing between

[1] *United Nations, General Assembly, Official Records*, 12th Session, 1957, *Plenary Meetings*, p. 233. (Italics added). A statement to the same effect was made by Mr. Shukairy in the Sixth Committee of the General Assembly at its 14th session. (See *United Nations, General Assembly, Official Records, 14th Session*, 1959, *Sixth Committee*, p. 227 *et seq.*). See also Mr. Shukairy's statement in the First Committee of the 1958 *United Nations Conference on the Law of the Sea, Official Records*, vol. III, p. 3.

Islam and the Gulf of Aqaba.[1] At the present stage of international law the Saudi Arabian claim is likely to strike one as an utter innovation, in support of which there do not seem to be any authorities. Thus, the term "Arab territorial waters" or any similar expression must be regarded as being devoid of any legal significance.

The only part of the Saudi Arabian delegate's statement which seems to rest on more traditional legal ground is the passage where it is claimed that, owing to the peculiar geographical configuration of the gulf, it does not belong to the class of international waterways, and that its narrowness causes rival national claims to overlap, thus eliminating the possibility of its being regarded as part of the high seas.

One of the main deficiencies inherent in this line of argument is, of course, the fact that the allegedly peculiar configuration of the gulf (namely, its narrow entrance which is dominated by two of the littoral States) does not lead the Saudi Arabian delegate to the conclusion that it is only those two littoral States that enjoy privileged rights at the entrance of the gulf. While Saudi Arabia is apparently willing to recognize the right of Jordan to innocent passage through the entrance of the gulf, she is denying the same right to Israel, which, like Jordan, possesses only a small coastal strip at the head of the gulf. The apparent contradiction in the rights suggested by Saudi Arabia for Jordan and Israel, respectively, cannot be explained away simply by the fact that the first happens to have a Moslem majority, while in the other the Moslems are the minority of the local population.

The assertion, according to which the legal status of a gulf is determined by the legal status which is presumed to prevail at its entrance, is equally fallacious. It is precisely the other way round: the juridical status of the gulf determines the rules governing the rights of passage through its entrance and the rights of the littoral State or States therein. If a given body of water is part of the open sea, then the strait linking this body of water with another part of the open sea cannot be blocked in time of peace[2] even if the waters within the strait constitute part of the

[1] Here again, there is considerable doubt whether the past history of the gulf does, in fact, bear out the assertions of Mr. Shukairy. According to Melamid, "due to the prevalence of strong northerly winds, the confined waters of the Gulf are very difficult to navigate by northbound sailing vessels. As a result, the Gulf was rarely used by ships prior to the advent of steam navigation.... For the same reason, Moslem pilgrim sailing ships do not appear to have used the Gulf." (Melamid, "Legal Status of the Gulf of Aqaba," 53 *AJIL* (1959), p. 412).

[2] It is not intended here to go into the argument, according to which there is no peace at present between Israel and her neighbours, because the Armistice Agreements concluded between the Arab States and Israel do not deprive the parties of their belligerent rights. This argument does not seem to affect the juridical status of the gulf as such, which is the question with which we are concerned here.

littoral State's territorial sea.[1] This rule has now found express recognition in article 16, paragraph 4, of the *Territorial Sea Convention*, which provides that

> there shall be no suspension of the innocent passage of foreign ships through straits which are used for international navigation between one part of the high seas and another part of the high seas or the territorial sea of a foreign State.[2]

However, this provision of the Convention is not an innovation of the Conference, but merely the restatement of a rule of law which had already been in force prior to the adoption of the Convention. Thus, Oppenheim maintains that a strait which connects two parts of the open sea cannot be blocked for innocent passage even if it is a territorial strait, i.e. when its width does not exceed twice the width of the marginal belt. He goes on to say that "it is irrelevant that the strait is not a necessary but only an alternative route between two parts of the high seas. It is sufficient that it has been a useful route for international maritime traffic."[3]

Thus, the most that can be achieved by putting forward an historic claim to the Gulf of Aqaba is to turn those parts of the gulf, which are outside the territorial sea of any of the littoral States, into the common property of *all* the coastal States, in accordance with the decision rendered in the *Gulf of Fonseca* case.[4] However, for the reasons given above, such a course would not appear to be commendable at all. The mere fact of the overlapping in certain parts of the gulf of various

[1] See the *Corfu Channel* case, *ICJ Reports*, 1949, p. 28.

[2] *Cmnd.* 584 (1959), p. 23. The adoption of article 16, paragraph 4, was vigorously opposed by the delegates of Saudi Arabia and the United Arab Republic (see *United Nations Conference on the Law of the Sea, Official Records*, vol. III, pp. 93–94; *ibid.*, vol. II, p. 65), who were well aware of the legal implications involved in the adoption of this paragraph.

According to Sørensen, "what was in everybody's mind, without being officially stated, was the Strait of Tiran at the entrance to the Gulf of Aqaba, giving access from the Red Sea to Israel's port of Eilath. A decision on the abstract question, which had been left open by ILC, would therefore also involve an expression of opinion as to the legality of Egyptian measures amounting to a blockade of this port. In this specific context, the vote became a test not only of attitudes toward the principle of free maritime communications but also of attitudes toward the Arab-Israel conflict. In committee, as well as in plenary, the more inclusive view, advocated by Israel, prevailed. An attempt was made in plenary to have a separate vote on the words describing straits of the Tiran type as distinct from straits between two parts of the high seas, but no majority could be mustered for a division of the vote. The whole rule, including the reference to straits of both types, was then adopted by a two-thirds majority." (Sørensen, *Law of the Sea*, International Conciliation No. 520, 1958, p. 236). See also to the same effect McDougal and Burke, *op. cit.*, pp. 211 and 440.

[3] Oppenheim, *op. cit.*, p. 512. This rule has also found recognition in the judgment rendered by the International Court of Justice in the *Corfu Channel* case. (*ICJ Reports*, 1949, p. 28).

[4] Cf. McDougal and Burke, *op. cit.*, p. 444, where the authors state that "one state or a group of states may not claim the waters of a bay or gulf to the exclusion of another bordering state."

national claims to marginal belts does not alter in the least the juridical status of the gulf. The general provisions for such an eventuality are to be found in article 12, paragraph 1, of the *Territorial Sea Convention.*[1]

The correct legal position as regards the juridical status of the Gulf of Aqaba seems to have been stated in 1957 by the various leading maritime Powers of the world, when at the 11th session of the U.N. General Assembly they rallied to the concept that the gulf was an international waterway, by reason of its being possessed by more than one littoral State. The delegate of the Netherlands asserted that

> inasmuch as the Gulf of Aqaba is bordered by four different States and has a width in excess of the three miles of territorial waters of the four littoral States on either side, it is, under the rules of international law, to be regarded as part of the open sea. ... The Straits of Tiran consequently are, in the legal sense, straits connecting two open seas, normally used for international navigation.[2]

Earlier in the debate the delegate of France had observed that, in the view of his Government,

> the Gulf of Aqaba, by reason partly of its breadth and partly of the fact that its shores belong to four different States, constitutes international waters.[3]

The United Kingdom delegate associated himself with this view when he declared that "the Gulf of Aqaba is not only bounded at its narrow point of entry ... by two different countries, Egypt and Saudi Arabia, but contains at its head the ports of two further countries: Jordan and Israel."[4] According to the United Kingdom delegate, this fact in itself suffices for putting the Gulf of Aqaba into a different category from those instances in which historic claims have been recognized in the past.[5]

On behalf of the United States of America Ambassador Cabot Lodge referred to a United States *aide-mémoire* to Israel of February 11th, 1957,[6] in which it had been stated that

[1] For the text of this paragraph, see above, p. 270, n. 4; true, the article does not apply "where it is necessary, by reason of historic title..., to delimit the territorial seas of the two States in a way which is at variance with this provision." (*Ibid.*). A careful perusal of the article's wording would, however, indicate that it excludes from its scope merely those cases where historic claims have already been recognized. It surely is not meant to apply to those cases in which an historic claim is based on the difficulty of delimiting the territorial seas.

[2] *United Nations, General Assembly, Official Records, 11th session,* 1957, *Plenary Meetings,* p. 1288.

[3] *Ibid.*, p. 1280.

[4] *Ibid.*, p. 1284.

[5] *Ibid.*

[6] U.N. Doc. A/3563 of February 26th, 1957.

the United States believes that the Gulf comprehends international waters and that no nation has the right to prevent free and innocent passage in the Gulf and through the Straits giving access thereto.[1]

A similar view was taken up by the delegates of Italy,[2] Belgium,[3] Sweden,[4] Denmark[5] and Canada.[6]

It is also worth mentioning in this connection that in the *Memorandum on Historic Bays* prepared by the United Nations Secretariat for the First Geneva Conference on the Law of the Sea, the Gulf of Aqaba does not appear among the bays which have been recognized as historic bays or are claimed as such.[7] This ominous omission – following closely the debate in the United Nations General Assembly on the status of the Gulf of Aqaba – cannot be regarded as devoid of any meaning.

The International Law Commission has in the past declined to put forward any suggestions as to the "historicity" of gulfs surrounded by more than one littoral State on the ground that "the Commission has not sufficient data at its disposal concerning the number of cases involved or the regulations at present applicable to them."[8]

Having regard to Resolution 1453 (XIV) adopted by the United Nations General Assembly on December 7th, 1959, in which it requested the International Law Commission "to undertake the study of the question of the juridical régime of historic waters, including historic bays,"[9] it is to be expected that the Commission will have to concern itself with the problem whether or not multinational bays are capable of being turned into historic bays.[10]

[1] *United Nations, General Assembly, Official Records, 11th session,* 1957, *Plenary Meetings*, pp. 1277–1278.

[2] *Ibid.*, p. 1287.

[3] *Ibid.*, p. 1296.

[4] *Ibid.*, p. 1303.

[5] *Ibid.*, p. 1303.

[6] *Ibid.*, p. 1296.

[7] See *United Nations Conference on the Law of the Sea, Official Records*, vol. I, *Preparatory Documents*, p. 1. See to the same effect Malek, "La théorie dites des "baies historiques," 6 *Revue de Droit International pour le Moyen Orient* (1957), p. 100.

[8] *ILC Yearbook*, 8th session, 1956, vol. II, p. 269.

[9] *Resolution 1453 (XIV)*, adopted on December 7th, 1959.

[10] Recent publications regarding the legal status of the Gulf of Aqaba include Bloomfield, *Egypt, Israel and the Gulf of Aqaba* in *International Law*, 1957; Selak, "A Consideration of the Legal Status of the Gulf of Aqaba," 52 *AJIL* (1958), p. 660 *et seq.*; Gross, "The Geneva Conference on the Law of the Sea and the Right of Innocent Passage through the Gulf of Aqaba," 53 *AJIL* (1959), p. 564 *et seq.*; Hartwig, "Der israelisch-ägyptische Streit um den Golf von Akaba," 9 *Archiv des Völkerrechts* (1961–1962), p. 27 *et seq.*; Strohl, *op. cit.*, pp. 389–397. For a presentation of this case by an Egyptian writer see Hammad, "The Right of Passage in the Gulf of Aqaba," 15 *Revue Egyptienne de Droit International* (1959), p. 118 *et seq.*

66. *The effects of territorial changes along the coast of a bay*

Owing to territorial changes occurring along the coast of a bay, it might well happen that a bay, which was formerly surrounded by a single State, becomes, as a result of such changes, enclosed by the territories of more than one coastal State (e.g. the Gulfs of Fonseca and Aqaba).

Conversely, there exists the possibility that a hitherto multinational bay is brought, as a result of territorial changes along its shores, under the sway of a single littoral State. Thus, the question arises how such changes are likely to affect the juridical status of a given bay.

The authorities available on this point are far from being plentiful. The reason for this dearth of learned authority seems to be the fact that during the last century or so – that is to say, since the crystallization of modern maritime international law – comparatively few instances of such changes have occurred. Thus, the arguments advanced on this point have a rather speculative character and the views expressed are of a purely tentative nature.

As far as the "splitting up" of a formerly "single-national" bay is concerned, the Gulf of Fonseca seems to provide an appropriate example. As will be recalled, this gulf was surrounded down to 1821 exclusively by the dependencies of the Spanish Crown, and in the period 1821–1839 by the Central American Federation. In 1839 this Federation was dissolved and the gulf has ever since been enclosed by three littoral States: Nicaragua, Honduras and El Salvador.

In its judgment relating to the juridical status of the gulf, the Central American Court of Justice held that the portions of water falling outside the marginal belts of the littoral States constituted the joint property of all three of them.[1] Thus, the Court seems – by implication – to have taken the view that the changes which had occurred along the coasts of the gulf did not affect its status at all, and, since the gulf formerly "belonged" to the State which possessed its shores in their entirety, the sole fact that that State was now replaced by a number of *States*, was no sufficient ground for altering the juridical status of the gulf. It also emerges from the Court's judgment as a matter of course that none of the littoral States was entitled to deprive any of the other littoral States of its rights in the gulf, even though not all the littoral States might enjoy possession over the entry of the bay.[2]

[1] 11 *AJIL* (1917), p. 716.

[2] The entrance to the Gulf of Fonseca is possessed by Nicaragua and El Salvador, while Honduras owns a part of the coast inside the gulf.

The decision reached in the *Gulf of Fonseca* case has, however, met with severe criticism and is still regarded as a sort of anomaly in international law, which does not reflect the general rule. According to Selak,

the Gulf of Fonseca situation appears to be unique. Water areas surrounded by the territory of a single coastal State, and thus having the status of 'closed seas,' which subsequently, because of political changes resulting in the establishment of more than one state on their shores, become multinational in character, generally have come to be regarded as essentially parts of the high seas, regardless of the narrowness of their entrances.[1]

The change of the character of such water areas from a closed sea into essentially high seas is, however, generally not brought about automatically through the territorial changes along the coast. As a rule, special treaty arrangements provide for the recognition of the new status of the maritime area in question. In this connection, Selak mentions the Black Sea as a case which aptly illustrates this point. From 1484 onwards – when the Turks completed the conquest of its entire littoral – until 1774 – when Russia secured a foothold on its southern coast – the Black Sea was a Turkish lake. By the Treaty of Kutchuk-Kainardji of 1774 Russia was not only recognized as a littoral State, but also obtained rights of navigation in the Black Sea and a right of passage through the Turkish Straits. Later developments culminated in the Montreux Convention of 1936 which provides for "freedom of transit and navigation in the Straits" without limit of time,[2] for all merchant vessels in time of peace.

Commenting on the significance of this Convention, Brüel observes that

the principle of freedom of navigation was proclaimed in the Montreux Convention as a principle of international law independent of the will of the parties.[3]

According to the same writer, the insistence on the freedom of navigation through such straits was necessary because

to apply the ordinary rules regarding national waters, territorial waters and the open sea to straits would be to confer upon the littoral state ... privileges in straits that would not seem compatible ... with the interests of sea-traffic in being able to use these waters as ways of communication independently and not subject to the discretion of the littoral state.... It would be all the more serious, as a great number of the commercially most important straits are navigable only in such a way that

[1] Selak, *loc. cit.*, p. 693.
[2] *League of Nations Treaty Series*, vol. 173, pp. 213-241, at p. 219.
[3] Brüel, *International Straits*, 1947, vol. II, p. 425.

shipping is bound to pass through the territorial waters, in one or more places, of one or several littoral states.[1]

As to the application of the above-mentioned principle to the Gulf of Aqaba, it would appear that ever since the dissolution of the Ottoman Empire and the emergence of more than one littoral State on the shores of the gulf, it has become an international waterway and its entrance – connecting as it does two parts of the open sea – cannot be blocked to the international maritime traffic on the ground that the navigable passage of the Strait of Tiran falls within the territorial sea of one or two of the littoral States. It also follows that the Palestine hostilities of 1948 and the establishment of the State of Israel in that year are immaterial facts from the point of view of the legal status of the gulf, as its juridical regime as an international waterway had already been determined some thirty years earlier and the succession of Israel to the former mandated territory of Palestine as one of the coastal States of the gulf in no way altered that regime.[2]

It is more difficult to speculate on the possible legal implications of territorial changes whereby a formerly multinational bay becomes surrounded by one State only. In fact, the general trend of the territorial changes that have taken place during the past 150 years has not been in this direction. The number of States has been steadily on the increase rather than on the decrease and year after year more new members have been seeking admission into the international community. On a purely academic basis two possible solutions suggest themselves:

(a) It may be argued that, since the waters of such a bay formerly constituted a part of the international maritime domain, no single State will be allowed to deprive the international community of this possession and to incorporate it into its own maritime domain. This principle has now also found expression in article 2 of the 1958 Geneva *Convention on the High Seas*, which stipulates that "the high seas being open to all nations, no State may validly purport to subject any part of them to its sovereignty."[3] Thus, it may be argued that the territorial changes along the shores cannot *eo ipso* alter the legal status of the water area and the littoral State will have to acquire an historic (adverse) title to these

[1] *Ibid.*, vol. I, p. 37.

[2] Cf. McDougal and Burke: "It would no doubt be argued,... that even if the claim to historic rights were justified the emergence of a new state bordering on the gulf altered the scope of authority normally associated with historic waters." (McDougal and Burke, *op. cit.*, p. 444). See also *ibid.*, p. 440.

[3] *Cmnd.* 584 (1959), p. 27.

waters, in compliance with the requirements laid down for the establishment of such a title.

(b) On the other hand, it may validly be maintained that the coastal State – which now possesses the whole of the bay's littoral – ought not to be put in a worse position than any other nation possessing the coast of a bay in its entirety merely by virtue of the fact that its possession is of comparatively recent standing.

These two conflicting points of view do, in fact, represent different approaches to the problem of the relationship between purely national and international interests. Those favouring the hegemony of international law would in all probability subscribe to the first suggestion, while others, more preoccupied with the specific interests of the littoral State, might prefer the latter concept. No clear-cut answer to this question is attempted here. Suffice it to say that the possible clash of opinions on this point may be regarded as yet another illustration of the strong impact which interests reaching far beyond the purely legal sphere are likely to have on the process of shaping the juridical rules governing international life.

67. Historic waters other than historic bays – Historic rights of delimitation

Following the emergence of the theory of historic bays, the doctrine of historic waters began to be applied also to other water areas which seemed to fulfil the requirements similar to those on which the claims to historic bays had been founded.

Generally speaking, it may be said that the various claims to historic waters are, in fact, claims to an *historic right of delimiting* territorial waters in a manner which constitutes a departure from the normal method of delimitation.[1]

[1] According to Johnson, "as regards the basic question of methods of delimiting territorial waters... three methods are theoretically possible...:
(a) The Norwegian method of using straight base lines connecting the headlands of bays and the outermost islands, islets and reefs, and of measuring the territorial sea from these base lines. ...This method may generally be described as the 'headland theory'....
(b) A method known as the *courbe tangente* or 'arcs of circles method'....
(c) A method, known as the *tracé parallèle*, which consists of drawing on the chart an exact replica of the coast-line so many miles out to sea from that coast-line." (See Johnson," The Anglo-Norwegian Fisheries Case," 1 *ICLQ* (1952), p. 145, at pp. 151-152; italics in original). Commenting on the applicability of the various methods of delimitation, Johnson remarks that "the so-called *tracé parallèle* method, although theoretically feasible along a very straight coast-line, becomes progressively impracticable along a very indented coast-line such as that of northern Norway.... The arcs of circles method of delimiting the territorial sea is really the inverse of the process used by a ship to discover whether she is inside or outside territorial waters.... Any person on the coast, wishing to draw the limit of territorial waters on a chart, draws arcs of four miles radius [assuming the breadth of the territorial sea to be

The 1930 Hague Codification Conference made an attempt to regulate the question of the manner of delimitation. The Conference, however, proved abortive and broke up without reaching agreement on any of the substantive points and the matter remained unsolved. The controversial nature of the subject was clearly brought out in the pleadings of the parties to the *Fisheries* case, where a great deal of the argument turned on the fact whether the method of delimitation by straight baselines, as applied by Norway, was valid in international law. The United Kingdom asserted that, from the replies that had been given by the various governments to the questionnaire submitted to them by the Preparatory Committee of the Hague Codification Conference, it emerged clearly that "the majority of... governments which replied to the question favoured the main principle that the tide mark on the coast is the base-line."[1] The United Kingdom thus challenged the validity in international law of the "Norwegian system" of straight baselines. It also contended that only Norway, Sweden, Poland and the Soviet Union had come out in favour of the "headland theory," and went on to submit that

> there does exist a general rule of international law requiring a State in principle to delimit its maritime belt by reference to the tide mark on its physical coast and ... any departures from this base-line have to be justified as falling under one of the specifically recognized exceptions. ... Norway is bound by this general rule except to the extent that she ... can establish an historic right entitling her to exceptional maritime territory.[2]

The United Kingdom at the same time denounced the method of "constituting an imaginary coast line by the joining of lines between the extreme points selected arbitrarily along the coast,"[3] as being contrary to international law.

Norway, on the other hand, maintained that "ni la méthode du tracé parallèle, ni celle de la courbe tangente ne peuvent... être considérées

four miles] from an infinite number of points along the coast. In technical language, the outer line of territorial waters is then formed by the outer 'envelope' of all these arcs." (*Ibid.*, pp. 152–153). For a general discussion of the problem of delimiting territorial waters, see Boggs, "Delimitation of Seaward Areas under National Jurisdiction," 45 *AJIL* (1951), p. 240 *et seq*; see also, by the same author, "Delimitation of the Territorial Sea," 24 *AJIL* (1930), p. 541 *et seq.*; see also Gidel, *op. cit.*, vol. III, pp. 503–516. For a critical analysis of the judgment in the *Fisheries* case as regards the various methods of delimitation, and the interpretation given to them by the parties to the dispute and by the Court, see Waldock, "The Anglo-Norwegian Fisheries Case," 28 *BYIL* (1951), p. 114, at pp. 133–136. For a more detailed explanation of the application of the arcs of circles method see also *ICJ*, *Fisheries* case, *Pleadings*, *Oral Arguments*, *Documents*, vol. II, pp. 752–753.

[1] *ICJ, Fisheries case, Pleadings, Oral Arguments, Documents*, vol. II, p. 446.

[2] *Ibid.*, p. 452.

[3] *Ibid.*

comme consacrées par une règle générale du droit international,"[1] and went on to say that the "headland theory" was the only practicable method where the coast was broken up by indentations and insular formations off the mainland.[2] While denying the existence of a rule of international law in favour of the *tracé parallèle* method, Norway claimed, that, even if such a rule existed, it would not be binding on her, because she "par une attitude constante et non équivoque a manifesté son refus de l'accepter."[3]

The Court found, by eight votes to four, that the "Norwegian system" of delimitation was not contrary to international law. In view of the peculiar geographical features of the Norwegian coast, the Court held that in the circumstances of the case

> the line of the low-water mark can no longer be put forward as a rule requiring the coast line to be followed in all its sinuosities; nor can one speak of exceptions when contemplating so rugged a coast in detail. Such a coast, viewed as a whole, calls for the application of a different method. Nor can one characterize as exceptions to the rule the very many derogations which would be necessitated by such a rugged coast. The rule would disappear under the exceptions.[4]

This passage of the Court's judgment has evoked criticism on the ground that it was not clear, to quote Johnson, "whether the Court intended to reject the coast-line rule as a rule of international law altogether [or merely rejected the coast-line rule as a binding rule on Norway]."[5] The same author expresses the view that the Court did, in fact, attempt to eliminate this rule entirely, but, in view of the considerable array of authorities in favour of this rule,[6] it preferred to undermine it by first equating it with the *tracé parallèle* method and then dismissing it as impracticable.[7]

The Court resorted instead to the "general direction of the coast" method, which consists, according to the Court, "of selecting appropriate points on the low-water mark and drawing straight lines between them."[8] This passage of the Court's judgment, as well as the principle underlying it, have since come under severe doctrinal criticism. The Court's statement, according to which the "general direction of the

[1] *Ibid.*, vol. I, p. 405.
[2] *Ibid.*, p. 406.
[3] *Ibid.*, p. 412.
[4] *ICJ Reports*, 1951, p. 129.
[5] Johnson, 1 *ICLQ* (1952), p. 155.
[6] For the main authorities on this point see Waldock, *loc. cit.*, p. 131.
[7] Johnson, *loc. cit.*, pp. 156–157.
[8] *ICJ Reports*, 1951, pp. 129–130. See, however, the Dissenting Opinions of Judges Read (*ibid.*, p. 187), and McNair (*ibid.*, p. 161), who both rallied to the coastline principle as to what they regarded as an established rule of international law.

coast" method, as interpreted by the Court, had been followed by several States and had "not encountered objections of principle by other States,"[1] has been met by Waldock who asserts that "*the Court appears to have made a minority practice the basis of a general rule of customary law.*"[2] Referring to the introduction by the Court of various economic-historic considerations as supplementary factors confirming and even legalizing the "general direction of the coast" method, the same writer points out that "the Court's criteria... are so flexible that they make the validity of many claims a matter of guesswork.... The general *direction* of the physical coast leaves much to mere opinion."[3]

The novelty of this judgment, from the point of view of the establishment of a maritime historic title, lies in the fact that the Court recognized an historic right to certain waters, deriving not from an historic claim to a given area of water – as is the case with historic claims over bays, for instance – but from an *historic right to delimit* territorial waters in a given manner. The Court found that

> the method of straight lines established in the Norwegian system ... had been consolidated by a constant and sufficiently long practice, in the face of which the attitude of governments bears witness to the fact that they did not consider it to be contrary to international law.[4]

It will be noted that in the establishment of the "Norwegian system" two factors were regarded as vital by the Court:

(a) a constant and sufficiently long practice; and

(b) the attitude of other governments.

These two requirements of manifestation of State authority, on the one hand, and acquiescence of the governments affected, on the other hand, are, in fact, the two concomitant factors which are indispensable in the establishment of any historic title. It thus emerges that the rules governing the acquisition of an historic right of maritime delimitation are subject to the same process as the building up of an "ordinary" historic title.

[1] *ICJ Reports*, 1951, p. 129.

[2] Waldock, *Loc. cit.*, p. 148. (Italics in original).

[3] *Ibid.*, p. 149. (Italics in original).

[4] *ICJ Reports*, 1951, p. 139. The application of the straight baselines method of delimitation affects the question of the acquisition of maritime historic rights in yet another way. A State can acquire not only an historic right of delimitation by straight baselines – as was held in the *Fisheries case* – but the adoption of this method of delimitation as a *novel* practice, in those cases in which article 4 of the *Territorial Sea Convention* has sanctioned such practice, may give rise to non-exclusive historic claims (such as rights of passage and fishing) on the part of other States. This aspect of the problem will be dealt with in more detail below, in sections 70, 71 and 73.

In justifying the application to the Norwegian coast of the straight baselines method, the Court referred, as has been mentioned above, to its peculiar geographical configuration as one of the reasons warranting the adoption of this course. The Court found that

since the mainland is bordered ... by the 'skjaergaard', which constitutes a whole with the mainland, it is the outer line of the 'skjaergaard' which must be taken into account in delimiting the belt of Norwegian territorial waters. This solution is dictated by geographic realities.[1]

The Court went on to say that the *tracé parallèle* method might be applied without difficulty to an ordinary, unbroken coast. "Where, [however]," the Court said, "a coast is deeply indented and cut into... or where it is bordered by an archipelago such as the 'skjaergaard' along the western sector of the coast here in question, the base-line becomes independent of the low-water mark, and can only be determined by means of geometric construction."[2]

Summing up its remarks on what may be termed the "geographical factor" in the acquisition of Norway's right to apply the "Norwegian system," the Court pronounced as follows:

the real question raised in the choice of base-lines is in effect whether certain sea areas lying within these lines are *sufficiently closely linked to the land domain* to be subject to the regime of internal waters.[3]

The Court also referred to the relevance of the economic factor to the acquisition of a maritime historic title and took into account the dependence of the Norwegian population in certain localities on the exploitation of the sea. Thus, the Court registered the fact that

in these barren regions the inhabitants of the coastal zone derive their livelihood essentially from fishing.[4]

It appears, however, that the economic factor was not regarded as a determining factor in the legal sense and was taken into account merely in conjunction with the geographical and other relevant aspects. It thus appears as an element of probative rather than of constitutive value.[5]

[1] *Ibid.*, p. 128.
[2] *Ibid.*, pp. 128–129.
[3] *Ibid.*, p. 133. (Italics added).
[4] *Ibid.*, p. 128. In another passage of the judgment the Court remarked: "There is one consideration not to be overlooked, the scope of which extends beyond purely geographical factors: that of certain economic interests peculiar to a region, the reality and importance of which are clearly evidenced by a long usage." (*Ibid.*, p. 133). See also *ibid.*, p. 142, where the Court refers to certain economic considerations relating to the Lopphavet.
[5] See to this effect Fitzmaurice, 31 *BYIL* (1954), pp. 400–402.

In his analysis of the *Fisheries* case, Sir Gerald Fitzmaurice reaches the conclusion that the Court had, in fact, laid down four criteria for determining the validity or otherwise of given straight baselines. They all are, according to Sir Gerald, "different expressions of [the] basic principle of the close dependence of the territorial sea on the land domain."[1] In the opinion of Sir Gerald, the baselines must

> (1) follow the general direction of the coast; (2) only enclose waters genuinely possessing the character of internal waters; (3) lie '*inter fauces terrarum*'; and (4) be moderate and reasonable, and drawn in a reasonable manner.[2]

On the whole, it would appear that the Court's judgment in the *Fisheries* case considerably reduced the scope of the theory of "historic waters" by its awarding recognition to the "general direction of the coast" rule and by sanctioning the straight baselines method whenever "more than mere curvatures" cut into the coast. This opinion is voiced, amongst others, by Johnson, when he asserts – rightly, it is believed – that

> by laying so much stress ... on the flexibility of the general rules of international law relating to delimitation, by rejecting the coast-line rule as a rule of law, and by including 'long usage' as a factor to be considered in assessing the validity, even under general international law, of straight base-lines drawn, not across bays only, but across sea areas, sufficiently closely linked to the land domain to be subject to the régime of internal waters,' the Court immeasurably reduced the scope of 'historic waters' as waters specially exempted, by virtue of an historic title, from the general rules of law.[3]

Seen now in retrospect, more than a decade after the pronouncement of the judgment in the *Fisheries* case, this prognosis seems indeed to have been borne out by subsequent trends in the law of the sea. The *Fisheries* case, no doubt, represented an attempt to incorporate, as it were, the doctrine of historic waters into *general* international law and to transform what was always considered as an exception to the rule into one aspect of the general norm.

The developments at the 1958 Geneva Conference on the Law of the Sea – and, in particular, the adoption of article 4 of the *Territorial Sea Convention*, dealing with situations in which the application of the

[1] *Ibid.*, p. 404.

[2] *Ibid.*, p. 404. (Italics in original). For a critical evaluation of each of these criteria, see *ibid.*, pp. 404–411.

[3] Johnson, 1 *ICLQ* (1952), pp. 163–164. The same view is expounded also by Fitzmaurice who claims that "the pronouncement of the Court... must considerably reduce the importance and scope of the historic bay principle." (31 *BYIL* (1954), p. 415). Waldock goes even further when he asserts that "there is now no room left for the distinction between historic and other bays." (28 *BYIL* (1951), p. 156).

straight baselines method of delimitation is permissible – do, in fact, amount to an indirect introduction of the theory of historic waters into the Convention. This is so despite the fact that the Conference professed to have excluded historic waters from the scope of its discussions and in one of its resolutions called on the General Assembly of the United Nations to arrange for a study of the juridical regime of historic waters, since the International Law Commission, and consequently the Conference itself, had not provided for the regime of historic waters.[1]

From the point of view of the subject-matter of this work it is also noteworthy that the Convention reaffirmed the general and well-established principle that "the normal baseline for measuring the breadth of the territorial sea is the low-water line along the coast,"[2] and that the application of the straight baselines method was relegated once more to a subordinate position, although its suitability was recognized for certain types of coastlines. The relevant provisions of article 4 of the Convention read as follows:

1. In localities where the coast line is deeply indented and cut into, or if there is a fringe of islands along the coast in its immediate vicinity, the method of straight baselines joining appropriate points may be employed in drawing the baseline from which the breadth of the territorial sea is measured.
2. The drawing of such baselines must not depart to any appreciable extent from the general direction of the coast, and the sea areas lying within the lines must be sufficiently closely linked to the land domain to be subject to the régime of internal waters.
3. ....
4. Where the method of straight baselines is applicable under the provisions of paragraph 1, account may be taken, in determining particular baselines, of economic interests peculiar to the region concerned, the reality and the importance of which are clearly evidenced by a long usage.[3]

Thus, the article seems to follow, on the whole, the principles laid down by the International Court of Justice in the *Fisheries* case. It accordingly requires that "the drawing of baselines must not depart to any appreciable extent from the general direction of the coast"[4] and that the sea areas lying within such baselines "must be sufficiently closely linked to the land domain to be subject to the régime of internal waters."[5]

A further indication of the impact of the Court's judgment on the

[1] *Cmnd.* 584 (1959), p. 50.
[2] Article 3 of the *Territorial Sea Convention, Cmnd.* 584 (1959), p. 20.
[3] Article 4 of the *Territorial Sea Convention, Cmnd.* 584 (1959), p. 20.
[4] Cf. *ICJ Reports,* 1951, p. 133.
[5] Cf. *ibid.*

drafting of this article is to be found in paragraph 4 stating that in cases in which the geographical configuration warrants the application of straight baselines, "account may be taken, in determining particular baselines, of economic interests peculiar to the region concerned, the reality and the importance of which are clearly evidenced by a long usage."[1]

It would appear that the adoption of article 4, and especially of paragraph 4 thereof, may be regarded as a triumph for those who, throughout the discussions preceding its adoption, wished to confine the scope of the principles laid down in the *Fisheries* case, by giving them the strictest possible interpretation.[2]

Commenting on the provisions contained in article 4, paragraph 4, of the *Territorial Sea Convention*, Sir Gerald Fitzmaurice pointed out that "they make it clear that economic interests are not *per se* a justification for the institution of straight baselines, thus correcting a very common misapprehension about the effect of the judgment in the *Norwegian* [*Fisheries*] case, namely that it indicated the existence of an economic interest as sufficing in itself to justify the use of straight baselines."[3]

Article 4 of the *Territorial Sea Convention* did at the same time secure, as Sir Gerald Fitzmaurice was quick to point out, a more favourable position for a State having an indented coast, inasmuch as such a State is not only allowed to apply the straight baselines method, but is also permitted to take into account, in drawing these baselines, its peculiar economic interests, a concession which is not normally made in favour of a State which, being less fortunate, has an "ordinary" coastline.[4]

Thus the pre-eminence of the geographical factor in the application of the straight baselines method has become evident and has been sanctioned by the overwhelming majority of the States which participated in the voting on this article.[5]

[1] Cf. *ibid.*

[2] See e.g. *ILC Yearbook*, 8th session, 1956, vol. I, p. 186, where Mr. Sandström and Sir Gerald Fitzmaurice expressed the wish that the wording of the article be brought into conformity with the findings of the International Court of Justice in the *Fisheries* case. Sir Gerald maintained there that "the Court's decision had not postulated economic interests as a ground *per se* for establishing a baseline system independently of the low water mark." See also further remarks to this effect made by Mr. Sandström (*ibid.*, p. 187), which met with the opposition of Mr. Krylov. (*Ibid.*, pp. 187–188).

[3] Fitzmaurice, "Some Results of the Geneva Conference on the Law of the Sea," 8 *ICLQ* (1959), p. 73, at p. 77. (Italics in original).

[4] See more generally on this point Fitzmaurice, 31 *BYIL* (1954), p. 420.

[5] In the First Committee of the Conference the article was carried by 44 votes to none, with 13 abstentions. (See *United Nations Conference on the Law of the Sea, Official Records*, vol. III, *First Committee*, p. 161). The article in question was adopted in plenary by 63 votes to 8, with 8 abstentions. (*Ibid.*, vol. II, p. 63).

It is worth mentioning that the requirement for the sea areas lying landwards of the straight baselines being "sufficiently closely linked to the land domain to be subject to the régime of internal waters" in fact amounts to a reference, though obliquely and in a paraphrased manner, to the test of effectiveness, which, as has been amply shown above, is a prerequisite for raising a presumption of acquiescence. As will be recalled from the previous sections – dealing specifically with historic bays – the relationship existing between the coastal State and the bay in question is of vital importance in the acquisition of an historic title to the bay: the stronger the relationship, as manifested in the exercise of State authority by the coastal State over the bay, the stronger the assumption that the international community, which refrained from raising any express objections to these State activities, did, in actual fact, acquiesce in the coastal State's pretensions to exclusive authority over the bay. The same considerations hold good with regard to other maritime areas too. It thus becomes apparent that the theory of historic waters is normally applicable merely to those areas of water which, owing to the geographical configuration of the adjacent land territories, may be considered as possessing a sufficiently close relationship with the land domain. Only then can they be subject to the regime of internal waters (i.e. exclusive State authority), the exercise of which is indispensable if an inference of international acquiescence is to be drawn.

Article 4, paragraph 1, of the *Territorial Sea Convention* expressly mentions two different situations which warrant the adoption of the straight baselines method, namely,

(a) localities where the coastline is deeply indented and cut into; and

(b) a fringe of islands along the coast in its immediate vicinity.

The first alternative possibility represents the normal case for the application of the straight baselines method. The reference to "localities" was inserted following a United Kingdom draft amendment, the intention of which was "to exclude the application of the straight baseline method in cases of isolated curvatures of a coast."[1]

The second alternative possibility mentioned in the article also has its root in the judgment of the International Court of Justice in the *Fisheries* case. Confronted with a coast which is almost entirely covered by a continuous island fringe, as is the case with Norway's *skjaergaard*,[2] the Court remarked that

[1] *Ibid.*, vol. III, p. 157 (by Sir Gerald Fitzmaurice).

[2] The western coast of Scotland, as well as parts of Canada's coast, display a similar geo-

the coast of the mainland does not constitute, as it does in practically all other countries, a clear dividing line between land and sea. What matters, what really constitutes the Norwegian coast line, is the outer line of the 'skjaergaard.'[1]

From this finding it followed that

the 'skjaergaard' ... constitutes a whole with the mainland, [and] it is the outer line of the 'skjaergaard' which must be taken into account in delimiting the belt of Norwegian territorial waters. This solution is dictated by geographic realities.[2]

Thus, by regarding the outer line of the island fringe as the starting-point for the delimitation of Norway's territorial sea, the Court did, in fact, convert all waters lying between the *skjaergaard* and the mainland into internal waters.

68. Historic waters other than historic bays – Water areas lying within and around island formations

Another, and more usual, possibility of island formations off the coast of the littoral State is that of "coastal archipelagoes," which was also canvassed at some length by the parties to the *Fisheries* case.[3] The Court itself remarked in its judgment that "the attempts that have been made to subject groups of islands or coastal archipelagoes to conditions analogous to the limitations concerning bays ... [requiring that the distance between such islands should not exceed twice the breadth of the territorial sea] have not got beyond the stage of proposals."[4] Thus, the Court declined to accept the United Kingdom submission, according to which the length of the baselines which may be drawn at the outer line of the *skjaergaard* should not exceed ten miles (a distance which at that time was believed to be the maximum permissible closing line for ordinary territorial bays). The Court associated itself on this point with the Norwegian contention, according to which there did not exist any upper limit as regards the length of such baselines.[5]

The *Territorial Sea Convention* follows the majority judgment in the

graphical configuration. See in this connection Judge Read's remarks in *ICJ Reports*, 1951, p. 193, and the observations made by Judge McNair, *ibid.*, pp. 169–170, where he also analyzes the linguistic similarity of the Norwegian term *skjaergaard* and the expression "skerry' which occurs in Scotland.

[1] *Ibid.*, p. 127.

[2] *Ibid.*, p. 128.

[3] See e.g. *ICJ, Fisheries case, Pleadings, Oral Arguments, Documents*, vol. II, pp. 517–553, where the United Kingdom introduced a distinction between coastal and mid-ocean archipelagoes; see also *ibid.*, vol. III, pp. 366–394, containing the Norwegian concept on this point.

[4] *ICJ Reports*, 1951, p. 131.

[5] The Court's decision on this point was vigorously challenged by the dissenting judges. Judge McNair's observations are to be found *ibid.*, pp. 163–164, and Judge Read's remarks at p. 194.

Fisheries case in allowing the drawing of baselines in such cases along the outer limit of the island fringe. No limit is fixed for the permissible length of baselines, nor does the Convention specify what distance is regarded as being within the "immediate vicinity" of the coast. The vagueness of these provisions and the looseness of the terminology employed are surely disturbing, because this lack of precision is likely to raise doubts and uncertainties as to what baselines do or do not "depart to an appreciable extent from the general direction of the coast."

It is felt that, in examining the juridical regime of historic waters, one of the main tasks of the International Law Commission might lie in this sphere rather than in the definition of historic bays and the determination of their juridical status. Should the International Law Commission's attempts on this point prove futile, and should no objective test for the length of baselines in such cases be forthcoming, then one can only envisage a series of controversies between States, which will have to be settled in accordance with the provisions laid down in Chapter VI of the Charter of the United Nations, dealing with the pacific settlement of disputes.[1]

The judgment of the International Court of Justice in the *Fisheries* case appears to have drawn a line of cleavage between "coastal archipelagoes," on the one hand, and "mid-ocean archipelagoes," on the other hand. Similarly, article 4 of the *Territorial Sea Convention* covers only the case of coastal island groups; the questions relating to the admissibility of drawing baselines between various mid-ocean islands allegedly composing one geographical unit, as well as the questions regarding the admissible length of such baselines and the juridical status of the waters enclosed by them, were left open by the Conference.

J. P. A. François, Special Rapporteur of the International Law Commission on the Law of the Sea, in his first report on the regime of the territorial sea, inserted a special article (draft article 10) dealing with problems relating to groups of islands, without distinguishing between island formations lying off the mainland or in the mid-ocean.[2] In subsequent drafts, submitted to the International Law Commission, various distances ranging between five and twenty-five miles were put forward as the maximum permissible distances for the drawing of straight baselines.[3] At later sessions of the Commission several members

[1] See Articles 33–38 of the Charter of the United Nations.

[2] *ILC Yearbook*, 4th session, 1952, vol. II, pp. 36–37.

[3] See on this point Sørensen, "The Territorial Sea of Archipelagos," in *Varia Juris Gentium – Liber Amicorum J. P. A. François*, Special Issue of *NTIR* of July, 1959, published on the occasion of François' 70th birthday, pp. 315–331, at p. 319.

proposed the omission of any maximum length at all, while others insisted on a numerical limitation. It was finally decided not to include any provision with regard to "mid-ocean" archipelagoes, and in its commentary on draft article 10 (islands), the Commission remarked that, concerning the problem of island formations,

> the Commission was unable to overcome the difficulties involved. The problem is singularly complicated by the different forms it takes in different archipelagos. ... It recognizes the importance of this question and hopes that if an international conference subsequently studies the proposed rules it will give attention to it.[1]

In a Memorandum prepared for the 1958 International Conference on the Law of the Sea,[2] Evensen gave a survey of State practice and past codificatory attempts on this question and recommended that the drawing of straight baselines be permitted, provided "[they do] not depart to any appreciable extent from the general direction of the coast of the archipelago viewed as a whole."[3] He also suggested that waters situated inside such baselines be considered as internal waters if they are so closely linked to the surrounding land domain as to be treated in much the same manner as the surrounding land. Those passages of water, however, which form "legal straits" (namely, straits connecting two parts of the open sea), should, notwithstanding their status as internal waters, remain open for the innocent passage of foreign ships.[4]

During the general debate held in the Second Committee of the Conference, the delegate of the Philippines, speaking on behalf of a country which consists of a group of islands, claimed that compact outlying archipelagoes should be treated as a whole and that the waters lying between and within the islands should be regarded as internal waters. He invoked on this point the theory of historic waters, which applied, according to him, to archipelagoes in much the same manner as to historic bays.[5] In support of his claim he relied on his country's legislation which stipulates that all the waters lying in, between and around the different islands formed an integral part of the Philippines' maritime domain, subject to its exclusive sovereignty, irrespective of their size.[6] He further maintained that there was no reason to deprive

[1] *ILC Yearbook*, 8th session, 1956, vol. II, p. 270.
[2] U.N. Document A/CONF. 13/18, *United Nations Conference on the Law of the Sea, Official Records*, vol. I, *Preparatory Documents*, pp. 289–302.
[3] *Ibid.*, p. 302.
[4] *Ibid.*
[5] *United Nations Conference on the Law of the Sea. Official Records*, vol. IV, *Second Committee*, p. 7.
[6] *Ibid.*

States consisting mainly or solely of archipelagoes of rights which were conceded to States with heavily indented coastlines.[1]

A similar attitude was taken up by the delegate of Indonesia representing – according to his own statement – a country consisting of 13,000 islands scattered over a vast area.[2] He asserted that his country's territorial sea should be measured from baselines drawn between the outermost points of the outermost islands.[3]

The fears of the leading maritime Powers, who were anxious to forestall any further encroachments on the principle of the freedom of the high seas were voiced in the statement made by Mr. Dean, the representative of the United States, in which he maintained that, if the straight baselines method were to apply to archipelagoes, then "areas of the high seas formerly used by ships of all countries would be unilaterally claimed as territorial waters or possibly even internal waters."[4] Such a course would, it was alleged, also contribute towards violating "historic rights" of innocent passage.[5]

At the Second United Nations Conference on the Law of the Sea, the representative of Australia, Sir Kenneth Bailey, observed that the extension of the maritime belt would impair also the freedom of flight over the high seas. "The right to fly over the high seas," he said, "was absolute, but there was no right of innocent passage for aircraft over the territorial sea except by permission of the State concerned."[6] Likewise, the representative of Israel, Mr. Rafael, pointed out that "any extension of the territorial sea would seriously harm air communications and might even endanger the safety of air travel."[7]

The Conference failed in its attempts to lay down any rules concerning the territorial sea of archipelagoes, just as the 1930 Hague Codification Conference had failed on this point some 28 years before.[8] In view of the fact that the doctrine of historic waters was invoked in the course of the Conference's proceedings as underlying the rights of the State possessing an archipelago to treat the waters enclosed by straight baselines as historic waters, and having regard to the Conference's wish not to look into the problem of historic waters, it would not be altogether

[1] *Ibid.*
[2] *Ibid.*, vol. III, pp. 43–44.
[3] *Ibid.*, p. 44.
[4] *Ibid.*, p. 25.
[5] *Ibid.*
[6] *Second United Nations Conference on the Law of the Sea, Official Records*, p. 82.
[7] *Ibid.*, p. 100.
[8] For a survey of the proceedings of the 1930 Hague Codification Conference on this question, as well as of the various drafts prepared by learned bodies and societies, see Waldock, 28 *BYIL* (1951), pp. 143–145.

surprising if the International Law Commission, which was requested by the United Nations General Assembly to arrange for a study of historic waters,[1] should give careful attention to the problems attendant on the juridical status of archipelagoes, while dealing with the problem of historic waters in general.[2]

The questions relating to the treatment of island formations and coastal archipelagoes also raised a further question, namely, that of the juridical status of the straits formed by such formations. The normal rules applicable to straits provide, as has already been mentioned before, that straits, the width of which does not exceed twice the breadth of the territorial sea, should be regarded as territorial straits.[3] A further rule provides, to quote Oppenheim, that "foreign merchantmen cannot be excluded from passage through territorial straits."[4] This rule, however, applies only "when they connect two parts of the open sea."[5] Where, however, a strait or channel connects the open sea with a territorial gulf or bay, foreign vessels can be excluded.[6] This provision, in fact, transforms such a strait into the littoral State's internal waters.

This problem too arose in the *Fisheries* case with regard to the Indreleia, a navigational route inside the Norwegian island fringe, which, according to the United Kingdom contention, connected two parts of the open sea, and through which there consequently existed a right of passage. The United Kingdom claimed that the Indreleia formed a continuous passage from the North Sea to the Arctic Sea and, since it was a waterway connecting two parts of the open sea ("legal strait"), a right of passage existed through it as in territorial waters.[7] Thus, the United Kingdom envisaged the possibility of territorial waters lying within a belt of internal waters,[8] a concept that did not commend itself to the majority of the Court, which declined to associate itself with this view. The Court held that

[1] *Resolution 1453 (XIV)*, adopted at the 847th plenary meeting, December 7th, 1959.

[2] For a detailed discussion of the various legal aspects surrounding the waters in and around archipelagoes, see Evensen, *loc. cit.*, and Sørensen, *loc. cit.*

[3] Oppenheim, *op. cit.*, vol. I, p. 510. The author refers there to straits "which are not more than six miles wide," on the obvious assumption that the breadth of the territorial sea is three miles. In view of the fluidity of present-day international law on this point, it was deemed appropriate not to indicate any precise numerical limit.

[4] *Ibid.*, p. 512.

[5] *Ibid.*

[6] *Ibid.* See also to this effect the judgment rendered in the *Corfu Channel* case, where the International Court of Justice held that, in the case of a channel belonging to the class of international waterways, "passage cannot be prohibited ... in time of peace." (*ICJ Reports*, 1949, p. 29).

[7] *ICJ, Fisheries case, Pleadings, Oral Arguments, Documents*, vol. II, p. 572.

[8] *Ibid.*, p. 556.

the Indreleia is not a strait at all, but rather a navigational route prepared as such by means of artifical aids to navigation provided by Norway.[1]

The Court therefore found that the juridical status of the Indreleia did not differ in any respect from that of the other waters included in the *skjaergaard*.[2]

The Court might have arrived, in all probability, at a different conclusion had it found that the Indreleia *was* a real strait, and it is thus difficult to see why some writers have taken the view that the Court's decision on this point is a potential clash with – or at any rate the nullification of – the decision given in the *Corfu Channel* case, which recognized the right of passage through "legal straits."[3]

69. *Historic waters other than historic bays – Historic rights to a greater breadth of the territorial sea*

Finally, yet another kind of "historic waters" ought to be mentioned, notably, the acquisition, on historic grounds, of a title to a wider marginal belt of territorial waters, irrespective of the method of delimitation to be applied for the measurement of this belt. In the *Fisheries* case, the United Kingdom, herself a staunch supporter of the three-mile limit, conceded that Norway had acquired, on historic grounds, a title to a four-mile limit, because the Norwegian claim could be traced back to the eighteenth century (i.e. to a period before the formulation of the three-mile limit rule), had persistently been asserted by Norway, had never been abandoned since, and had met with a more or less general acquiescence.[4] Thus, the problem of the precise breadth of Norway's territorial sea was not in issue before the Court and the majority judgment did not fail to recognize this fact when it stated that

the Parties being in agreement on the figure of four miles for the breadth of the territorial sea [of Norway], the problem which arises is from what base-line this breadth is to be reckoned.[5]

Owing to the United Kingdom's admission of a four-mile limit for the Norwegian territorial sea, the Court did not have to pronounce on this point. Although such admission *inter partes* does not, of course, bind

[1] *ICJ Reports*, 1951, p. 132.
[2] *Ibid.*
[3] See e.g. Waldock, 28 *BYIL* (1951), p. 158, n. 3; see also Fitzmaurice, 31 *BYIL* (1954), p. 419.
[4] *ICJ, Fisheries case, Pleadings, Oral Arguments, Documents*, vol. II, pp. 421–423.
[5] *ICJ Reports*, 1951, p. 128.

any third State, there is indeed little likelihood that any State will in the future challenge the Scandinavian concept of the four-mile territorial sea; this is particularly so in view of the fact that in the meantime a considerable number of States have raised claims to a territorial sea of six and even twelve miles, claims which have made the formerly excessive Scandinavian pretensions look modest indeed.[1]

The fact should be registered, however, that historic claims to wider marginal belts are, in all probability, the only claims of maritime historic titles, where the requirement for a close geographical link with the adjacent land domain may be dispensed with. The juridical basis, though, for the validity of such claims is the same as in all other cases in which maritime historic claims are advanced: acquiescence in such claims on the part of the international community.

70. The juridical status of historic waters – Historic waters are internal waters

Water areas which form the maritime domain of the coastal State fall into two categories:

(1) internal waters; and

(2) the territorial sea.

Waters belonging to the first category consist, according to Oppenheim, of "lakes, ... canals, ... rivers together with their mouths, ... ports and harbours, and... some of... [the] gulfs and bays."[2]

The territorial sea consists, to quote again the same author, of "the waters contained in a certain zone or belt, called the maritime or marginal belt, which surrounds a State and thus includes a part of the waters in some of its bays, gulfs and straits."[3]

The distinction between these two categories is important for several reasons, among which the main ones are the following:

(a) Internal waters are assimilated in law to the land territory of the State and the rights which the littoral State enjoys over this portion of water are equivalent to those which it enjoys over its land territories;

(b) Consequently, the right of passage for foreign ships – which is generally admitted to exist in respect of territorial waters – does not

[1] For the various national claims as regards the breadth of the territorial sea, see the *Synoptical Table concerning the Breadth and Juridical Status of the Territorial Sea and Adjacent Zones*, prepared by the United Nations Secretariat for the Second Geneva Conference on the Law of the Sea, U.N. Document A/CONF. 19/4 of February 8th, 1960 (mimeographed).

[2] Oppenheim, *op. cit.*, p. 460. Other expressions employed to denote internal waters are "*national waters*" or "*inland waters.*" Article 1 of the *Territorial Sea Convention* refers to "*internal waters*" (*Cmnd.* 584 (1959), p. 20), and this term is accordingly used in this study.

[3] Oppenheim, *op. cit.*, p. 461.

apply to internal waters, and the littoral State is entitled to exclude such vessels from its internal waters;

(c) In cases where certain portions of water, such as bays, are recognized as being internal waters, the measurement of the territorial sea – by means of baselines – will start at the point where the internal waters end.[1]

Thus, it can readily be seen that the fixing of the juridical status of historic waters – i.e. the determination of their status as either internal waters or territorial waters – has far-reaching legal implications and is not merely a matter for academic discussion, for on the answer given to this question turn the rights of the claimant States in their allegedly "historic" waters.[2]

It must be stressed from the outset that this answer, in turn, depends almost exclusively on the definition given to the term "historic waters." Given a narrow interpretation, historic waters *stricto sensu* are only those waters, over which the littoral State claims *full sovereignty*, with all the rights pertaining to such a claim, and not merely a claim for *certain* rights, which do not entail a claim to the exclusive possession by the claimant State. It is in this sense that Gidel, for instance, conceives the notion of historic waters, when he observes:

> Les 'eaux historiques' ne sont donc pas, on ne saurait y insister trop fortement, des eaux où l'Etat adjacent revendique *certains* droits, certaines compétences distraites du faisceau de celles dont l'ensemble constitue ce qu'on appelle 'la souveraineté'.... Il faut se tenir très fermement à ce point capital de la matière des 'eaux historiques' que les 'eaux historiques' sont des eaux intérieures.[3]

Gidel admits at the same time that normally the State putting forward an historic claim will not intend to enforce over the area in question *all* the rights which flow from the status of sovereignty, and will content itself with the utilization of certain rights, such as the right of excluding foreign fishermen. The enforcement of such rights by the littoral State does not presuppose, according to Gidel, any historic claim, for it is perfectly legitimate for States to prohibit fishing by foreigners not only in their internal waters, but also in their territorial seas. Therefore,

[1] This rule has been laid down expressly in article 5, paragraph 1, of the *Territorial Sea Convention*, which provides that "waters on the landward side of the baseline of the territorial sea form part of the internal waters of the State." (*Cmnd.* 584 (1959), p. 21).

[2] The discussion in this chapter on the juridical status of historic waters does not touch upon the question of the juridical status of the territorial sea, the width of which exceeds, on historic grounds, the normal breadth of territorial waters. (See above, section 69). This category of "historic waters" does not present any problems as to the juridical status of the waters in question. They form part of the *territorial* sea of the littoral State, with all the rights and duties flowing therefrom to the riparian State.

[3] Gidel, *op. cit.*, vol. III, p. 625–626. (Italics in original).

Gidel goes on to say, a State wishing to extend the marginal belt of *exclusive* fishing rights will be tempted either to extend the width of its territorial sea or to draw new baselines further out to sea, thereby automatically advancing the limit of its territorial sea. In the opinion of Gidel, States will normally resort to the second method, because the extension of internal waters can be done administratively, whereas the legislative measures required for the extension of the territorial sea are frequently the subject of a lengthy and not always friendly exchange of Notes between the coastal State and other States, the latter protesting against such an extension of the territorial sea at the expense of the high seas.[1]

In another passage Gidel explains the inherent contradiction between, and incompatibility of, the concept of historic waters – being, as they are, internal waters – and the right of innocent passage through historic waters. He says:

La baie une fois tenue pour 'historique,' la totalité de ses eaux deviennent des eaux intérieures avec toutes les conséquences que comporte le statut des eaux intérieures. L'Etat riverain n'est plus tenu notamment d'y admettre le 'passage inoffensif' des navires étrangers.[2]

Admittedly, State authorities dealing with this problem in the past were not always precise enough in the terminology employed by them and would thus often confuse territorial waters with internal waters. This confusion is clearly evidenced by the authorities quoted in the *Memorandum on Historic Bays* prepared by the United Nations Secretariat for the First Geneva Conference on the Law of the Sea,[3] where it is attributed to "the looseness of the terminology employed rather than to differences of opinion on the actual principle."[4]

[1] *Ibid.*, p. 625, n. 1.

[2] *Ibid.*, p. 625. The same view is expressed by Cavaré who holds that the juridical status of historic waters "se confond avec celui des eaux intérieures. En conséquence, le droit de passage inoffensif n'existe pas." (Cavaré, *op. cit.*, vol. II, p. 684). According to Colombos, "the rights of jurisdiction of the littoral State over its territorial gulfs and bays are identical to those it enjoys over its national waters." (Colombos, *op. cit.*, p. 174). Rousseau expresses the same view when he says: "une dernière catégorie de baies traditionnellement qualifiées de baies historiques... sont *des baies considérées comme nationales* par suite d'un usage continu et incontesté, plus que séculaire. ...Ces baies sont considérées comme étant placées sous la souveraineté de l'Etat riverain. Au point de vue du *statut juridique, ce sont des eaux intérieures*." (Rousseau, *Droit international public approfondi*, 1961, p. 244; italics added).

The Soviet international lawyer Kozhevnikov is of the same opinion and he too asserts that "so-called historical bays... are considered to be the internal territory of a State." (See *International Law*, a textbook for use in law schools, Academy of Sciences of the U.S.S.R., Institute of State and Law, translated from the Russian by Dennis Ogden, Foreign Languages Publishing House, Chapter VI, by F. I. Kozhevnikov, p. 205).

[3] See *United Nations Conference on the Law of the Sea, Official Records*, vol. I, *Preparatory Documents*, U.N. Document A/CONF. 13/1, pp. 21–27.

[4] *Ibid.*, p. 27.

The various draft codes, prepared either by learned societies or under the auspices of international organizations, draw a sharp distinction between the legal regime of historic waters and the territorial sea. True, these various drafts do not refer to historic waters in general, but confine themselves solely to "historic bays"; however, this is accounted for, according to Gidel, by the fact that it was never envisaged that the theory of historic waters might apply except in areas which, by reason of their configuration, are not normally used as major international routes of transit.[1] Thus, it may safely be assumed that the considerations underlying the juridical regime of historic bays do apply to the same extent to historic waters in general. From the fact that the datum line for the measurement of the territorial sea in territorial bays – and historic bays belong to this category – is a fictitious and imaginary baseline drawn at a certain distance from the coast, it necessarily follows that the waters landwards of this baseline are to be regarded as internal waters.

Article 4 of the Draft Convention prepared by Schücking for the 1930 Hague Codification Conference – as amended following the discussions held in the Committee of Experts appointed by the Assembly of the League of Nations in 1924 – expressly provides that the waters of bays, as defined in that article (i.e. bays bordered by a single State, where the distance between the two shores does not exceed ten marine miles, "unless a greater distance has been established by continuous and immemorial usage"[2]) are to be assimilated to internal waters.[3] Likewise, article 7, paragraph 4, of the *Territorial Sea Convention* stipulates that the waters enclosed by a baseline drawn across the entrance of a bay, the width of which does not exceed twenty-four miles, "shall be considered as internal waters."[4] Although paragraph 6 of the same article expressly excludes historic bays from the scope of the provisions of this article,[5] it is clearly understood that the intention of this stipulation was to recognize some departure from the restrictive rules envisaged for ordinary bays, the entrance of which – if claimed as territorial bays – could not exceed a certain width. This question does not arise in respect of historic bays.

It may therefore be confidently assumed that this provision is not meant to indicate any distinction between the legal regime of the waters

[1] Gidel, *op. cit.*, p. 626.
[2] *Ser. L.o.N.P.*, 1927, V. 1, p. 72.
[3] *Ibid.*
[4] *Cmnd.* 584 (1959), p. 21.
[5] *Ibid.*

of ordinary bays, recognized as territorial bays, and the regime accorded to historic bays. Both categories of bays are to be regarded as internal waters.

In this connection articles 4 and 5 of the Convention also appear to have some bearing on the subject-matter of the present section, although the term "historic waters" does not occur in them at all. Article 4 deals with those cases in which the coastal State is entitled to draw – for reasons specified in the article – straight baselines,[1] following the general rule laid down in article 3, which stipulates that "the normal baseline for measuring the breadth of the territorial sea is the low-water line along the coast."[2]

Article 4 refers, as will be recalled, to those instances in which the baseline may be drawn in a different manner, and expressly recognizes the possibility for a State to acquire a belt of territorial waters wider than that which would have normally accrued to it in accordance with the general rule enunciated in article 3. Paragraph 1 refers to a somewhat unusual geographical configuration of the coastline (such as deep indentations into the coast or coastal archipelagoes), which warrant a departure from the general rule. Lest the "geographical factor" be abused by the unjustified exploitation of an allegedly unusual configuration, paragraph 2 contains what in actual fact amounts to a proviso to paragraph 1, stipulating that "the drawing of... baselines must not depart to any appreciable extent from the general direction of the coast."[3] It is also noteworthy that the paragraph requires for the drawing of straight baselines that "the sea areas lying within the lines... be sufficiently closely linked to the land domain to be subject to the régime of *internal waters*."[4] These words are significant for two reasons:

(a) they expressly lay down the rule – similar to that which appears in article 7, paragraph 4, as regards bays – that all areas on the landward side of the baselines are to be treated as internal waters; and

(b) they make it clear at the same time that no drawing of straight baselines will be justified unless the sea areas lying within the lines can be regarded as sufficiently closely linked to the land domain to be subject to the regime of internal waters.

This latter requirement is, as is well known, the main condition for the recognition of a claim to an historic title. There can be no recognition of such a claim if the coastal State cannot prove "a sufficiently close link

[1] *Ibid.*, p. 20.
[2] *Ibid.*
[3] *Ibid.*
[4] *Ibid.* (Italics added).

to the land domain" and the various elements which are indicative of such a link are the means by which the existence of such a title is proved. Article 4, paragraph 4, which permits the taking into account, in all the cases in which the straight baselines method is applicable, of economic interests peculiar to the region concerned, the reality and importance of which are clearly evidenced by "long usage," is a clear expression of the idea that the economic factor in isolation has been rejected as a constitutive element of an historic title, and that it is only through its interplay with various other elements that it may be considered. (The precise role of the economic factor in the establishment of an historic title was discussed at some length above[1]).

Most illuminating, perhaps, from the point of view of the juridical status of historic waters, is the provision contained in article 5, paragraph 2, which reads as follows:

> Where the establishment of a straight baseline in accordance with article 4 has the effect of enclosing as internal waters areas which previously had been considered as part of the territorial sea or of the high seas, a right of innocent passage ... shall exist in those waters.[2]

The wording of this paragraph is self-explanatory and does not require elucidation. It appears at the same time pertinent to recall briefly the historical evolution of this provision. The problem of the right of passage through waters which were hitherto regarded as part of the high seas or the territorial sea, and which became internal waters as a result of the application of the straight baselines method, was first raised by the United Kingdom Government in its comments on the provisional articles concerning the regime of the territorial sea, as adopted by the International Law Commission at its 6th session.[3] At the 7th session of the Commission, Mr. François, Special Rapporteur, rejected the United Kingdom proposal for preserving the right of innocent passage through such water areas.[4] One of the reasons given by François for his viewing unfavourably the United Kingdom proposal was his belief that it might give rise to a complex situation in which there would be, in fact, three types of water within the littoral State's marginal belt, namely,

(a) internal waters properly so called;
(b) internal waters subject to the right of passage; and
(c) the territorial sea.

[1] See above, section 52.
[2] *Cmnd.* 584 (1959), p. 21.
[3] *ILC Yearbook*, 7th session, 1955, vol. II, p. 58.
[4] *ILC Yearbook*, 7th session, 1955, vol. I, pp. 196–197.

It would be extremely difficult, Professor François argued, to draw a proper demarcation line between the first and second of these two categories of water, particularly in the case of a deeply indented coastline.[1]

The matter was again raised at the 8th session of the Commission by Sir Gerald Fitzmaurice,[2] and after lengthy discussions which ensued, Sir Gerald's proposal was carried by 9 votes to 1, with 2 abstentions.[3]

In the course of the general debate held in the First Committee of the First Geneva Conference on the Law of the Sea, the United Kingdom Attorney-General of the day, Sir Reginald Manningham-Buller (now Lord Dilhorne), came out in support of the insertion into the Convention of a provision safeguarding the right of innocent passage through water areas which became internal waters through the application of the straight baselines method. He rightly pointed out that one of the effects of drawing straight baselines was "to enclose what might be large stretches and to convert them into internal or national waters; the areas in question would previously have been territorial waters through which a right of innocent passage existed, or even part of the high seas. It seemed very doubtful whether a coastal State could deprive other countries of *established rights* by action of that kind."[4]

The italicized words of Sir Reginald's statement are interesting in that they seem to convey the idea of "historic rights in reverse" to which further reference will be made below.[5] Suffice it to say here that Sir Reginald's remarks aimed at safeguarding historic rights acquired by States *against* the littoral State.

The United Kingdom proposal met with some opposition[6] and the paragraph in question, as revised by the United Kingdom, was finally adopted by the Committee by 44 votes to 15, with 8 abstentions.[7] At the 19th plenary meeting of the Conference the paragraph was carried by 55 votes to 16, with 6 abstentions.[8] It thus created a new kind of

[1] *Ibid.*

[2] *ILC Yearbook*, 8th session, 1956, vol. I, pp. 8–9; for the discussion see *ibid.*, pp. 9–11.

[3] *Ibid.*, pp. 187–190. See also the Special Rapporteur's comments on this problem, *ibid.*, vol. II, pp. 8–9, and the Commission's report on its 8th session to the General Assembly, containing draft article 5 with commentary, *ibid.*, pp. 267–268. The Commission recommended the preservation of the right of innocent passage only through internal waters "where the waters have normally been used for international traffic." (*Ibid.*)

[4] *United Nations Conference on the Law of the Sea, Official Records*, vol. III, *First Committee*, p. 9. (Italics added).

[5] See below, section 73.

[6] See e.g. the statement made by the Yugoslav delegate, Mr. Katicic, *United Nations Conference on the Law of the Sea, Official Records*, vol. III, *First Committee*, p. 158.

[7] *Ibid.*, p. 160.

[8] *Ibid.*, vol. II, p. 63. For a more detailed discussion of the question o f the right of innocen

internal waters, which are subject to the right of innocent passage of foreign vessels, thus assimilating such internal waters in this respect to the territorial sea.

71. The juridical status of historic waters – The distinction between internal inland waters and internal non-inland waters

The idea of distinguishing between two categories of internal waters had already been canvassed at the 1954 session of the Institute of International Law held at Aix-en-Provence. In a report submitted to the Tenth Commission of the Institute on "the distinction between the territorial sea and internal waters," the Rapporteur, Mr. Castberg, observed that

un Etat peut être autorisé, en se fondant sur des raisons historiques, économiques ou sociales, à fixer de longues lignes de base entre les îles et les rochers lorsqu'il s'agit de calculer la limite extrême de la mer territoriale, et surtout lorsqu'il est question de la limite territoriale du droit acquis exclusif de la population aux pêches côtières. *Il n'est toutefois pas certain que l'Etat juge opportun de considérer toutes les eaux en deçà des lignes de base comme des eaux intérieures au sens du droit international.* Il peut estimer équitable ou utile d'étendre le droit de passage des navires d'autres Etats, en temps de paix aussi, à une partie des eaux qui se trouve en deçà des lignes de base.[1]

In his conclusions Castberg submitted that

les limites des eaux intérieures de l'Etat riverain peuvent être tracées de manière différente dans des buts différents, par des dispositions législatives édictées pour cet Etat, à condition toutefois qu'il ne soit pas porté atteinte par cette mesure aux droits des autres Etats, surtout à leur droit de libre passage inoffensif dans la mer territoriale.[2]

In lending his support to this concept of Castberg, which recognizes different kinds of internal waters for different purposes, Sir Gerald Fitzmaurice, in a letter written to the Rapporteur, states:

I share this basic idea with you, but I would express it rather differently. I would prefer to say that all waters inside the base line from which territorial waters are measured, are internal waters; but that a further distinction is to be drawn between

passage through internal waters in general, as well as for a survey of the developments that led to the adoption of article 5 of the *Territorial Sea Convention*, see McDougal and Burke, *op. cit.*, pp. 117–126.

[1] 45 *Annuaire de l'Institut de Droit International*, Aix-en-Provence session, April-May, 1954, vol. I, pp. 126–127. (Italics added). In a footnote Castberg invokes the support of Raestad who, in an article published in 1931, discussing the problem of internal waters, as it had posed itself at the 1930 Hague Codification Conference, declared that "il est naturel que les Etats étrangers intéressés s'opposent à ce que toutes les portions d'eaux qui se trouvent à l'intérieur des lignes de base soient déclarées être des eaux intérieures dans toute l'acception de ce terme." (Raestad, 7 *RDI* (1931), p. 134).

[2] 45 *Annuaire de l'Institut de Droit International*, Aix-en-Provence session, April-May, 1954, vol. I, p. 172. (Italics added).

those internal waters which are genuinely *inland* waters (e.g. rivers, creeks, inland lakes, canals, etc.), and those which are not (e.g. large bays and waters between the mainland and islands off the coast). Generally speaking, there is no right of passage through the former waters, but there is, or should be, through the latter. (If this idea were adopted, the expressions 'internal waters' and 'inland waters,' instead of meaning the same thing, as they do at present, would each have a distinct meaning). Under no circumstances should the extension of internal waters made possible by the new base line method, operate so as to impede the right of innocent passage through what would be territorial sea if the older coast-line (or tide-mark) rule were still applied.[1]

Thus, Fitzmaurice suggested not only the adoption of a new terminology, which would distinguish between *internal inland waters* and *internal non-inland waters*, but also suggested that internal non-inland waters be in all cases assimilated to the territorial sea as far as the right of innocent passage of foreign vessels through such waters is concerned. It is noteworthy that this suggestion went considerably further than that eventually adopted in article 5, paragraph 2, of the *Territorial Sea Convention*, where the right of innocent passage was conceded only through those internal waters, which had previously been considered as part of the territorial sea or the high seas, and whose status was altered as a result of the application of the straight baselines method.

The Castberg-Fitzmaurice concept met with the vigorous opposition of François who objected to the introduction into international law of a new category of waters having a status halfway between internal waters and the territorial sea. In his letter to Castberg, François pointed out that

dans le système que vous préconisez on adopterait trois zones de mer différentes: la mer territoriale, les eaux intérieures et une troisième zone, qui est ni mer territoriale, ni eaux intérieures et dont le régime juridique reste quelque peu indécis. Je voudrais contester que le droit international reconnaisse l'existence de cette troisième zone.... Il ne suffit point de démonstrer à cet effet, comme vous le faites, que certains Etats n'exercent pas les droits qui leur reviennent dans les eaux intérieures, sur toute l'étendue de ces eaux. Il appartient toujours à l'Etat de ne pas faire usage, sur des parties de son territoire, de la plénitude de ses droits sans qu'il en résulte une modification essentielle du statut juridique de cette partie du territoire.... Il prête à confusion de créer de nouvelles 'zones' ... et de vouloir, comme vous le proposez, 'reconnaître que la limite des eaux intérieures peut être tracée de manière différente sous différents rapports.' ... Il faut ... maintenir la règle nette et pratique du droit international en vertu de laquelle la limite extérieure des eaux intérieures coïncide avec la limite intérieure de la mer territoriale....[2]

The opposition to the Castberg-Fitzmaurice concept was further strengthened by Gidel who threw the whole weight of his authority

[1] *Ibid.*, p. 206. (Italics in original).
[2] *Ibid.*, p. 208.

behind the line taken up by François. In his letter to the Rapporteur he maintained:

Le morcellement que vous suggérez d'établir dans les eaux intérieures serait, je le crains, infiniment dangereux et ne ferait que jeter le trouble là où nous avons la bonne fortune de voir régner l'accord dans la pratique comme parmi les auteurs. Ce morcellement impliquerait que chaque Etat riverain pourrait composer à sa guise pour *ses* eaux intérieures un statut juridique particulier; il retiendrait dans ce statut individuel des eaux intérieures toutes les compétences qu'il estimerait lui être avantageuses et éliminerait toutes celles auxquelles correspondrait une charge .... Il n'est pas au pouvoir d'un Etat riverain de se créer pour ses eaux intérieures un statut juridique particulier dérogatoire à la catégorie juridique du droit international 'eaux intérieures.' Mais l'Etat riverain demeure libre de renoncer soit conventionnellement soit législativement à l'exercice de telle ou telle des compétences que le droit international commun reconnaît à l'Etat riverain comme tel dans ses eaux intérieures.[1]

In view of the disagreement which arose among the various members of the Institute on this point, the Rapporteur, in his revised report, submitted to the 1956 session held at Granada, refrained from including any provision to this effect, and he suggested, referring to the right of access and passage through internal waters, that "sauf l'obligation contractuelle contraire, l'Etat riverain peut refuser aux navires étrangers tout accès aux *eaux intérieures*."[2] Sir Gerald Fitzmaurice did, however, take up this subject once more in his comments on the Rapporteur's revised report. He maintained that "the right of innocent passage, at any rate for merchant ships in time of peace, is so universally recognised, and so indispensable to the freedom and convenience of world communications, that... countries whose vessels have been accustomed... to enjoy rights of innocent passage in certain waters on the basis that they are territorial waters, must be regarded as having acquired a vested interest in, or acquired a right to continue to enjoy, such passage for their vessels, through the same waters, notwithstanding the fact that, by the establishment of a baseline, these waters have technically ceased to be territorial waters and have become internal waters."[3]

Invoking the doctrine of the abuse of rights, Sir Gerald expressed the view that it would be in such cases an abuse of right if the *full* regime of internal waters were applied to such waters and if certain acquired

[1] *Ibid.*, pp. 219 and 223. (Italics in original).

[2] 46 *Annuaire de l'Institut de Droit International*, Granada session, April 1956, pp. 51–60, at p. 51. (Italics in original).

[3] *Ibid.*, p. 69.

rights (such as the right of innocent passage) were not taken into account.[1]

When the revised draft was discussed at the plenary meeting of the Institute at its 1957 session in Amsterdam, Lord McNair supported the views put forward by Sir Gerald Fitzmaurice.[2] Colombos, likewise, criticized the wording of the revised draft as a retrograde measure, being contrary to the applied principles of international law.[3]

At a later stage of the debate, François supported a concept, which eventually found favour with the 1958 Geneva Conference on the Law of the Sea, and is now embodied in article 5, paragraph 2, of the *Territorial Sea Convention.* He asserted that

on ... puisse ... accepter un régime spécial pour une *certaine partie* des eaux intérieures. Il peut exister un droit de passage non général qui existerait lorsque les eaux territoriales ont été transformées en eaux intérieures.[4]

Following the words of François, Jenks suggested the adoption of an amendment which read as follows:

Sous réserve des droits de passage consacrés par l'usage, L'Etat riverain peut, sauf obligation contractuelle contraire, refuser aux navires étrangers l'accès aux eaux intérieures généralement reconnues comme telles....[5]

The italicized portion of this draft amendment is intended to safeguard traditional rights of passage which rest solely on usage and are not founded on any treaty provisions.

Wright tabled an amendment in which the right of innocent passage was recognized to foreign ships in all the "eaux *maritimes* intérieures,"[6] thus adopting the distinction suggested by Sir Gerald Fitzmaurice between internal inland waters and internal non-inland waters.

In an obvious attempt to reconcile these conflicting views, Quadri suggested that a right of passage in internal waters be denied to foreign vessels "sous réserve des droit acquis, soit par l'usage, soit par convention."[7]

De La pradelle, on the other hand, came out with a draft amendment sanctioning the right of free passage for foreign vessels in internal waters,

[1] *Ibid.*
[2] 47 *Annuaire de l'Institut de Droit International,* Amsterdam session, September 1957, vol. II, pp. 173–174.
[3] *Ibid.,* p. 180.
[4] *Ibid.,* p. 194. (Italics in original).
[5] *Ibid.,* p. 195. (Italics added). See also to the same effect the words of Winiarski (*ibid.,* p. 204), and Badawi (*ibid.,* p. 205).
[6] *Ibid.,* p. 203. (Italics added). See also the statement made by Ripert (*Ibid.,* p. 206).
[7] *Ibid.,* p. 207.

except where there exists an exceptional title and for a period as limited as possible.[1]

After protracted discussions, the Institute, by 42 votes to 6, with 7 abstentions, adopted a draft amendment tabled by the Rapporteur which, in its relevant passage, reads as follows:

Sous réserve des droits de passage consacrés, soit par l'usage, soit par convention, l'Etat riverain peut refuser aux navires étrangers l'accès aux *eaux intérieures*, à moins qu'ils ne se trouvent en état de danger.[2]

One cannot fail to notice the striking similarity which exists between this article and article 5, paragraph 2, of the *Territorial Sea Convention*.[3]

72. *The juridical status of historic waters – Multinational bays*

It is noteworthy that throughout the proceedings of the Institute and of the various international bodies, leading up to the *Territorial Sea Convention*, the discussions were invariably confined to bodies of water enclosed by a single littoral State. The question of the juridical status of waters surrounded by more than one littoral State was not touched upon at all. François, in his capacity as the International Law Commission's Special Rapporteur on the Law of the Sea, referred to this matter when he commented on the remarks made by various governments on the draft articles submitted to them by the Commission. He informed the Commission that

the Israeli Government inquired, *inter alia*, what was the position of bays whose coast line was shared by more than one State. The problem was one of the many which the Commission, aware that it was making a first effort to codify the matter, had deliberately refrained from attempting to solve.[4]

The same approach is also clearly reflected in the *Territorial Sea Convention*. Article 7, paragraph 1, as adopted by the Conference (article 7 is the article dealing with bays), prefaces the provisions contained therein by stating that

this article relates only to bays the coasts of which belong to a single State.[5]

[1] *Ibid.*, p. 208.
[2] *Ibid.*, p. 220. (Italics in original). The proviso regarding ships in distress was not disputed and was included in most of the draft proposals submitted during the debate.
[3] For a description of the developments leading up to the adoption of article 5, see above, section 70.
[4] *ILC Yearbook*, 8th session, 1956, vol. I, p. 190. (Italics in original).
[5] *Cmnd.* 584 (1959), p. 21.

Thus, the article, while explicitly excluding historic bays from its scope, followed the pattern set by earlier deliberations of international bodies and learned societies, a pattern which was described by Gidel in the following words:

Ni le Comité des Experts, ni aucune des compagnies savantes qui ont examiné la question des 'baies historiques' n'ont jamais, à son propos, relevé que l'hypothèse d'une baie bordée par les territoires d'un seul Etat riverain.[1]

The *Gulf of Fonseca* case therefore appears to be to the present day the only instance in which the possibility of a multinational historic bay was envisaged and, being what Gidel calls "une anomalie tout à fait notable dans le système logique des baies historiques,"[2] it can hardly be taken as the last word on this point.

Referring to the right of passage through the waters of that bay, the judgment in the *Gulf of Fonseca* case accorded to the waters falling outside the exclusive property of each of the riparian States the status of territorial waters, in which the right of passage of foreign vessels is not contested.[3] This decision of the Court has been criticized by Gidel on the ground that it

n'attribue pas aux eaux de ce golfe le caractère d'eaux intérieures comme l'exigerait ce caractère de baie historique, mais le caractère d'eaux territoriales.[4]

The decision rendered in the *Gulf of Fonseca* case has been criticized on several occasions in the course of this chapter. For the sake of completeness it should be added, however, that this decision might perhaps be best understood bearing in mind the unique *legal* characteristics of the case. Historically, the Gulf of Fonseca was encompassed for several centuries by the dominions of the Spanish Crown, and in the period 1821–1839 it was surrounded entirely by the Federal Republic of Central America. These historical facts, however, could have hardly warranted in themselves the Court's decision in favour of El Salvador, had it not been for the existence of two legal considerations of the highest significance, namely,

(a) that the parties to the dispute were agreed that the gulf is a closed sea.[5] Following the agreement between the parties on this point the Court was not called upon to consider whether or not the gulf

[1] Gidel, *op. cit.*, p. 627.
[2] *Ibid.* For a discussion of the *Gulf of Fonseca* case, see also Anzilotti, "Baie storiche: loro caratteri; rapporti fra gli Stati costieri," published in *Opere di Dionisio Anzilotti, Scritti di diritto internazionale pubblico*, vol. I, 1956, p. 707, at p. 723–729.
[3] As to the relevant passage of the judgment, see 11 *AJIL* (1917), p. 716.
[4] Gidel, *op. cit.*, p. 627.
[5] 11 *AJIL*, (1917), p. 693.

formed part of the high seas (a problem which normally faces a tribunal confronted with an historic claim to maritime areas), and was able to exclude this question from the scope of its deliberations. The only remaining legal problem that had to be settled by the Court was whether the waters of the bay outside the territorial seas of the three littoral countries were divided into separate parts, each of which belonged to one of the coastal States, or whether they came, in their entirety, under the joint ownership of the three States; and

(b) that both parties to the litigation were signatories to the General Treaty of Peace and Amity, concluded by the Central American Republics at Washington in 1907. Article II of the said Treaty imposed upon the signatory States the duty not to alter in any form their constitutional order, because any alteration of that order was conceived as a menace to the peace and security of each of the States and of Centrla America in general.[1] This provision, in turn, was based on the principle that the signatory States were disintegrated parts of the Republic of Central America. Accordingly, the conclusion by Nicaragua of the Bryan-Chamorro Treaty constituted, in the opinion of El Salvador, a menace to "the transcendental interests that the Salvadorean people have always held, and still hold, constantly in mind as one of their greatest and most legitimate aspirations: that of the reconstitution, undiminished, with the brother peoples, of the great country that was once the master of the ancient Central American domain."[2] The Court found, by four votes to one, that the conclusion of the Bryan-Chamorro Treaty constituted a violation on the part of Nicaragua of the 1907 General Treaty of Peace and Amity.[3]

It is against this background that the Court's decision must be viewed, and, having regard to these exceptional and unusual circumstances, it is hardly surprising that a tribunal composed exclusively of Central American judges should have found as it did. Thus, if the Court's decision is limited to the case itself, without being regarded as a precedent to be applied under different circumstances, the *Gulf of Fonseca* case might perhaps appear to be less unjustified in law than most writers have hitherto been prepared to assume.

More recently the late Mr. John Foster Dulles, when United States Secretary of State, seems to have had the example set in the *Gulf of Fonseca* case in mind when he declared:

[1] For the text of this article, see *ibid.*, p. 725.
[2] *Ibid.*, p. 680.
[3] *Ibid.*, p. 694.

If the four littoral states which have boundaries upon the gulf [of Aqaba] should all agree that it should be closed, then it could be closed.[1]

He did not specify, however, what would be the juridical status of such a closed multinational historic bay, outside the territorial waters of each of the littoral States.

It is at least debatable whether Mr. Dulles did, in fact, give a correct picture of the law as it *is*, for, according to Gidel, even the littoral States' agreement to "close" a multinational bay is not sufficient to achieve this legal effect unless such measure receives the recognition, or at least the acquiescence, of other States.[2]

Thus, it would be far more in accordance with the prevailing concepts of modern maritime international law if the waters surrounded by more than one littoral State would be considered as falling *ex definitione* outside the category of historic bays, and if the waters beyond the marginal belts of each of the littoral States were regarded as part of the high seas.[3]

73. Non-exclusive historic rights over maritime areas

In the foregoing chapters, as well as in the foregoing sections of the present chapter, the acquisition of exclusive State rights based on an historic title was discussed. It was submitted that the State, which succeeded in proving the existence of an historic title, was to be regarded as the territorial sovereign over the territory in question, enjoying the aggregate of rights flowing from territorial sovereignty. Thus, historic titles were classified among the valid territorial titles which form the juridical basis of the sovereignty of States over their territories.

The term "historic waters," likewise, has been employed so far to denote maritime areas which, to quote the International Court's judgment in the *Fisheries* case, "are treated as internal waters but which would not have that character were it not for the existence of an historic

[1] News Conference statement of February 19th, 1957, 36 *Department of State Bulletin* (January-June, 1957), p. 404.

[2] Gidel, *op. cit.*, p. 604. See also to the same effect Oppenheim, *op. cit.*, p. 508. See, however, Jessup who takes the view that a bay bordered by more than one State "is properly considered by the bordering states as their common property." (Jessup, *The Law of Territorial Waters and Maritime Jurisdiction*, 1927, p. 476).

[3] In fact, the 1958 Geneva Conference of the Law of the Sea appears to have adopted this view. According to McDougal and Burke, "the decision of the 1958 Conference prohibiting suspension of the right of innocent passage through a strait which connects one part of the high seas with the territorial sea of a foreign state... seems incompatible with acceptance of a claim to historic waters on the part of [the riparian] states since there would be no such right of innocent passage if the claim were regarded as acceptable." (McDougal and Burke, *op. cit.*, p. 444).

title."[1] As has been shown above, internal waters are regarded as part of a State's territory, over which it is entitled to exercise full rights of sovereignty,[2] subject to minor qualifications, which were also referred to above.

In addition to the acquisition of historic titles *stricto sensu* there are, however, also claims of a more limited character which also purportedly rest on an historic basis. In contradistinction to the *exclusive* claims of sovereignty, which characterize an historic claim properly so called, historic claims belonging to this second category will be termed henceforth "*non-exclusive* historic rights." Historic claims falling into the first group are normally claims *erga omnes*, while those falling into the second group are raised *inter partes* only.[3]

By non-exclusive rights we understand rights falling short of sovereignty, which are acquired by a State at the expense of another State, this latter being the sovereign over the area over which the non-exclusive rights are asserted. To this category of non-exclusive rights belong the rights of passage through another State's territory, or through its internal waters, as well as traditional fishing rights acquired by the nationals of one State in waters which are claimed by another State as part of its maritime belt (the so-called "historic rights in reverse").

Non-exclusive historic rights may be acquired, needless to say, not only in respect of maritime areas, but over land territories also. A recent example for the recognition by the International Court of Justice of such non-exclusive historic rights is the judgment given by the Court in the case concerning *Right of Passage over Indian Territory*,[4] in which the Court recognized the existence of traditional Portuguese rights of passage through certain parts of Indian territory.[5]

The problem of the existence of non-exclusive historic rights in general was given passing reference in chapter III, section 24, above, where it was pointed out that, since non-exclusive historic rights prevail in our days mainly in the maritime sphere, it was deemed appropriate to deal with this matter at some length in the chapter devoted to the specific problems surrounding maritime historic rights.

Non-exclusive State rights, which are basically rights conferred upon the "dominant" State, such as would not normally accrue to it under the general rules of international law, are frequently termed "*international*

[1] *ICJ Reports*, 1951, p. 130.
[2] Gidel, *op. cit.*, vol. III, pp. 625–626.
[3] This matter has been briefly dealt with above, in chapter III, section 24.
[4] *ICJ Reports*, 1960, p. 6.
[5] *Ibid.*, p. 40.

servitudes." The existence of the institution of servitudes in the sphere of international law has often been criticized in the past both for reasons of substance and terminology,[1] and some writers went as far as to deny its very existence.[2]

Commenting on the status of servitudes in international law, Lauterpacht maintains that "of all attempts to apply to relations between States conceptions taken from private law, none has caused more confusion or has brought the recourse to analogy into more disrepute than the efforts made to introduce the conception of servitudes into international public law."[3]

Similarly, Váli points out that "the 'servitude' of international law is the traditional scapegoat of international jurisprudence."[4] The same writer goes on to say that this doctrine "has suffered... contemptuous criticism and blunt rejection, and at the same time enjoyed... unsubstantiated approval and wanton praise."[5] Recent textbooks of international law, he further points out, "while often maintaining a cautious reserve, generally approved of the existence... of the concept of international servitudes."[6]

Whatever attitude one is tempted to adopt as to the suitability of this doctrine to meet the requirements of international life, as well as regarding the propriety of the terminology involved, it is felt that, as far as non-exclusive *historic* rights are concerned, the doctrine of international servitudes should not be invoked as the legal basis underlying such rights. The reason for this contention is that, according to the generally accepted definition of international servitudes, they are based on *treaty* provisions, whereas the source of historic rights is to be found, *ex definitione*, in *customary* international law.

The source of historic rights is a certain practice which was followed for a period of time sufficiently long to warrant the conclusion that it has been recognized by the parties affected by such practice. An international servitude, on the other hand, is, according to Váli, "a permanent (durable) legal relationship *established by a particular international treaty* whereby one State, or a certain number of States, is or are entitled to exercise rights within part or the whole of the territory of another

[1] Váli, *Servitudes of International Law*, 2nd ed., 1958, p. 43. For a criticism of the terminological aspect see also McNair, "So-called State Servitudes," 6 *BYIL* (1925), p. 111 *et seq.*

[2] See e.g. Nys, "Les prétendues servitudes internationales," 7 *RDILC* (*Deuxième série*) (1905), p. 118; see also the same writer in 13 *RDILC* (*Deuxième série*) (1911), p. 314.

[3] Lauterpacht, *Private Law Sources and Analogies in International Law*, 1927, p. 119.

[4] Váli, *op. cit.*, p. 42.

[5] *Ibid.*

[6] *Ibid.*, p. 43.

State, for a special purpose or interest relating to the territory in question."[1]

Now, as has been said before, it is clear, that if an international treaty regulating such a relationship were in existence, the need for invoking an historic claim would not arise at all. The theory of historic rights comes into play, as was submitted elsewhere, only in those cases where no such conventional source of rights and correlative obligations exists.

Thus, non-exclusive historic rights are rights akin to international servitudes, but differing from the latter as to their source: while international servitudes arise out of a contractual relationship between the States concerned, non-exclusive historic rights are based on special norms of customary international law and find their justification in the tacit acquiescence of the affected States in certain practices exercised at the expense of their sovereignty.

It is worth distinguishing non-exclusive historic rights in this sense from the so-called "natural restrictions" on State sovereignty. By "natural restrictions" we mean those limitations which are imposed on a State *eo ipso*, as a corollary to its sovereignty. These are "general restrictions upon territorial supremacy which, according to certain rules of the Law of Nations, concern all States alike.... Thus, for instance, it is... a 'natural' restriction on territorial supremacy that a State is obliged to admit free passage of foreign merchantmen through its territorial maritime belt."[2]

By non-exclusive historic rights, however, we understand rights of a different nature, i.e. rights which *do not* normally accrue to the claimant State by virtue of any general rule of law, but which are the outcome of an exceptional local and isolated process, which creates rights in favour of the "dominant" State, at the expense of the "servient" State (e.g. the right of passage through the internal waters of another State).

In at least one important respect the acquisition of non-exclusive maritime historic rights differs from the acquisition of an historic title in general. Among the requirements for the establishment of an historic title (involving the acquisition of exclusive rights of sovereignty), the requirement for the possession of the claimant State being *à titre de souverain* was already mentioned, and it was submitted that an historic title can be acquired only through the acts of persons in the service of

[1] *Ibid.*, p. 309 (Italics added). See also to the same effect Oppenheim, *op.cit.*, vol. I, p. 536; Starke, *An Introduction to International Law*, 5th ed., 1963, p. 195; Cavaré, *op. cit.*, vol. II, p. 618; Sibert, *Traité de droit international public*, 1951, vol. I, p. 383.

[2] Oppenheim, *op. cit.*, p. 536.

the State or authorized to act on its behalf.[1] This, however, is not the case, where a State claims merely non-exclusive historic rights.

According to Fitzmaurice, such rights may also be acquired through the private acts of individuals acting on their own. "Thus," says Fitzmaurice, "if the fishing vessels of a given country have been accustomed from time immemorial, or over a long period, to fish in a certain area, on the basis of the area being high seas and common to all, it may be said that their country has through them (and although they are private vessels having no specific authority) acquired a vested interest that the fisheries of that area should remain available to its fishing vessels (of course on a non-exclusive basis) – so that if another country asserts a claim to that area as territorial waters, which is found to be valid or comes to be recognized, this can only be subject to the acquired rights of fishery in question, which must continue to be respected."[2]

The reason for the distinction between the acquisition of non-exclusive rights over land territory and maritime areas, respectively, lies, according to Sir Gerald, in their different legal status. The sea being *res communis*, international law confers a positive and substantive right on all to exploit its resources, and not merely a faculty to do something which is not prohibited by international law. Thus, a State interfering with the activities performed by another State's nationals on the high seas will obviously commit an international wrong. On the other hand, a State occupying land territory, which was hitherto *res nullius*, will be allowed to interfere with the private acts of exploitation undertaken there by private individuals, nationals of another State, without committing an international wrong.[3]

Fitzmaurice therefore arrives at the conclusion that exploitation by private individuals of a land territory which is *res nullius*, even if continued for a long period of time, cannot give rise to any acquired rights which would be valid in the face of a subsequent appropriation of the territory by another State. Such exploitation of a maritime area may,

[1] See above, chapter IV, section 37.

[2] Fitzmaurice, 30 *BYIL* (1953), p. 51. According to the same author, "there would seem to be justice in this idea – for if a State can by a long-continued usage and practice build up a prescriptive or historical right to the waters of an area originally and in its essence *res communis*, so equally should a State which has specifically exercised its communal rights in respect of that area as such, over a long period of time, be entitled to continue to do so, notwithstanding the change in the status of the area. Indeed, it could be said, that the latter claim is the stronger – since it only involves the retention and continued exercise of an existing right, not the acquisition of a new one." (*Ibid.*; italics in original). See also above, chapter IV, section 37.

[3] *Ibid.*, p. 52.

however, lead to the formation of a vested interest, conferring special rights in relation to that area.[1]

Non-exclusive maritime historic rights fall into two main groups:

(a) historic rights of passage;

(b) historic fishing rights.

The existence of "historic rights of passage" through certain maritime areas was already dealt with when discussing the problems relating to the transformation of given bodies of water into internal waters, by means of applying the straight baselines method of delimitation. For reasons of convenience it was deemed fit to discuss this type of non-exclusive maritime historic rights in previous sections – rather than in the present one. Owing to the fact that the problem of the preservation of maritime historic rights of passage normally arises through the application of the straight baselines method and the resulting incorporation into the riparian State's maritime domain (as internal waters) of what was hitherto regarded as part of the open sea, or of the territorial sea, it was felt that the juridical problems attendant on such historic rights of passage could hardly be separated from the problems surrounding the application of the straight baselines method and from the questions relating to the juridical status of historic waters in general.[2]

It is therefore proposed to turn now to the main remaining aspect of maritime historic rights, namely, historic rights of fishing.

74. Historic rights of fishing

Claims of non-exclusive historic rights of fishing have in recent years been among the most controversial features of the law of the sea and the impossibility of securing the necessary two-thirds majority for any proposal on this topic caused the Second Geneva Conference on the Law of the Sea to break up without any tangible results.

According to the general rules of international law, a State is entitled to exclude from its territorial waters all foreign fishermen and to reserve the fishing banks within that area for the fishing activities of its own population. Such rights, do not, however, accrue beyond the territorial sea, although the littoral State has certain rights to legislate on fishing matters beyond those limits.[3]

Owing to the recent, and almost universal, trend which may be discerned in State practice for States to extend their territorial seas,

[1] *Ibid.*

[2] See above, sections 70 and 71.

[3] See the 1958 Geneva *Convention on Fishing and Conservation of the Living Resources of the High Seas, Cmnd.* 584 (1959), p. 34.

fishermen of different countries – and mainly those who used to engage in distant-water fishing – find themselves deprived of fishing rights in areas, which were formerly recognized as part of the high seas, but which are now claimed as part of the territorial sea of the littoral State. Thus arises the question of the historic rights of foreign fishermen to fish in what has allegedly become part of the maritime domain of the coastal State, rights which are frequently based on time-honoured practice and age-long exercise of fishing activities. Such rights have been frequently termed "historic rights in reverse," thereby indicating that, in contradistinction to the "ordinary" claim of historic character, where the littoral State endeavours to assert certain rights to be acquired at the expense of the international community at large, here the international community, or one of its members, insists that its acquired rights be respected and protected from any possible encroachment by the coastal State.

Since the 1958 Geneva Conference on the Law of the Sea proved unable to agree on the question of historic fishing rights, the 1960 Geneva Conference took up the matter again. At the Second Conference Canada put forward a proposal, under which each nation would have a three-mile territorial sea, with an adjacent nine-mile belt, in which the coastal State would be entitled to reserve fishing for its nationals. It was realized from the outset – and the Canadian proposal bears witness to this effect – that the problem of exclusive fishing rights was inextricably linked up with the problem of the breadth of the territorial sea. This was also clearly reflected in the words of Señor García Amador, who, speaking on behalf of Cuba in the Committee of the Whole of the Conference, pointed out that the recognition of any historic fishing rights would inevitably lead to a clash with the coastal State's rights, whenever the latter extended its territorial sea beyond the traditional limits, thereby claiming exclusive fishing rights over areas of the high seas, in which the nationals of another State had been fishing in the past. According to Señor García Amador,

> the State whose nationals had thus traditionally fished an area of the high seas could be said to have acquired prescriptive rights in that area; those rights could carry even greater weight than those of the coastal State itself – for example, where the latter's nationals engaged in little or no fishing activity in the area. And the argument was even more cogent where the activities of the nationals of the coastal State were such that they could not possibly affect the productivity of the local fish stock or stocks.[1]

[1] See *Second United Nations Conference on the Law of the Sea, Official Records*, U.N. Document A/CONF. 19/8, p. 41.

The United States delegate, Mr. Dean, also supported the preservation of historic fishing rights of foreign nationals in the zone between 6 and 12 miles from the coast, provided that no increase in foreign fishing would be permitted, and that all increased productivity would thus benefit exclusively the riparian State.[1] He also suggested that a five-year practice be considered as sufficient for the establishment of such a right;[2] this suggestion was a departure from the original American proposal submitted to the First Geneva Conference on the Law of the Sea, where the United States had suggested a ten-year practice.[3]

The Peruvian delegate opposed the five-year dead-line on the ground that historic rights could not be acquired in ten, let alone five years, because "only in the context of centuries could the term 'historic rights' be meaningful."[4]

The delegate of Canada based his country's opposition to the perpetuation of historic fishing rights on the ground that "to do so would discriminate against newly emergent States and those countries which did not yet possess the economic resources needed for building up long-distance fishing fleets."[5] The same idea was conveyed in a more radical manner by the delegate of Iceland, who denounced "such 'historic rights' as [being] on par with colonial rights, a concept that was fortunately obsolescent."[6] The delegate of Bulgaria, likewise, saw in the concept of historic rights "a product of an invidious tendency... to elevate the dominant position of technically advanced countries into a system of legally sanctioned privileges."[7]

Another reason given by the Canadian delegate for his rejection of the theory of historic rights was the fact that

> it would penalize countries which had sought to establish a rule of law through international agreement under United Nations auspices, and which had accordingly refrained during the past few years from taking unilateral action to extend their territorial sea beyond three miles.[8]

[1] *Ibid.*, p. 46. For the text of the American proposal, see *ibid.*, p. 166; the United States proposal was supported by the United Kingdom (*ibid.*, p. 58), the Netherlands (*ibid.*, p. 59), Italy (*ibid.*, p. 64), Portugal (*ibid.*, p. 72), the Federal Republic of Germany (*ibid.*, p. 74), Australia (*ibid.*, pp. 81–82) and Ceylon (*ibid.*, p. 99).

[2] *Ibid.*, p. 166. (U.N. Document A/CONF. 19/C. 1/L.3).

[3] See *United Nations Conference on the Law of the Sea, Official Records*, vol. III, *First Committee*, p. 253, Annexes, U.N. Doc. A/CONF. 13.C. 1/L. 159.

[4] *Second United Nations Conference on the Law of the Sea, Official Records*, p. 62.

[5] *Ibid.*, p. 50; the Canadian delegate was supported by the delegates of Colombia (*ibid.*, p. 60), Poland (*ibid.*, p. 68), Yugoslavia (*ibid.*, p. 70), Guatemala (*ibid.*, p. 78), Norway (*ibid.*, p. 84), and South Korea (*ibid.*, p. 103).

[6] *Ibid.*, p. 79.

[7] *Ibid.*, p. 113.

[8] *Ibid.*, p. 50. See also to the same effect the statement made by the delegate of Uruguay, *ibid.*, p. 90.

The Australian delegate, while supporting the United States proposal, criticized the application in this context of the term "historic rights," saying it might create confusion as to the juridical nature of the rights involved. "Under the general law of nations," he said, "all States could fish as of right in that specified zone of the high seas, and therefore the fishing rights currently exercised by distant-water fishing had been, and were, perfectly lawful by definition and their present validity did not depend on the duration of their exercise."[1]

This approach to the problem of acquired fishing rights was wholeheartedly supported by M. Gros, the delegate of France, who observed that "the expression 'historic rights' meant nothing. The only thing historic about it was the coastal State's eagerness to colonize the high seas. The States which practised distant water fishing fished in the high seas and it was incorrect to speak of 'historic rights' in that connexion."[2]

The New Zealand delegate introduced the idea of the gradual lapse of historic rights within a period to be specified,[3] and was supported in this approach by the delegate of Israel.[4] This notion of the gradual expiry of historic rights was the basis of the joint American-Canadian proposal, envisaging the lapse of historic fishing rights – which had been in existence for at least five years – after a transition period of ten years.[5] This proposal received 54 votes, 28 voting against, and 5 abstaining;[6] it thus failed by an odd vote to receive the necessary two-thirds majority, and the Conference broke up without having achieved anything on this point.

Commenting on the deliberations of this Conference, Bowett has pointed out – rightly, it is believed – that the term "historic rights" was perhaps an unfortunate choice when applied to the preservation of fishing rights in what was hitherto regarded as part of the high seas, "for... the sponsors of this proposal never intended any relation with the doctrine of prescription.... As the Australian delegate pointed out,... these fishing rights, having been exercised on the high seas, were *per se* lawful."[7] The unsuitability of the term "historic rights" in this connection is further increased by the fact that, contrary to the original proposals which had been laid before the 1958 Geneva Conference on

[1] *Ibid.*, p. 82.
[2] *Ibid.*, p. 118.
[3] *Ibid.*, p. 97.
[4] *Ibid.*, p. 100.
[5] *Ibid.*, p. 169, U.N. Document A/CONF. 19.C. 1/L.10.
[6] *Ibid.*, p. 30.
[7] Bowett, "The Second United Nations Conference on the Law of the Sea," 9 *ICLQ* (1960), 415 at p. 424. (Italics in original).

the Law of the Sea, the draft resolutions tabled at the 1960 Conference envisaged the introduction of "historic rights" which would fade away after a transition period of ten years. It is difficult to see how rights of such a temporary nature, which are to be enjoyed only for a definite period of time and not in perpetuity, are to be regarded as "historic rights" in the meaning normally attached to this term.

The reasons for this novel approach and for the proposals advocating the introduction of a "phasing out" period lay outside the legal sphere and the problem essentially was, according to Bowett, "to find a compromise period which would allow the coastal State to look forward to exclusive rights in the not-too-distant future and, at the same time, allow the fishing States to make the appropriate adjustments to their economy."[1] The main purpose of those who suggested an allowance for such a transition period was to enable the States affected by the extension of the exclusive fishing zones of the coastal States to re-equip their fishing industry and to prepare it in time to meet the new situation.[2]

The attempts of the Conference to regulate the problem of historic fishing rights in the form of a multilateral convention having proved abortive, it should be expected that the affected States will now seek their remedy in the form of bilateral agreements. This is what, in fact, seems to have happened since 1958 and the tendency to rely on bilateral treaties rather than to await the possible, but now unlikely, conclusion of an international convention has gained momentum since the deliberations of the Second Geneva Conference on the Law of the Sea have come to nought. This, in effect, had been the practice of States even before the 1958 Geneva Conference on the Law of the Sea. One of the pertinent examples is the Anglo-Soviet Fisheries Agreement which was signed in Moscow on May 25th, 1956.[3]

Under this Agreement British trawlers were enabled to fish up to three miles from the Soviet coast in certain areas of the Barents Sea. (The Soviet Union claims a twelve-mile limit for its territorial sea). The Agreement, which came into force on March 12th, 1957 – following the exchange of the instruments of ratification between the parties – was concluded for a period of five years and was terminable by one year's notice. The Soviet Government denounced the Agreement on

[1] *Ibid.*, p. 426.

[2] It has been estimated, for example, that about ten per cent of the total British catch came from the four-twelve mile zone off Iceland. (See Alexander, 14 *YBWA* (1960), p. 252, n. 17).

[3] *Cmnd.* 148 (1957), *United Kingdom Treaty Series* No. 36 (1957). This Agreement superseded the Anglo-Soviet Fisheries Agreement of May 22nd, 1930. (See *League of Nations Treaty Series*, vol. 102, p. 103).

March 2nd, 1961,[1] and it therefore expired on March 12th, 1962. According to reports published in June, 1962, talks were held in Moscow on the possible renewal of the 1956 Agreement; no results, however, were reached in the negotiations which took place between the parties.[2]

In 1959 the United Kingdom and Denmark reached an Agreement regulating off-shore fishing in a six-mile zone off the Faroe Islands. (Denmark is responsible for the external relations of the archipelago). The conclusion of this Agreement was precipitated by the decision of June 6th, 1958, adopted by the *Lagting* of Thorshavn, to extend the territorial sea of the Faroe Islands from three to twelve miles, a decision which affected adversely the activities of British fishermen who used to fish outside the three-mile limit.[3] The Agreement reached between the parties after secret negotiations, on April 27th, 1959, provided that British fishermen would be allowed to fish outside a marginal belt of six miles during certain seasons of the year.[4] This agreement was terminable after four years, by one year's notice. On April 28th, 1962, the Danish Chargé d'Affaires in London officially notified the British Foreign Office that the Danish Government wished to terminate, with effect from April 28th, 1963, the 1959 Agreement.[5] At the request of the Faroe Government, the Danish Government had previously sent an *aide-mémoire* to Britain suggesting fresh negotiations on the fishery limits off the Faroes; in reply, the British Government had informed the Danish Government on April 17th, 1962, that they agreed to negotiations for the amendment of the 1959 Agreement.[6]

It appears pertinent at this juncture to mention the *Red Crusader* incident which aptly illustrates the high degree of sensitiveness displayed in international life in the sphere of fishery rights. On May 29th, 1961, the Scottish trawler *Red Crusader* was allegedly found trawling inside the six-mile limit off the Faroe Islands and was signalled to stop by the Danish frigate *Niels Ebbesen*. The Danes then put a boarding party of two on board the *Red Crusader* and ordered her to proceed to Thorshavn. The *Red Crusader* obeyed at first, but later the skipper, having concerted with the crew to seclude the boarding party still on board, decided to evade Danish jurisdiction. He accordingly made off for Aberdeen. The

[1] *The Times* of July 1st, 1961.

[2] *The Times* of June 12th, 1962. For the report on a previous round of talks on the renewal of the 1956 Agreement, see *The Times* of February 24th, 1962.

[3] For the text of the resolution adopted by the *Lagting*, see 28 *ASJG* (1958), p. 207, doc. 11.

[4] For the text of the exchange of Notes between the two Governments, see *Cmnd.* 776 (1959); *United Kingdom Treaty Series*, No. 55 (1959).

[5] *The Times* of April 30th, 1962.

[6] *Ibid.*

Niels Ebbesen pursued the Scottish trawler and fired at her several shots, holing her bowls and damaging her masts and antennae. Later two British vessels (the minesweeper *Wotton* and the frigate *Troubridge*) met the trawler, caused the Danish boarding party to be released and escorted the *Red Crusader* to Aberdeen. An exchange of Notes ensued between the two Governments. It was finally decided to submit the matter for investigation by a Commission of three, appointed by the Governments of Denmark and the United Kingdom. The Commission (consisting of M. de Visscher of Belgium, M. Gros of France and Captain Moolenbourgh of the Netherlands) started its investigations on March 5th, 1962, at The Hague and its findings were published on March 30th, 1962. The Commission's Report gave the two Governments an opportunity to let the matter drop. Both sides were found to have been in the wrong. The *Red Crusader*, although not found to have been actually fishing inside the six-mile fishery limit, had her trawl inside that limit for several minutes. The Commission rejected the skipper's claim that he had misunderstood the Danish frigate's signals, but found that the *Niels Ebbesen* had exceeded the legitimate use of armed force in firing at the trawler without warning and with danger to human life. It expressed the view that, while the *Red Crusader's* violation of the order received and at first obeyed was a possible explanation for the action taken by the *Niels Ebbesen*, it was not a justification for it. The conduct of the *Wotton* and the *Troubridge* was found by the Commission to have been "impeccable," and their actions (i.e. the causing of the Danish boarding party to be released and the escorting of the *Red Crusader* to Aberdeen) were described by the Commission as "the best solution."[1]

Thus, the tension which arose as a result of the *Red Crusader* incident may be said to have subsided.[2] The whole case, however, seems to serve as a good illustration for the serious repercussions and complications on the international level which may be caused by seemingly unimportant fishery issues.

[1] For a report on the *Red Crusader* incident, see *The Times* of May 31st, 1961, and 65 *RGDIP* (1961), pp. 824–827. For the Report of the Commission see *The Times* of March 31st, 1962, and 66 *RGDIP* (1962), pp. 597–600. See also *Keesing's Contemporary Archives*, vol. XIII, 1961–1962, p. 18738. For a discussion of the Anglo-Danish Fisheries Agreement of 1959 in general and of the *Red Crusader* incident in particular, see Johnson, 10 *ICLQ* (1961), pp. 594–597.

[2] On January 23rd, 1963, the British and Danish Governments announced that they had agreed to an amicable settlement of the incident in which each side would waive all its claims and charges against the other. (See *The Times* of January 24th, 1963). According to press reports from Copenhagen, this announcement was received with some resentment in the Faroe Islands, where Denmark has been accused of lacking in will to protect the island's vital interests. (See *The Times* of January 25th, 1963). A twelve-mile fishery limit for the Faroe Islands went into effect on March 12th, 1964.

Shortly after the failure of the 1960 Geneva Conference on the Law of the Sea, Norway intimated that she contemplated the extension of her maritime belt, which is reserved for the exclusive fishing activities of her nationals, so as to include a twelve-mile zone, measured from the baselines. After three rounds of talks held alternately in Oslo and London, an Agreement was reached on November 17th, 1960, on the lines of the joint American-Canadian proposal which had failed to get the necessary majority at the Second Law of the Sea Conference, and which had been supported by both the United Kingdom and Norway. According to the terms of this Agreement, the United Kingdom acquiesced in the extension of the Norwegian exclusive fishing belt up to twelve miles, if and when Norway saw fit to decide on such extension; Norway at the same time agreed that British fishermen should exercise their traditional rights of fishing in the outer six-mile zone for a transitional period of ten years, starting from October 31st, 1960.[1]

On January 11th, 1961, the Norwegian Prime Minister, Mr. Gerhardsen, announced the extension of the Norwegian fishery limits, during 1961, in two stages: the first extension, from four to six miles was introduced on April 1st, 1961, and the second, from six to twelve miles, on September 1st, 1961.[2]

A similar pattern was followed in the settlement of the much-publicized *Anglo-Icelandic Fisheries* Dispute, which had clouded the relations between the two States for over a decade. Denmark, which had been formerly the sovereign of Iceland, claimed from 1859 onwards a territorial sea of four miles. After the accession of Iceland to independence in 1944, a law dated April 5th, 1948, empowered the Government to establish within the limits of Iceland's continental shelf areas, in which fishing would be subjected to Icelandic jurisdiction.[3] A Fisheries Convention concluded in 1901 between Great Britain and Denmark – in which the latter had limited her exclusive rights of fishing off the coasts of Iceland and the Faroe Islands as against Great Britain to a three-mile zone[4] – was terminated by Iceland as from 1951. A series of regulations, which came into force since 1950, first prohibited fishing by foreign fishermen within a marginal belt of four miles, as measured from newly-drawn straight baselines,[5] and later culminated in the

[1] *Cmnd.* 1224 (1960).

[2] See *Keesing's Contemporary Archives*, vol. XIII, 1961–1962, p. 17884; see also *ibid.*, p. 18293.

[3] For the English text of this law, see *United Nations Legislative Series, Laws and Regulations on the Regime of the Territorial Sea* (ST/LEG/SER.B/6), 1957, p. 513.

[4] 94 *BFSP*, p. 29.

[5] Iceland did not, however, enforce these regulations as against the United Kingdom pending litigations in the *Fisheries* case.

Icelandic order of June 30th, 1958, which fixed a twelve-mile "fisheries limit" within which "all fishing activities by foreign vessels" were prohibited.[1] This order evoked strong protests on the part of a number of States.[2] Subsequently, British trawlers found fishing within the four to twelve-mile zone were frequently fired on by Icelandic coast guards and trawling was carried on under the protection of the Royal Navy.

Following the failure of the Second Geneva Conference on the Law of the Sea, the parties to the dispute started negotiations with a view to reaching a bilateral solution of the problems in issue. Under an Agreement published in London on February 27th, 1961, and simultaneously laid before the *Althing* in Reykjavik for approval, the United Kingdom Government undertook not to object to a twelve-mile fishing zone round Iceland; the Icelandic Government, on its part, dropped its objections to fishing by British vessels in certain parts of the six to twelve-mile zone for a transitional period of three years. The United Kingdom also agreed not to object to the re-drawing of the baselines from which the twelve-mile marginal belt was to be measured in a manner favourable to Iceland; the new baselines are to be applied both during the transitional period and afterwards. In establishing a transitional period of only three years, the Agreement is clearly more favourable to Iceland than the Agreement reached with Norway, which, it will be recalled, allows for a transitional period of ten years.

The Icelandic Government have not dropped their ultimate objective of extending the limits of the exclusive fishing zone over the whole of Iceland's continental shelf – which has in some places a breadth of even fifty miles – but agreed to give six months' notice before claiming any extension beyond the twelve-mile zone, and accepted the jurisdiction of the International Court of Justice in any future dispute in respect of such claim.[3]

The *Althing* of Reykjavik approved the Agreement on March 9th, 1961, by 33 votes to 27, and two days later the Agreement was given effect by an exchange of Notes between the two Governments.[4] Thus,

[1] For the English text of this order see 28 *ASJG* (1958), p. 365; at p. 355 there see also the *Memorandum on the Fishing Question* submitted by Iceland in September, 1958, to the United Nations General Assembly.

[2] For a list of the protesting States see Goy, "L'affaire des pêcheries islandaises," 87 *Journal du Droit International* (1960), p. 371, at pp. 392–394. Among recent publications referring in detail to the *Anglo-Icelandic Fisheries* Dispute see also Alexander, "Offshore Claims and Fisheries in North-West Europe," 14 *YBWA* (1960), p. 236 *et seq.*

[3] For a report on this Agreement see *The Times* of February 28th, 1961. See also Johnson, 10 *ICLQ* (1961), pp. 592–594.

[4] See *The Times* of March 13th, 1961. The exchange of Notes between the United Kingdom and Iceland has been published in *Cmnd.* 1328 (1961), *United Kingdom Treaty Series*, No. 17 (1961).

it may confidently be assumed that this dispute, which marred the relations between the two countries for over a decade, has finally found a settlement satisfactory for both parties.

Following negotiations held at the Soviet Union's request, a Soviet-Norwegian Fisheries Agreement was signed in Moscow on February 22nd, 1962. Similar to the Anglo-Norwegian Fisheries Agreement of November 17th, 1960, the Soviet-Norwegian pact gives Soviet fishermen the right to operate between six and twelve nautical miles off the Norwegian coast until October 31st, 1970. In return, Norwegian fishermen will enjoy special fishing rights in certain Soviet waters within the twelve-mile limit, including the Nordfargrunden fishing bank in the Soviet part of the Varanger Fjord area and the Henöy banks off Cape Niemetski.[1]

75. Are claims to the sea-bed and subsoil of an "historic" character?

It now remains to be seen whether the rights of States over their continental shelves may properly be regarded as "historic rights" in the meaning given to this term in the present study.

The continental shelf has been defined by the 1958 Geneva *Convention on the Continental Shelf* (hereinafter referred to as the "*Continental Shelf Convention*") – for the purposes of the Convention – as including:

(a) the sea-bed and subsoil of the submarine areas adjacent to the coast but outside the area of the territorial sea, to a depth of 200 metres or, beyond that limit, to where the depth of the superjacent waters admits of the exploitation of the natural resources of the said areas;

(b) the sea-bed and subsoil of similar submarine areas adjacent to the coasts of islands.[2]

This definition represents a major step forward, in spite of its obvious deficiencies. (E.g. it is uncertain whether all submarine areas adjacent to the coast, which are capable of exploitation, are covered by the definition, including portions of water of a depth greater than 200 metres before a shallower depth is reached; equally, the introduction of the concept of exploitability, being in itself a test subject to changes,

[1] See *The Times* of February 24th, 1962, and *Keesing's Contemporary Archives*, vol. XIII, 1961–1962, p. 18674. Likewise, in the European Fisheries Convention, signed in March-April 1964 by the U.K., Ireland, Portugal, Spain, France, Italy, West Germany, the Benelux countries, Denmark and Sweden, the "6 plus 6" formula was adopted for fishing purposes. (*Cmnd.* 2335 (1964), p. 8). The U.K. *Fishery Limits Act*, 1964, giving effect to the Convention's provisions, came into force on September 30th, 1964.

[2] See article 1 of the *Continental Shelf Convention*, *Cmnd.* 584 (1959), p. 40. See also Gutteridge, "The 1958 Geneva Convention on the Continental Shelf," 35 *BYIL* (1959), p. 102 *et seq.*, containing a brief survey of the various stages which preceded the adoption of this definition. (*Ibid.*, pp. 107–110).

owing to growing scientific and technical knowledge, is not sufficiently precise and is likely to give rise to doubts and disputes). Still, allowing for all its vagueness and looseness of terminology, this definition is by far superior to the one resorted to only a few years ago. As late as 1952 Mouton defined the continental shelf as "the part of the sea-bottom and the soil underneath, which is covered by shallow waters up to a depth where the slope of the sea-bottom increases noticeably in steepness, which fringes large parts of the continents, over varying distances from the coasts."[1]

The problems relating to the continental shelf are of comparatively recent standing. As has been observed by Johnson, "before 1939 this problem was little discussed, except in connexion with special questions such as the Ceylon pearl fishery or the Channel Tunnel."[2]

The first instrument concerning the continental shelf was a treaty concluded between the United Kingdom and Venezuela in 1942, regarding the submarine areas of the Gulf of Paria[3] which was followed by the *Submarine Areas of the Gulf of Paria (Annexation) Order, 1942.* The real impetus to the development of this concept was, however, given only three years later by the Truman Proclamation of September 28th, 1945,[4] which formed the starting-point for a series of similar proclamations by the Latin-American and other States.

The novelty of this problem is relevant inasmuch as "historic rights" have been defined in an earlier chapter[5] as being either rights, the origins of which cannot be traced, or adverse rights, acquired at the expense of the former owner of the title. Neither of these assumptions would appear to apply in respect of the continental shelf. This statement necessitates, of course, a closer investigation of the nature of States' rights over their continental shelves and an examination of the basis of the title on which State claims to the continental shelf rest.

The precise nature of State rights over the continental shelf formed for years one of the focal points of controversy.[6] Various suggestions

[1] Mouton, *The Continental Shelf,* 1952, p. 1. Writing in 1950, Lauterpacht remarked that the expression "continental shelf" was "no more than a general indication of title to *areas of indeterminate extent.*" (27 *BYIL* (1950), pp. 384–385; italics added). This opinion truly reflects the confusion that pervaded this sphere until recently. For a detailed investigation of the various tests suggested in an attempt to find a working definition see also Johnson, "The Legal Status of the Sea-bed and Subsoil," 16 *ZRV* (1955–1956), pp. 451–500.

[2] Johnson, *loc. cit.,* p. 451; for further references on this point see n. 2 there.

[3] *Cmnd.* 6400 (1942); *United Kingdom Treaty Series,* No. 10 (1942).

[4] Published in 40 *AJIL* (1946), Supplement, pp. 45–46. See also *United Nations Legislative Series, Regulations on the Regime of the High Seas* (ST/LEG/SER. B/1), 1951, vol. I, pp. 38–39.

[5] See above, chapter III, sections 22 and 23.

[6] See the award rendered in the arbitration between *Petroleum Development (Trucial Coast)*

were put forward as to the basis of these rights; occupation, prescription and sovereignty *ipso jure* were mentioned on different occasions as possible roots of title to these areas. The clarification of this problem was greatly hampered by the inconsistent terminology employed by the various national proclamations. Some of them asserted rights of *sovereignty* of the coastal State,[1] while others contented themselves with assertions of "*jurisdiction and control*."[2]

The various national pretensions to exclusive rights of one kind or another over the continental shelf have been divided by Mouton as falling into three categories:

(a) claims to limited rights over the continental shelf outside the territorial sea (mainly over mineral resources);

(b) claims assuming the form of full sovereignty over the sea-bed and subsoil; and

(c) claims amounting to an extension of the territorial sea to distances going much beyond its normally accepted limits.[3]

As has been pointed out by Johnson, "the distinction between the first group and the second group is far less marked than that between the second and the third group. As a matter of practice it would be difficult for a country to assert a claim to the mineral resources of the continental shelf without also exercising control over all the natural resources of that shelf".[4]

Having regard to the provisions of article 3 of the *Continental Shelf Convention*, there is little doubt that the third group (namely, the group claiming sovereignty over the superjacent waters of the continental shelf) may be disregarded from the point of view of international law. Article 3 stipulates that

> the rights of the coastal State over the continental shelf do not affect the legal status of the superjacent waters as high seas, or that of the airspace above those waters.[5]

Moreover, as has been pointed out by Mouton, these claims were already considered as being contrary to international law even prior to the adoption of that Convention.[6]

The concept, according to which the title of the coastal State is based

Ltd. v. *the Sheikh of Abu Dhabi*, where Lord Asquith, the Umpire, discusses at some length the doctrine of the continental shelf, its substance and history. (1 *ICLQ* (1952), p. 247).

[1] Cf. Lauterpacht, *loc. cit.*, p. 389.

[2] Cf. *ibid.*, p. 388.

[3] Mouton, "The Continental Shelf," 85 *Hague Recueil* (1954), vol. I, pp. 367–379.

[4] Johnson, *loc. cit.*, p. 476.

[5] *Cmnd.* 584 (1959), p. 40.

[6] Mouton, 85 *Hague Recueil* (1954), vol. I, p. 424.

on "occupation," in the meaning habitually given to this term in international law, appears to be untenable for different reasons.

Firstly, it is at least debatable whether the sea-bed and subsoil are capable of "occupation," i.e. appropriation, in the sense in which land territory can be brought under the effective occupation of a State. These doubts persist even if we are to assume that the sea-bed and subsoil do, in fact, constitute a "territory" in the legal sense of this term – an assumption which is far from being unquestioned.[1]

Secondly – and this seems to be the stronger practical reason for denying "occupation" as the root of title to the continental shelf – the invocation of this concept invariably presupposes that the territory in question was hitherto *res nullius*, capable of appropriation by the first newcomer. The adoption of this concept with regard to the continental shelf would entail that in all those cases, in which the coastal State did not appropriate its continental shelf, any other State would be entitled to do so. It is not difficult to foresee the chaotic conditions which would follow, were such a course of action sanctioned by international law. Moreover, such a policy would clearly be to the disadvantage of the new and emerging nations as well as of those who, for the lack of economic means and technical and scientific knowledge, are unable – for the time being at least – to exploit their continental shelves in the manner in which this is being done by the "rich" countries.[2] In fact, all the State proclamations relating to the continental shelf have explicitly referred to the fact that the submarine areas in question border on their territories, thus stressing the special relationship linking them – to the exclusion of all other States – to their continental shelves.[3]

The reliance on an historic title or on a title akin to prescription must be equally dismissed. If it is true that, in the appropriation of its continental shelf, the coastal State has an exclusive and monopolistic status – and this assumption seems to be the correct one ever since the inception of this doctrine – then clearly the right of the coastal State over its continental shelf cannot be regarded as an *adverse* right, acquired as against a former possessor. Historic rights, however, do in the majority of cases belong to this category, as has amply been illustrated above.

[1] Cf. Lauterpacht, *loc. cit.*, p. 416.

[2] Cf. *ibid.*, p. 420.

[3] Article 2, paragraph 3, of the *Continental Shelf Convention* does not appear to be relevant on this point. It reads as follows: "The rights of the coastal State over the continental shelf do not depend on occupation, effective or notional, or on any express proclamation." (*Cmnd.* 584 (1959), p. 40). From the context it would appear that the term "occupation" is not employed here in the sense of meaning one of the modes of acquiring territory, but refers rather to a factual situation, i.e. the exercise of State authority.

The acquisition of such adverse rights is effected through the acquiescence of the party or parties affected and this acquiescence habitually expresses itself through the lack of protest against the exercise of effective authority by the newcomer. Article 2, paragraph 3, of the *Continental Shelf Convention*[1] makes it, however, sufficiently clear that the coastal State's rights do not presuppose the exercise of such authority – neither effective, nor notional.

In a minority of cases, it has been shown, historic rights are founded on "immemorial possession," i.e. on a situation which has lasted for so long that it is impossible to provide proof of a different situation; the origins of this situation remain at the same time uncertain. For obvious reasons, this test cannot be applied to a situation which seems to have originated only about a quarter of a century ago.

Yet another possibility for justifying the rights of the coastal State over its continental shelf would be by resorting to the concept of the "inchoate title," given a specific connotation, differing from that with which this notion is normally associated.[2] In this connection the invocation of this theory would mean that the littoral State is entitled *ipso jure* to the adjacent submarine areas, but that so long as it has not perfected its title by claiming it formally through the issue of a proclamation, declaratory of an existing right, the title is merely inchoate.[3]

This theory has been rejected by Mouton on the ground that the continental shelf – being a comparatively new conception – could not be justified on such a basis. "How," he asks, "could rights concerning a geographical formation exist before people were aware of its existence? ... And who had heard of resources in the continental shelf 30 years ago?"[4]

The wording of article 3 of the *Continental Shelf Convention* also seems to militate against this concept of an inchoate title which has to be followed up by proclamation, since it explicitly lays down the rule that "the rights of the coastal State do not depend... on any express proclamation."[5] Paragraph 2 of the same article, however, stipulates at the same time that the rights of the coastal State are not affected by their non-exercise and the fact that the littoral State chooses not to undertake

[1] *Ibid.*

[2] By "inchoate title" international law usually understands the acquisition of an imperfect title, the perfection of which is subject to the fulfilment of some further requirements. Thus, discovery, for instance, was considered in the past as an inchoate title which could be perfected if followed up within a reasonable period of time by an effective taking of possession.

[3] Lauterpacht, *loc. cit.*, p. 422.

[4] Mouton, *op. cit.*, p. 269.

[5] *Cmnd.* 584 (1959), p. 40.

the activities to which it is entitled does not confer such right on any other State. Thus, it can still be maintained that the littoral State does possess a sort of title *ipso jure*, which is a result of its owning the coast to which the continental shelf is adjacent. The title thus invoked would appear to be a mixture of a claim *ipso jure* coupled with the doctrine of contiguity. This idea was advanced by Waldock when he suggested that "we should recognise an entirely new doctrine of customary law under which the continental shelf vests *ipso jure* in the coastal State on the analogy of territorial waters or territorial air space.... The suggested new doctrine of the continental shelf, therefore, is not merely novel, but involves a reversal of existing customary law."[1] Mouton, while admitting that this is an attractive idea, has his doubts as to its usefulness in explaining the juridical status of the continental shelf. He contends that the theory of contiguity has not acquired the status of a generally recognized rule of international law and, whatever its value in the past, it is now obsolete.[2]

The theory which regards contiguity as the legal basis underlying the national claims to rights over the continental shelf has met with the approval and support of Lauterpacht who observes that most of the proclamations on this topic have invoked the fact of contiguity and of geographical unity.[3] He stresses at the same time the fact that "the basis of title appears to be not contiguity in the accepted sense, i.e. as connoting horizontal prolongation of the already occupied territory, but a different, and apparently more intense, degree of unity – a unity provided by the fact that the shelf is supposed to constitute the base, the platform, on which the continent rests."[4] Referring to the objections that are usually raised against this concept – namely, (a) that it has never become part of international law and that it was rejected by international tribunals; and (b) that it represented a theory which, because of its vagueness and comprehensiveness, was full of dangerous implications – Lauterpacht remarks that neither of these objections can be regarded as valid. Basing himself on doctrine, State practice and international case-law alike,[5] he reaches the conclusion that this concept may legitimately be resorted to even to-day. He warns at the same time that this theory – like that of "effective occupation" – is one

[1] Waldock, "The Legal Basis of Claims to the Continental Shelf," *Grotius Transactions*, vol. 36 (1950), p. 115, at pp. 142–143.
[2] Cf. Mouton, *loc. cit.*, p. 428. On the problem of contiguity, see above, chapter IV, section 51.
[3] Lauterpacht, *loc. cit.*, pp. 423–424.
[4] *Ibid.*, p. 424.
[5] *Ibid.*, pp. 425–427.

of relative value, and he suggests that it should be used "with such discretion as the equities of the case and considerations of stability require."[1]

As to the second objection, Lauterpacht remarks that "no device can prevent the abuse of a rule or principle, however otherwise useful and reasonable, by unilateral claims of states which refuse to submit disputed issues to impartial adjudication."[2]

Gidel, likewise, regards the title of the littoral State to its continental shelf as based on a "droit inhérent," flowing from the fact of geographical proximity.[3]

The International Law Commission adopted a similar view, when, in its Report to the General Assembly covering the work of its 8th session, it remarked that it was impossible

> to disregard the geographical phenomenon whatever the term – propinquity, contiguity, geographical continuity, appurtenance or identity – used to define the relationship between the submarine areas in question and the adjacent non-submerged land.[4]

These views seem to have found substantial support in the provisions contained in the *Continental Shelf Convention*. Article 3, paragraph 3, has already been referred to above. The article embodies the principle that the rights of the coastal State over its continental shelf should not depend on occupation, effective or notional, or on any express proclamation. Paragraph 1 of the same article provides that "the *coastal* State exercises over the continental shelf sovereign rights."[5] The italicized word of the passage just quoted seems to convey the idea that the rights of the State are a result of its being in possession of the coast, which, in fact, amounts

[1] *Ibid.*, p. 429.

[2] *Ibid.*, p. 430. See however, Böhmert, "Meeresfreiheit und Schelfproklamationen," 5 *Jahrbuch für internationales Recht* (1954), pp. 25–26, where the author criticizes the views propounded by Lauterpacht on the ground that the theory of contiguity never achieved the degree of a legal norm of international law. See also the same author, *ibid.* vol. 6 (1955), pp. 88–92. See also the criticism levelled by Waldock against this doctrine, as applied to the claims to the continental shelf, in *Grotius Transactions*, vol. 36 (1950), pp. 137–142, where he claims that the concept of contiguity is "a thoroughly dangerous principle, being one of the banners under which nationalist expansion has frequently sought to justify itself." (*Ibid.*, p. 139). He also points out that contiguity "once adopted as a legal principle, would sooner or later be used to attack established titles." *(Ibid.)*.

[3] Gidel, "A propos des bases juridiques des prétentions des Etats riverains sur le plateau continental: les doctrines du 'droit inhérent,'" 19 *ZRV* (1958), pp. 81–101, where he claims that, since the continental shelf is "une extension de la masse continentale riveraine, il est juste que l'Etat riverain ait le droit d'exploiter... les ressources naturelles du plateau continental; il serait dangereux pour la sécurité de l'Etat riverain que le plateau continental fût l'objet, à cet effet, d'activités de la part d'autres Etats...; l'exploitation *optima* du plateau continental ne peut se faire qu'... avec le consentement de l'Etat riverain." (*Ibid.*, p. 99, italics in original).

[4] *ILC Yearbook*, 8th session, 1956, vol. II, p. 298.

[5] *Cmnd.* 584 (1959), p. 40. (Italics added).

to the adoption of the theory of contiguity in disguise. This argument only gains additional weight in view of the provisions of paragraph 2 of the same article which stipulates that the rights of the coastal State "are exclusive in the sense that if the coastal State does not explore the continental shelf or exploit its natural resources, no one may undertake these activities or make a claim to the continental shelf, without the express consent of the coastal State."[1]

It may be pertinent to add that, according to article 2, paragraph 4, of the Convention, the natural resources, the exploration and exploitation of which are the exclusive right of the coastal State, include, in addition to the mineral and other non-living resources of the sea-bed and subsoil, also living organisms belonging to the sedentary species, which are defined as "organisms which, at the harvestable stage, either are immobile on or under the sea–bed or are unable to move except in constant physical contact with the sea-bed or the subsoil."[2] Thus, all those forms of sedentary fisheries, which are performed within the continental shelf of the coastal State – in so far as they are covered by the definition given in the Convention – are merged in the doctrine of the continental shelf and are reserved exclusively for the littoral State. The remaining forms of sedentary fisheries, as well as those carried out on the high seas, and the relevance of historic claims to such fisheries, will be discussed in the next section.

76. Sedentary fisheries as historic rights

The term "*sedentary fisheries*" has been used in the past in a twofold meaning:

(a) to denote fisheries of sedentary *species*, i.e. organisms which are found on or under the sea-bed or are unable to move except in constant physical contact with the sea-bed or the subsoil;

(b) to denote fisheries carried out by means of *structures* erected on the sea-bed for mobile species.

The former kind of sedentary fisheries will be referred to hereinafter as "natural sedentary fisheries," while the latter will be termed "structural sedentary fisheries."

The origins of known sedentary fisheries go back as far as the sixth century A.D. The best-known instances of ancient sedentary fisheries are the pearl fisheries off the coasts of Ceylon and India, in the Persian

[1] *Ibid.*
[2] *Ibid.*

Gulf (Bahrein, Kuwait, Quatar), as well as sponge fishing off the coasts of Tunisia and pearl fishing off the coasts of Australia.[1]

The rights of exclusive sedentary fisheries on the high seas of States whose nationals have been engaged in such activities do not appear to have been seriously questioned by writers on international law. "Qui doutera," asks Vattel, "que les pêcheries de perles de Bahrem et de Ceylan ne puissent légitimement tomber en propriété?"[2]

The nature of the coastal State's exclusive rights to sedentary fisheries has been less clear. Certain writers have invoked "occupation" as the basis of such rights,[3] while others have relied on the doctrine of prescription.[4]

Oppenheim takes the view that these fisheries form an exception to the doctrine of the freedom of the high seas. Referring to the Ceylonese and Bahreini pearl fisheries, he asserts that we are faced with an historically recognized anomaly of customary international law, based on the absolute and general recognition by the international community.[5]

Whatever the juridical basis of exclusive State claims to sedentary fisheries on the high seas, it would appear that the process of formation of these rights is, in fact, identical with that observed in the emergence of historic rights in general, namely, assertion of exclusive State authority, on the one hand, and acquiescence in such exercise of authority, on the other hand. Gidel, who considers the right to exclusive sedentary fisheries outside the territorial sea of the State as irreconcilable with the general notion of the freedom of the high seas, maintains that such rights can be acquired only through "*l'usage effectif et prolongé* d'une partie de la haute mer aux fins de pêcheries sédentaires, *sans* que les autres Etats, et spécialement ceux qui pourraient du fait leur situation géographique faire valoir des objections particulières, aient opposé a cet usage des *protestations* formelles et persistantes."[6]

The above-quoted passage from Gidel, and in particular its italicized words, clearly bring out his conviction that the rights to exclusive sedentary fisheries on the high seas are acquired in precisely the same manner as historic rights in general.

[1] For a detailed study of State practice on this point in general see Papandréou, "La situation juridique des pêcheries sédentaires en haute-mer," 11 *Revue Hellénique de Droit International* (1958), pp. 1–148, at pp. 40–73. See also McDougal and Burke, *op. cit.*, pp. 642–663.

[2] Vattel, *op. cit.*, book I, chapter XXIII, para. 287.

[3] See e.g. Westlake, *op. cit.*, part I, pp. 190–191. See also Hurst, "Whose is the Bed of the Sea?," 4 *BYIL* (1923–1924), pp. 34–43.

[4] See e.g. Lindley, *op. cit.*, p. 169.

[5] Oppenheim, "Der Tunnel unter dem Ärmelkanal und das Völkerrecht," *Zeitschrift für Völkerrecht und Bundesstaatsrecht* (1908), pp. 6–10.

[6] Gidel, *op. cit.*, vol. I, pp. 500–501. (Italics added).

When the problem of sedentary fisheries was first discussed by the International Law Commission, it was agreed there that "sedentary fisheries should be regulated independently of the problem of the continental shelf."[1] The reason for this distinction was, according to the comments contained in the 1951 Report of the Commission, that "the proposals relating to the continental shelf are concerned with the exploitation of the *mineral resources* of the subsoil, whereas, in the case of sedentary fisheries, the proposals refer to fisheries regarded as sedentary because of the species caught or the equipment used, e.g. stakes embedded in the sea-floor. This distinction justifies a division of the two problems."[2] The Commission at the same time recognized the historic rights of coastal States to regulate sedentary fisheries in areas where such fisheries have long been maintained and conducted by the nationals of that State.[3]

In 1953 the International Law Commission reversed its former opinion on this question when it concluded that "the products of sedentary fisheries, in particular to the extent that they were natural resources permanently attached to the bed of the sea, should not be outside the scope of the régime adopted... [and] the sovereign rights of the coastal State over its continental shelf cover also sedentary fisheries."[4] The former draft article on sedentary fisheries was accordingly dropped. After much discussion in the Fourth Committee of the First United Nations Conference on the Law of the Sea it was decided to include natural sedentary fisheries also in the definition of "natural resources," the exploration and exploitation of which are reserved for the coastal State.[5] The relevant provision was carried in the plenary meeting of the Conference by 59 votes to 5, with 6 abstentions.[6]

Thus, it would appear that the coastal State's rights to sedentary fisheries in its continental shelf were assimilated by the Conference to the rights accruing to the coastal State in that area in general.

As to traditional rights of sedentary fisheries outside the continental shelf, i.e. on the high seas, the relevant provision is to be found in article 13, paragraph 1, of the 1958 Geneva *Convention on Fishing and Conservation of the Living Resources of the High Seas*, which reads as follows:

[1] *ILC Yearbook*, 3rd session, 1951, vol. II, p. 143.
[2] *Ibid.* (Italics added).
[3] *Ibid.*
[4] *ILC Yearbook*, 5th session, 1953, vol. II, p. 214.
[5] *Cmnd.* 584 (1959), p. 40, article 2, paragraph 4.
[6] *United Nations Conference on the Law of the Sea, Official Records*, vol. II, *Plenary Meetings*, p. 15

The regulation of fisheries conducted by means of equipment embedded in the floor of the sea in areas of the high seas adjacent to the territorial sea of a State may be undertaken by that State where such fisheries have long been maintained and conducted by its nationals, provided that non-nationals are permitted to participate in such activities on an equal footing with nationals *except in areas where such fisheries have by long usage been exclusively enjoyed by such nationals*. Such regulations will not, however, affect the general status of the areas as high seas.[1]

Thus, this provision – if and when it comes into force[2] – will have the effect of safeguarding traditional structural sedentary fisheries rights on the high seas. It does not provide, however, for natural sedentary fisheries rights in such areas. The silence of the Convention on this point may be interpreted either as amounting to a denial of the existence of such rights or as indicating that, inasmuch as such rights have been based till now on customary norms of international law, this situation is not intended to be altered by the Convention.

It may confidently be asserted that the legal problems attendant upon sedentary fisheries in general have considerably lost momentum since the incorporation of this problem within the general question of the juridical status of the continental shelf. One is therefore tempted to subscribe to the proposition made by Young, in whose view "[the] proponents of national claims to sedentary fisheries were rescued from an increasingly precarious position by the timely advent of the continental shelf concept."[3] It may also be doubted whether this concept of traditional sedentary fisheries rights has ever acquired such notoriety as to make a lack of challenge equivalent to acquiescence. According to Young, from time to time some examples of State practice ran against the concept.[4]

Thus, it can safely be predicted that henceforth the status of sedentary fisheries will have to be considered as part and parcel of the continental shelf doctrine.[5]

[1] *Cmnd.* 584 (1959), p. 38. (Italics added). According to paragraph 2 of the same article, "the expression 'fisheries conducted by means of equipment embedded in the floor of the sea' means those fisheries using gear with supporting members embedded in the sea floor, constructed on a site and left there to operate permanently, or, if removed, restored each season on the same site."

[2] By September 1964 the Geneva *Convention on Fishing and Conservation of the Living Resources of the High Seas* was signed by 37 States; 17 States also ratified the Convention.

[3] Young, "Sedentary Fisheries and the Convention on the Continental Shelf," 55 *AJIL* (1961), p. 359, at p. 369.

[4] *Ibid.*, p. 360, n. 7, and p. 369, n. 38.

[5] This has been the course followed by the Government of Australia in an attempt to exclude Japanese fishermen from areas which Australia considered to be traditional fishing grounds of her nationals. For a discussion of the legal problems involved there see O'Connell, "Sedentary Fisheries and the Australian Continental Shelf," 49 *AJIL* (1955), p. 185 *et seq.*; See also Mouton, 85, *Hague Recueil* (1954), vol. I, pp. 445–449; see also Papandréou, *loc. cit.*, pp. 40–49.

CHAPTER VII

CONCLUSIONS

77. *Consolidation as the legal root of historic titles*

The term "historic title" – the emphasis being on the qualifying adjective "historic" – clearly brings out, in spite of the deficiencies inherent in the employment of this term, the distinctive feature which distinguishes this international territorial title from the remaining modes of acquisition of territory. This difference is marked by the fact that, while all the other titles rest on an instantaneous act having an immediate effect, to which act the origins of such titles can be traced, the historic title is the outcome of a lengthy process comprising a long series of acts, omissions and patterns of behaviour which, in their entirety, and through their cumulative effect, bring such a title into being and *consolidate* it into a title valid in international law. In these final remarks it is proposed to focus attention on the italicized word of the foregoing phrase, because recent writers seised of the problems attendant on historic titles have, with increasing frequency and with a steadily growing emphasis, referred to the notion of "historical consolidation" as to the legal concept which underlies the process of the formation of an historic title.[1]

The term "historical consolidation" with regard to the acquisition of an historic title was first resorted to in a dictum in the *Fisheries* case where the International Court of Justice justified the juridical validity of the application by Norway of the "Norwegian method" of straight baselines on the ground of "an historical consolidation which would make it enforceable as against all States."[2]

It was this dictum that encouraged recent writers to make it the starting-point for a new presentation of the topics relating to international titles in general and to historic titles in particular. De

[1] Among recent contributions on this subject, see de Visscher, *op. cit.* See also Johnson, "Consolidation as a Root of Title in International Law," *Cambridge Law Journal* (1955), p. 215 *et seq.* See also Schwarzenberger, *op. cit.*, pp. 290–292 and 51 *AJIL* (1957), pp. 310–311. See also Roche, *op. cit.*, pp. 68–73.

[2] *ICJ Reports*, 1951, p. 138.

Visscher, who had been one of the judges in the *Fisheries* case, took the lead when, in a book first published in 1953, he interpreted the term "consolidation" as resting on a process of historical evolution and based on the maxim *quieta non movere*, which had already found favour with the Permanent Court of Arbitration in the *Grisbadarna* case.[1] He pointed out that "proven long usage, which is its foundation, merely represents a complex of interests and relations which in themselves have the effect of attaching a territory or an expanse of sea to a given State."[2] He distinguished "consolidation" from "prescription" by stating that, while the latter is based on the notion of adverse possession, the former can apply also to territories that could not be proved to have belonged to another State; the distinction between "consolidation" and "occupation" lies in the fact that "consolidation" applies not only to land territories, but can also be resorted to with regard to the acquisition of maritime areas. Finally, it differs from recognition, which has an instantaneous effect, in that it normally comes about through the acquiescence of States, which, in turn, is evidenced through a sufficiently prolonged absence of opposition by interested States.[3] The time factor as such, however, has no creative force of its own and, where acquiescence can be otherwise proved, lapse of time is not required.

De Visscher has thus embraced under a single heading of "consolidation" both "prescription" and "immemorial possession," by founding both on the juridical basis of acquiescence.

The introduction of the notion of "consolidation" as a mode of acquiring territory has, according to Schwarzenberger, thrown light on the process of "evolution and expansion of international society."[4] He makes the point that, by having recourse to the concept of consolidation, three essential features of this process become apparent:

(a) the acquisition of an international title is a gradual process;
(b) during the period of its initiation a territorial title is a relative one and its holder aspires to transform it into an absolute title, to be valid *erga omnes*; and
(c) the more absolute the title becomes, the more multiple its legal foundations.

The gradual evolution of the territorial title through a continuous and sometimes lengthy process of *consolidation* is merely a reflection on

[1] Scott, *Hague Court Reports*, 1st series, 1916, p. 130; *UNRIAA*, vol. XI, p. 161.
[2] De Visscher, *op. cit.*, p. 200.
[3] *Ibid.*, pp. 200–201.
[4] Schwarzenberger, *op. cit.*, p. 292.

the present imperfect stage of international law. It underlines, to quote once more Schwarzenberger, "the unsatisfactory character of any attempt to put the operative rules into the strait jacket of private law analogies. Owing to the existence of a central authority in highly developed communities, absolute titles can be granted with immediate effect *erga omnes*. International society lacks such a central authority,"[1] and the result is that territorial rights are, in their beginnings, frequently only relative rights which are perfected in the course of time and thus become absolute rights.

In order to achieve this degree of absolute validity, titles acquired by a process of consolidation must be constantly *maintained*, and it is one of the additional merits of the theory of consolidation that it combines under the same heading both the *acquisition* of a territorial title and its subsequent *maintenance*. This aspect of the approach putting forward historical consolidation as a valid root of title appears to be particularly welcome, because the relative longevity of international persons has often made it necessary – in accordance with the rules of intertemporal law – to apply different norms to the establishment of titles on the one hand, and to their maintenance and extinction on the other hand, thus further obscuring the already complex rules governing this branch of international law.[2] To quote the award rendered by Judge Huber in the *Island of Palmas* case, "if the contestation is based on the fact that the other Party has actually displayed sovereignty, it cannot be sufficient to establish the title by which territorial sovereignty was validly acquired at a certain moment; it must also be shown that the territorial sovereignty has *continued* to exist."[3]

This virtue of the doctrine of consolidation (i.e. that it makes the validity under international law of a territorial title contingent not merely on the proper *acquisition* of rights, but also on their *maintenance*, carries with it, incidentally, the seeds of the weakness of a title acquired by consolidation, and is one of the major sources of its vulnerability, in that it might compel a State to examine constantly its title to each portion of its territory.[4] The rigours of this criticism are, however,

[1] *Ibid.* (Italics in original).

[2] For a more detailed discussion of this problem in relation to the application of intertemporal law, see above, chapter V, section 55.

[3] *UNRIAA*, vol. II, p. 839. (Italics added).

[4] Cf. Jessup, 22 *AJIL* (1928), pp. 740–741. For a criticism of the concept of historical consolidation see also Jennings, *op. cit.*, pp. 26–28, where he asserts, *inter alia*, that "the name *historical* consolidation is indeed in some measure a misnomer, for the tendency of consolidation is rather to augment the significance of relatively recent possession." (Italics in original).

considerably reduced and mitigated by the fact that the manifestations required for the "maintenance" of an already acquired title vary in accordance with circumstances.[1]

78. Critical appraisal of the doctrine of historic titles

Seen in this light, the process of consolidation, rather than upsetting the territorial structure of international society and shaking the legal foundations of territorial titles, would appear to represent a welcome contribution towards the promotion of international stability. Here again, however, one has to be mindful of the danger inherent in the excessive recourse to any legal device which is basically intended to fulfil the role of a safety valve. The doctrine of historic titles was originally invoked to provide for a smooth transfer of international law from the now obsolete notions of the Middle Ages to the more dynamic concepts of modern international law. With the emergence of the new sets of norms governing the rules of sovereignty, it became apparent that many a title, which was formerly held valid under a different regime of law, would be invalidated by the superseding rules of international law.

Thus, in order to achieve a necessary measure of stability in international relations and to ensure the harmonious co-operation of the Powers whose acquired rights might have been affected by too stringent an application of the new rules of law and a stubborn and indiscriminate insistence on their enforcement, international law was prepared to recognize the juridical validity of otherwise unlawful situations. It can hardly be denied that the invocation of the doctrine of historic titles and the resulting sanctioning of certain acquired privileged situations tends to operate to the advantage of what Westlake calls the "old countries,"[2] (meaning essentially the European Powers, and applied both to the territories of the mother countries and to their overseas dependencies), to the exclusion of the "new countries," i.e. all those countries which, owing to the brevity of their existence, were unable to build up such a privileged claim.

Against this background one might perhaps feel more sympathetic towards the assertion made by the delegate of Bulgaria at the Second Geneva Conference on the Law of the Sea. As will be recalled, the

[1] Cf. Johnson, *Cambridge Law Journal* (1955), pp. 224–225.
[2] Westlake, *op. cit.*, p. 90.

delegate of Bulgaria saw in the doctrine of historic rights "a product of an invidious tendency... to elevate the dominant position of technically advanced countries into a system of legally sanctioned privileges."[1] Utterances such as this are, of course, not motivated by purely legal reasons, and it is not difficult to detect in them the familiar ring of argumentation characteristic of one of the major political trends of our days. Whether the Bulgarian delegate was right in accusing the supporters of the doctrine of historic rights of wishing to perpetuate, under the cloak of this legal theory, a dominant position acquired under an out-dated and now obsolescent international regime, is a question which has its roots outside the sphere of law. He was doubtless entitled to warn that certain States might be tempted to abuse a legal device, which was originally contemplated as an emergency solution to be applied in rare and exceptional circumstances. The dispassionate observer will have to admit, however, that any dangers inherent in the tendency to inflate the doctrine of historic rights are not circumvented at all when for the "historic" element is substituted the "vital" factor, a tendency which has been frequently displayed in the policies of the "new" countries. This practice is surely yet another proof of what has always been a truism for the impartial and unbiased observer, namely, that the vigilant and selfish preservation of special advantages is by no means the monopoly of the "old" countries. One has therefore to recognize the danger of excessive national pretensions, one of whose manifestations may be an exaggerated "historic" claim, whatever its origin, purpose and motivation.

The doctrine of historic rights must be regarded as a necessary, though undesirable, device ensuring a measure of stability and good order required for the smooth functioning of the international community. It should be borne in mind at the same time that the ultimate objective of international law is a uniform world-wide legal system and that any regional, local or otherwise exceptional arrangement, however indispensable at present, constitutes an obstacle in the way of attaining this goal. The true interests of the international community lie therefore not in the perpetuation – let alone extension – of a regime which aims at disrupting the trends of unifying international law, but rather in an unflinching effort to reduce to a bare minimum the number of rules which are derogatory of the uniform rules of general international law and are relics of an ancient and more particularist legal order. Thus,

[1] *Second United Nations Conference on the Law of the Sea, Official Records*, p. 113.

the diminishing significance and eventual fading away of the doctrine of historic rights – should this ever occur – might be regarded as a further milestone reached by international society in its efforts to shake off the yoke of particularism and to pave the way for the blessings of true internationalism.

UTI POSSIDETIS IN INTERNATIONAL LAW

The term *uti possidetis* should be used with caution in international law. The term is derived from Roman law in which it was used to denote an edict of the *praetor*, the purpose of which was to preserve, pending litigation, an existing state of possession of an immovable *nec vi, nec clam, nec precario,* as between individual claimants. The meaning of this term, when used with regard to international boundaries in Latin America, is somewhat different from that ascribed to it in civil law and is intended to denote *permanent* rather than temporary possession. In the words of the Uruguayan diplomatist Guani, it means "que les pays formant notre continent ont domination et sont considérés comme possesseurs des territoires qui leur appartenaient respectivement... au moment de la déclaration d'indépendance [en 1810], conformément aux limites, spécialement d'ordre administratif, que les couronnes d'Espagne et du Portugal avaient assignées à leurs provinces."[1]

When Spanish control over Hispanic America came to an end, each of the new States tended to follow the lines of cleavage which had previously divided the Spanish administrative units. However, the demarcation of these units had rarely been defined by the Spaniards and the resulting uncertainty caused a series of boundary disputes. In many instances the arbitrators appointed to settle these disputes were called upon by the parties to apply as their criterion the rule of *uti possidetis* of the period of independence. The assumption in all these cases was that it was possible to trace, by a study of the Spanish decrees, the precise lines of division of the former administrative units. However, more often than not, this assumption was not borne out by the realities; it was found that in many instances the new States exercised at the time of the cessation of the Spanish rule – sometimes *bona fide* and without intentional usurpation – State authority beyond the border lines apparently designated as the limit of their territorial jurisdiction. The State which had expanded in this manner was prone to insist that the meaning of *uti possidetis* was administrative possession as it *actually* existed at the time of independence, while the opposing party to the dispute usually contended that the principle implied the restriction of sovereignty to those areas which were *rightfully* occupied by the antecedent colonial unit. The two conflicting theories of *uti possidetis* became accordingly known as "*uti possidetis de facto*" and "*uti possidetis juris,*" respectively, and the resulting confusion has led Lapradelle to suggest that the theory of *uti possidetis* be discarded altogether.[2]

According to the award rendered in the *Guatemala-Honduras Boundary* Arbitration, a tribunal called upon to pronounce in a territorial dispute which is to be decided in accordance with the principle of *uti possidetis*, "must have regard (1) to the facts of actual possession; (2) to the question whether possession by one Party has been acquired in

[1] Guani, "La solidarité dans l'Amérique Latine," 8 *Hague Recueil* (1925), vol. III, p. 207 *et seq.*, at p. 293.

[2] Lapradelle, *La frontière*, 1928, p. 86.

good faith, and without invading the right of the other Party; and (3) to the relation of territory actually occupied to that which is as yet unoccupied."[1]

In any event, the doctrine of *uti possidetis* can be considered merely as "a principle by which the American Republics have decided to adjust their boundary differences. But in no case has the International Community recognized, as an institution of international law, the principle of *uti possidetis*.... It remains... derogatory to general international law... binding only on those... [who] have, by a convention, expressly agreed to it."[2]

More recently, it has been pointed out by Schwarzenberger that "even so obvious a 'loan' from Roman law as is the use of *uti possidetis* in the Latin-American practice... is more indicative of the differences between this remedy in Roman law and its application on the inter-state level than of any supposed likeness between these two institutions".[3]

[1] *UNRIAA*, vol. II, p. 1352; this passage of the award is also quoted in Green, *International Law through the Cases*, 2nd edition, 1959, at p. 369.

[2] Bloomfield, *The British Honduras-Guatemala Dispute*, 1953, p. 94. (Italics in original).

[3] Schwarzenberger, 51 *AJIL* (1957), p. 309. As to more detailed discussions on the theory of *uti possidetis*, see Moore, *Memorandum on Uti Possidetis*, 1913; see also Guani, *loc. cit.*, pp. 293–310; see also Fisher "The Arbitration of the Guatemalan-Honduran Boundary Dispute," 27 *AJIL* (1933), p. 403 *et seq.*, at p. 415 and the references mentioned there at p. 416, note 50; see also Waldock, 25 *BYIL* (1948), pp. 325–326; see also Bloomfield, *op. cit.*, pp. 78–96.

SELECTED BIBLIOGRAPHY

(A) TREATISES, MANUALS, DIGESTS AND OTHER GENERAL WORKS OF INTERNATIONAL LAW

Anzilotti, D., *Cours de droit international* (translated from the Italian by Gidel), Paris, 1929, vol. I.

Balladore Pallieri, G., *Diritto internazionale pubblico*, 7th rev. ed., Milano, 1956.

Brierly, J. L., *The Law of Nations*, 6th edition, edited by Waldock, Oxford, 1963.

Calvo, C., *Le droit international théorique et pratique*, 5th edition, Paris, 1896, 6 volumes.

Cavaré, L., *Le droit international public positif*, 2nd rev. ed., Paris, 1961–2, 2 volumes.

Cobbett, W. P., *Leading Cases on International Law*, 4th edition, London, 1922–4, 2 volumes.

Fauchille, P., *Traité de droit international public*, 8th edition, Paris, 1921–1926, 2 volumes.

Grotius, H., *De Jure Belli ac Pacis (libri tres)*, the Classics of International Law, edited by J. B. Scott, translated by F. W. Kelsey, Oxford, London, 1925.

— *De Jure Praedae Commentarius*, the Classics of International Law, edited by J. B. Scott, translated by G. L. Williams, Oxford, London, 1950, vol. I.

— *Mare Liberum*, the Classics of International Law, edited by J. B. Scott, translated by Magoffin, New York, 1916.

Guggenheim, P., *Traité de droit international public*, Geneva, 1953–1954, 2 volumes.

Hackworth, G. H., *Digest of International Law*, Washington, 1940–1943, 8 volumes.

Hall, W. E., *A Treatise on International Law*, 8th ed. (edited by Higgins), Oxford, 1924.

Heffter, A. W., *Das europäische Völkerrecht der Gegenwart*, 8th ed. (edited by Geffcken), Berlin, 1888.

Hershey, A. S., *The Essentials of International Public Law*, New York, 1912.

Hertslet, L., *A Complete Collection of the Treaties and Conventions... between Great Britain and Foreign Powers*, London, 1840–1925, 31 volumes.

Hyde, C. C., *International Law Chiefly as Interpreted and Applied by the United States*, 2nd rev. ed., Boston, 1945, 3 volumes.

Kelsen, H., *Principles of International Law*, New York, 1952.

La Fontaine, H., *Pasicrisie internationale*, Berne, 1902.

Lapradelle, A. G. de, and Politis N., *Recueil des arbitrages internationaux*, Paris, 1905–1954, 3 volumes.

Lawrence, T. J., *The Principles of International Law*, 7th revised edition (edited by Winfield), London, 1923.

Louter, J. de, *Le droit international public positif* (translated from the Dutch), London, New York, 1920, 2 volumes.

Martens, G. F., *Nouveau recueil de traités... des Puissances et Etats de l'Europe, 1808–1839*, Göttingen, 1817–1841, 16 volumes.

— *Nouveau recueil général de traités (Deuxième série), 1853–1907*, Göttingen, 1876–1910, 36 volumes.

— *Précis du droit des gens moderne de l'Europe*, revised edition, Paris, 1858.

Moore, J. B., *A Digest of International Law*, Washington, 1906, 8 volumes.

— *History and Digest of International Arbitrations to which the United States has been a Party*, Washington, 1898, 6 volumes.
— *International Adjudications (Modern Series)*, New York, 1929–1933, 6 volumes.
Nys, E., *Le droit international* (revised edition), Bruxelles, 1912.
Oppenheim, L. F. L., *International Law; a Treatise*, 8th ed., edited by Lauterpacht, London, New York, 1955, vol. I.
Phillimore, R. J., *Commentaries upon International Law*, 3rd ed., London, 1879–1888, 4 volumes.
Rivier, A. P. O., *Principes du droit des gens*, Paris, 1896, 2 volumes.
Ross, A., *A Text-Book of International Law*, London, New York, 1947.
Rousseau, Ch., *Droit international public approfondi*, Paris, 1961.
— *Principes généraux du droit international public*, Paris, 1944, vol. I.
Scelle, G., *Droit international public*, Paris, 1944.
Schwarzenberger, G., *International Law*, 3rd ed., London, 1957.
Scott, J. B., *Cases on International Law*, St. Paul, 1922.
— *Hague Court Reports*, 1st Series, New York, 1916.
Sibert, M., *Traité de droit international public*, Paris, 1951, vol. I.
Smith, H. A., *Great Britain and the Law of Nations*, London, 1932–1935, 2 volumes.
Starke, J. G., *An Introduction to International Law*, 5th edition, London, 1963.
Strupp, K., *Eléments du droit international public*, 2nd ed., Paris, 1930, 2 volumes.
— *Grundzüge des positiven Völkerrechts*, Bonn, 1921.
Strupp, K., *Wörterbuch des Völkerrechts*, 2nd edition, edited by Schlochauer, Berlin, 1960, vol. I.
Vattel, E. de, *Droit des gens*, the Classics of International Law, edited by J. B. Scott, translated by C. G. Fenwick, Washington, 1916.
Verdross, A., *Völkerrecht*, 4th ed., Wien, 1959.
Westlake, J., *International Law*, 2nd ed., Cambridge, 1910, 2 volumes.
Wheaton, H., *Elements of International Law*, 8th American ed. (edited by Dana), Boston, 1866.
Wilson, G. G., *The Hague Arbitration Cases*, Boston, 1915.

(B) MONOGRAPHS OF INTERNATIONAL LAW

Adamiyat, F., *Bahrein Islands*, New York, 1955.
Bianchi, W. J., *Belize: The Controversy between Guatemala and Great Britain over the Territory of British Honduras in Central America*, New York, 1959.
Bleiber, F., *Die Entdeckung im Völkerrecht*, Greifswald, 1933.
Bloomfield, L. M., *Egypt, Israel and the Gulf of Aqaba in International Law*, Toronto, 1957.
— *The British Honduras-Guatemala Dispute*, Toronto, 1953.
Brüel, E., *International Straits*, London, 1947, 2 volumes.
Charpentier, J., *La reconnaissance en droit international et l'évolution du droit des gens*, Paris, 1956.
Colombos, C. J., *The International Law of the Sea*, 5th rev. ed., London, 1962.
Gidel, G., *Le droit international public de la mer; le temps de paix*, Paris, 1932–1934, 3 volumes.
Goebel, J. Jr., *The Struggle for the Falkland Islands*, New Haven, 1927.

Hartingh, F. de, *Les conceptions soviétiques du droit de la mer*, Paris, 1960.
Heimburger, K., *Der Erwerb der Gebietshoheit*, Karlsruhe, 1888, Part I.
Hudson, M. O., *The Permanent Court of International Justice 1920–1942*, New York, 1943.
Jenks, C. W., *The Prospects of International Adjudication*, London, New York, 1964.
Jennings, R. Y., *The Acquisition of Territory in International Law*, Manchester, New York, 1963.
Jessup, P. C., *The Law of Territorial Waters and Maritime Jurisdiction*, New York, 1927.
Lapradelle, P. de, *La frontière: étude de droit international*, Paris, 1928.
Lauterpacht, H., *Private Law Sources and Analogies in International Law*, London, New York, 1927.
— *The Development of International Law by the International Court*, London, 1958.
— *The Function of Law in the International Community*, Oxford, 1933.
Lindley, M. F., *The Acquisition and Government of Backward Territory in International Law*, London, New York, 1926.
McDougal, M. S., and Burke, W. T., *The Public Order of the Oceans*, New Haven and London, 1962.
Mochot, J., *Le régime des baies et des golfes en droit international*, Paris, 1938.
Mouton, M. W., *The Continental Shelf*, The Hague, 1952.
Ortolan, E., *Des moyens d'acquérir le domaine international*, Paris, 1851.
Perels, F., *Das internationale öffentliche Seerecht der Gegenwart*, 2nd revised edition, Berlin, 1903.
— *Manuel de droit maritime international* (translated from the German, edited by Arendt), Paris, 1884.
Raestad, A., *La mer territoriale*, Paris, 1913.
Roche, A. G., *The Minquiers and Ecrehos Case*, Geneva, 1959.
Rosenne, Sh., *The International Court of Justice*, Leyden, 1957.
Sørensen, M., *Law of the Sea*, International Conciliation, No. 520, New York, 1958.
— *Les sources du droit international*, Copenhagen, 1946.
Suy, E., *Les actes juridiques unilatéraux en droit international public*, Paris, 1962.
Váli, F. A., *Servitudes of International Law*, 2nd edition, London, 1958.
Versfelt, W. J. B., *The Miangas Arbitration*, Utrecht, 1933.
Verykios, P. A., *La prescription en droit international public*, Paris, 1934.
Visscher, Ch. de, *Theory and Reality in Public International Law* (translated from the French by P. E. Corbett), Princeton, 1957.
Wenzel, M., *Die Hoheitsrechte in der Lübecker Bucht*, Rostock, 1926.

(c) ARTICLES IN PERIODICALS

including lectures delivered at the Hague Academy of International Law and papers read before the Grotius Society.

Alexander, L. M., "Offshore Claims and Fisheries in North-West Europe," 14 *YBWA* (1960), p. 236.
Audinet, E., "De la prescription acquisitive en droit international public," 3 *RGDIP* (1896), p. 313.
Baade, H. W., "Intertemporales Völkerrecht," 7 *Jahrbuch für internationales Recht* (1956), p. 229.

Baldoni, C., "Les navires de guerre dans les eaux territoriales étrangères," 65 *Hague* Recueil (1938), vol. III, p. 185.

Beckett, W. E., "Les questions d'intérêt général au point de vue juridique dans la jurisprudence de la Cour Permanente de Justice Internationale (Juillet 1932–Juillet 1934)," 50 *Hague Recueil* (1934), vol. IV, p. 189.

Boggs, S. W., "Delimitation of Seaward Areas under National Jurisdiction," 45 *AJIL* (1951), p. 240.

— "Delimitation of the Territorial Sea," 24 *AJIL* (1930), p. 541.

Böhmert, V., "Meeresfreiheit und Schelfproklamationen," I. 5 *Jahrbuch für internationales Recht* (1954), p. 1; II. 6 *Jahrbuch für internationales Recht* (1955), p. 7.

Bouchez, L. T., "The Concept of Effectiveness as Applied to Territorial Sovereignty over Sea-Areas, Air Space and Outer Space," 9 *NTIR* (1962), p. 150.

Bourquin, M., "Les baies historiques," *Mélanges Georges Sauser-Hall*, Geneva, 1952, p. 38.

Bowett, D. W., "Estoppel before International Tribunals and its Relation to Acquiescence," 33 *BYIL* (1957), p. 176.

— "The Second United Nations Conference on the Law of the Sea," 9 *ICLQ* (1960), p. 415.

Brüel, E., "La protestation en droit international," 3 *ASJG* (1932), p. 75.

Cavaglieri, A., "Règles générales du droit de la paix," 26 *Hague Recueil* (1929), vol. I, p. 311.

Drago, L. M., "Un triomphe de l'arbitrage," 19 *RGDIP* (1912), p. 5.

Fisher, F. C., "The Arbitration of the Guatemalan–Honduran Boundary Dispute," 27 *AJIL* (1933), p. 403.

Fitzmaurice, G. G., "Some Results of the Geneva Conference on the Law of the Sea," 8 *ICLQ* (1959), p. 73.

— "The General Principles of International Law Considered from the Standpoint of the Rule of Law," 92 *Hague Recueil* (1957), vol. II, p. 1.

— "The Law and Procedure of the International Court of Justice, 1951–54: General Principles and Sources of Law," 30 *BYIL* (1953), p. 1.

— "The Law and Procedure of the International Court of Justice, 1951–54: Points of Substantive Law, Part I," 31 *BYIL* (1954), p. 371.

— "The Law and Procedure of the International Court of Justice, 1951–54: Points of Substantive Law, Part II," 32 *BYIL* (1955–1956), p. 20.

— "The Law and Procedure of the International Court of Justice: Treaty Interpretation and Certain Other Treaty Points," 28 *BYIL* (1951), p. 1.

Friede, W., "Das Estoppel-Prinzip im Völkerrecht," 5 *ZRV* (1935), p. 517.

Gidel, G., "A propos des bases juridiques des prétentions des Etats riverains sur le plateau continental: les doctrines du 'droit inhérent,'" 19 *ZRV* (1958), p. 81.

Goy, R., "L'affaire des pêcheries islandaises," 87 *Journal du Droit International* (1960), p. 371.

Gross, L., "The Geneva Conference on the Law of the Sea and the Right of Innocent Passage through the Gulf of Aqaba," 53 *AJIL* (1959), p. 564.

Guani, A., "La solidarité dans l'Amérique Latine," 8 *Hague Recueil* (1925), vol. III, p. 207.

Guggenheim, P., "Contribution à l'histoire des sources du droit des gens," 94 *Hague Recueil* (1958), vol. II, p. 1.

Gutteridge, J. A. C., "The 1958 Convention on the Continental Shelf," 35 *BYIL* (1959), p. 102.

Hammad, B. W., "The Right of Passage in the Gulf of Aqaba," 15 *Revue Egyptienne de Droit International* (1959), p. 118.
Hanessian, J., "The Antarctic Treaty," 1959, 9 *ICLQ* (1960), p. 436.
Hartwig, B., "Der israelisch-ägyptische Streit um den Golf von Akaba," 9 *Archiv des Völkerrechts* (1961), p. 27.
Hayton, R. D., "The 'American' Antarctic," 50 *AJIL* (1956), p. 583.
Hurst, C. J. B., "Whose is the Bed of the Sea?," 4 *BYIL* (1923–1924), p. 34.
Jenks, C. W., "An International Regime for Antarctica?," 32 *International Affairs* (1956), p. 414.
Jessup, P. C., "The Palmas Island Arbitration," 22 *AJIL* (1928), p. 735.
Johnson, D. H. N., "Acquisitive Prescription in International Law," 27 *BYIL* (1950), p. 332.
— "Consolidation as a Root of Title in International Law," *Cambridge Law Journal*, (1955), p. 215.
— "Notes on the Case concerning the Arbitral Award made by the King of Spain on December 23, 1906," 10 *ICLQ* (1961), p. 328.
— "The Anglo-Norwegian Fisheries Case," 1 *ICLQ* (1952), p. 145.
— "The Legal Status of the Sea-bed and Subsoil," 16 *ZRV* (1955–1956), p. 451.
— "The Minquiers and Ecrehos Case," 3 *ICLQ* (1954), p. 189.
Johnston, V. K., "Canada's Title to Hudson Bay and Hudson Strait," 15 *BYIL* (1934), p. 1.
Kelsen, H., "Théorie du droit international coutumier," *Revue Internationale pour la Théorie du Droit* (1953), p. 253.
Khadduri, M., "Iran's Claims to Sovereignty over Bahrayn," 45 *AJIL* (1951), p. 631.
Kopelmanas, L., "Custom as a Means of the Creation of International Law," 18 *BYIL* (1937), p. 127.
Kulski, W. W., "Soviet Comments on International Law and International Relations," 47 *AJIL* (1953), p. 125.
Kunz, J. L., "Sanctions in International Law," 54 *AJIL* (1960), p. 324.
— "The Nature of Customary International Law," 47 *AJIL* (1953), p. 662.
Laband, P., "Lippe-Detmold-Schaumburg-Lippe affaire des bailliages de Schieder, Blomberg et Lipperode," Lapradelle-Politis, *Recueil des arbitrages internationaux*, Paris, 1905, vol. I, p. 423.
Lauterpacht, H., "Decisions of Municipal Courts as a Source of International Law," 11 *BYIL* (1929), p. 65.
— "Nationality of Denationalized Persons," *Jewish Yearbook of International Law* (1948), p. 164.
— "Sovereignty over Submarine Areas," 27 *BYIL* (1950), p. 376.
McDougal, M. S., "The Hydrogen Bomb Tests and the International Law of the Sea," 49 *AJIL* (1955), p. 356.
MacGibbon, I. C., "Customary International Law and Acquiescence," 33 *BYIL* (1957), p. 115.
— "Estoppel in International Law," 7 *ICLQ* (1958), p. 468.
— "The Scope of Acquiescence in International Law," 31 *BYIL* (1954), p. 143.
McNair, A. D., "So-called State Servitudes," 6 *BYIL* (1925), p. 111.
— "The Legality of the Occupation of the Ruhr," 5 *BYIL* (1924), p. 17.

Malek, Ch., "La théorie dites des 'baies historiques,'" 6 *Revue de Droit International pour le Moyen Orient* (1957), p. 100.
Melamid, A., "Legal Status of the Gulf of Aqaba," 53 *AJIL* (1959), p. 412.
Meyer-Lindenberg, H., "Seerechtliche Entwicklungstendenzen," 21 *ZRV* (1961), p. 38.
Morelli, G., "Cours général de droit international public", 89 *Hague Recueil* (1956), vol. I, p. 437.
Mouton, M. W., "The Continental Shelf," 85 *Hague Recueil* (1954), vol. I, p. 347.
Nys, E., "Les prétendues servitudes internationales," I. 7 *RDILC* (*Deuxième série*) (1905), p. 118; II. 13 *RDILC* (*Deuxième série*) (1911), p. 314.
O'Connell, D. P., "Sedentary Fisheries and the Australian Continental Shelf," 49 *AJIL* (1955), p. 185.
Oppenheim, L. F. L., "Der Tunnel unter dem Ärmelkanal und das Völkerrecht," 2 *Zeitschrift für Völkerrecht und Bundesstaatsrecht* (1908), p. 1.
Papandréou, A., "La situation juridique des pêcheries sédentaires en haute-mer," 11 *Revue Hellénique de Droit International* (1958), p. 1.
Pinto, R., "La prescription en droit international," 87 *Hague Recueil* (1955), vol. I, p. 387.
Raestad, A., "Le problème des eaux territoriales à la Conférence pour la Codification du Droit International," 7 *RDI* (1931), p. 107.
Rau, K. K., "The Sino-Indian Boundary Question and International Law," 11 *ICLQ* (1962), p. 375.
Schwarzenberger, G., "The Fundamental Principles of International Law," 87 *Hague Recueil* (1955), vol. II, p. 191.
— "Title to Territory: Response to a Challenge," 51 *AJIL* (1957), p. 308.
Scott, J. B., "The Swiss Decision in the Boundary Dispute between Colombia and Venezuela," 16 *AJIL* (1922), p. 428.
Selak, C. B. Jr., "A Consideration of the Legal Status of the Gulf of Aqaba," 52 *AJIL* (1958), p. 660.
Sørensen, M., "La prescription en droit international," 3 *ASJG* (1932), p. 145.
— "The Territorial Sea of Archipelagos, *Varia Juris Gentium – Liber Amicorum J. P. A. François*, Special Issue of *NTIR*, July 1959, p. 315.
Tunkin, G. I., "Co-existence and International Law," 95 *Hague Recueil* (1958), vol. III, p. 5.
Verzijl, J. H. W., "Territorial Controversies before the International Court of Justice," 1 *NTIR* (1953–1954), p. 234.
Visscher, Ch. de, "Observations sur l'effectivité en droit international," 62 *RGDIP* (1958), p. 601.
— "Reflections on the Present Prospects of International Adjudication," 50 *AJIL* (1956), p. 467.
Waddell, D. A. G., "Developments in the Belize Question 1946–1960," 55 *AJIL* (1961), p. 459.
Wade, E. C., "The Minquiers and Ecréhous Case," *Grotius Transactions*, vol. 40 (1954), p. 97.
Waldock, C. H. M., "Disputed Sovereignty in the Falkland Islands Dependencies," 25 *BYIL* (1948), p. 311.
— "The Anglo-Norwegian Fisheries Case," 28 *BYIL* (1951), p. 114.
— "The Legal Basis of Claims to the Continental Shelf," *Grotius Transactions*, vol. 36 (1950), p. 115.

Woodhouse, J. T., "The Principle of Retroactivity in International Law," *Grotius Transactions*, vol. 41 (1955), p. 69.

Young, R., "Sedentary Fisheries and the Convention on the Continental Shelf," 55 *AJIL* (1961), p. 359.

INDEX OF NAMES

GENERAL INDEX

GPSR Compliance

The European Union's (EU) General Product Safety Regulation (GPSR) is a set of rules that requires consumer products to be safe and our obligations to ensure this.

If you have any concerns about our products, you can contact us on ProductSafety@springernature.com

In case Publisher is established outside the EU, the EU authorized representative is:

Springer Nature Customer Service Center GmbH
Europaplatz 3
69115 Heidelberg, Germany

Batch number: 10830943

Printed by Printforce, the Netherlands